AutoCAD Civil 3D 2011
ESSENTIALS

ASCENT – Center for Technical Knowledge®
autodesk®
authorized author

ISBN: 978-1-58503-557-1

SDC
PUBLICATIONS

Schroff Development Corporation

www.SDCpublications.com

Schroff Development Corporation
P.O. Box 1334
Mission KS 66222
(913) 262-2664
www.**SDCpublications**.com

Publisher: Stephen Schroff

Examination Copies:

Books received as examination copies are for review purposes only and may not be made available for student use. Resale of examination copies is prohibited.

IT IS A VIOLATION OF UNITED STATES COYRIGHT LAWS TO MAKE COPIES IN ANY FORM OR MEDIA OF THE CONTENTS OF THIS BOOK FOR EITHER COMMERCIAL OR EDUCATIONAL PURPOSES WITHOUT EXPRESS WRITTEN PERMISSION

Electronic Files:

Any electronic files associated with this book are licensed to the original user only. These files may not be transferred to any other party.

Trademarks

AutoCAD® and Civil 3D® are registered trademarks of Autodesk Inc.

Printed in the United States of America

Table of Contents

Preface

The *AutoCAD Civil 3D 2011 Essentials* course is designed for Civil Engineers and Surveyors who want to take advantage of AutoCAD Civil 3D's interactive, dynamic design functionality. AutoCAD Civil 3D permits the rapid development of alternatives through its model-based design tools. You will learn techniques enabling you to organize project data, work with points, create and analyze surfaces, model road corridors, create parcel layouts, perform grading and volume calculation tasks, and lay out pipe networks.

Upon completion of the course, students will be able to:

- Import data through AutoCAD LandXML and from an Autodesk Land Desktop Project

- Create and manage Points and Point Groups

- Create, edit, view, and analyze surfaces

- Create parcels and parcel tables

- Create sites, create and edit alignments, and create profiles and cross-sections

- Create assemblies, corridors, and cross-sections, and calculate corridor volumes

- Create complex grading solutions

- Create pipe networks

Module 1

The AutoCAD Civil 3D Interface

This module introduces:

Section 1: AutoCAD Civil 3D Interface

✓ **Product Overview**

✓ **AutoCAD Civil 3D Workspaces**

✓ **AutoCAD Civil 3D User Interface**

✓ **AutoCAD Civil 3D Toolspace**

✓ **AutoCAD Civil 3D Panorama**

Section 1: AutoCAD Civil 3D Interface

1.1 Product Overview

AutoCAD Civil 3D supports a wide range of Survey and Civil Engineering tasks. This application creates intelligent relationships between objects so that design changes can be dynamically updated.

- AutoCAD Civil 3D makes use of dynamic objects for points, alignments, profiles, terrain models, pipe networks, and more. Objects can update when data changes. For example, if an alignment changes, its associated profiles and sections update automatically. Commands can be safely undone in AutoCAD Civil 3D without causing the graphics to become out of date with survey and design data.

- These objects are style-based and dynamic, which streamlines object creation and editing.

- AutoCAD Civil 3D objects (surfaces, alignments, etc.) are often stored directly inside drawing files. The only time they are not is when working with the Autodesk Data Management System (Vault), shortcuts, or a survey database.

- AutoCAD Civil 3D, unlike AutoCAD Land Desktop, supports a multiple document interface. This means that more than one drawing file can be open in the same session of AutoCAD Civil 3D at the same time. Users of AutoCAD Land Desktop moving into AutoCAD Civil 3D should be aware that, by default, opening a second drawing does not automatically close any currently open drawings.

- AutoCAD Civil 3D can be launched by selecting its icon from the desktop or by accessing the command through the Start Bar. Depending on the installed version of AutoCAD Civil 3D the icon will indicate Imperial or Metric, as shown in Figure 1-1. Once launched, the AutoCAD Civil 3D application initiates with the standard AutoCAD Civil 3D profile. It is also possible to customize the shortcut to initiate the Civil 3D application to launch with project based setting, this is accomplished by using a custom profile.

Figure 1–1

1.2 AutoCAD Civil 3D Workspaces

When AutoCAD Civil 3D is launched for the first time, you are presented with a Welcome Screen dialog box, as shown in Figure 1–2. From here, you can view information about the User Interface, Learning Resources, New Features Workshop, and Best Practices. You can also watch the new Getting Started Movies from this screen.

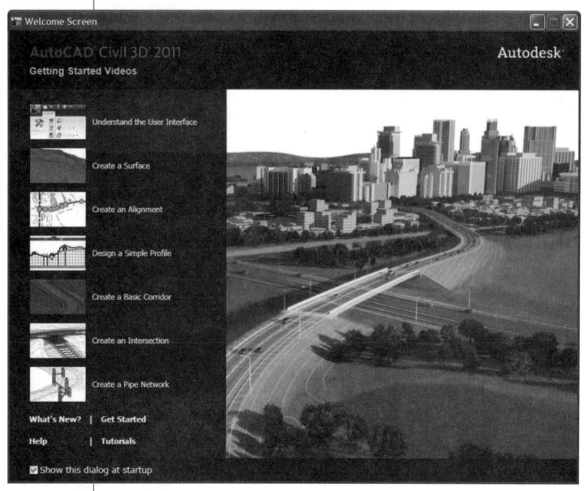

Figure 1–2

It is recommended that you stay in the Civil 3D Workspace most of the time. As a review, AutoCAD Workspaces are saved groupings of menus, toolbars, palettes, and Dashboard control panels organized as needed for specific tasks. You can edit the stock Workspaces supplied with AutoCAD Civil 3D or create your own. In this material, you work with the Civil 3D Workspace, which includes a complete list of AutoCAD Civil 3D-specific Ribbons, pull-down menus, and tools.

Workspaces can be changed using the Workspaces switching icon on the Status Bar, located in the lower left corner, as shown in Figure 1–3. They can also be modified using the **CUI** command.

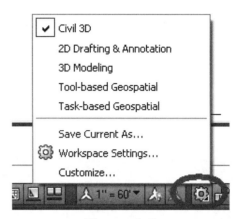

Figure 1–3

1.3 AutoCAD Civil 3D User Interface

The AutoCAD Civil 3D user interface is shown in Figure 1–4. The numbered areas are described in this topic.

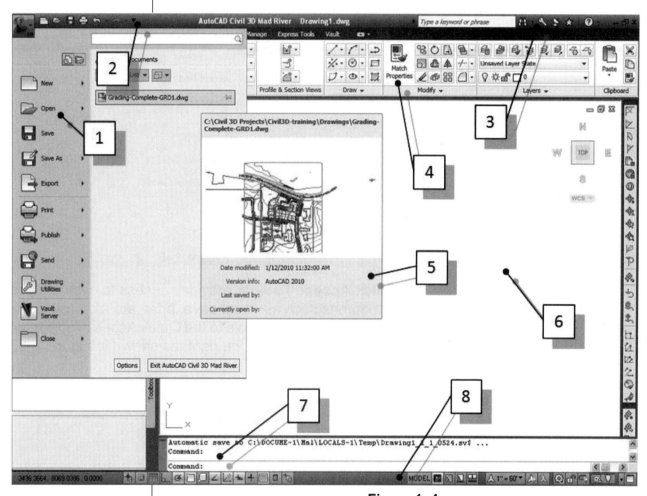

Figure 1–4

1.   Application Menu

2.   Quick Access Toolbar

3.   InfoCenter

4.   Ribbon

5.   Tooltips

6.   Drawing Window

7.   Command Line

8.   Status Bar

1. **Application Menu** provides access to commands, settings, and documents. With the Application Menu you can: 1) Browse menus available in AutoCAD Civil 3D; 2) Perform a search of menus, menu actions, tooltips, and command prompt text strings; and 3) Browse for recent documents, currently open documents, and commands you recently executed. An example is shown in Figure 1–5.

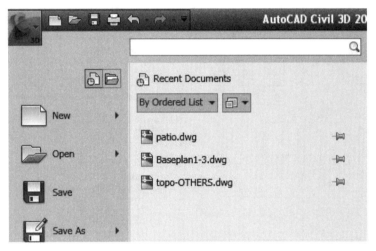

Figure 1–5

2. **Quick Access Toolbar** provides access to commonly used commands such as open, save, print, etc. You can add an unlimited number of tools to the Quick Access Toolbar by clicking on the down arrow on the right, as shown in Figure 1–6.

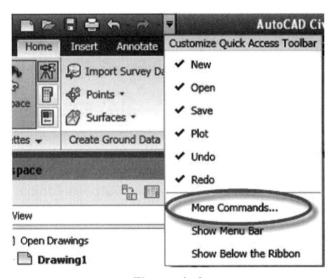

Figure 1–6

3. **InfoCenter** enables you to quickly search for help. You can specify which Help documents to search, and collapse or expand the search field, as shown in Figure 1–7, to save screen space.

Figure 1–7

4. **Ribbon** provides a single, compact location for *commands* that are relevant to the current task. It contains tools in a series of *tabs* and *panels* to reduce clutter in the application and maximize drawing space. Selecting a tab displays a series of panels. The panels contain a variety of tools, grouped by function, as shown in Figure 1–8.

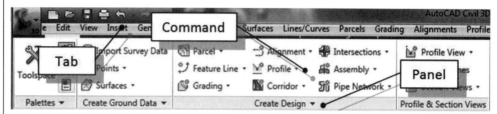

Figure 1–8

Clicking the drop-down icon expands the panel to display additional tools, as shown in Figure 1–9. Clicking an arrow pointing to the bottom right opens the tools dialog box for additional controls.

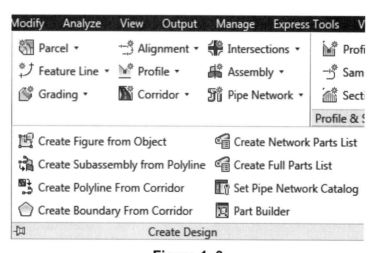

Figure 1–9

You can minimize the Ribbon by clicking on the arrow successively, as shown in Figure 1–10.

Figure 1–10

There are two classifications of Ribbons: static and contextual.

Static Ribbons display the most often used tabs, panels, and commands, whereas the contextual Ribbons display the tabs, panels, and commands that are applicable only to the selected object. A Static Ribbon is shown in Figure 1–11.

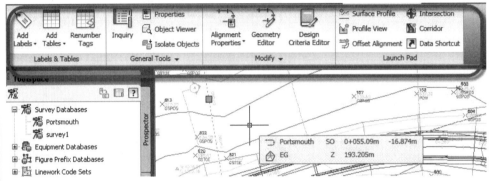

Figure 1–11

5.   **Tooltips** display the item's name, a short description, and sometimes a graphic. They provide information about tools, commands, and drawing objects, as shown in Figure 1–12.

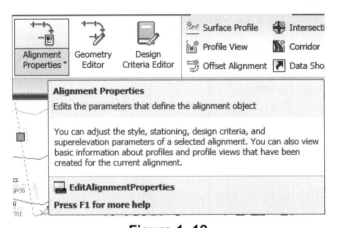

Figure 1–12

6.   **Drawing Window** is the area of the screen where the drawing appears.

7. **Command Line** is a text window located at the bottom of the screen that shows command prompts and a history of commands, as shown in Figure 1–13. To toggle the command line display, press <Ctrl> + <9> on the keyboard.

Figure 1–13

8. **Status Bar** enables you to change many of AutoCAD's drafting settings, such as snap, grid, and object snap, as shown in Figure 1–14.

Figure 1–14

1.4 AutoCAD Civil 3D Toolspace

AutoCAD Civil 3D uses a Toolspace to manage objects, settings, and styles. The Toolspace can have up to four tabs: *Prospector*, *Settings*, *Survey*, and *Toolbox*. Each uses a hierarchical tree interface to manage objects, settings, and styles. Branches in these hierarchical trees are referred to in AutoCAD Civil 3D as "collections". The Toolspace is an interactive data management tool. Right-clicking on a collection or on an individual object provides many commonly used commands in the shortcut menus.

Toolspace operates similar to an AutoCAD tool palette in that it can be resized, set to dock or float, and when floating can be set to auto-hide. The Toolspace is shown docked on the left of Figure 1–15 and floating on the right.

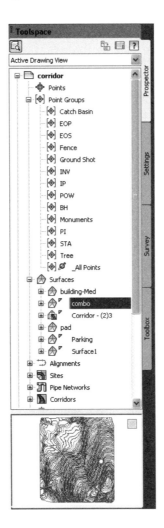
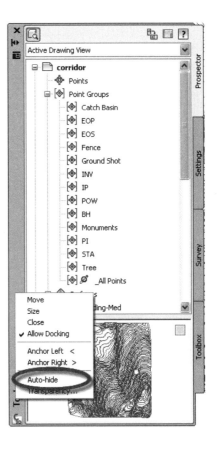

Figure 1–15

The Toolspace can be closed by clicking on the **X** in the upper left or right corner. Once closed, it can be opened by selecting the *Home* tab > Toolspace on the Ribbon, as shown in Figure 1–16.

Figure 1–16

Prospector Tab

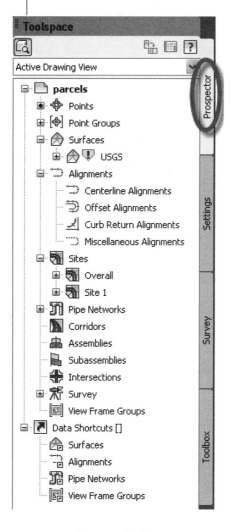

The *Prospector* tab lists the AutoCAD Civil 3D objects present in open drawings as well as other important information, as shown in Figure 1–17. Its hierarchical structure dynamically manages and displays objects and their data. As objects are created or deleted, they are removed from the *Prospector*. A pull-down menu at the top offers the following options:

Active Drawing View displays only the AutoCAD Civil 3D objects present in the active drawing. If you switch to another drawing, the tree is updated to reflect the currently active drawing.

Master View displays a list of all open drawings and their objects, project information, and a list of drawing templates. The name of the active drawing is highlighted.

Figure 1–17

Each object type (Points, Point Groups, Alignments, Surfaces, etc.) is allotted a collection, and objects present in a drawing are listed below the respective collection.

The bottom of the *Prospector* tab alternately shows a list view of items in the highlighted collection or a preview of an object selected in the *Prospector*.

The icon at the top of the *Prospector* tab controls how items in the *Prospector* tree are displayed. Icons next to objects give you additional information about the object. A list of common icons is shown below:

	Turns the Toolspace item preview on or off.
	Displays (or closes) the Panorama window. This window only appears if there are vistas to be displayed in the Panorama.
	Opens the AutoCAD Civil 3D Help system.
	Indicates the object is currently locked for editing.
	Indicates the object is referenced by another object. In the *Settings* tab, this also indicates that a style is in use in the current drawing.
	Indicates the object is being referenced from another drawing file (such as through a shortcut or Vault reference).
	Indicates the object is out of date and needs to be rebuilt, or is violating specified design constraints.
	Indicates a project object (such as a point or surface) has been modified since it was included in the current drawing.
	Indicates you have modified a project object in your current drawing and those modifications have yet to be updated to the project.

Settings Tab

The *Settings* tab is used to configure how AutoCAD Civil 3D operates and the way AutoCAD Civil 3D objects are displayed and printed, as shown in Figure 1–18. You do not create or modify AutoCAD Civil 3D objects here (use the *Prospector* and *Survey* tabs instead); rather, you control how objects are created and how they behave afterwards.

Different settings are accessed by right-clicking on the name of a drawing file or on one of the collections located inside this tab.

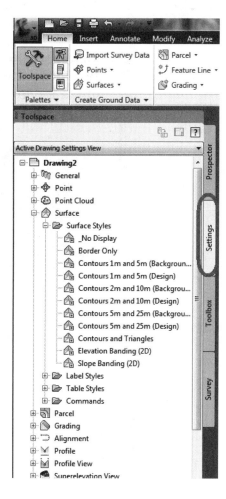

Figure 1–18

The collections (such as the Surface collection shown in Figure 1–18) can contain object styles, label styles, command settings, and related controls.

Changes to settings affect all lower items in the tree. For example, assigning an overall text height in the drawing's Edit Label Style Defaults dialog box applies that height to all other settings and styles in the drawing. Applying the same setting in the Surface collection's Edit Label Style Defaults only applies the text height to the surface label styles. (Lower items in the tree and styles can be set to override these changes individually as needed.)

All drawing settings originate from the template used to create an AutoCAD Civil 3D drawing.

Survey Tab

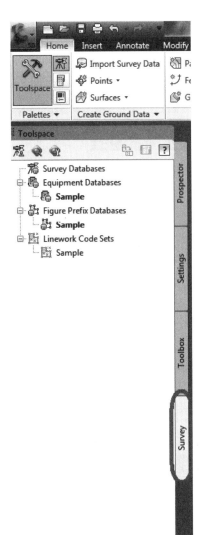

The *Survey* tab is used to manage survey observations data, as shown in Figure 1–19. Selecting this tab enables you to create a survey database, create a survey network, points, and figures, and import and edit survey observation data.

To toggle the display of the *Survey* tab, select the Survey Toolspace icon in the top left area of the screen, as shown in Figure 1–20.

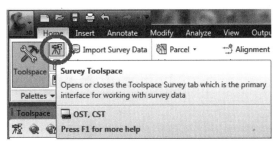

Figure 1–20

Figure 1–19

Toolbox Tab

The *Toolbox* tab is used to access the Reports Manager and to add custom tools to the AutoCAD Civil 3D Interface, as shown in Figure 1–21. The Toolbox can be toggled on and off by selecting the drop-down arrow below the Toolspace icon (located in the top right area of your screen), as shown in Figure 1–22.

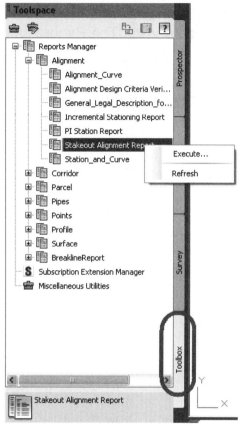

Figure 1–21

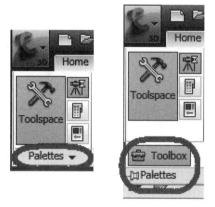

Figure 1–22

The Reports Manager, the only set of tools that appears in the toolbox by default, enables you to generate a large variety of survey and design reports. For example, to launch a Stakeout Alignment Report, right-click on it under the Alignments collection and select **Execute**.

The icons in the upper left area of the *Toolbox* tab enable you to:

 Open the Edit Report Settings dialog box, where you can assign settings for all report types. These settings include items such as the name to display in the report.

 Open the Toolbox Editor, where you can add custom reports and other tools.

1.5 AutoCAD Civil 3D Panorama

AutoCAD Civil 3D includes a multi-purpose grid data viewer called the Panorama. The dialog box is similar to an AutoCAD tool palette in that it can be docked or floating, and set to auto-hide. Each tab in the Panorama is called a Vista. The Panorama can be opened from the

AutoCAD Civil 3D Toolspace using this toggle: , and can be closed clicking on the **X** in the upper left or right corner of the window. You can only display the Panorama after launching a command that uses it, such as **Edit Points** (right-click on a Point Group in the *Prospector* tab of the Toolspace to access this option). The Panorama can display many different kinds of data, such as point properties, alignment, and profile data, as shown in Figure 1–23.

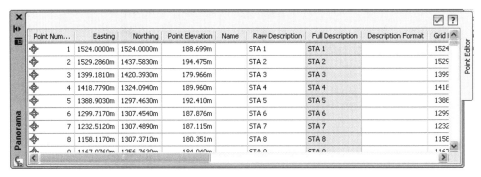

Figure 1–23

The Panorama can also show a special Vista called the event viewer, as shown in Figure 1–24. The event viewer appears when AutoCAD Civil 3D encounters a processing error, such as when surface breaklines cross or a road model passes over the edge of the existing ground surface. When working through a large number of events, clearing all of the old entries through the **Action > Clear All Events** option in the Panorama can be helpful.

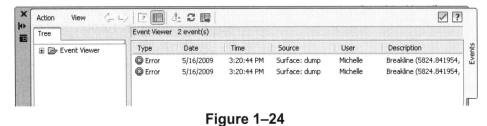

Figure 1–24

If a Panorama contains multiple Vistas, clicking on the green checkmark closes only the current Vista. To close (hide) the Panorama, click on the **X** in its mast.

Practice 1a

Overview of AutoCAD Civil 3D and its User Interface

In this practice you will become familiar with AutoCAD Civil 3D's capabilities and learn about its interface.

Task 1: Set up the practice.

1. If necessary, start AutoCAD Civil 3D by double-clicking on the desktop icon (AutoCAD Civil 3D). If presented with the Welcome Screen window, click ✕ to close it.

2. On the Status Bar, confirm that **Civil 3D** is the active Workspace. The Workspace icon is located in the Status Bar to the left, as shown in Figure 1–25.

⚙ Civil 3D ▾

Figure 1–25

3. Select the *Home* tab and ensure that the Layers panel is displayed. If it is not, right-click anywhere on the Ribbon and select **Layers**, as shown in Figure 1–26.

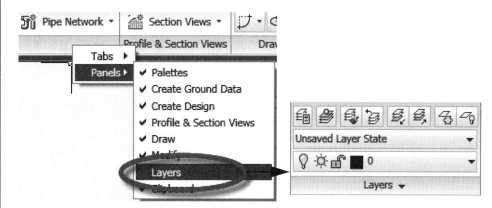

Figure 1–26

4. If a blank drawing is open (**Drawing1.dwg**), close the current default drawing by selecting the **Application Menu** > **Close**.

5. Open an existing drawing by selecting the **Application Menu** ![icon] > **Open** and browse for **INTRO-Introduction.dwg** in the following folder: *C:\Civil 3D Projects\Civil3D-training\Drawings*.

6. You can add a shortcut to the folder in the bar on the left side of the dialog box. This will enable quick access to the class folder when in the Open dialog box. Select the **Application Menu** ![icon] > **Open** again. The Select File dialog box should still be pointing to the *C:\Civil 3D Projects\Civil3D-training\Drawings* folder, as shown on the left in Figure 1–27. In the dialog box, select **Add Current Folder to Places** in the Tools pull-down menu, as shown on the right.

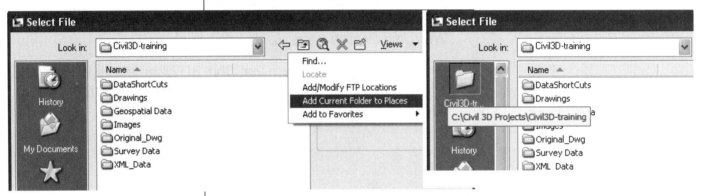

Figure 1–27

7. Close the Open dialog box by clicking **Cancel**. When prompted to save the changes to your Places List, click **Yes**.

8. Locate the Civil 3D Toolspace, as shown in Figure 1–28, which by default appears docked to the left side of your screen. If you cannot find it, select **Home > Toolspace**. This command is useful to remember if you ever close the Toolspace accidentally.

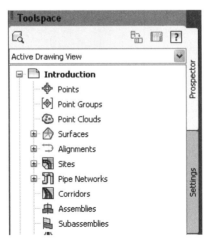

Figure 1–28

9. Save the drawing as **Example 1.dwg**. Select **Application Menu**
    , click in the Search field, and type **save**, as shown in
    Figure 1–29. Select **Save As...**, type in **Example 1** in the File
    Name field, and click **Save**.

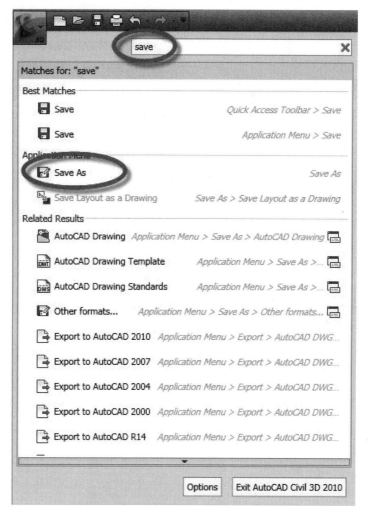

Figure 1–29

Task 2: Review the Prospector tab.

In this task, you will explore the tabs in the Civil 3D Toolspace.

1. Ensure that the Civil 3D Toolspace is visible. If the Toolspace is
    not visible, click the Toolspace icon located at the top left
    corner of the Ribbon on the *Home* tab.

2. Click in the *Prospector* tab to make it active. (The tabs are listed
    vertically along the right side of the Toolspace.)

3. Click on the "+" signs to open the collections and the "-" signs to close them. Items shown in the *Prospector* tab are the design data currently in the drawing file (such as points, alignments, and a surface).

4. Collections like Points do not have a "+" or "-" sign because they are not intended to be expanded in the tree view of the *Prospector*. Click on the **Points** collection and the list view appears below, describing the AutoCAD Civil 3D points currently in the drawing file.

5. Under the Surfaces collection, look for the surface called **Existing Ground**. Expand its branch and the *Definition* area inside it. Highlight the items below (breaklines, boundaries, etc.) and notice the components shown in the list view.

6. With Existing Ground's breaklines highlighted in the list view, right-click on Ditch and note the commands available in the shortcut menu, as shown on the left in Figure 1–30. Select **Zoom to**.

Similar shortcut menus are available for nearly all objects shown in the *Prospector*. Expand the Point Groups, select the **Bdy Survey** point group, and then press the <Shift> key to select point numbers **2** and **3**, as shown on the right in Figure 1–30. Right-click and select **Zoom To**. This enables the *Prospector* to serve as the primary control center for creating, editing, and managing design objects.

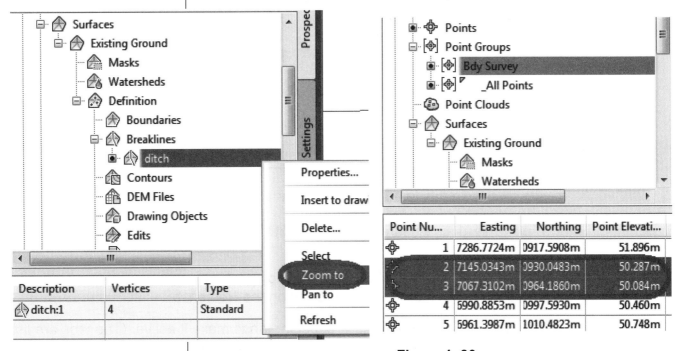

Figure 1–30

Task 3: Review the Settings tab.

1. Switch to the *Settings* tab in the Civil 3D Toolspace, as shown in Figure 1–31.

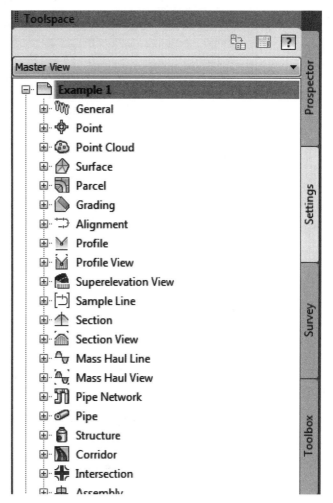

Figure 1–31

2. In the *Settings* tab, right-click on the drawing's name (Example 1.dwg, at the top), and select **Edit Drawing Settings…**.

3. In the Drawing Settings dialog box, select the *Units and Zone* tab, as shown in Figure 1–32.

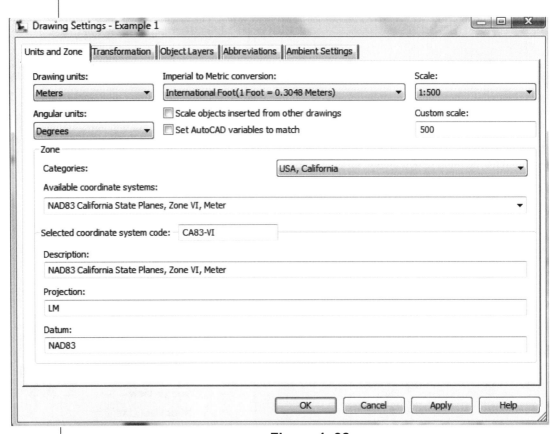

Figure 1–32

4. Change the *Scale* to **1:1000** in the pull-down menu on the upper right corner.

5. Note the coordinate systems available in the *Zone* area, such as CA83-VI, NAD83 California State Planes, Zone VI, or Meter.

6. Click [OK] to close the dialog box. Because Civil3D labels are annotative, the point label annotation size has changed to match the new Drawing Scale.

7. You can also change the Model Space display scale using the **Annotation** icon in the Status Bar. Change it to read **1:500**. Notice as you change the scale, all labels also change in size, as shown in Figure 1–33.

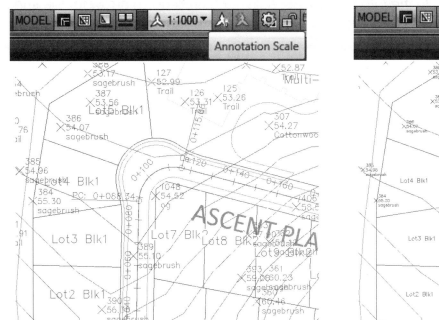
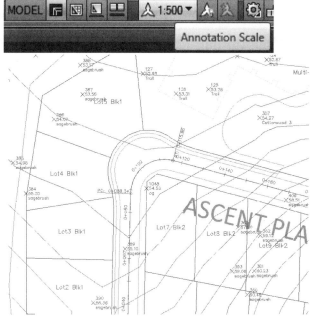

Figure 1–33

8. You can change the display of the contours by changing the style of the surface. Select the surface object in the AutoCAD window, and the Ribbon will display the contextual Ribbon, as shown in Figure 1–34.

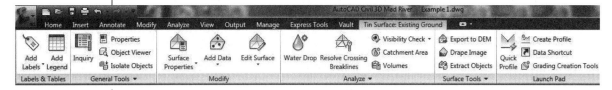

Figure 1–34

9. Select **Surface Properties** in the *Modify* tab or right-click and select **Surface Properties**.

10. In the *Information* tab, select the drop-down arrow for the surface style, as shown in Figure 1–35. Select one of the predefined styles and click Apply to apply the selected style to the surface.

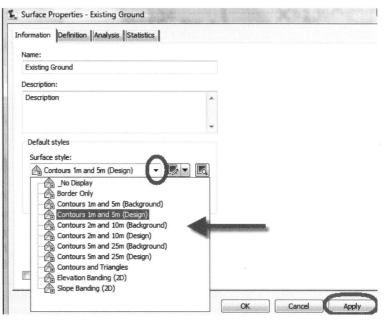

Figure 1–35

11. Click OK to exit the Surface Properties dialog box.

12. View the label style default. Select the *View* tab in the Ribbon and in the Views panel, select **Named views**. In the View Manager under Model Views, select **Contour label**, select **Set Current**, and click OK. This will zoom into a preset view of the contour labels, as shown in Figure 1–36.

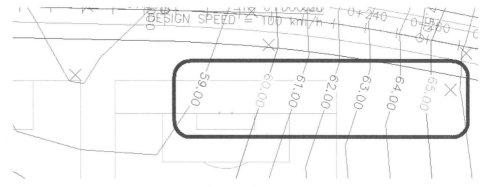

Figure 1–36

Note that the labels are not rotated to the correct drafting standards. The contour label style being used is rotating the text so that it remains plan readable (so they do not appear upside down). The highlighted labels are rotated more than 90 degrees from horizontal. This is caused by the *Readability Bias* setting being larger than 90 degrees. This setting controls the viewing angle at which the contour text should be flipped, and is presently set to the default 110°.

13. You could change the setting in only this particular contour label style, if needed. To assign this new value to *all* surface label styles, right-click on the Surface collection in the *Settings* tab and select **Edit Label Style Defaults**.

14. Under the *Plan Readability* property, set the *Readability Bias* to 91°, as shown in Figure 1–37, and click [OK].

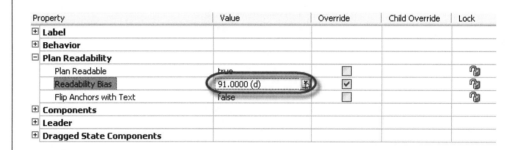

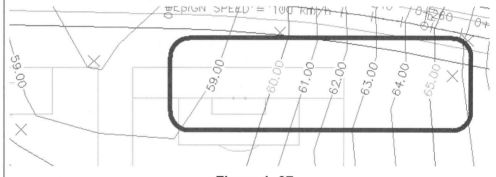

Figure 1–37

Task 4: Review AutoCAD Civil 3D's Dynamic Object Model.

1. Select the *View* tab in the Ribbon and in the Views panel, select **Named views**. In the View Manager under Model Views, select **Alignment Profile**, select **Set Current**, and click [OK]. This will zoom into a preset view of the alignment and the surface to the right.

2. Select the **Jeffries Ranch Rd** alignment to activate its grips, as shown in Figure 1–38. Left-click on the lowest grip and reposition it. The alignment and profile update as well. (If the alignment had labels displayed, they would also update).

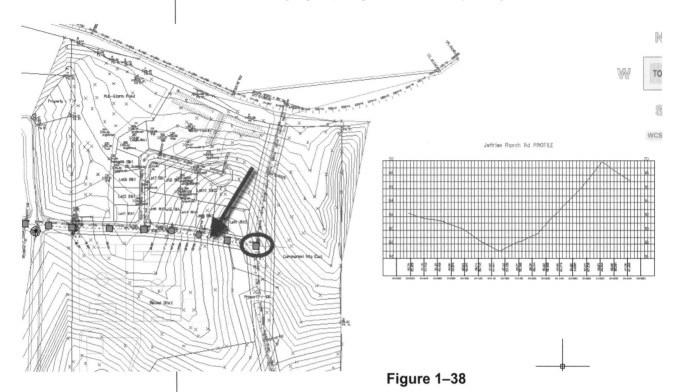

Figure 1–38

3. Float your crosshairs near the alignment in its new position. The station, offset, and surface elevation information are provided through tooltips.

4. Save the drawing.

Task 5: Review AutoCAD Civil 3D's Reports Manager.

1. Select the *Toolbox* tab in the Civil 3D Toolspace. Expand the Report Manager, as shown in Figure 1–39, by selecting the "+" sign.

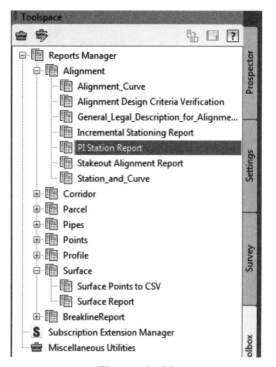

Figure 1–39

2. Expand the Alignment collection. Select **PI Station Report**, right-click, and select **Execute**, as shown in Figure 1–40. **Note:** As a shortcut, you can double-click to execute the Report command without having to select the Execute command.

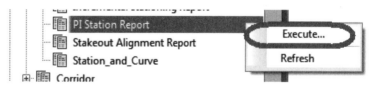

Figure 1–40

3. Accept all the defaults and click **Create report**. The report appears as shown in Figure 1–41.

Alignment PI Station Report

Client:
Client
Client Company
Address 1
Date: 15/02/2010 5:07:51 PM

Prepared by:
Preparer
Your Company Name
123 Main Street

Alignment Name: Ascent Blvd
Description:
Station Range: Start: 0+000.00, End: 0+560.24

PI Station	Northing	Easting	Distance	Direction
0+000.00	620,951.8490m	1,907,201.7791m		
			227.440m	S15° 19' 55"W
0+227.44	620,732.5039m	1,907,141.6411m		
			337.754m	S12° 37' 15"E
0+560.24	620,402.9107m	1,907,215.4396m		

Figure 1–41

4. Expand the Surface collection. Select **Surface Report**, right-click, and select **Execute**, as shown in Figure 1–42.

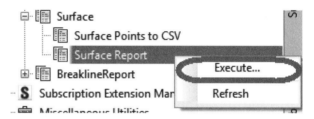

Figure 1–42

5. Accept all the defaults and click **Create report**. The report appears as shown in Figure 1–43. Enter a file name for the saved report or accept the default.

Your Company Name

123 Main Street

Suite #321

City, State 01234

Surface Report
Project Name: C:\Civil 3D Projects\Civil3D-training\Drawings\Example 1.dwg
Report Date: 15/02/2010 5:13:25 PM

Client: Client Company
Project Description:
Prepared by: Preparer

Linear Units: meter	Area Units: squareMeter	Volume Units: cubicMeter

Surface: Existing Ground
Description: Description

Area 2D: 247269.606	Area 3D: 248981.671
Elevation Max: 88.732	Elevation Min: 47.824
Number of Points: 330	Number of Triangles: 628

Figure 1–43

Review Questions

Question 1   How is AutoCAD Civil 3D different from traditional Survey and Civil Engineering packages, such as AutoCAD Land Desktop?

Question 2   Which Workspace do you use in this Student Guide?

Question 3   What does the *Prospector* tab do?

Question 4   What does the *Settings* tab do?

Question 5   How do you access the Edit Drawing Settings dialog box?

Question 6   What is the main function of the Panorama window?

Module 2

Parcels Level 1

This module introduces:

Section 1: Parcels Overview

✓ **Introduction to Parcels**

Section 2: Subdividing Parcels

✓ **Creating and Editing Parcels by Layout Overview**

✓ **Creating and Editing Parcels**

✓ **Renumbering Parcels**

Section 3: Parcel Reports, Annotation, and Tables

✓ **Parcel Reports**

✓ **Parcel Labels**

✓ **Parcel Tables**

Section 1: Parcels Overview

2.1 Introduction to Parcels

A Site under development, as shown in Figure 2–1, is the starting point for defining smaller parcels. The development's agreement or covenants determine the size, setback, and other criteria for the new parcels. If a parcel is residential, there could be restrictions affecting minimum parcel areas, setbacks, and where to locate a house. If it is a commercial property, there could be restrictions or specific mandates for access, traffic control, parking spaces, etc. The Parcel Layout commands are used for subdividing larger parcels.

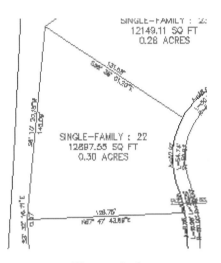

Figure 2–1

Sites, parcels, and alignments are closely related. Each can exist by itself and you do not need to have any alignments associated with the parcels. However, you often start with a site boundary and then divide the site into smaller parcels by placing alignments within its boundary.

- Parcels are listed in the *Prospector* tab in the Sites branch, as shown in Figure 2–2.

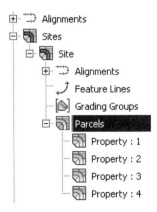

Figure 2–2

- When adding alignments to a site, the Parcels list is updated in the *Prospector* tab.
- As in all other Civil 3D objects, Parcel object layers are controlled in the Drawing Settings dialog box, *Object Layers* tab, as shown in Figure 2–3.

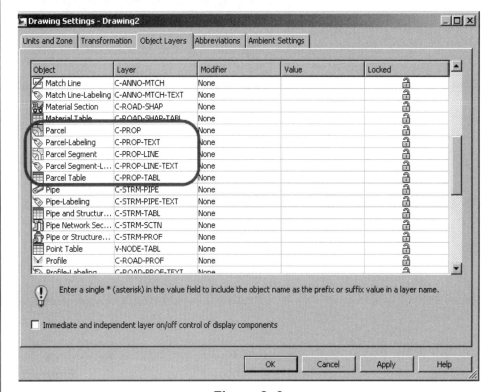

Figure 2–3

ROW Parcel

The right-of-way (ROW) parcel is related to the alignment and parcels. This special parcel represents land that is owned, maintained, and used for the community by a regulatory body (usually the local municipality). The ROW contains the road, sidewalks, and distribution and removal systems for potable water, storm water runoff, and sewage. The contents of the ROW depend on the covenants or agreements made before the site is developed.

- AutoCAD Civil 3D contains a **ROW** command that creates a parcel using offsets from an alignment.
- A ROW parcel can represent the front yard definition of several potential parcels.

- While normal parcels automatically adjust to changes to an alignment, ROW parcels are static, as shown in Figure 2–4. Therefore, you should create ROW parcels only after settling on a final location for an alignment.

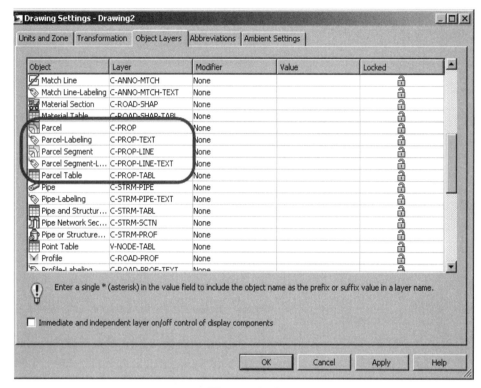

Figure 2–4

Parcel Style Display Order

Parcel segment display is controlled by parcel styles, and parcel lines can abut parcels with different styles. Select the **Parcels** collection (under *Sites*), right-click, and select **Properties**, as shown in Figure 2–5, to open the Site Parcel Properties dialog box. You can select which parcel style should take preference in the *Parcel style display order* area of the Site Parcel Properties dialog box, as shown in Figure 2–5. Placing the style for the overall parent tract (the Site Parcel Style) at the top of the list causes the outside parcel lines to display differently than those inside.

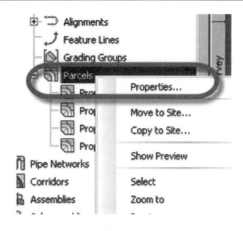

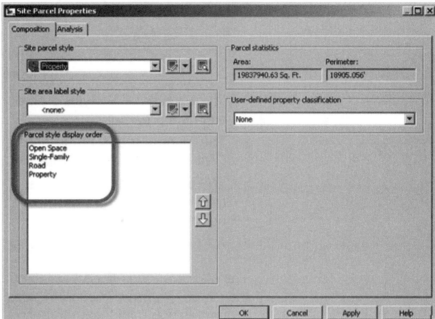

Figure 2–5

Parcel Properties

The properties of a parcel include its name, style, and an *Analysis* tab containing the parcel's area, perimeter, and point-of-beginning (POB). The Parcel Property's *Composition* tab shows the label style, area, and perimeter, as shown in Figure 2–6.

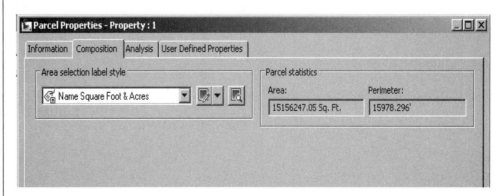

Figure 2–6

The *Analysis* tab contains a parcel boundary Inverse or Mapcheck analysis. In the upper right side of the tab, you can change the POB location and the analysis direction, as shown in Figure 2–7.

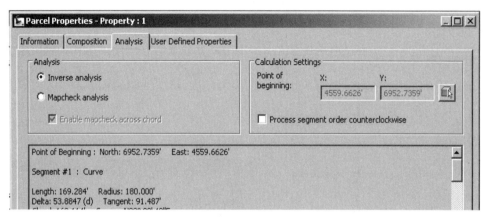

Figure 2–7

- The Mapcheck analysis precision is the same as the drawing distance precision.
- The Inverse report precision is set to the precision of AutoCAD Civil 3D (10-12 decimal places).
- The default direction of a Mapcheck or Inverse analysis is clockwise. You can change the direction to counter-clockwise, if needed.
- A POB can be any vertex on the parcel's perimeter.

The *User Defined Properties* tab contains site-specific details, such as the *Parcel Number, Parcel Address, Parcel Tax ID,* and other properties you might want to define, as shown in Figure 2–8. Custom properties can be assigned to a drawing through the *User Defined Property Classifications* section of the *Settings* tab, under the *Parcels* collection.

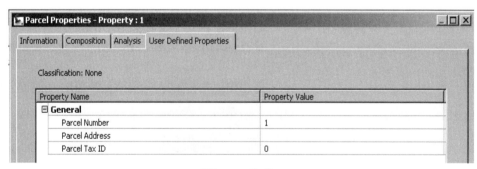

Figure 2–8

Parcel Labels and Styles

There are two types of parcel annotation: an area label for the parcel itself and the segments defining the parcel.

A parcel area label usually consists of a parcel's number or name, area, and perimeter, as shown in Figure 2–9. Most offices define their own parcel label styles. A parcel label style can include several additional parcel properties, address, PIN, Site name, etc. In AutoCAD Civil 3D, you graphically select a parcel by selecting a parcel area label, not parcel segments.

SINGLE-FAMILY : 16
10200.00 SQ FT
0.23 ACRES

Figure 2–9

Create Parcels from Objects

AutoCAD Civil 3D can create parcels from AutoCAD objects, such as closed polylines and closed sequences of lines and arcs. Be careful to avoid gaps, multiple polyline vertices at the same location, and polylines that double-back over themselves, which might lead to errors in parcel layouts.

These objects can be selected in the current drawing or from an XREF. Keep in mind that AutoCAD Civil 3D parcel lines in an XREF cannot be selected-only lines, arcs, and polylines. Also note that AutoCAD Civil 3D parcels created from AutoCAD objects maintain no relationship to the objects after creation.

Creating Right-of-Way Parcels

Once a site has the property defined as a parcel and alignments are generated, you are ready to start creating subdivision plans. One command that can speed up the process is **Parcels > Create ROW**. This command automatically creates Right-of-Way parcels based on alignment setbacks.

Keep in mind that ROW parcels do not automatically update when alignments change. Therefore, you might want to create ROWs after you are fairly certain where you want the alignments to be for this alternative.

Hint: Multiple Alternatives in the Same Drawing

Sites enable you to organize alignments, parcels, and related data into separate containers, so that parcel lines from one site alternative do not clean up with parcel lines in others. However, sites do not offer layer or any other kind of visibility control. Therefore, if you intend to have multiple parcel layout alternatives in the same drawing, you should consider placing parcel area labels and parcel segments on different layers

Practice 2a | Beginning a Subdivision Project

Task 1: Create a Site parcel from objects and renumber parcels.

1. Open the file **PCL1-Sec1-Parcel.dwg** from the following folder:

   C:\Civil 3D Projects\Civil3D-training\Drawings.

2. To make the annotation easier to read, change the current drawing scale. In the Status Bar, set the Annotation Scale to **1:1000**, as shown in Figure 2–10.

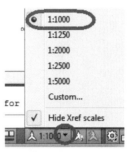

Figure 2–10

3. Create a parcel from existing objects in Model Space. In the *Home* tab > Create Design panel, select **Parcel > Create Parcels** from Objects, as shown in Figure 2–11.

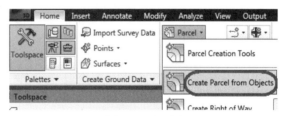

Figure 2–11

4. In the model, select all the objects that represent the property boundary and press Enter when done selecting. Set the following parameters:

   - Site: **Site 1**
   - Parcel style: **Property**
   - Area Label style: **Name Area & Perimeter**
   - Erase existing entities: Select this option.

5. Refer to Figure 2–12 for the remaining values, then click OK to accept and close the dialog box.

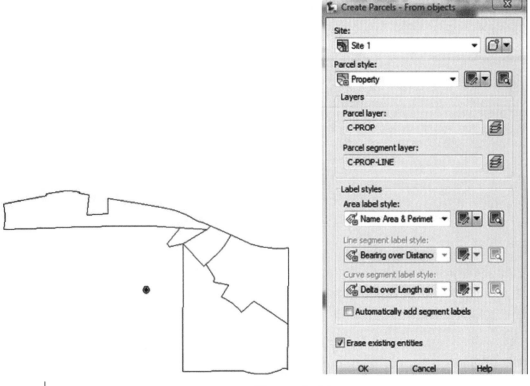

Figure 2–12

6. Five parcels will be created. In the *Prospector* tab, expand the **current drawing branch**, as well as the **Sites** branch by selecting the **+** sign. Continue to expand until you reach the *Parcels* branch, as shown in Figure 2–13. **Note**: If the **+** is not showing next to *Parcels*, press the <F5> key to refresh the *Prospector* tab view.

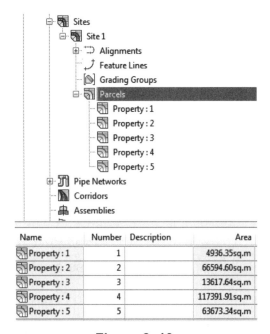

Name	Number	Description	Area
Property : 1	1		4936.35sq.m
Property : 2	2		66594.60sq.m
Property : 3	3		13617.64sq.m
Property : 4	4		117391.91sq.m
Property : 5	5		63673.34sq.m

Figure 2–13

7. Change the style of two properties. In Model Space, select the parcels shown in Figure 2–14. Select **Property 1** and in the *Parcel* tab > Modify panel, select **Parcel Properties**. In the *Information* tab of the dialog box that opens, change the *Object style* to **Single-Family**.

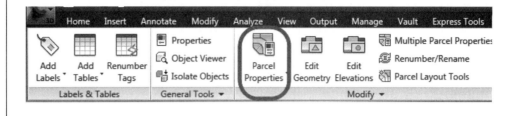

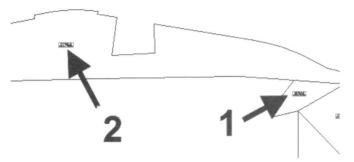

Figure 2–14

8. Repeat the previous step for **Property 2** and change the *Object style* to **Open Space**.

9. In the *View* tab > Views panel, select the preset view **C3D-Parcel-Split Parcel**.

10. Note the north boundary of the Single-Family parcel that shares the parcel line with the Open Space parcel displays this parcel line with the style assigned to the Open Space, as shown in Figure 2–15.

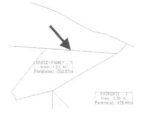

Figure 2–15

11. Display the Single-Family parcel so that its assigned style takes precedence over all other shared parcel line styles. In the *Prospector* tab, expand the *Sites* collection, and then the *Site 1* collection. Select the **Parcels** collection, right-click, and select **Properties**.

12. In the Site Parcel Properties dialog box, select **Single-Family** in the Parcel style display order section, as shown in Figure 2–16.

   Click 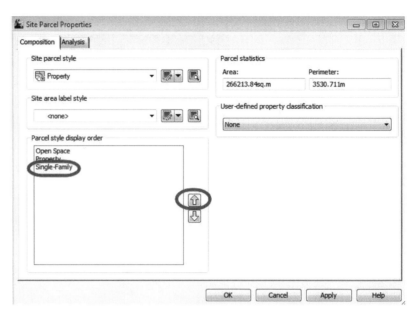 to move it up in the list.

Figure 2–16

13. Click  to close the dialog box and save the drawing.

Task 2: Split and Merge Parcels.

As part of the development, you will need to acquire or purchase a partition of land from Property 2 (Open Space:2) and Property 1 (Single-Family:1).

1. Continue working with the drawing from the previous task.

2. In the *View* tab > Views panel, select the preset view **C3D-Parcel-Split Parcel**, as shown in Figure 2–17.

Figure 2–17

3. You will extend the blue property line until it intersects the north green property line. Select the blue property line to display the grips. Select the grip and move it to the apparent intersection. Press <Ctrl>, right-click, and select **Apparent Intersection**. When prompted for apparent of, select **line 1** and then **line 2**, as shown in Figure 2–18.

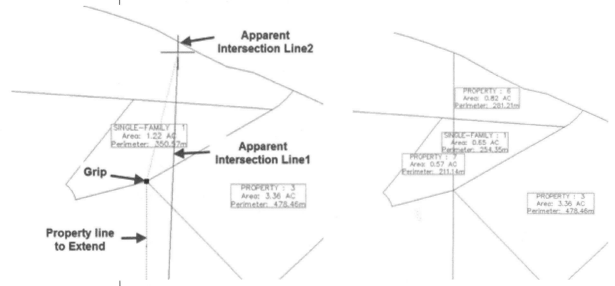

Figure 2–18

4. Select the parcel label **Property 6** and in the contextual Ribbon, select **Parcel Properties**. In the Parcel Properties dialog box, select the *Analysis* tab and select the **Mapcheck analysis** option. Scroll down the list and you should see the *Error Closure* or *Precision*, as well at the total *Area*, as shown in Figure 2–19. This is the area of land you will need to purchase. Perform the same steps to determine the area you will need to purchase from the single-family lot.

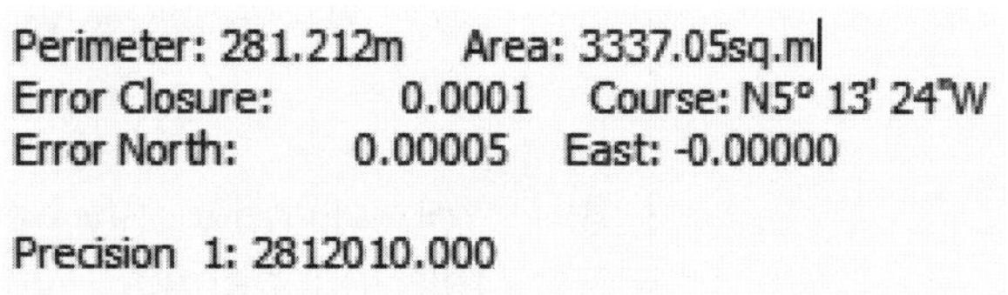

Perimeter: 281.212m   Area: 3337.05sq.m|
Error Closure: 0.0001   Course: N5° 13' 24"W
Error North: 0.00005   East: -0.00000

Precision 1: 2812010.000

Figure 2–19

5. To create one parcel based on your development site, you have to erase and modify all property lines that split the site. Since you are performing a land transfer of Single-Family:1 and Property:6 to the main parcel site, you need to adjust the property line that divides the two parcels.

6. Select the north property line to display the grips. Select the east grip and move it to the intersection. Press <Ctrl>, right-click, and select **Intersection**. When prompted for intersection of, select **point 1**, as shown in Figure 2-20.

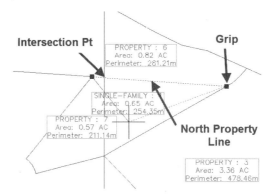

Figure 2–20

7. Use the AutoCAD **Erase** command to erase all of the internal property lines, as shown in Figure 2–21.

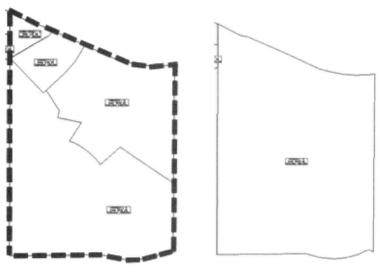

Figure 2–21

8. You will now only have three properties. Rename them to relevant names. Type **ZE** <Enter> at the Command Line for Zoom Extents. In the Status Bar, enable the Quick Properties icon, as shown in Figure 2–22.

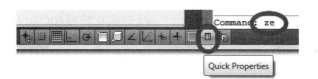

Figure 2–22

9. Select the **Open Space:2** property (at the west end) and in the Quick Properties dialog box, change the *Name* to **Private AR** (agricultural reserve) and leave the *Style* as **Open Space**, as shown in Figure 2–23. Press <Esc> when finished.

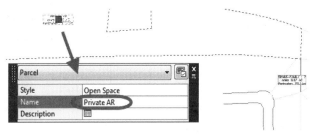

Figure 2–23

10. Select the pie-shaped parcel located in the middle area between the two parcels. Rename it to **Single Family R1** and enter **Single-Family** for the *Style*, as shown in Figure 2–24.

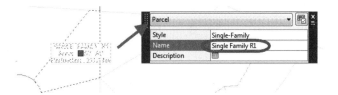

Figure 2–24

11. Select the main parcel that is to the east. Rename it to **Main Property** and enter **Property** for the *Style*.

Task 3: Create a new Site and Site parcel from referenced objects.

You have received a drawing from the Land planning department that shows the street layout and different parcels. Using this plan, you will create parcels.

1. Continue working with the drawing from the previous task.

2. To enable a preset view, in the *View* tab > Views panel, select the preset view **C3D-Parcel-Site**.

3. In the *Insert* tab > Reference panel, click the arrow to the right, as shown on the left in Figure 2–25, to start the **Manage Xrefs** command. In the External References dialog box, click 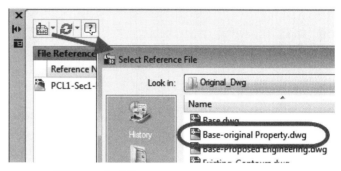 (Attach Dwg). In the Select Reference File dialog box, select **Base-original Property.dwg**, located in *C:\Civil 3D Projects\Civil3D-training\Original_Dwg*, as shown on the right.

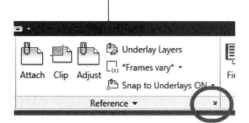

Figure 2–25

4. In the Attach External Reference dialog box, as shown in Figure 2–26, select the **Locate using Geographic Data** option and click OK to reference the drawing. In the External References dialog box, click on the **X** to close it.

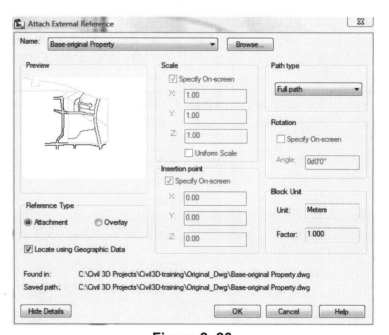

Figure 2–26

5. In the *Home* tab > Layers panel, select the preset layer setting **C3D-Parcel Proposed**.

6. Create a new site branch where you can store all parcels that are relevant to the Main development site. In the *Prospector* tab, right-click on the Sites branch and select **New**. Enter **C3D Training** as the name and click [OK] to close the dialog box.

7. You now need to move the Parcel Main Property from Site 1 to the C3D Training site. Expand the *Site1* collection, expand the *Parcels* collection, right-click on Main Property parcel and select **Move to Site**, as shown on the left in Figure 2–27. In the Move to site dialog box, select **C3D Training**, as shown on the right. Click [OK] to close the dialog box.

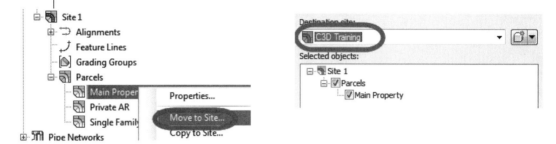

Figure 2–27

8. In the AutoCAD Layer Manager, freeze the layer **Base-original Property|A-Property-Existing**.

9. Create parcels from the x-referenced file. In the *Home* tab > Create Design panel, select **Parcel > Create Parcels from Objects**. Type **X** (for **xref**) <Enter> at the Command Line.

10. When prompted to select the xref objects, type **WP** (for window poly) <Enter> at the Command Line. Draw a boundary that encompasses all of the polylines that define the internal site, as shown on the left of Figure. Once you are finished defining the boundary, end the WP selection command by pressing <Enter>. Press <Enter> again to end the xref selection command.

11. In the Create Parcels - From objects dialog box, ensure that the Site name is **C3D Training** and accept the remaining defaults, as shown on the right in Figure 2–28. Click [OK] to close the dialog box.

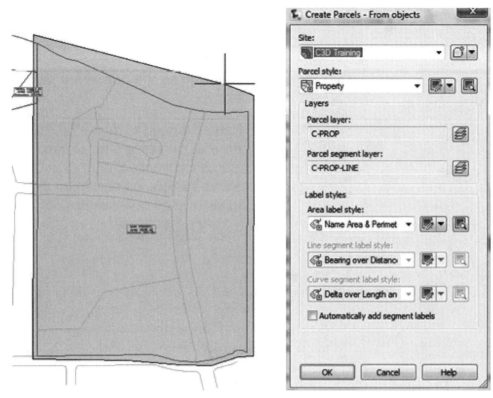

Figure 2–28

12. The project site has nine parcels. Select each of the **parcel labels** and in the Quick Properties dialog box, rename the parcels according to Figure 2–29.

1. Commercial C1

2. Multi Family MF

3. Municipal Reserve MR

4. Pond PUL

5. Residential BLK2 R1

6. Residential BLK1 R1

7. Residential BLK3 R1

8. Right Of Way

9. School MSR

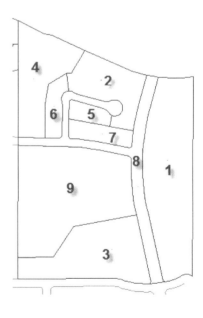

Figure 2–29

13. Save the drawing.

Review Questions

Question 1 | Where are parcels listed?

Question 2 | What does the ROW contain?

Question 3 | What does a parcel style assign in the Display tab?

Question 4 | What is the default direction of a Mapcheck or Inverse report?

Question 5 | How do you adjust parcel display order?

Section 2: Subdividing Parcels

2.2 Creating and Editing Parcels by Layout Overview

In addition to creating parcels from polylines, arcs, and lines, AutoCAD Civil 3D can also intelligently create (and adjust) parcels using commands in the Parcel Layout Tools toolbar. To open the Parcel Layout Tools toolbar, click the down arrow next to the **Parcel** icon on the Create Design panel, and select **Parcel Creation Tools** in the drop-down list, as shown in Figure 2–30.

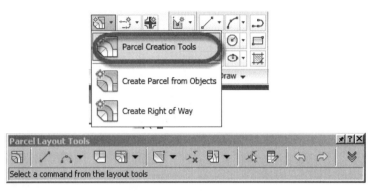

Figure 2–30

- (Create Parcel) assigns parcel creation settings, such as parcel type, labeling styles, and other parameters.

- The **Line** and **Curve** commands ( ) can be used to create individual line and curve parcel segments. Segments created with these tools are considered *fixed* (see the *Alignment* course material for a definition of the fixed vs. free or floating segment types).

- (Draw Tangent - Tangent with No Curves) enables you to create a series of connected parcel line segments.

- The Parcel Sizing flyout, as shown in Figure 2–31, contains a list of commands for creating and editing parcels. The methods used to create parcels include defining the last parcel segment by slide direction, slide angle, swing line, or freehand drawing of a parcel boundary. The most frequently used method is **Slide Line**.

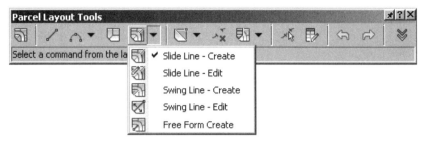

Figure 2–31

- The commands at the center of the toolbar, as shown in Figure 2–32, enable you to further edit parcel segments. These commands include inserting or deleting PIs (points of intersection), deleting parcel segments, or creating or dissolving parcel unions.

Figure 2–32

- (Pick Sub-Entity) enables you to select a parcel line and view its details in the Parcel Layout Parameters dialog box.

- (Sub-entity Editor) opens and closes the Parcel Layout Parameters dialog box.

- The next two commands enable you to **Undo** and **Redo** parcel edits ( ).

- The drop-down arrow (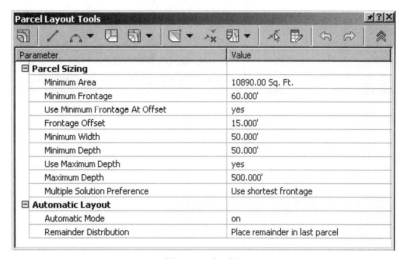) expands the toolbar to show the Parcel Creation parameters, as shown in Figure 2–33 (also accessible through the Command Settings of *CreateParcelByLayout* in the *Settings* tab).

Figure 2–33

- The *Parcel Sizing* section sets the minimum area for parcels to be laid out. The *Minimum Frontage* sets the minimum width of a parcel at the ROW or at a setback from the ROW.

- The *Use Minimum Frontage At Offset* specifies whether or not to use frontage offset criteria.

- The *Frontage Offset* sets the default value for the frontage offset from the ROW.

- The *Minimum Width* sets the default minimum width at the frontage offset.

- The *Minimum Depth* sets the minimum depth of new or existing parcels at the mid-point and is perpendicular to the frontage of the parcel.

- The *Use Maximum Depth* specifies whether or not to use maximum depth criteria.

- The *Maximum Depth* sets the maximum depth for new parcels or when editing parcels.

- The *Multiple Solution Preference* specifies whether or not to use the shortest frontage or the smallest area when multiple solutions are encountered.

- The *Automatic Layout* section affects how parcel auto-sizing subdivides a parcel block.

2.3 Creating and Editing Parcels

The Create Parcel by Layout tools can quickly help you create a subdivision plan. Although these tools can make your job easier and are faster than manual drafting, they are only effective in creating the last side of new parcels. In other words, you might need to create additional (or adjust) parcel lines manually to guide AutoCAD Civil 3D to the best solution. The area shown in Figure 2–34, for example, requires you to create minimum 950 sq m parcels.

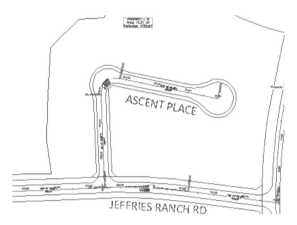

Figure 2–34

The back parcel lines (those along the west and south of the Cul-De-Sac area, and between Jeffries Ranch Rd and Ascent Place) were drawn manually and saved in a separate drawing file. Once inserted, they will be used to guide the creation of the parcels adjacent to Ascent Place. If you ask AutoCAD Civil 3D to automatically subdivide this area, the result is a total of 15 parcels, as shown in Figure 2–35.

Figure 2–35

The various creation and editing techniques available in the Create Parcel by Layout toolbar are described below.

Freehand

The **Line** and **Curve** commands (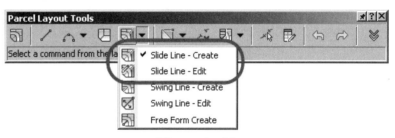) and (Draw Tangent - Tangent with No Curves) command enable you to create lot lines without having to specify an area. In contrast, the commands below all create parcels based on a specified area.

Slide Line

The **Slide Line - Create** command enables you to subdivide a larger parcel by creating new parcel lines that hold a certain angle relative to the Right-of-Way, such as 90° or a specific bearing or azimuth. The **Slide Line - Edit** command enables you to modify a parcel to a specified area while holding the same angle from the ROW or a specific bearing or azimuth. They are shown in Figure 2–36.

Figure 2–36

Swing Line

The **Swing Line - Create** command enables you to create a new parcel by creating a parcel segment that connects to a specified point, such as a property corner. The **Swing Line - Edit** command enables you to resize a parcel while specifying a lot corner. These commands are shown in Figure 2–37.

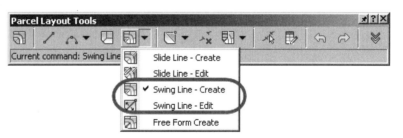

Figure 2–37

Free Form Create

The **Free Form Create** command enables you to create a new lot by specifying an area, an attachment point and angle, or two attachment points.

Frontage

When using these routines, you are prompted to select a parcel interior point and trace its frontage geometry. This is a critical step. As you trace the frontage, the command creates a jig (heavy highlight) that recognizes the changing geometry of the frontage line work.

2.4 Renumbering Parcels

Creating parcels using the methods explained in the previous examples results in inconsistent parcel numbering. AutoCAD Civil 3D parcels can be renumbered individually using Parcel Properties, or in groups using **Modify > Parcel > Renumber/Rename**.

This command enables you to specify a starting parcel number and the increment you would like between parcels. (It also enables you to rename your parcels based on a different name template.) When renumbering, the command prompts you to identify parcels in the order in which you want to have them renumbered. The Renumber/Rename Parcels dialog box is shown in Figure 2–38.

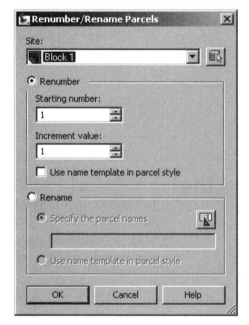

Figure 2–38

Practice 2b | Creating and Editing Parcels

You have three parcels zoned as single-family residential: Block 1 (1.31ac), Block2 (0.94ac), and Block3 (1.47ac). Your client, the land developer, requires you to maximize the number of lots in these three parcels, keeping in mind the minimum area and frontages as required by the Land Use bylaws.

Task 1: Create parcels by slide angle.

1. Continue working with the drawing from the previous practice or open the file **PCL1-Sec2-Parcel.dwg** from the following folder:

    C:\Civil 3D Projects\Civil3D-training\Drawings

2. In the *View* tab > Views panel, select the preset view **C3D-Parcel-Create parcels**.

3. In the *Home* tab > Create Design panel, select **Parcel > Parcel Creation Tools**. The Parcel Layout Tools toolbar is displayed, as shown in Figure 2–39.

Figure 2–39

4. Click and enter the values shown in Figure 2–40. As you enter each value, notice the graphics below in the dialog box. They visually identify what the values you enter are used for.

Parameter	Value
⊟ **Parcel Sizing**	
Minimum Area	950.00sq.m
Minimum Frontage	20.000m
Use Minimum Frontage At Offset	Yes
Frontage Offset	6.000m
Minimum Width	20.000m
Minimum Depth	6.000m
Use Maximum Depth	Yes
Maximum Depth	1500.000m
Multiple Solution Preference	Use shortest frontage
⊟ **Automatic Layout**	
Automatic Mode	On
Remainder Distribution	Place remainder in last parcel

Figure 2–40

5. In the Parcel Layout Tools toolbar, expand  and select **Slide Line - Create**, as shown in Figure 2–41.

Figure 2–41

6. In the Create Parcels - Layout dialog box, set the following parameters, as shown in Figure 2–42:

    - Site: **C3D Training**

    - Parcel style: **Single-Family**

    - Area label style: **Parcel Name - Area**

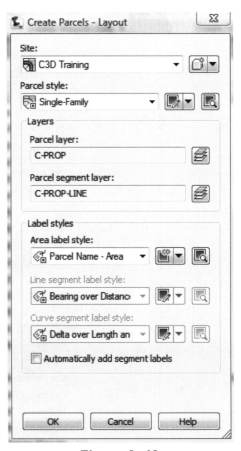

Figure 2–42

7. Click ⬚ OK ⬚ to accept the changes and close the dialog box.

8. When prompted to select the parcel to be subdivided, select the label for parcel **RESIDENTIAL BLK1 R1**, as shown in Figure 2–43.

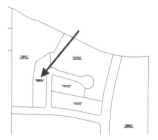

Figure 2–43

9. When you are prompted for the *starting point on frontage*, select the south end of the corner cut. Press the <Ctrl> key, right-click, and select **endpoint**. Then select the corner cut, Pt1, shown in Figure 2–44.

10. When prompted for the *end point of the frontage*, set the end point of the property line to the north, Pt 2, as shown in Figure 2–44. Use the same process as the previous step to set the end point.

11. When prompted for the *angle of the property line* that will be used to define each lot, select a point east of the parcel near Pt 3, shown in Figure 2–44. For the second point, press the <Ctrl> key, right-click, and select **Perpendicular**. Then select the line at Pt 4.

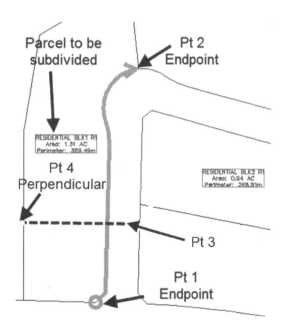

Figure 2–44

12. When prompted to *Accept results*, press <Enter>.

13. When prompted to select another parcel to subdivide, press <Enter> to end the command.

14. Enter **X** at the Command Line to exit the layout tool.

15. Save the drawing.

Task 2: Rename and renumber parcels.

1. Continue working with the drawing from the previous task.

2. Rename and renumber the lots so that you have the same numbering system. In the *Modify* tab > Design panel, select **Parcel**. This displays the *Parcel* Ribbon tab.

3. In the *Parcel* tab > Modify panel, select **Renumber/Rename**, as shown in Figure 2–45.

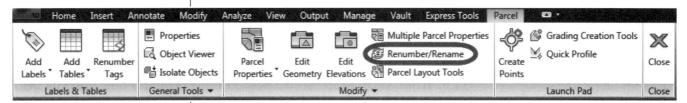

Figure 2–45

4. In the Renumber/Rename Parcel dialog box, select the **Rename** option. Select the **Specify the parcel names** option and click

, as shown in Figure 2–46.

Figure 2–46

5. In the Name Template dialog box, enter **Blk1 - Lot** with a space after it in the *Name* field, as shown in Figure 2–47. Select **Next Counter** in the *Property Fields* drop-down list and click Insert . Click OK to apply the changes and close the dialog box.

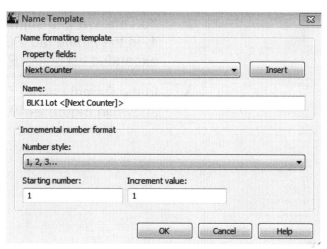

Figure 2–47

6. In the Renumber/Rename Parcel dialog box, click OK to accept the changes and close the dialog box.

7. When prompted for the points, select all of the parcels to be renumbered. Select the three points shown in Figure 2–48 and press <Enter> to complete the selection. Press <Enter> again to exit the command.

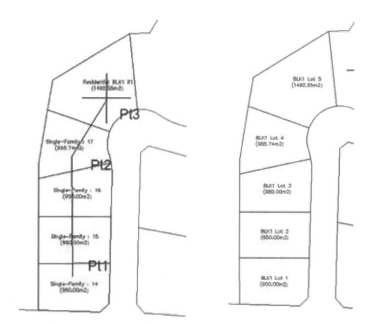

Figure 2–48

8. Save the drawing.

Task 3: Edit parcels using Swing Line - Edit.

In this task, you adjust the last three lots of the parcel (or lotting plan) so that they are more marketable.

1. Continue working with the drawing from the previous task.

2. You first want to adjust the Lot line between Parcel 3 and Parcel 4. In the *Home* tab > Create Design panel, select **Parcel**. In the expanded list select **Parcel Creation Tools**.

3. In the Parcel Layout Tools toolbar, select **Swing Line - Edit**, as shown in Figure 2–49.

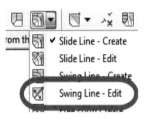

Figure 2–49

4. In the Create Parcel - Layout dialog box, set the following parameters, as shown in Figure 2–50:

   • Site: **C3D Training**

   • Parcel Style: **Single-Family**

   • Area Label style: **Parcel Name - Area**

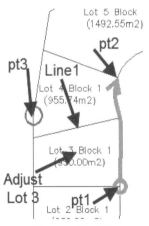

Figure 2–50

5. At this point, you do not want to label segments so do not enable this option. Click ⬚ OK ⬚ when done.

6. When prompted to select the parcel line to adjust, select the parcel line between Lot 3 and Lot 4.

7. When prompted for the parcel to adjust, select Lot 3.

8. When prompted for the *start frontage*, select the bottom right corner of Lot 3, pt1. When prompted for the *end of the frontage*, select the top right corner of lot 4, pt2.

9. When prompted for the *swing point*, select the end point of pt3.

10. When prompted to accept the results. enter **yes** and press <Enter>.

11. You have the desired results for Lot 3. However, Lot 4 is 955.74 m2 and Lot 5 is 1492.55m2. You want to somewhat even-sized lots, each being approximately 1224 m2. Show the Parcel Layout Tools toolbar if it is not visible.

12. You should still be in the **Swing Line - Edit** command. (If not, repeat steps 2-3 of this task.)

13. In the Parcel Layout Tools toolbar, click ⌄⌄ to expand it. Change the minimum area to **1224**. Collapse the toolbar if needed by clicking ⌃⌃ .

14. When prompted to select the parcel line to adjust, select the parcel line between Lot 4 and Lot 5 (Line 1).

15. When prompted for the parcel to adjust, select Lot 4.

16. When prompted for the *start frontage*, select the bottom right corner of Lot 4, pt1. When prompted for the *end of the frontage*, select the top right corner of lot 5, pt2.

17. When prompted for the *swing point*, select the end point of pt3, as shown in Figure 2–51.

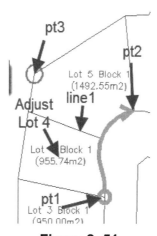

Figure 2–51

18. When prompted to accept the results, enter **yes** and press <Enter>.

19. Press <Esc> or click the **X** in the Parcel Layout Tools dialog box to close it.

20. If time permits, perform the same steps as described above to subdivide Parcels Block 2 and Block 3.

21. Save the drawing.

Review Questions

Question 1 How do you create or subdivide parcels interactively?

Question 2 Which Parcel Create command enables you to hold a specified angle relative to the Right-Of-Way?

Section 3: Parcel Reports, Annotation, and Tables

2.5 Parcel Reports

AutoCAD Civil 3D has several types of parcel reports. Parcel Inverse and Mapcheck data is available through the *Analysis* tab of the Parcel Properties dialog box, as shown in Figure 2–52. The report can be generated clockwise or counter-clockwise, and the point of beginning can be specified.

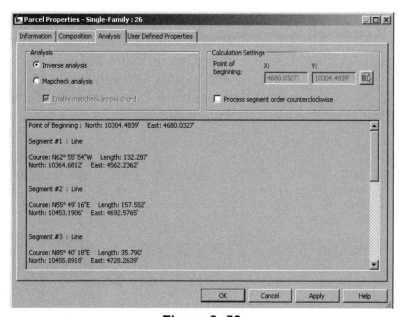

Figure 2–52

This dialog box does not enable output. If you want to generate a printable report, use AutoCAD Civil 3D's Toolbox. It includes several stock Parcel-related reports (such as Surveyor Certificates, Inverse and Mapcheck reports, Metes and Bounds), as shown in Figure 2–53.

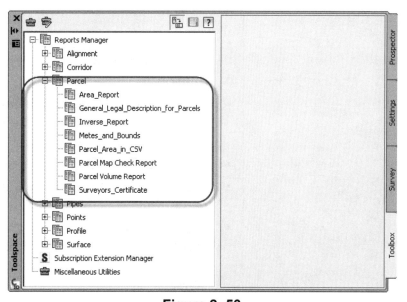

Figure 2–53

2.6 Parcel Labels

Parcel area labels are a means of graphically selecting a parcel, such as when creating Right-of-Ways. In the Parcel creation and editing examples, you had parcel segment labels created for you automatically. This section explores the functionality of these labels in more depth.

The Add Labels dialog box (**Annotate > Add Labels > Parcel > Add Parcel Labels...**) can be used to assign the desired label styles and place labels in the drawing. It can set the line, curve, and spiral styles and toggle between single and multiple segment labeling, as well as access the Tag Numbering Table. The dialog box is shown in Figure 2–54.

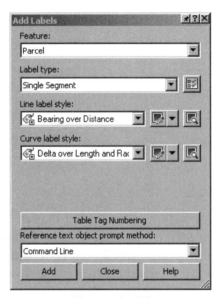

Figure 2–54

- Parcel labels, as with all AutoCAD Civil 3D labels, are capable of rotating and resizing to match changes in the viewport scale and rotation.
- A segment label has two definitions: composed and dragged state. A dragged state can be quite different from the original label definition.
- AutoCAD Civil 3D can label segments while sizing parcels.
- Labeling can be read clockwise or counter-clockwise around the parcel.
- Labels can be added through an external reference file using the same commands that label objects in their source drawing. This makes it easier to have multiple plans that need different label styles.

- The **Replace Multiple Labels** option is useful when you want to replace a number of parcel segment labels with another style. However, if you are labeling through an external reference file, labels created in the source drawing cannot be modified.

Parcel Area labels are controlled using Parcel Area Label Styles, which control the display of custom information (such as the parcel number, area, perimeter, address, etc.). You can create more than one parcel area label, for example, if you need to show different parcel information on different sheets. An example is shown in Figure 2–55.

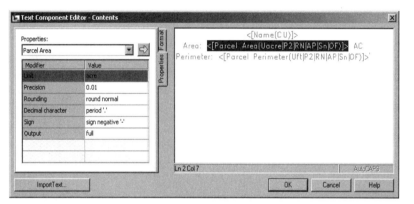

Figure 2–55

Parcel Segment labels annotate the line and curve segments of a parcel, as shown in Figure 2–56. You can label all segments of a parcel with one click or label only selected parcel segments.

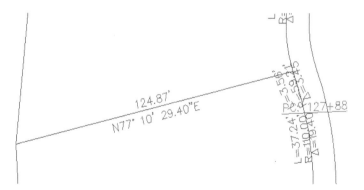

Figure 2–56

All labels have two definitions: one for the original location, and another when it is moved from its original location. A dragged label can remain as originally defined or can be changed to stacked text.

2.7 Parcel Tables

Parcel tables are an alternative to labeling individual parcel areas and segments. An example is shown in Figure 2–57.

Parcel Line and Curve Table			
Line #/Curve #	Length	Bearing/Delta	Radius
L76	112.01	N4° 08' 12.22"W	
L77	395.08	N85° 33' 05.19"E	
L78	471.49	N85° 33' 05.19"E	
L79	210.99	N4° 17' 33.13"W	
L80	211.55	N4° 17' 33.13"W	
L81	115.43	S25° 31' 05.98"W	

Figure 2–57

When creating a table, AutoCAD Civil 3D changes the parcel segment labels to a letter-number combination, called a *tag*. A tag with **L** stands for line and **C** stands for curve. A segment's tag has a corresponding entry in the table.

- A table can only represent a selected set of label styles.
- The **Add Existing** option, as shown in Figure 2–58, creates a table from existing objects. New objects will not be added to the table. The **Add Existing and New** option will create a table with existing as well as new objects.

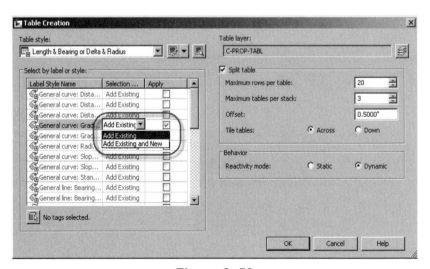

Figure 2–58

- A table can have a dynamic link between a segment's tag and table entry. If the segment changes, the table entry updates.
- AutoCAD Civil 3D switches a label to a tag by changing the *Display* mode from **Label** to **Tag**, as shown in Figure 2–59.

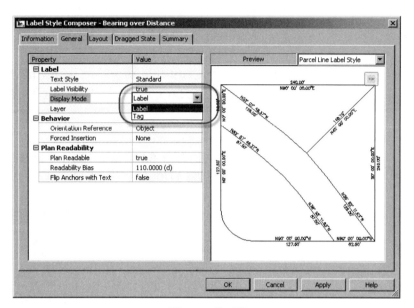

Figure 2–59

Practice 2c | Reporting on and Annotating the Parcel Layout

Task 1: Add Parcel labels.

1. Continue working with the drawing from the previous practice or open the file **PCL1-Sec3-Parcel.dwg** from the following folder:

   C:\Civil 3D Projects\Civil3D-training\Drawings

2. In the *Annotate* tab > Labels & Tables panel, select **Add Labels**, as shown in Figure 2–60.

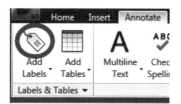

Figure 2–60

3. In the Add Labels dialog box, set the following parameters, as shown in Figure 2–61:

   - Feature: **Parcel**

   - Label type: **Multiple Segment**

   - Line label style: **Azimuth over Distance**

   - Curve label style: **Delta over Length and Radius**

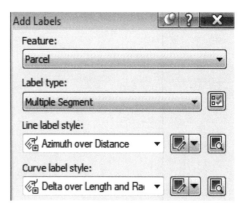

Figure 2–61

4. Click [Add].

5. When prompted to select the Parcels you want to annotate, select all of the single-family parcels in Model Space.

6. When prompted for the label direction, enter **CL** for clockwise and press <Enter>.

7. Repeat the previous three steps for all remaining parcels.

8. Press <Enter> when done labeling the parcels.

9. Click the **X** in the Add Labels dialog box or click [Close] to close the dialog box.

Parcels can also be labeled in an XREF file.

10. Save the drawing.

Task 2: Create Line and Curve Segment Tables.

Labels are overlapping in a number of locations, making the drawing difficult to read. In this task, you try two methods to fix this. In the first method, you simply drag the label to a location where there is no conflict. In the second method, you add a label tag and an associated table.

1. Continue working with the drawing from the previous task.

2. In the Ribbon *View* tab > Views panel, select the preset view **C3D-Parcel Add Tag1**.

3. Select the label **3.64m**, select the square grip, and drag to place the label in a location where there is no conflict. Do the same for the label **6.37m**, as shown in Figure 2–62.

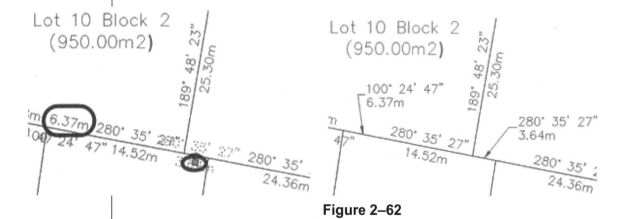

Figure 2–62

4. In the Ribbon *View* tab > Views panel, select the preset view **C3D-Parcel Add Tag2**.

5. You will now add tags and a table. In the *Annotate* tab > Label & Tables panel, select **Add Tables > Parcel > Add segment**, as shown in Figure 2–63.

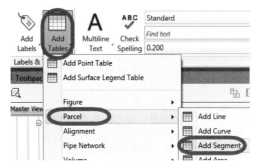

Figure 2–63

6. In the Table Creation dialog box, click 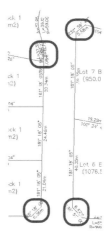 and select the labels shown in Figure 2–64.

Figure 2–64

7. When prompted to convert labels to tags or to not add labels, select **Convert all selected label styles to tag mode**.

8. Click [OK] to close the Table Creation dialog box.

9. When prompted for a location for the table, select a location in an open space, as shown in Figure 2–65.

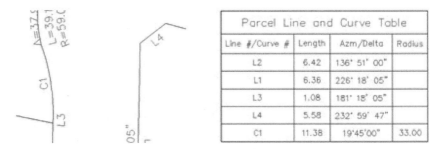

Figure 2–65

10. Save the drawing.

Task 3: Create a Parcel Area Table.

1. In the *Annotate* tab > Label & Tables panel, select **Add Tables > Parcel > Add Area**.

2. In the Table Creation dialog box, select the style name **Parcel Name - Area** in the *Select by label* or *style* section, as shown in Figure 2–66. All parcels with this style will be selected.

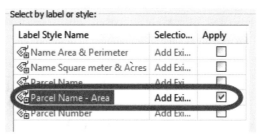

Figure 2–66

3. Click a location to insert the table into the drawing, as shown in Figure 2–67.

Parcel Area Table				
Lot	Area	Perimeter	Segment Lengths	Segment Bearings
BLK1–Lot 1	950.00m²	124.09	126.51 69.02 20.88 109.83 80.86	89° 58' 04" 181° 18' 05" 226° 18' 05" 271° 18' 05" 359° 58' 04"
BLK1–Lot 2	950.00m²	126.61	128.38 80.26 126.51 80.24	89° 58' 04" 181° 18' 05" 269° 58' 04" 359° 58' 04"
BLK1–Lot 3	950.00m²	127.67	132.28 66.72 128.38 91.50	100° 46' 26" 181° 18' 05" 269° 58' 04" 359° 58' 04"

Figure 2–67

4. Save the drawing.

Task 4: Create a Parcel Report.

1. Continue working with the drawing from the previous task.

2. If the *Toolbox* tab is not visible, go to the *Home* tab > Palettes panel, and click  (Toolbox), as shown in Figure 2–68.

Figure 2–68

3. In the *Toolbox* tab, expand the Reports Manager and Parcel collections. Right-click on Surveyor's Certificate and select **Execute**.

4. In the Export to LandXML dialog box, click (Pick from drawing), located at the bottom left of the dialog box.

5. When prompted to select a parcel, select one of the single-family lots created earlier and press <Enter>.

6. In the Export to XML Report dialog box, notice that only the Lots you selected now have a check mark. Click OK to close the dialog box.

7. In the Save As dialog box, enter the desired file name for the report and click Save to close.

8. Review the report, as shown in Figure 2–69, and close the web browser.

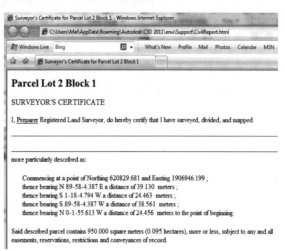

Figure 2–69

9. Save the drawing.

Either of these formats can be opened in word processors such as Microsoft Word, which can read all of the formatting displayed in the web browser. Report settings, such as the Preparer's name, can be assigned by clicking **Report Settings** in the Toolspace.

Review Questions

Question 1 What are the two types of AutoCAD Civil 3D Parcel labels?

Question 2 What does the Add Labels dialog box do?

Question 3 What are parcel tables an alternative to?

Module 3

Survey Level 1

This module introduces:

Section 1: Civil 3D Survey Toolspace
- ✓ **Survey Workflow Overview**
- ✓ **Introduction to the Survey Toolspace**
- ✓ **The Survey Toolspace**
- ✓ **Survey Networks**

Section 2: Civil 3D Points
- ✓ **Points Overview**
- ✓ **Point Label Styles**
- ✓ **Styles and Templates**
- ✓ **Point Settings**
- ✓ **Creating Points**

- ✓ **Transparent Command**
- ✓ **Description Key Sets**
- ✓ **Importing and Exporting Points**
- ✓ **Point Groups**
- ✓ **Reviewing and Editing Points**
- ✓ **Locking/Unlocking Points**
- ✓ **Point Reports**

Section 3: Civil 3D Survey Figures
- ✓ **Survey Figures**
- ✓ **Importing a Field Book**
- ✓ **Working with Figures**

Section 1: Civil 3D Survey Toolspace

3.1 Survey Workflow Overview

This module focuses on automated *Field to Finish* tools that aid in drafting an accurate and efficient "Existing Condition Plan". These tools create a correct existing topography, property lines, right-of-way, and center line locations.

Workflow

To create linework from coordinate files use the following survey workflow:

1. Data needs to be entered into the data collector. The proper language, methodology, and basic rules regarding data entry into the data collector begin with an understanding of Figure Commands and Codes (raw descriptions).

2. Data can be transferred from the data collector to the computer using an ASCII file. An ASCII file can be opened in Notepad and data can be separated or delineated by spaces or commas. The most popular transferred format is Point Number, Northing, Easting, Elevation, Description. This material focuses on the different types of Descriptions that can be entered into a data collector so that the user obtains the desired automated symbology and linework.

3. If using a field book file (a type of ASCII file), data needs to be converted from the raw coordinate file to a field book (*.fbk) using AutoCAD Civil 3D's Survey Link or other methods. Autodesk has collaborated with major survey equipment vendors to develop API and drivers that will interface their specific survey equipment (Trimble Link, TDS Survey Link, Leica X-Change, TOPCON Link, etc.) to AutoCAD Civil 3D.

    If following the Linework Code Set command format, you do not need to convert the coordinate file to a field book. All that is required is to import the file with linework processing turned on.

4. AutoCAD Civil 3D needs to have all the necessary Styles, Settings, and Figure Prefixes to create, sort, and place points and linework on the desired layers.

The surveying department can substantially increase productivity and efficiency by standardizing codes and figure commands, as well as learning some new fundamentals. This new knowledge enables field and office staff to better coordinate their efforts.

Data Entry in the Field

Entering field data using methodology that takes advantage of AutoCAD Civil 3D analysis and drafting tools (that utilizes automated linework connectivity) can save a significant amount of time in the office. As the figure is essentially created during the survey field pick up, this workflow reduces discrepancy and interpretation as to what exists in the field. The linework can be part of the final deliverable building outlines, surface breakline center line of pavement, parcel segment, control lines, etc.

Retracement methodology used to establish boundary, traverse closure and adjustments, and error findings are not always the surveyor's focus. Many of these functions are easily calculated in AutoCAD Civil 3D. Third party software and data collectors can also perform these same functions out in the field during the survey. With the rise in popularity of GPS units, the need for traverse, setups, or back sights is reduced.

Field crews are the "witnesses" to a site and should be responsible for drawing the lines. Errors are made by office surveyors and draftsman when analyzing hand-drawn field sketches and many hours can be spent connecting points and solving connection errors.

Survey Results as Coordinate Files

There are two methods of importing point files containing the Point Number, Northing, Easting, Elevation, and Description. One is through the point creation tool and the other is through the Survey Database.

When importing point files outside the Survey Database through the point creation tool, the Description Key Sets, Point Groups, and Point and Label Styles work together to categorize points into layers, organize points into groups, and display symbols. However no line work is generated. When importing files through the Survey Database, you have all the benefits of importing through the point creation tool, as well as automatic line generation and additional features.

Preparing Coordinate Files for Linework

A coordinate file produces linework when it contains survey figure codes that match preset figure prefixes in AutoCAD Civil 3D and/or have the proper figure commands before or after them. Survey codes are field-entered values and when processed correctly, will create the desired linework within the AutoCAD Civil 3D drawing.

There are two strategies to processing the files to generate figures (linework). The first is to convert the coordinate file to a field book file. The resulting field book contains figure control commands that create the linework. For some time, this was the only option to create figures. The major disadvantages to the field book language is that it requires the user to only input commands defined by Autodesk. These commands are hard-coded and the user cannot customize them to conform to legacy methodology. The most popular method used to create a field book is with Autodesk's Survey Link, which was created before the MCE and MCS (multiple curve start and end commands) came into existence; therefore, it does not recognize these commands. Lastly, curve observations in the field must be consecutive. This means that when a curve is started the rodman has to complete the curve before another non-curve shot can be taken. One of the major advantages of the use of a field book format is the ability to use the analysis tools within the networks created in the Survey Database.

An innovation in Survey is the introduction of Linework Code Sets. A code set is by default the traditional field book language codes. A coordinate file with valid Linework Code Set commands produces the same figure that comes from importing a field book without having to convert the file to a field book.

A Linework Code Set is changeable, whereas the field book language is not. For example, in a field book, B is the only way to begin a figure. In a Linework Code Set, you can enter almost any character as a starting figure command. Offices that use numbers for descriptions can now use numbers to start a figure. In the following portion of code, the number 1 starts a figure:

7,631397.3883,2208901.6900,809.6300,1 EPA

By default, the letter 'B' starts a figure instead of number 1, as shown in the following portion of code:

7,631397.3883,2208901.6900,809.6300,B EPA

The second advantage to Linework Code Sets is when importing, they manage all the starts, ends, and continues without actually being in the coordinate file. Finally, Line Code Sets support multiple point curves without the points having to be consecutive points. You can now create multiple point curves (more than three points) with other described points between the points creating the curve. The field book method does not support this.

In the practice for this section, you will process a coordinate file to a field book, import it, and review the resulting linework. In the second practice, you import the coordinate file directly without having to create a field book and get the same results.

These two methods assume no adjustment is needed since the files contain coordinates, not observations. A later section will use a survey with observations to create linework. From the import of this file type, you are able to perform an adjustment if desired.

3.2 Introduction to the Survey Toolspace

The Survey Toolspace displays a panel through which all surveys are processed. Survey uses graphics to display field book imports, figure and network previews, and points. If you toggle off these graphics, you can process a survey without a drawing being open. If you want to view these graphics, you will have to have a drawing open. Survey will remind you if you not have one open.

Displaying the Survey Toolspace

To display the Survey Toolspace, click the Survey Toolspace icon on the Ribbon's *Home* tab. Clicking this icon toggles the Toolspace on and off.

Survey Database Tree

The *Survey* tab displays a tree that contains a list of local Survey Databases, the Equipment, Figure Prefix, and Linework Code Set databases. The local surveys are in a user-defined working folder. This folder does not have to contain any drawings.

The Equipment, Figure Prefix, and Linework Code Set databases reside in a *Survey* folder that is in the local or network folder. Survey settings enable you to point to a relocated folder and its databases.

Typical Survey Database Settings

Surveys are either in a State Plane Coordinate system or an assumed coordinate system (e.g., 5000 for Northing and 5000 for Easting). Either of these coordinates systems are typed into a data collector at the first survey control found by the field crew. In AutoCAD Civil 3D, these different settings can be stored as definitions that the user assigns when creating a database, or assigned by editing a survey's settings.

Survey Protocol

Only one Survey Database can be edited at a time. When opened for editing, this prepares the survey for reading and writing. The process is analogous to Autodesk's previous Civil/Survey software, AutoCAD Land Desktop, where an external database in a project folder stored all the various data that was created in the drawing.

There are options to set the path or location for the Survey Database project files, as well as all the settings. When the user creates a new Survey Database, a Windows folder is created with the same name. If you close a drawing with a survey open, the Survey Database will close automatically. You must start a new drawing and then open the desired Survey Database.

3.3 The Survey Toolspace

After collecting and coding the data, downloading and converting it, the next step in Survey is to import the survey data, review it, and place the survey points and figures into a drawing.

Survey is a Toolspace, accessed through a panel in the Ribbon, in the Toolspace, or the Survey pull-down menu. It contains Survey settings, Equipment defaults, Figure Prefixes, and Linework Code Sets. Survey's settings can be on a local or network folder. Using a network folder is preferred for larger offices because all users can then standardize the file values.

A working folder defines where the local Survey Database resides. Again, the preferred location is a network folder, in which you place the local Survey Databases.

If your Toolspace does not display the *Survey* tab, click the Survey Toolspace icon in Ribbon's *Home* tab > Palettes panel to display it, as shown in Figure 3–1.

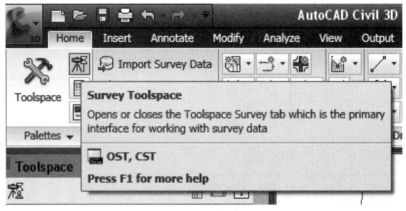

Figure 3–1

The *Survey* tab accesses the Survey settings and databases.

The Survey User Settings dialog box sets the defaults for all new Survey Databases. You should set these before starting Survey.

The Survey Working Folder is the location for all Survey Databases and can be local or on the network. The default working folder is *C:\Civil 3D Projects*.

Survey Database

A Survey Database is a subfolder in the working folder. The Survey Working Folder contains the Survey's settings and observation database. This database contains the Survey's Networks, Figures, and Survey Points.

Each local Survey Database references files to perform some of its tasks. The Equipment Database is an *.edb file and the Figure Prefix Database is an *. fdb file. The Equipment settings file contains values to estimate errors for the Least Squares adjustment process. The Figure Prefix Database lists definitions for Survey figures (figure style and layers).The default location for these files is *C:\Documents and Settings\All Users\Application Data\Autodesk\C3D 2011\enu\Survey.*

> **Note:** Survey Database folders cannot be deleted within AutoCAD Civil 3D Survey. If you want to delete the working folder, for example, this process must be manually done external to AutoCAD Civil 3D.

Survey has four nodes: *Import Events, Networks, Figures,* and *Survey Points. Import Events* is where files are imported into the Survey's networks. The files can be a coordinate, a field book, a LandXML file, and points from a drawing. When importing a file, depending on its contents, the import results in figures and points. Information in the file also populates portions of a Survey's Network.

When importing a coordinate or field book file containing only coordinates, the *Figures* and *Survey Points* nodes are your focus.

When processing a file with observations, turned angles, zenith angles, slope distances, and setups, your focus is the network and its nodes.

Practice 3a | Creating a Survey Database

In this practice you will set up a Survey project.

1. Open the file **SUV1-Sec1-Survey.dwg** from the following folder:

    C:\Civil 3D Projects\Civil3D-training\Drawings

2. You might have to change the draw order to be able to view the other objects. In Model Space, select the image, right-click, and select **Display Order > Send to Back**, as shown in Figure 3–2.

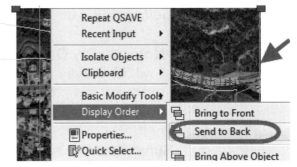

Figure 3–2

3. To toggle on the *Survey* tab, click the Survey Toolspace icon in the Ribbon's *Home* tab > Palettes panel, as shown in Figure 3–3.

Figure 3–3

4. Select the *Survey* tab on the Toolspace.

5. The Survey Toolspace displays four nodes: *Survey Databases*, *Equipment Databases, Figure Prefix Databases*, and *Linework Code Sets*. Each has a Sample database with default values. Expand the *Equipment Database* until you see the *Sample* database.

6. To create an Equipment database, right-click on the *Equipment Database* and select **New**, as shown on the left in Figure 3–4. Enter **Training** as the equipment database name, as shown on the right, and click ⌷ OK ⌷ to accept and close the dialog box.

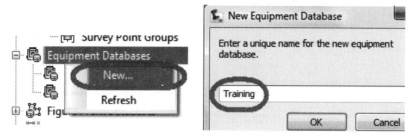

Figure 3–4

7. To open the Equipment Properties dialog box, select **Training**, right-click, and select **Manage Equipment database…**. Civil 3D saves the Equipment database files in the folder shown in Figure 3–5.

Name	Path
Sample	C:\ProgramData\Autodesk\C3D 2011\enu\Survey\Sample.edb_xdef
Training	C:\ProgramData\Autodesk\C3D 2011\enu\Survey\Training.edb_xdef

Figure 3–5

8. Review the settings. When done, click 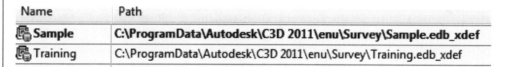 to close the dialog box.

9. To set the working folder for the Survey Database, in the Survey tab, select **Survey Databases**, right-click, and select **Set working folder...**, as shown on the left in Figure 3–6. Browse and select folder *C:\Civil 3D Projects\Civil3D-training\Geomatics*, as shown on the right. When done, click OK to close the dialog box.

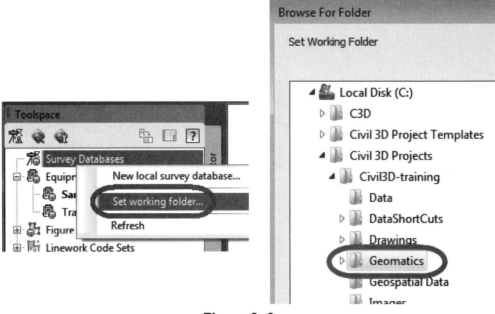

Figure 3–6

10. To create a new local Survey Database, select **Survey Databases** in the *Survey* tab, right-click, and select **New local survey database...**, as shown on the left in Figure 3–7. Enter **Survey Data1** as the name of the Survey Database, as shown on the right. Click OK to accept and close the dialog box

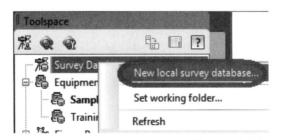

Figure 3–7

11. A Survey Database is now created in the *Survey* tab, as shown on the left in Figure 3–8. This Survey Database is actually a folder that exists under the specified Geomatics working folder, as shown on the right.

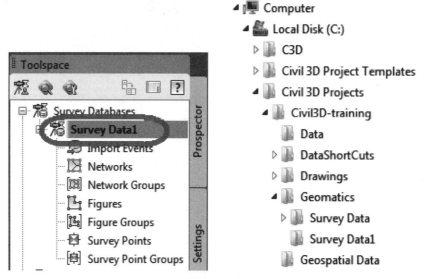

Figure 3–8

12. To edit the Survey Database settings, select **Survey Data Training**, right-click, and select **Edit survey database settings...**, as shown in Figure 3–9.

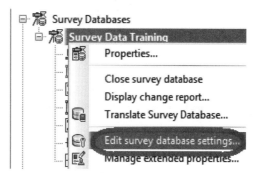

Figure 3–9

13. Under *Units* in the dialog box, click 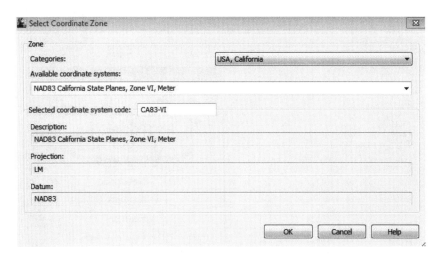 for the *Coordinate Zone* and set the zone to **NAD83 California State Planes, Zone VI, Meter**, as shown in Figure 3–10, and click [OK].

Figure 3–10

14. Set the *Distance* to **Meter**, the *Direction* to **North Azimuths**, the *Temperature* to **Celsius**, and the *Pressure* to **Millimeters Hg**, as shown in Figure 3–11. When done, click [OK] to close the dialog box.

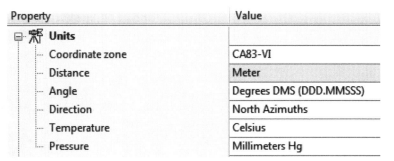

Figure 3–11

15. Save the file.

3.4 Survey Networks

A local Survey Database has one or more networks. You can import one or more field books or point files into a network when the Survey spans more than one field book or point file. Networks are usually a day of field work, for example. The larger the area of interest, the greater number of networks needed. At least one network is necessary when importing files to create linework and points.

Before importing a Survey, you must have a named network. To create a new network, select the Survey's network heading, right-click, select **New**, and enter the network's name. After creating a named network, Survey creates five nodes below its name: Control Points, Non-Control Points, Directions, Setups, and Traverses, as shown in Figure 3–12.

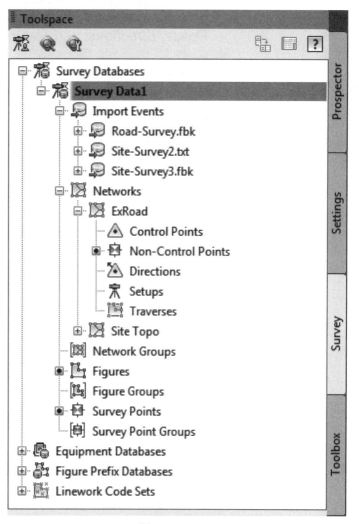

Figure 3–12

You can import one or several field books or LandXML files into the same network. By default, each import supplements the previous import. When you re-import a file, Survey automatically deletes the information from the original file import and recalculates the observations from the re-imported file.

Importing multiple files with the correct settings creates a single network whose data is the combination of the imported files. This allows you to create traverse(s), or perform a Least Squares analysis from data that spans more than one file.

When importing a file, Survey sequentially processes each line, creating setups and processing the setup's observations. When processing the setup's observations, Survey stores them in the observation database and calculates a point's preliminary coordinates from the observation values.

When toggling on interactive graphics, Survey displays the setups, draws figure linework, and populates the *Control Points*, *Non-Control Points*, *Directions*, and *Setups*.

When completing the import, Survey populates all or some of the nodes under the *Networks* heading.

Control points are NE or NEZ entries in a field book. Directions are azimuth entries between points used in the stationing process. Survey points are initially calculated coordinates from the file's setups and observations. Any NE SS entries become non-control points. These points have coordinates, but are not control points (not used in a setup or as stationing points). You can promote them to control points by using them as part of a traverse or referencing them as part of a setup.

Non-control points can also be the result of importing a point coordinate file instead of an observation-based file.

Practice 3b | Creating a Survey Network

In this practice you will create a Survey network. This practice assumes that you have successfully created a Survey Database.

Task 1: Open drawing and database.

---

1. Continue working with the drawing from the previous practice or open the file **SUV1-Sec1-Survey-.dwg** from the following folder:

   C:\Civil 3D Projects\Civil3D-training\Drawings

2. Select the *Survey* tab.

3. If you have not created the survey database, refer to *Practice 3a Creating a Survey Database*

4. Select **Survey Data1**. If this Survey project is not open (the label will not be bold), right-click and select **Open for edit**.

Task 2: Create a network.

---

1. In the *Survey* tab, under *Survey Data1*, select the **Networks** heading, right-click, and select **New**.

2. In the New Network dialog box, enter **Site Topo** for the network name, as shown on the left in Figure 3–13, and click ▭ OK ▭ to create the network. The new network appears under the *Survey Data1>Networks* collection, as shown on the right. Expand the *Site Topo* network by clicking on its adjacent + sign.

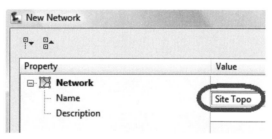
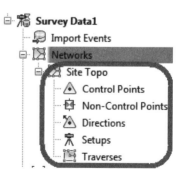

Figure 3–13

Review Questions

1. If you need linework, do the point files have to be brought into AutoCAD Civil 3D through the Survey Database? Or can the linework be created by importing points through the *Prospector*?

2. What are the major differences between using field books for creating linework and using text files with the P,N,E,Z,D format that use Linework Code Sets?

3. If you need to analyze the field data using the analysis tools available in the Survey Database, does this require a field book or a text file?

Section 2: Civil 3D Points

3.5 Points Overview

Points are often most heavily used at the beginning and end of a project. Surveyors collect data about existing site conditions (elevations, utilities, ownership, etc.) and set out the points for those who are going to build the design. Their world is coordinates, which are represented by points. Each point has a unique number (or name) and a label containing additional information (usually the elevation at the coordinate and a short, coded description).

There are no national standards for point descriptions in the Surveying industry. Each company or survey crew needs to work out its own conventions. There are no standards for symbols either; each firm can have its own set of symbols. The symbols used in a submission set can be specified by the firm contracting the services.

The lack of standard descriptions and symbols adds time to preparing and converting contracted work. AutoCAD Civil 3D contains a layer and point description translator to assist in preparing a project's point data. These tools export the points and layer data needed by those who build the design.

In the design process, points might not be part of the tasks performed in the office; they could instead be reference material that does not need to change or be displayed. In other cases, points are data for a surface and after building it, are not needed for later tasks.

At the end of the design process, points can be used to represent critical coordinates of the design. These points and their coordinates become the cornerstone of the design construction process. Again, these tasks might never be a part of an office's daily routine.

In other Civil/Survey software, coordinate geometry (cogo) points are commonly a node or block. When using a block, its insertion point is the point's coordinates. Associated with the node or block is text that labels the point's number, elevation, and description. A point's marker and label can have different layers. Civil 3D cogo points are a single object with two elements: a point style and a point label style. A cogo point definition is shown in Figure 3–14.

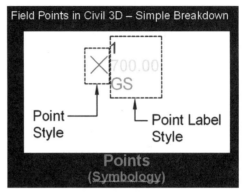

Figure 3–14

The following is important cogo point information:

A point style (no matter what it displays), an AutoCAD node, a custom marker, or a block is selectable with AutoCAD NODE object snaps.

A point label is not limited to the point's number, elevation, and description. A point label can contain lines, blocks, and other point properties. For example, point labels may display only an elevation or description. This text can be manually overridden (as shown in the example in Figure 3–15) or it can consist of intelligent variables that represent point characteristics (such as its convergence angle). In state plane coordinate systems, the convergence angle is the difference between a geodetic azimuth and the projection of that azimuth onto a grid (grid azimuth) of a given point.

Figure 3–15

Creating the first point automatically creates a point group named _All Points_. This point group is similar to layer 0; it cannot be renamed or deleted. Every drawing point resides in this point group.

Additional point groups can use all or a subset of drawing points. Usually, additional point groups contain a subset of all points. Each of these groups can display the originally assigned point style and label, or change one or both through overrides.

The *Point* collection in the Settings panel manages all of the styles affecting points: *Point Styles, Label Styles, Description Key Sets, Table Styles*, and *Commands*, as shown in Figure 3–16.

Figure 3–16

AutoCAD Civil 3D point styles define a cogo point's visibility, layer, color, and linetype. A style can use the layer properties or override them. To use AutoCAD layer properties, a style sets the properties' value to **ByLayer**, as shown at the top in Figure. To have the style control layer properties, the style sets a specific color, linetype, etc., as shown at the bottom in Figure 3–17.

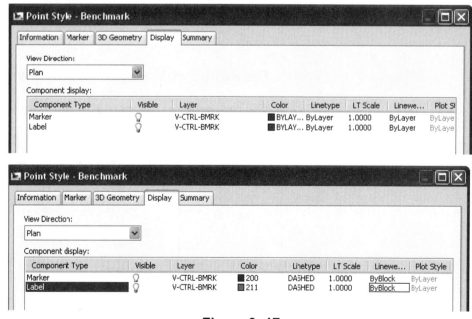

Figure 3–17

Point Marker Styles

A surveyor interacts with points daily and to easily use Civil 3D points, you need a basic understanding of them and the related styles.

If opening a drawing with no Civil 3D content, or starting a drawing from a template with no Civil 3D content, AutoCAD Civil 3D will provide a single style (Standard) using one layer 0. Every new style will start from this point style and can be edited, copied, and renamed.

AutoCAD Civil 3D provides metric and imperial template files that contain several point styles: Civil 3D Imperial (NCS) and Civil 3D Metric (NCS). These two templates use the National CAD standards for their layers and provide examples of styles you can use in a project. To customize these styles, you will have to modify and expand the list of point styles. When installing AutoCAD Civil 3D, the first thing you should do is set one of these two templates as your default template. Alternatively, you can develop your styles and use your template.

A point style defines a point's display, its 3D elevation, and its coordinate marker size. In the example shown in Figure 3–18, the point style is an X for a ground shot.

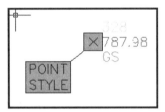

Figure 3–18

The Point Style dialog box top has five tabs, as described below.

The *Information* tab sets the point style's name and description, as shown in Figure 3–19.

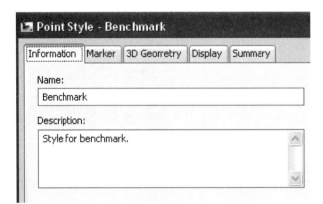

Figure 3–19

The *Marker* tab supports three marker definition methods, as shown in Figure 3–20, and as described below.

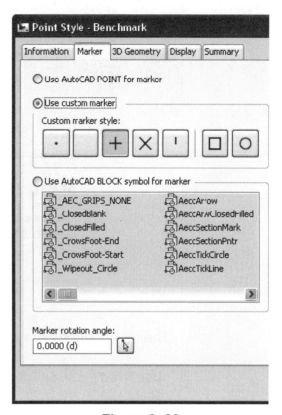

Figure 3–20

- **Use AutoCAD POINT [node] for marker:** All points in the drawing follow AutoCAD's PDMODE and PDSIZE system variables. You have no independent control over points using this method.

- **Use custom marker:** This method creates markers similar to an AutoCAD point (node), but the marker is under AutoCAD Civil 3D's control, and each point style can display a different combination of marker styles. When using this method, you select the components of the style from the list of Custom marker style shapes. A custom marker can have shapes from the left and right sides. The first comes from one of the five icons on the style's left side, and you can optionally add one or both shapes from the right.

- **Use AutoCAD BLOCK symbol for marker:** This method defines the marker by using a block (symbol). The blocks listed represent definitions in the drawing. When your cursor is in this area and you right-click, you can browse to a location containing drawings you want to include as point markers.

At the marker panel's top right corner are options to scale the marker. The most common option is **Use drawing scale**, as shown in Figure 3–21, which takes the marker size (0.100) and multiplies it by the current drawing's annotation scale, resulting in the final marker size. When the annotation scale changes, AutoCAD Civil 3D automatically resizes the markers and their labels to be appropriate for the scale.

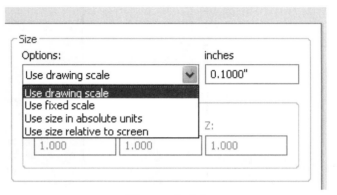

Figure 3–21

The other options are described in the table below.

Use fixed scale	Specifies user-defined X, Y, and Z scale values.
Use size in absolute units	Specifies a user-defined size.
Use size relative to screen	Specifies a user-defined percentage of the screen.

The 3D Geometry panel affects the point's elevation. The default is **Use Point Elevation**, as shown in Figure 3–22, which displays the point at its actual elevation value.

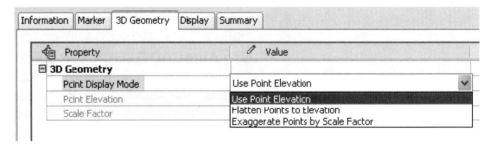

Figure 3–22

The other options are described in the table below.

Flatten Points to Elevation	Specifies the elevation to which the point is projected (flattened). The Point Elevation cell will highlight if this option is selected and by default is 0 elevation. When using an AutoCAD object snap to select a marker using this option, the resulting entity's elevation will be the default elevation: 0 (zero). If selecting by point number or point object, the resulting entity will be the point's actual elevation.
Exaggerate Points by Scale Factor	Exaggerates the point's elevation by a specified scale factor. When selecting this option, the Scale Factor cell highlights.

The *Display* tab assigns the marker and label layers, and sets their visibility and properties. Setting the property to **ByLayer** uses the layer's properties. Alternatively, you override the original layer properties by setting a specific color, linetype, or lineweight.

A style's view direction value affects how the point and label components display in the plan, model, profile, and section views, as listed in Figure 3–23.

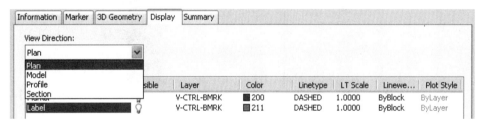

Figure 3–23

The *Summary* tab is a report of all the style's settings. You can also edit style variables in this tab.

| Practice 3c | # Point Marker Styles |

In this practice you will create a new point style and apply it to an existing group of points.

Task 1: Add a Block Symbol.

1. Continue working with the drawing from the previous practice.

   In the previous practice, you only set up the working environment and created a survey database. No changes have been made to the drawing.

2. You might have to change the draw order to be able to view the other objects. In Model Space, select the image, right-click, select **Display Order > Send to Back**, as shown in Figure 3–24.

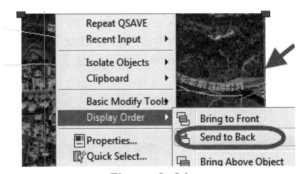

Figure 3–24

3. In the Toolspace, select the *Settings* tab, expand the *Point* collection until you see *Point Styles*. Expand the *Point Styles* collection.

4. Review the *Point Styles* list and notice that there is no light pole style.

5. From the *Point Styles* list, select the **Guy pole** style, right-click, and select **Copy....**

6. In the *Information* tab, change the point style's name to **Light Pole**, as shown in Figure 3–25.

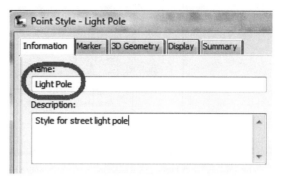

Figure 3–25

7. Select the *Marker* tab. Select the **Use AutoCAD BLOCK symbol for marker** option. In the block list, scroll across as needed and select the AutoCAD block **ST-Light**, as shown in Figure 3–26.

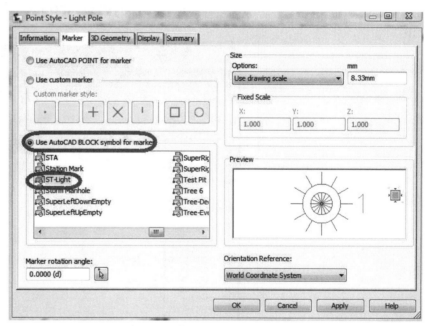

Figure 3–26

8. Select to the *Display* tab and notice the layer settings are from the Light Pole point style, as shown in Figure 3–27.

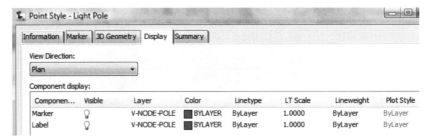

Figure 3–27

9. You can reassign the marker and/or label layer by clicking the layer name. **Select the layer name** to view the drawing layer list.

10. If you need to create a new layer, **click** **New...** in the top right corner of the Layer Selection dialog box. The Create Layer dialog box opens, as shown in Figure 3–28, enabling you to create new layers without having to use the Layer Manager.

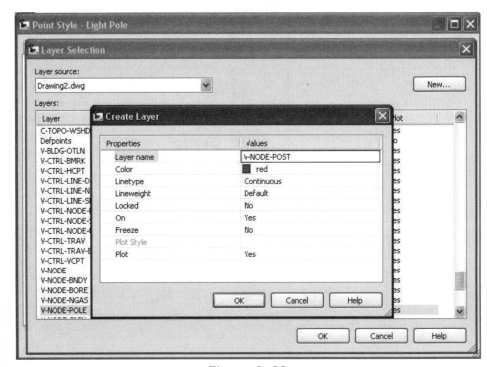

Figure 3–28

11. Click **Cancel** to exit the Create Layer dialog box. Click **Cancel** to exit the Layer Selection dialog box.

12. Click **OK** to create the point style.

13. Review the *Point Styles* list and notice that Light Pole is now a point style, as shown in Figure 3–29.

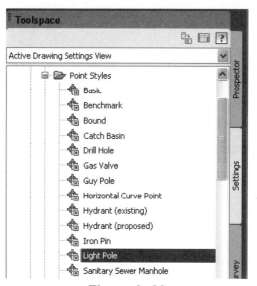

Figure 3–29

14. Select **Application Menu** 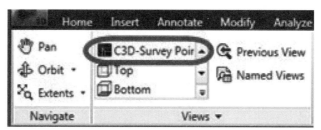 > **Save As**. Enter **Training** for the file name and save it. Ensure that the correct folder is selected: *C:\Civil 3D Projects\Civil3D-training\Drawings*.

Task 2: Apply the point style.

---

1. Continue working with the drawing from the previous task.

2. In the *View* tab > Views panel, select the preset view **C3D-Survey Point style**, as shown in Figure 3–30.

Figure 3–30

3. In the Toolspace, select the *Prospector* tab, expand the *Point Groups* collection until you see the *Street Light* point group. Select the **Street Light** group, right-click, and select **Properties**.

4. In the *Information* tab, in the *Default styles* section, select **Light Pole** in the *Point style* drop-down list, as shown in Figure 3–31.

Figure 3–31

5. Click [OK] to accept the changes and close the dialog box. The symbols for the Light pole points have now been changed.

6. Save the drawing.

3.6 Point Label Styles

The AutoCAD Civil 3D point label style annotates point properties beyond the typical point number, elevation and description. A typical point label style is shown in Figure 3–32.

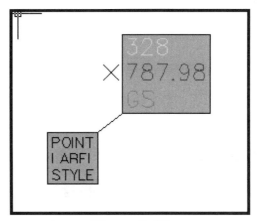

Figure 3–32

All AutoCAD Civil 3D label style dialog boxes are the same. The basic behaviors for a label come from the setting found in the Edit Label Style Defaults dialog box. The values in this dialog box define the label layer, text style, orientation, plan readability, size, dragged state behaviors, and more.

In the *Settings* tab, the drawing name and object collections control these values for the entire drawing (at the drawing name level) or for the selected collection (*Surface, Alignment, Point,* etc.) To display the Edit Label Style Defaults dialog box, select the drawing name or a heading, right-click, and select **Edit Label Style Defaults...**, as shown in Figure 3–33.

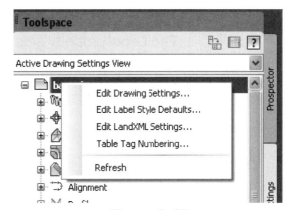

Figure 3–33

The Label Style Composer dialog box contains five tabs, each defining specific label behaviors. They are described below.

Information Tab

The *Information* tab names the style, as shown in Figure 3–34.

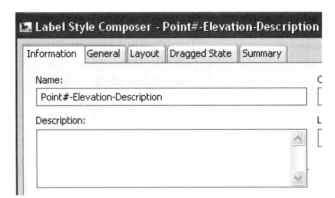

Figure 3–34

General Tab

The General tab contains three properties: *Label* (text style and layer), *Behavior* (orientation), and *Plan Readability* (amount of view rotation before flipping text to read left to right), as shown in Figure 3–35.

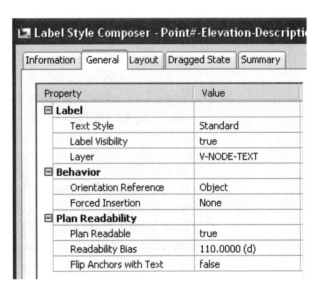

Figure 3–35

The *Label* property sets the *Text Style*, the *Label Visibility*, and the label's *Layer*. Click in the *Value* cell beside the *Text Style* and *Layer* to activate browsers to change their values. Clicking in the *Label Visibility* cell displays a drop-down list with the options **true** and **false**.

The *Behavior* property sets two variables that control the label's location. The *Orientation Reference* variable offers three label orientation options, as described in the table below.

Object	Rotates labels relative to the object's zero direction. The object's zero direction is based on its start to end vector. If the vector changes at the label's anchor point, the orientation updates automatically. This is the default setting.
View	Forces labels to realign relative to a screen-view orientation in both model and layout views. This method assumes the zero angle is horizontal, regardless of the UCS or Dview twist. If the view changes, the label orientation updates with it.
World Coordinate System	Labels read left to right using the WCS X axis. Changing the view or current UCS does not affect label rotation; the label always references the world coordinate system.

Under the *Behavior* property, the *Forced Insertion* variable has three optional values that specify the label's position relative to an object. This setting applies only when the *Orientation Reference* is set to **Object** and the objects are lines, arcs, or spline segments.

None	Maintains label position as composed relative to the object.
Top	Adjusts label position to be above an object.
Bottom	Adjusts label position to be below an object.

Note: If you select **Top** or **Bottom**, the value of *Plan Readable* should be **True**.

The *Plan Readability* property has three variables that affect how text flips when rotating a drawing view. The result of these settings is to flip text to be left-to-right readable.

Under the *Plan Readability* property, the *Plan Readable* variable has two options, as described in the table below.

True	Allows text to rotate to maintain left-to-right readability.
False	Does not allow text to flip. The resulting text maybe upside down or read from right to left.

The *Readability Bias* variable is the amount of rotation required to flip a label to become left-to-right readable. The angle is measured counter-clockwise from the WCS 0 (zero) direction.

The *Flip Anchors with Text* variable has two options, as described in the table below.

True	If the text flips, the text anchor point also flips.
False	The label flips, but maintains the original anchor point. The behavior is similar to mirroring the original text.

Layout Tab

The *Layout* tab defines the label contents, as shown in Figure 3–36. A label component is an object property it labels. Point properties include northing, easting, raw description, etc. A label may have one component with several properties, or several components each containing an object property.

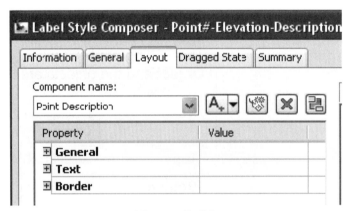

Figure 3–36

A label component can be text, lines, or blocks. To add a component, click the drop-down arrow next to the icon shown in Figure 3–37 and select the component type.

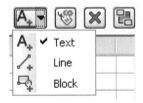

Figure 3–37

The remaining icons in the *Layout* tab are described in the table below.

	Copies the current component and its properties.
	Deletes the current component.
	Affects a label's components display order. For example, use this icon to change the draw order of the label's components (such as text above a mask).

Depending on the label component type, it may have any combination of three sections: *General*, *Text*, and *Border*. *General* defines how the label attaches to the object or other label components, its visibility, and its anchor point.

If the label component is text, the *Text* property values affect how it displays its object property. To set or modify a label's text value, click in the cell beside *Contents* to display the ⠤ icon shown in Figure 3–38. Click ⠤ to open the Text Component Editor dialog box.

Property	Value
⊞ **General**	
⊟ **Text**	
Contents	<[Full Description. ⠤
Text Height	0.1000"
Rotation Angle	0.0000 (d)
Attachment	Top left
X Offset	0.0000"
Y Offset	0.0000"
■ Color	■ BYLAYER
Lineweight	ByLayer
⊞ **Border**	

Figure 3–38

The Text Component Editor dialog box, as shown in Figure 3–39, defines what property the label annotates. When creating a label component, first double-click on the text in the right side panel to highlight it. Select the property to add from the left side panel, set the property's format values, and click 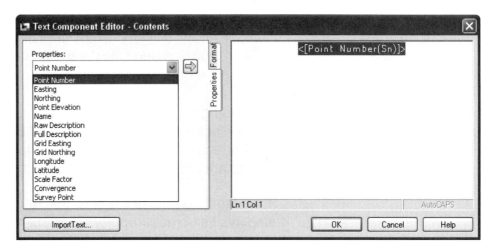 to add the new property to the label component.

Figure 3–39

It is important to maintain the process order and to remember that the text on the right within brackets needs to be highlighted before revising its format values on the left.

Dragged State Tab

The *Dragged State* tab has two properties: *Leader* and *Dragged State Components*, as shown in Figure 3–40. This tab defines how a label behaves when dragging a label from its original insertion point.

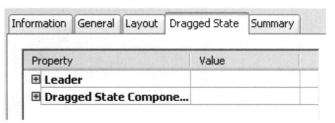

Figure 3–40

The *Leader* property defines if a leader appears and what properties it displays. You can use the label's layer properties in the *General* tab (**ByLayer**) or override them by specifying a color, as shown in Figure 3–41.

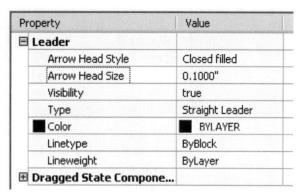

Figure 3–41

The *Dragged State Components* property defines the label component's display after it is dragged from its original position. Click in the cell beside *Display* to view the two display options, as shown in Figure 3–42.

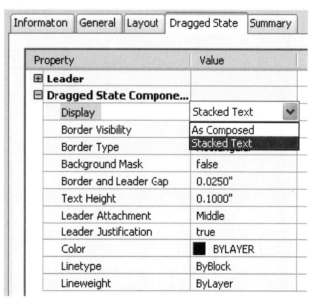

Figure 3–42

These two options are described in the table below.

As Composed	The label maintains its original definition and orientation from the settings in the Layout panel. When you select **As Composed**, all other values become unavailable for editing.
Stacked Text	The label text becomes left-justified and label components are stacked in the order listed in Layout's Component Name list. When you select **Stacked Text**, all blocks, lines, ticks, and direction arrows are removed.

The *Summary* tab lists the label component, general, and dragged state values for the label style. The label components are listed numerically in the order they were defined and report all of the current values.

Practice 3d | Point Label Styles

In this practice, you will create a label style and use it with the point style from the previous practice.

Task 1: Create a Point Label Style's Components.

1. Continue working with the drawing from the previous practice.

2. Select the *Settings* tab.

3. Expand the *Point* collection until you see the *Point Label Styles* list.

4. From the list of point styles, select **Point#-Elevation-Description**, right click, and select **Copy…**.

5. In the *Information* tab, change the name to **Point#-Description-N-E**.

6. Select the *Layout* tab. Select **Point Number** from the *Component name* drop-down list. Because you want the Point Number label to link to the point object, set the *Anchor Component* to **<Feature>** and the *Anchor Point* to **Top Right**, as shown in Figure 3–43. Finally, set the *Attachment* to **Bottom left**. These settings will attach the bottom left of the label to the top right of the point object.

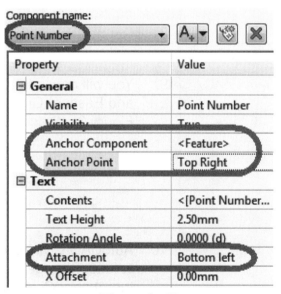

Figure 3–43

7. Because you do not need the elevation label, you can delete it. Select **Point Elev** in the *Component name* drop-down list and click , as shown in Figure 3–44. When prompted "Do you want to delete it?" click [Yes].

Figure 3–44

8. To set the properties for the description label, select **Point Description** in the *Component name* drop-down list. Set the *Anchor Component* to **<Feature>**, the *Anchor Point* to **Bottom Right**, and the *Attachment* to **Bottom left**, as shown in Figure 3–45.

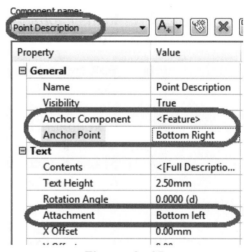

Figure 3–45

9. You will now add a new text component to display the Northing and Easting. Click the **Create Text Component** icon shown in Figure 3–46 and select **Text** to create a text component.

Figure 3–46

10. AutoCAD Civil 3D creates a text component with some default values. Change the default *Name* **text.1** to **Coordinates** and set the *Anchor Component* to **<Feature>**. Then set the *Anchor Point* to **Bottom Right** and the *Attachment* to **Top left**.

11. You will now change the contents from the default label set by AutoCAD Civil 3D to display the coordinates. Click in the *Contents* cell, next to *Label Text*, as shown in Figure 3–47.

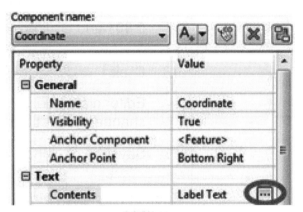

Figure 3–47

12. In the Text Component Editor dialog box, double-click on the text in the right side panel to highlight it and type in **N**.

13. Select **Grid Northing** in the *Properties* drop-down list. Change the *Precision* to **0.001** and click , as shown in Figure 3–48, to add the code to display the northing.

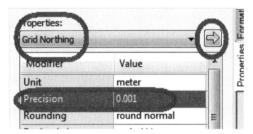

Figure 3–48

14. To place the easting on a new line below the northing, you need to insert a line feed at the end of the code of the northing. Click at the end of the code. Press <Enter> to insert a new line followed by the letter **E**. Then select **Grid Easting** in the *Properties* drop-down list and add it to post the code in the right side panel. You should see the following:

- N<[Grid Northing(Um|P3|RN|AP|GC|UN|Sn|OF)]>

- E<[Grid Easting(Um|P4|RN|AP|GC|UN|Sn|OF)]>

15. In the easting, the value will be displayed to the 4th decimal, "P4". You need to change it so that it matches the northing. The only way to do this is re-insert the code. AutoCAD Civil 3D does not yet have the ability to edit or add a specific section of code. Select all of the code for the easting. Change the *Precision* to **0.001** and click ⇨ to revise the easting code.

16. Click [OK] to accept the changes in the Text Component Editor dialog box, and click [OK] again to accept the changes in the Label Style Composer.

17. Save the drawing.

Task 2: Apply a Point Label Style's Components.

1. Continue working with the drawing from the previous task.

2. In the Toolspace, select the *Prospector* tab, expand the *Point Groups* collection until you see the *Street Light* point group. Select the **Street Light** group, right-click, and select **Properties**.

3. In the *Information* tab, select **Point#-Description-N-E** in the *Point label style* drop-down list, as shown in Figure 3–49.

Figure 3–49

4. Click [OK] to accept the changes and close the dialog box.

5. The symbols for the Light pole points have now been changed. Also, both the point symbols and point labels are annotative. In the Status Bar at the bottom, click the drop-down arrow next to the annotation scale and change the scale of the drawing from 1:1000 to **1:500**, as shown in Figure 3–50. The size of the labels and point symbols change.

Figure 3–50

6. Save the drawing.

3.7 Styles and Templates

A drawing template (.dwt extension) contains all blocks, Paper Space title sheets, settings, and layers for a new drawing. For AutoCAD Civil 3D, templates contain all AutoCAD template values, plus Civil 3D styles and content-specific settings. AutoCAD Civil 3D's Settings panel manages these values.

To use AutoCAD Civil 3D efficiently and effectively, you need to configure these styles and settings to control AutoCAD Civil 3D's object display. All of these styles and settings affect the final delivered product and allow you to deliver a product with consistent quality. Once a Civil 3D style is created, it can be transferred between drawings and templates by selecting the style and dragging it to the desired file. When dragging a style to a drawing, any associated style layers also transfer.

One method of transferring styles is to use the *Setting* tab's **Master View**. The Master View shows all open drawings and their settings with the current drawing as the first (top) entry of the open drawing list. Access the **Master View** by expanding the drop-down list at the top of the *Settings* tab, as shown in Figure 3–51. This example shows two open files. The current drawing, Baseplan, is in bold and at the top of the list.

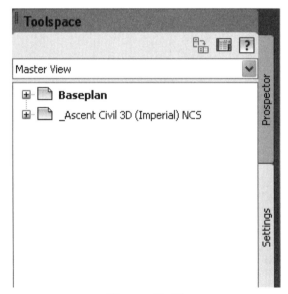

Figure 3–51

To transfer a style, you need two open files: a source drawing (containing the style) and a destination drawing (the drawing receiving the style). A source or destination drawing can also be a template.

Transfer a style from the inactive source drawing by selecting it from the list, then dragging and dropping it into the destination drawing.

In the example shown in Figure 3–52, the **Light Pole** point style is transferred from the baseplan (the source drawing) to the template file, which is the active drawing.

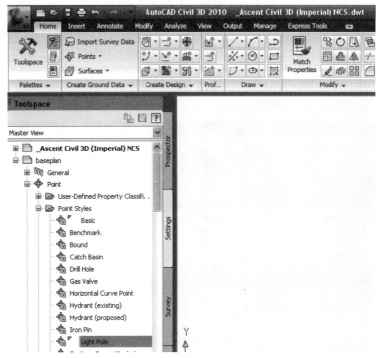

Figure 3–52

To drag and drop the style into the destination drawing, select the point style in the source drawing's *Settings* tab, hold down the left mouse button, and drag the style into the other file. When the cursor displays as a pointer with a square, release the left mouse button to drop the style into the file. Use the same process to transfer a style between drawings.

Transferring More than One Style

When you want to transfer more than one style to a drawing, insert a drawing containing the styles. When the insertion process is done, the styles that were in the source drawing are then in the destination drawing.

Creating Template Files

To create a template file, use the **Save As** command and in the Save As dialog box, change the *File of Type* to **DWT**.

3.8 Point Settings

When creating new points, you must determine the next point number, as well as what elevations and descriptions to assign and how to assign them. To set the current point number, default elevations, descriptions, and other similar settings, you use the Create Points

toolbar's expanded area. Display this area by clicking 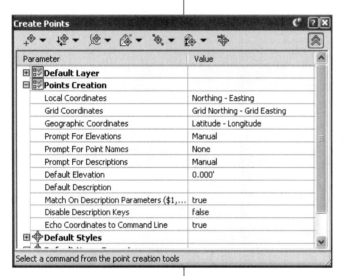 on the Create Points toolbar. The two sections, *Points Creation* and *Point Identity*, as shown in Figure 3–53, contain the most commonly used values.

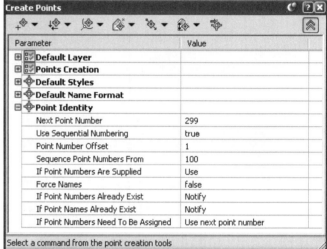

Figure 3–53

Points Creation Values

The *Points Creation* section affects prompting for elevations and/or descriptions. The two properties in this section are *Prompt For Elevations* and *Prompt For Descriptions*. These properties can be set as described in the table below.

None	Does not prompt for an elevation or description.
Manual	Prompts for an elevation or description.
Automatic	Uses the Default Elevation or Default Description value when creating a point.
Automatic-Object	Creates points along an alignment whose description consists of the Alignment name and Station. This description is not dynamic and does not update if the alignment changes or the point is moved.

Point Identity Values

The *Point Identity* section sets the default method of handling duplicate point numbers. If there are duplicate point numbers, you have three ways to resolve the duplication. You can overwrite the existing point data, ignore the new point, or assign it a new number.

This section's most critical property is *Next Point Number.* It is set to the first available number in the point list. If a file of imported point data uses point numbers 1-131 and 152-264, the current point number is 132 after importing the file. This value should be set manually to the next desired point number before creating new points with the Create Points toolbar.

3.9 Creating Points

You create points using commands in the Create Points toolbar. The commands include:

- **Miscellaneous - Manual:** Creates a new point at specified coordinates.
- **Alignments - Station/Offset:** Creates a point at an alignment's specific station and offset. These points and their descriptions do not update if the alignment is modified or the point is moved. If you prefer a dynamic station and offset labels, consider an Alignment label instead.
- **Alignments - Measure Alignment:** Creates point objects at a set interval, which is useful for construction staking. Again, these points do not update if the alignment changes.
- **Surface - Random Points:** Creates points whose elevation is from a specified surface. These points do update, but you must manually force the update. If you prefer a dynamic spot label, consider a Surface label instead.

Each icon in the Create Points toolbar has a drop-down list. If you expand this list, you can select a command from the list to run, as shown in Figure 3–54.

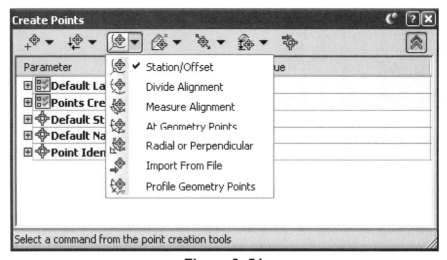

Figure 3–54

3.10 Transparent Command

Several methods for placing points can use other existing points to help define the location of a new point. For example, you may want to locate a new point at given distances from two existing points. AutoCAD Civil 3D uses the point filters in the Transparent Commands toolbar to reference point objects in a drawing. The Transparent Command toolbar is shown in Figure 3–55.

Figure 3–55

The point filters reference points by Point Name, Point Number, or by selecting a point on the screen (Point Object). You can access the transparent commands from their respective toolbars or type an apostrophe letter pair: **'PA** for Point Name, **'PN** for Point Number, and **'PO** for point object. Point Object is the easiest, because you only need to select a point on the screen.

The AutoCAD Civil 3D transparent commands work with most AutoCAD Civil 3D and AutoCAD commands that can use a point's coordinates. AutoCAD commands using transparent commands include **Line**, **Pline**, and **Circle**. To exit a transparent command, press <Esc> or <Enter>.

Practice 3e | Creating AutoCAD Civil 3D Points

In this practice, a fire hydrant was located by GPS. You will add a point object to locate it manually.

1. Continue working with the drawing from the previous practice.

2. In the *Home* tab > Create Ground Data panel, select **Points-Point Creation Tools** to access the Create Points toolbar. Expand the toolbar by clicking ![expand icon], as shown in Figure 3–56.

Figure 3–56

3. Note: Alternatively, you can select the *Settings* tab and expand the *Commands* collection under the *Point* collection. Select **CreatePoints**, right-click, and select **Edit Command Settings...**, as shown in Figure 3–57.

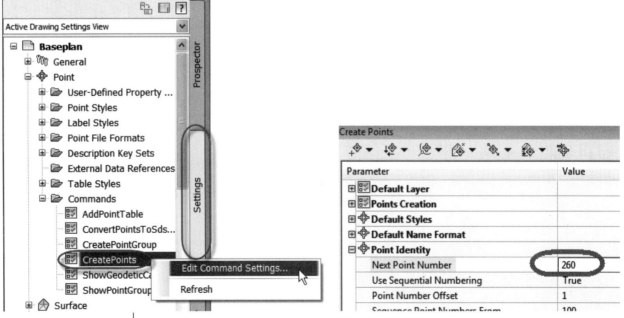

Figure 3–57

4. In the *Point Identity* section of the dialog box, set the *Next Point Number* to **260** and collapse the toolbar.

5. Select the **Manual** option from the miscellaneous group on the toolbar as shown in Figure 3–58.

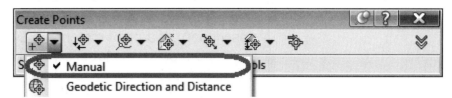

Figure 3–58

6. When prompted for a location, enter **1906852.13, 620768.56** <Enter> at the Command Line, for easting, northing. When prompted for a description, enter **HYD** <Enter>. When prompted for an elevation, press <Enter> to accept the default value **<.>** (period), since it is unknown. The period is simply a placeholder for the elevation field. Inputting a zero is not correct because 0 is a valid elevation.

7. Press <Enter> again to finish the command and click on the **X** in the Create Points dialog box to close it. In the *Prospector* tab, under the *Point* collection, locate and select point **260**, right-click, and select **Zoom to**, as shown in Figure 3–59.

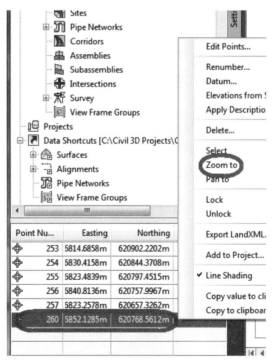

Figure 3–59

8. Save the drawing.

3.11 Description Key Sets

Description Keys categorize points by their field description (raw description). If a point matches a Description Key entry, the point is assigned a point and label style, and a full description (possibly a translation of the raw description). Description Key Sets can also scale and rotate points. The *Description Key Sets* collection is shown in Figure 3–60.

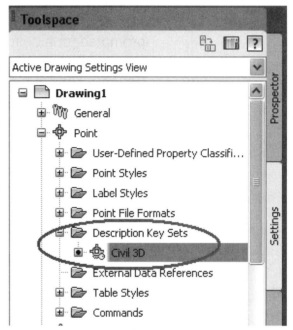

Figure 3–60

The Description Key's first five columns are the most used entries, as shown in Figure 3–61.

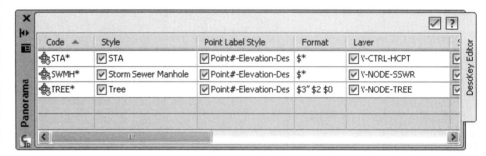

Figure 3–61

Note: To create a new Description Key row, select an existing code, right-click, and select **New...** To edit a code, double-click in the cell.

Code, Point, and Label Style

Description code is a significant part of data collection. Code assigned to a raw description will trigger action by the Description Key Set. Each entry in the set represents all possible descriptions a field crew would use while surveying a job. When a raw description matches a code entry, the Key Set assigns all of the row's values to the matching point, point, and label style, translates the raw description, and possibly assigns a layer. Codes are case-sensitive and must match the field collector's entered raw description.

A code may contain wildcards to match raw descriptions that contain numbering or additional material beyond the point's description. For example, MH* would match MH1, MH2, etc. or UP* would match UP 2245 14.4Kv Verizon. Look up "wild cards, in description keys" in the Help menu for more information.

Matching a Key Set entry for the code assigns a Point Style at the point's coordinates. If the *Point Style* is set to **Default**, the *Settings* tab's Point feature *Point Style* is used (set in the Edit Feature Settings dialog box), as shown in Figure 3–62.

Matching a Key Set entry for the code assigns a point label style to annotate important point values; usually, this is the number, elevation, and description. If the *Point Style* is set to **Default**, the *Settings* tab's Point feature *Point Label Style* is used (set in the Edit Feature Settings dialog box), as shown in Figure 3–62.

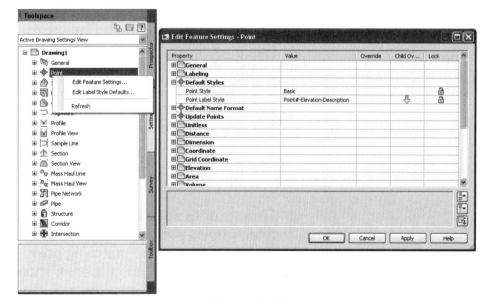

Figure 3–62

Format

The *Format* column translates the raw description into a full description. When including spaces in a raw description, AutoCAD Civil 3D assigns parameter numbers to each description element. Parameters are represented by a $ sign followed by a number. For example, the description *PINE 6* has two elements: PINE and 6, with PINE as parameter 0 ($0) and 6 as parameter 1 ($1). To use the raw description as the full description, the *Format* column contains $* (use the raw description as the full description). The *Format* column can reorder the parameters and add characters to create a full description. For example, the raw description *PINE 6* can be translated to 6" PINE by entering **$1" $0**.

The function of parameters in the Format column is to translate a cryptic raw description into a more readable full description. Parameters are defined by spaces in a raw description. The first element is assigned **$0** and the maximum number of elements is 9 (i.e., **$0...$9**). The following is a complex raw description:

- TREE D MAPLE 3

For the raw description to match the Description Key Set entry, the entry **TREE** must have an asterisk (*) after TREE (see the example shown in Figure 3–63). The raw description elements and their parameters are TREE ($0), D ($1), Maple ($2), and 3 ($3). The *Format* column entry of **$3" $2 $0** creates a full description of 3" MAPLE TREE.

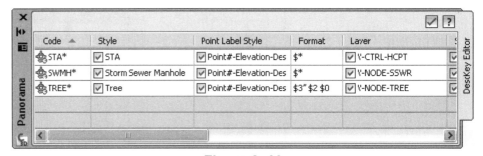

Figure 3–63

If a point does not match any Description Key Set entry, it receives the default styles assigned by the _All Points group. The *Layer* column assigns a layer to the matching point. If the Point Style already has a marker and label layer, this entry should be toggled off. The Description Key Set also contains the *Scale* and *Rotate Parameter* columns. In the above example, the 3 for the trunk diameter can also be a tree symbol scaling factor when applied to the symbol's X-Y.

Practice 3f | Creating a Description Key Set

In this practice you will learn to create a new Description Key Set entry and apply it to an existing point. In addition you will update the Description Key Set to use parameters.

Task 1: Reset the _All Points point style.

1. Continue working with the drawing from the previous practice.

2. In the *Prospector* tab, select the point group **_All Points**, right-click, and select **Properties...**.

3. In the _All Points Properties dialog box, select the *Information* tab.

4. Select **Basic** from the *Point style* drop-down list.

5. As the Hydrant is the only point that is exclusively in the _All Points group, it is the only point that is impacted by the style. This concept is explained in more detail in the Point Groups material.

6. Click [OK] to exit the Properties dialog box.

Task 2: Create a new Description Key Set entry.

1. In the Toolspace, select the *Settings* tab.

2. Expand the *Point* collection until you see the *Description Key Set* collection and its list.

3. Select **C3D-Training** from the list, right-click, and select **Edit Keys...**

4. Right-click in any *Code* cell and select **New...**, as shown in Figure 3–64.

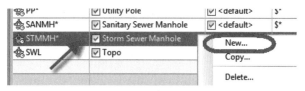

Figure 3–64

5. Double-click in the *Code* cell of the newly created row and enter **HYD**, as shown in Figure 3–65.

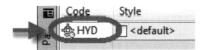

Figure 3–65

6. In the *Style* cell, toggle on (check box) the Point Style and click in the Style cell to open the Point Style dialog box, as shown in Figure 3–66. Select **Hydrant (existing)** from the drop-down list and click [OK] to assign the style to the code.

Figure 3–66

7. Leave **<default>** selected as the *Point Label Style* and **$*** as the *Format*. This means that the label will be the same as what was entered by the surveyor. Leave the check box toggled off in the *Layer* column. You do not have a scale parameter and will not be using a fixed scale. However, you want to scale the symbol based on the drawing scale, so toggle on the **Yes** option in the *Use drawing scale* column, as shown in Figure 3–67.

Code	Style	Point Label ...	F...	Layer	Scale Param...	Fixed ...	Use dra
HYD	☑ Hydrant (existing)	☑ <default>	$*	☐	☐ Parameter 1	☐ 1.000	☑ Yes

Figure 3–67

8. Close the DescKey Editor vista by clicking in the top right corner of the dialog box, as shown in Figure 3–68.

Figure 3–68

Task 3: Apply the new Description Key Set to an existing point.

1. Zoom in to the hydrant so that you will see the changes to the hydrant symbol when you apply the updates. In the *Prospector* tab, expand the *Point Groups* collection and select the **_All Points** group, as shown in Figure 3–69. In the grid view, select the hydrant point number **260**, right-click, and select **Zoom to**.

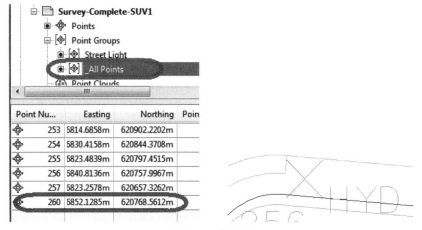

Figure 3–69

2. In the *Prospector* tab, select the **_All Points** group, right-click, and select **Apply Description Keys**. The point updates to show the Hydrant symbol and new description, as shown in Figure 3–70.

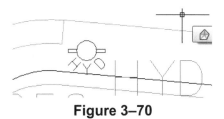

Figure 3–70

3. Save the drawing.

Task 4: Update the Description Key Set to use parameters.

1. In this task you will use the Parameters feature to control the display properties of symbols in your drawings. The most common parameter is the *Scale* parameter. With this parameter, a surveyor will enter the size of a tree as part of the description and the description key file will insert a symbol scaled to the value provided by the surveyor. In this case, you want the pumpers on the hydrant to display correctly (i.e., running parallel to the road).

2. In the *Settings* tab, expand the *Point* collection and expand the *Description Key Sets* collection. Select **C3D-Training**, right-click, and select **Edit Keys...**, as shown in Figure 3–71.

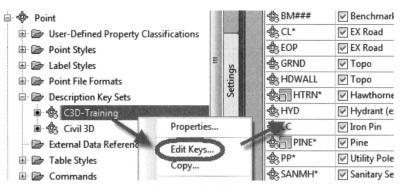

Figure 3–71

3. In the *HYD* row, toggle on the check box in the *Rotate Parameter* column, then click in the cell to select **Parameter1** from the drop-down list. The selected parameter is shown in Figure 3–72.

Figure 3–72

4. Click ☑ in the top right corner of the dialog box to close the Panorama view

5. In the graphics screen (Model Space), select the Hydrant point object, right-click, and select **Edit point**. Set the *Raw Description* from HYD to **HYD -5**. The -5 indicates the required rotation.

6. Select the row, right-click, and select **Apply Description Keys**, as shown in Figure 3–73.

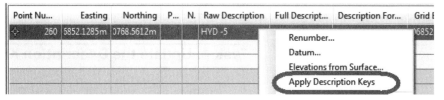

Figure 3–73

7. Click ☑ in the top right corner of the dialog box to close the Panorama view.

8. The hydrant has now been rotated to show the hydrant pumpers following the rotation of the road, as shown in Figure 3–74.

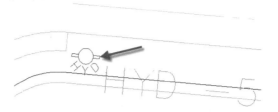

Figure 3–74

9. The label also displays the rotation angle text -5, which you do not want. In the *Settings* tab, expand the *Point* collection and expand the *Description Key Sets* collection. Select **C3D-Training**, right-click, and select **Edit Keys…**

10. In the *HYD* row, change the *Format* from $* to **Hydrant**, as shown in Figure 3–75.

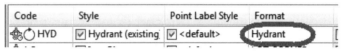

Figure 3–75

11. You still need to apply the changes. In the graphics screen (Model Space), select the Hydrant point object, right-click, and select **Apply Description Keys**. The changes are now applied, as shown in Figure 3–76.

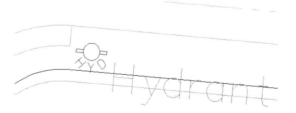

Figure 3–76

12. Save the drawing.

3.12 Importing and Exporting Points

AutoCAD Civil 3D has methods to import point data from ASCII text files, AutoCAD Land Desktop point databases, Autodesk LandXML files, as well as methods to convert AutoCAD Land Desktop points to AutoCAD Civil 3D points. The Survey tab also inserts points from a survey to a drawing.

To Import Points

There are two methods of invoking the import point feature, one is via the Ribbon Insert tab and the other is through the Points creation tool in the prospector tab.

Ribbon Insert tab method

1. On the Ribbon's *Insert* tab, select **Points from File**. Alternatively, you can click on the Create Points toolbar. This opens the Import Points dialog box.
2. In the Import Points dialog box, set the file format, select the files to import, set any advanced options, and click OK to import the points.

Point Creation tools method

1. Open the Create Points dialog box by expanding Points on the Ribbon's *Home* tab, and selecting a *Create Points* option from the drop-down list, as shown on the left in Figure 3–77. Alternatively, in the *Prospector* tab, select **Points**, right-click, and select **Create...**, as shown on the right.

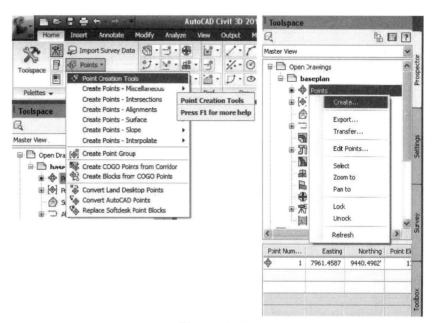

Figure 3–77

All commands on the Create Points toolbar can also be accessed through the **Points** pull-down menu, as shown in Figure 3–78.

Figure 3–78

2. Click  (Import Points) to open the Import Points dialog box.
3. In the Import Points dialog box, select a point file format from the *Format* drop-down list.

4. After setting the format, click to the right to open the Select Source File dialog box.

5. In the Select Source File dialog box, browse to the import point file, select it, and click **Open**. You can select multiple files as long as they have the same file format. You can assign the imported points to a new or existing point group by selecting the **Add Points to Point Group** option and selecting the point group from the drop-down list. Select any *Advanced options* as needed. The Import Points dialog box is shown in Figure 3–79.

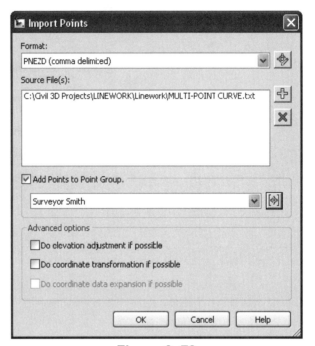

Figure 3–79

The Duplicate Point Number dialog box opens if there is a conflict between point numbers in the ASCII file and the drawing (e.g., both contain Point Number 1).

To import points directly from an AutoCAD Land Desktop point database, select the External Project Point Database format and browse for the project's COGO subfolder. Then locate and select the **Points.mdb** file.

If a drawing contains all or a subset of all points, you only need to convert the points into Civil 3D cogo points.

Duplicate Point Numbers

If an imported file creates duplicate point numbers, AutoCAD Civil 3D overwrites, merges, or reassigns them during the import process. When encountering duplicate point numbers, AutoCAD Civil 3D can assign the next available number, add an offset (add 5000 to each point number that conflicts), overwrite (replaces the current point values with the file's values), or merge (add the file's values to an existing point's values). If using the offset method, the new point numbers are kept unique in the drawing. If using the next available number method, the new points blend into the original points and are difficult to identify.

The offset method is preferred when resolving duplicate point numbers. When importing points that will potentially duplicate point numbers, the Create Points toolbar's *Point Identity* settings, as shown in Figure 3–80, is the default when handling duplicate point numbers.

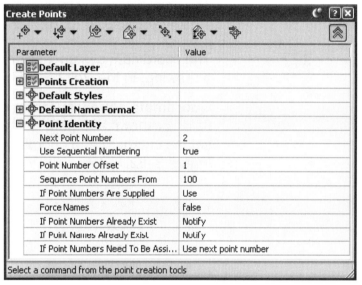

Figure 3–80

In the *Point Identity* settings, set the duplicate point resolution method for the *If Point Numbers Already Exist* variable. The four methods are Renumber, Merge, Overwrite, and Notify, as shown in Figure 3–81. The import process never overwrites point data unless you specify it.

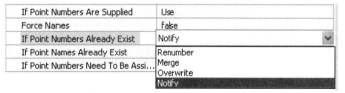

Figure 3–81

When encountering a duplicate point, the Duplicate Point Number dialog box opens. After you define a resolution, it can be assigned to the current duplicate point or to all encountered duplicate points.

Transforming Points on Import or Export

When importing points, the assumption is that the file's and drawing's points are in the same coordinate system. When the file's points are in a different coordinate system, you must define a point file format identifying the point file's coordinate system.

To identify that a point file contains coordinates from a different system, you must define a new point file format. When using this file to import points, the import routine knows the points are from one system and the drawing is assigned another. Therefore, when importing the points, it transforms them to the drawing's coordinate system.

When using the file format to export points, the export routine transforms the points from the drawing's coordinate system to the point file format's coordinate system.

The point file format must have two values: the coordinate system and the keywords **Grid Northing** and **Grid Easting**.

The coordinate system assignment is similar to assigning a system to a drawing. In the Point File Format dialog box, toggle on the

Coordinate zone transform option and click ⊕ beside the *Zone* field, as shown in Figure. In the Select Coordinate Zone dialog box, set the category and coordinate system, as shown at the bottom in Figure 3–82.

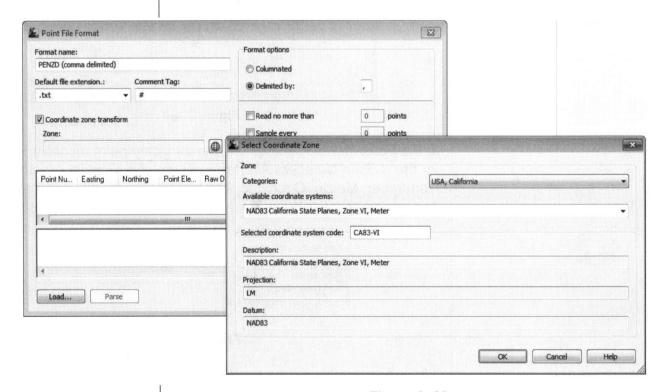

Figure 3–82

You then need to change the Northing and Easting headings to Grid Northing and Grid Easting. Select the heading and in the Select Column Name dialog box, select the new heading: **Grid Northing** or **Grid Easting**, as shown in Figure 3–83.

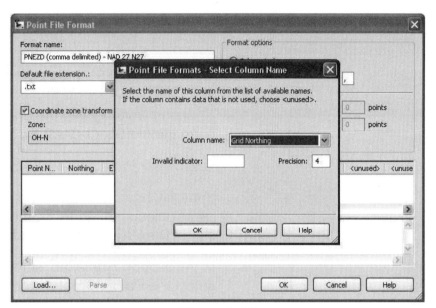

Figure 3–83

Practice 3g

Importing and Exporting Points Part I

In this practice you will import an ASCII file created in the field.

Task 1: Import an ASCII file using the Create Points toolbar.

1. Continue working with the drawing from the previous practice or open the file **SUV1-Sec2-Survey.dwg** from the following folder:

    C:\Civil 3D Projects\Civil3D-training\Drawings

2. You may have to change the draw order to be able to view the other objects. In Model Space, select the image, right-click, select **Display Order > Send to Back**.

3. In the Ribbon *Home* tab, select **Points** and in the drop-down list select the Points Creation tool.

4. Click ⬥ (Import Points) on the toolbar.

5. In the Import Points dialog box, select **PNEZD (comma delimited)** from the *Format* drop-down list.

6. Click ⊕ and in the Select Source File dialog box, browse to the ASCII file's location, *C:\Civil 3D Projects\Civil3D-training\Data*. The survey of the property pins is the file you want to import.

7. Select the file **Site-Property.txt** and click **Open** to select the file and return to the Import Points dialog box, as shown in Figure 3–84.

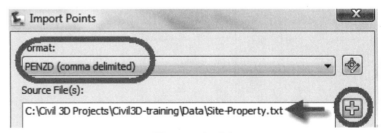

Figure 3–84

8. Click OK to import the file. When done, click on the **X** to close the Import Points dialog box.

9. Save the drawing.

Task 2: Review points.

1. In the *Prospector* tab, select **Points** to preview the points in the *Prospector's* preview area.

2. From the point list, select point **249,** right-click, and select **Zoom to**.

3. In the *Prospector's* point preview list, select point **249**, right-click, and select **Delete...** Click [Yes] in the dialog box that opens to delete the point.

4. In the *View* tab > Views panel, select the preset view **C3D-Survey Main**.

5. Save the drawing.

Task 3: Create a new point file format.

In AutoCAD Civil 3D, you are able to create an output format based on an independent coordinate system. Using this output file, you can then open multiple drawings that each have their own coordinate systems and export the points to one common coordinate system.

1. Select the *Settings* tab.

2. Expand the *Point* collection until you see the *Point File Formats* collection and its format list. From the *Point File Formats* list, select **PNEZD (Comma delimited)**, right-click, and select **Copy...**

3. In the Point File Format dialog box, change the format name to **PNEZD (Comma delimited) Lat-Long**.

4. Toggle on the **Coordinate zone transform** option and click 🌐 beside the Zone field.

5. In the Select Coordinate Zone dialog box, set the *Categories* to **Lat Longs** and the *Available coordinate systems* to **WGS84 datum, Latitude-Longitude; Degrees**, as shown in Figure 3–85. Click [OK] to return to the Point File Format dialog box.

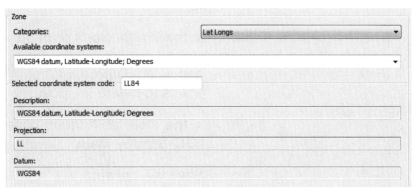

Figure 3–85

6. Select the **Northing** heading, as shown in Figure 3–86, and in the Select Column Name dialog box, select **Latitude** from the *Column name* drop-down list and click [OK].

7. Select the **Easting** heading, as shown in Figure 3–86, and in the Select Column Name dialog box, select **Longitude** from the *Column name* drop-down list and click [OK].

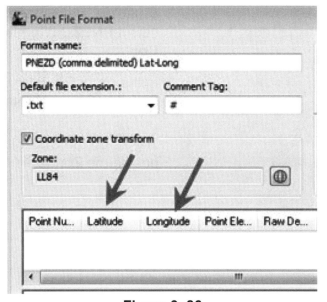

Figure 3–86

8. Click [OK] to create the new point file format.

Task 4: Export a Lat Longs point file.

1. Select the *Prospector* tab.

2. If necessary, expand the *Point Groups* collection.

3. From the list of point groups, select **_All Points**, right- click, and select **Export…** to open the Export Points dialog box.

4. In the Export Points dialog box, change the file format to **PNEZD Comma delimited) Lat-Long**.

5. Click [icon] to open the Select Destination File dialog box.

6. Browse to the *C:\Civil 3D Projects\Civil3D-training\Geomatics\ Survey Data1* folder. Enter **Site-Lat-Long** for the file name and

   click [**Open**] to create the file.

7. In the Export Points dialog box, toggle on the **Limit to Points in Point Group** option and select **Street Light** from the drop-down list on the left.

8. Toggle on the **Do coordinate transform if possible** option, and

   click [OK] to export the points.

9. Open Windows Explorer and browse to the *C:\Civil 3D Projects\Civil3D-training\Geomatics\Survey Data1* folder. Open the file **Site-Lat-Long.txt** using Notepad and review its lat and long coordinates.

Practice 3h | Importing and Exporting Points Part II

One method of importing points is to import a points file directly into AutoCAD Civil 3D. In this practice you will examine another method. You will use the Survey Database features to import a points file.

Task 1: Set the Survey Database and import points.

1. Continue working with the drawing from the previous practice or open the file **SUV1-Sec3-Survey.dwg** from the following folder:

    C:\Civil 3D Projects\Civil3D-training\Drawings

2. In the preceding practice, **Creating a Survey Database** you set up a survey database. Ensure that the *Survey Database* working folder is set and that the Survey Database **Survey Data1** is open, as shown in Figure 3–87. If not, follow the next three steps.

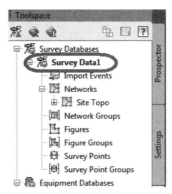

Figure 3–87

3. In the *Survey* tab, select **Survey Databases**, right-click, and select **Set working folder...**, as shown in Figure 3–88.

Figure 3–88

4. Browse to the folder *C:\Civil 3D Projects\Civil3D-training\ Geomatics* and click [OK].

5. To open the Survey Database, select **Survey Data1**, right-click, and select **Open for edit**, as shown in Figure 3–89.

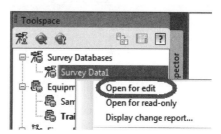

Figure 3–89

6. You will now import a point file into the Site Topo network. Expand the *Networks* collection until you see the network *Site Topo*. Select **Site Topo**, right-click, and select **Import>Import point file...**, as shown in Figure 3–90.

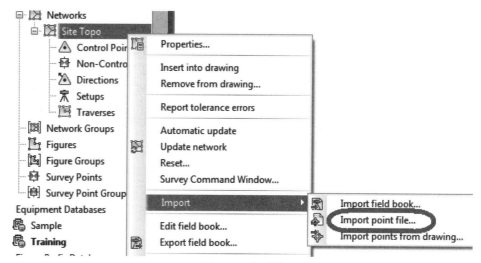

Figure 3–90

7. From the Select Source File dialog box, browse to *C:\Civil 3D Projects\Civil3D-training\Data* and select **Site-Survey2.txt**, and open it.

8. In the Import Points dialog box, set the *Point file format* to
    PNEZD (comma delimited) and the *Insert survey points* to **Yes**.
    Ensure that all other defaults are set as shown in Figure 3–91.

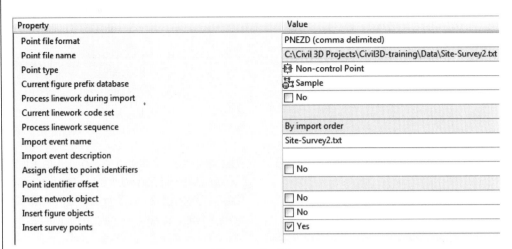

Figure 3–91

9. Note that AutoCAD Civil 3D has created an import event that can
    be used to re-process the points files when changes are made to
    them, as shown in Figure 3–92.

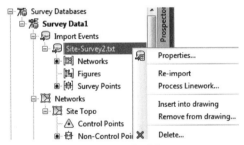

Figure 3–92

10. Save the drawing.

3.13 Point Groups

Point groups organize points that share common descriptions and characteristics (such as existing storm, gas lines, building corners, etc.). Point groups also allow points to display different point or label styles. For example, a Landscape Architect wants to see different symbols for each tree species, while an Engineer only needs to see a generic tree symbol. The Description Key Set enables you to assign the tree species symbols for the Architect, and a point group enables generic tree symbols to override the symbols for the Engineer. Another function of a point group is to hide all points.

In AutoCAD Civil 3D, point groups can be defined in the template along with a Description Key Set. When you create a new drawing from this template and import points, they will be assigned their symbols and be sorted into point groups.

All points in a drawing belong to the _All Points_ point group. Consider this point group as the point database. It cannot be deleted and initially, it is not in a drawing until you add points. All new point groups will include all drawing points or a subset of drawing points (copied points from the _All Points_ point group).

Defining Point Groups

To create a new point group, go to the *Prospector* tab, right-click on the *Point Groups* collection and select **New...** Alternatively, in the *Home* tab, select **Points>Create Point Group**.

After selecting **New...** or **Create Point Group**, the Point Group Properties dialog box displays. This dialog box has nine tabs, each affecting the point group's definition.

The *Point Groups*, *Raw Desc Matching*, *Include*, and *Query Builder* tabs add points to the point group. The *Exclude* tab removes points from a point group.

The *Information* tab defines the point group's name. The *Point style* and *Point label style* should remain at their defaults, unless you want to use either style to override the assigned styles of the points in the point group. The points in the point group will display their originally assigned styles until you toggle on the override. A point group can be locked by toggling on the **Object locked** option to prevent any changes to the group. The Point Group Properties dialog box appears as shown in Figure 3–93.

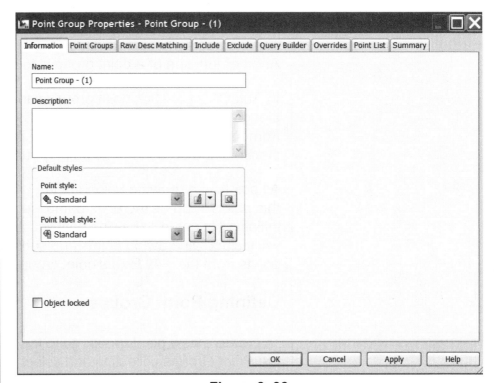

Figure 3–93

The *Point Groups* tab lists the drawing's groups. A point group can be created from other point groups. By toggling on a point group name, the group and its points become members of the new point group. For example, the point group *Trees* is created from the point groups *Maple*, *Walnut*, *Oak*, etc.

The *Raw Desc Matching* tab lists codes from the Description Key Code set. When you toggle on the code, any point matching the code becomes part of the point group.

If you cannot select a point with the previous two methods, the *Include* tab enables you to include points by specifically entering in the selection criteria. The criteria include the point number (point number list or by selection), elevation, name, raw description, full description, and all points.

- **With numbers matching:** This option selects points by a point number range or list. When creating a list, sequential point numbers are hyphenated (1-20) and individual numbers are in a comma delimited list. A point list can include sequential and individual points (1-20, 14, 44, 50-60). Click **Selection Set in Drawing** to select the points in the drawing and list their point numbers at the top of the Include tab.

- **With elevations matching:** This option enables you to select points by entering a specific elevation or by specifying a minimum and/or maximum elevation. For example, valid entries include >100,<400 and >100. The first entry includes only points whose elevation is above 100, but less than 400. The second entry includes only points whose elevation is greater than 100. A point with NO elevation cannot be selected using this method. An elevation range, defined by separating the start and end numbers with a hyphen, includes points whose elevation falls within the range (1-100). This can be combined with greater or less than symbols.

- **With names matching:** This option selects points based on matching their point names. Enter one or more point names separated by commas.

- **With raw/full descriptions matching:** This option selects points based on matching an entered raw or full description. Enter one or more descriptions separated by commas. You can use the same wildcards as the Description Key Set. Generally, this method uses the asterisk (*) as the wildcard after the description (e.g., PINE*, CTV*, CL*, etc.).

- **Include all points:** This option assigns all points in the drawing to the point group. When this option is toggled on, all other Include options are disabled.

The *Exclude* tab has the same options as the *Include* tab, except for the **Include All Points** option.

The *Query Builder* tab creates one or more expressions to select points. Each query is a row selecting points. As with all SQL queries, you combine expressions using the operators AND, OR, and NOT. You can also use parentheses to group expressions.

The *Overrides* tab overrides the points in the point group's raw description, elevation, point style, and/or point label style. For example, you can override specific tree species symbols with a generic tree symbol, override a label style when displaying this group, or override the point and label style with none (to hide all points).

The point group display order affects points and their overrides. To change how the point groups display, manipulate the Point Group display order.

The *Point List* tab displays the point group's points. This tab enables you to review points currently in the point group.

The *Summary* tab displays the point group's settings. You can print this tab as a report by cutting and pasting it into a document.

Updating Out-of-Date Point Groups

After defining point groups and then adding points to a drawing, the group goes out of date before assigning the points to the group. This allows you to verify that the point(s) should become a part of the group. To review why a group is out of date, select the group, right-click, and select **Show Changes…** If the changes are correct, click **Update** to add the points to the group. If you know all the groups showing as out of date should be updated, right-click on the *Point Groups* collection and select **Update**. At this level, the command updates all point groups.

Overriding Point Group Properties

When working with points, you may want them to display different labels, not be visible, or show different symbols. Each desired change is a function of a point group override. A point group that contains all points and overrides their symbols and labels with none displays no points. This is similar to freezing all layers involved with points. A point group that changes what symbols a group displays overrides the label styles assigned to the point in the point group. To display a different symbol, the point group overrides the assigned point styles. To set the style and override the assigned styles, toggle on the point group in the *Overrides* tab and set the styles in the *Override* column of the point group, as shown in Figure 3–94.

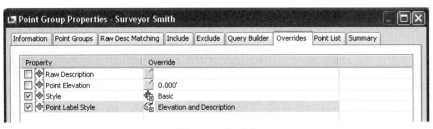

Figure 3–94

Point Groups Display Properties

When creating a point group, it is placed at the top of the point group list. The point group list is more than a list of point groups; it is also AutoCAD Civil 3D's point draw order. AutoCAD Civil 3D draws the point groups on the screen starting from the bottom of the list to the top. If _All Points is the first drawn point group and the remaining point groups are subsets of all points, you will not see the individual point group, just all of the points.

To view point groups that are a subset of all points, you must create a point group whose purpose is to hide all points. Many users call this popular point group *No Display*. With this group, any point group drawn after it displays its members without 'seeing' the other points.

As mentioned above, AutoCAD Civil 3D draws point groups from the bottom to the top of the list. To manipulate the display order, right-click on the Point Groups collection in the *Prospector* tab and select **Properties**. The Point Groups dialog box opens, enabling you to modify the point group display order with the arrows on the right side, as shown in Figure 3–95.

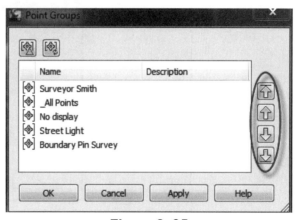

Figure 3–95

These arrows enable you to select the desired point group and move it up or down in the list (or all the way to the top or bottom of the list with one click, ⬆) in the hierarchy for display purposes. The Point Groups dialog box has two additional icons at the top. The first icon displays the difference between point groups and the second icon updates them all.

If you use Description Key Sets, a point will show the assigned point and label style when it is part of any point group. The only time the point displays another style is when you override the style (in the Point Group Properties dialog box, in the *Overrides* tab).

With the Description Key Set and display order shown in Figure 3–96, the points will show their originally assigned point label styles.

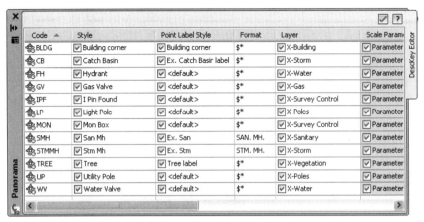

Figure 3–96

The *No Display* point group includes all points, but overrides the originally assigned point style and point label styles with **<none>**. When *No Display* is moved to the list's top, no points display. The Point Groups dialog box is shown in Figure 3–97.

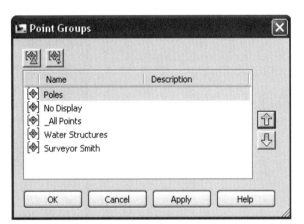

Figure 3–97

Practice 3i | Creating Point Groups

In this practice you create point groups.

Task 1: Create Point Groups (Boundary Pin Survey)

1. Continue working with the drawing from the previous practice.

2. In the *Prospector* tab, select **Point Groups**, right-click, and select **New...**, as shown in Figure 3–98.

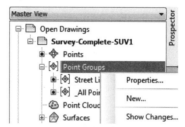

Figure 3–98

3. In the Point Group Properties dialog box, in the *Information* tab, enter **Boundary Pin Survey** in the *Name* field, set the *Point style* to **Iron Pin**, and set the *Point label style* to **Elevation and Description**, as shown in Figure 3–99.

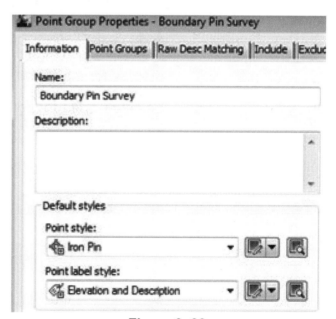

Figure 3–99

4. Select the *Include* tab. Select the **With raw description matching** option and set it to **yes** (check mark). Enter ***IP.** In the field to select all points that have the last three characters "IP." (iron pin). You can confirm this by going to the *Point List* tab, as shown in Figure 3–100.

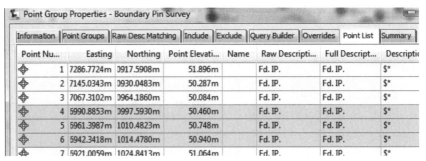

Figure 3–100

5. Click [OK] to close the dialog box and apply the changes.

Task 2: Create point groups (No display).

Continue working with the drawing from the previous task. In this task you will use the point group to control the points display. Not only will you be able to display the same point differently, but you will also be able to control the visibility of the points. This eliminates having to use the **Layer** command to thaw and freeze layers.

1. As in *Task 1*, select **Point Groups**, right-click, and select **New...** to create a new point group. In the *Information* tab, enter **No display** for the *Name*.

2. Select **<none>** for both the *Point style* and the *Point label style*, as shown in Figure 3–101.

Figure 3–101

3. Select the *Overrides* tab and select the check boxes for *Style* and *Point Label Style*, as shown in Figure 3–102.

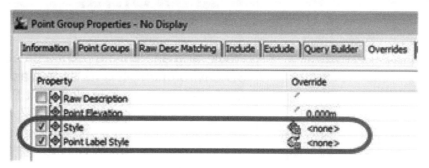

Figure 3–102

4. Select the *Include* tab and select the **Include all points** option and set it to **True** (check mark). Select the *Point List* tab to confirm that all points have been included.

5. Click [OK] to create the point group. Notice the points have disappeared.

6. To control the hierarchy and the display of the point group style, go to the *Prospector* tab, select **Point Groups**, right-click, and select **Properties**.

7. In the Point Groups dialog box, select the **Boundary Pin Survey** point group and move it to the top of the list by using the ⤒ icon, located to the right. Click [OK] to apply the changes. Only the points in the Boundary Pin point group are now displayed. If you do not see the property pins, the image may be hiding them. You may have to change the draw order to be able to view the other objects. In Model Space, select the image, right-click, and select **Display Order > Send to Back**.

8. Experiment with moving point groups up and down the list to control the display of points.

9. Save the drawing

3.14 Reviewing and Editing Points

Reviewing and editing point data occurs throughout the AutoCAD Civil 3D environment. It is as simple as selecting a point in the drawing, right-clicking, and selecting **Edit Points...**. You can also edit points using the shortcut menu of the *Points* heading in the *Prospector* tab, as shown in Figure 3–103. Alternatively, you can click in a point entry in the *Prospector's* preview area.

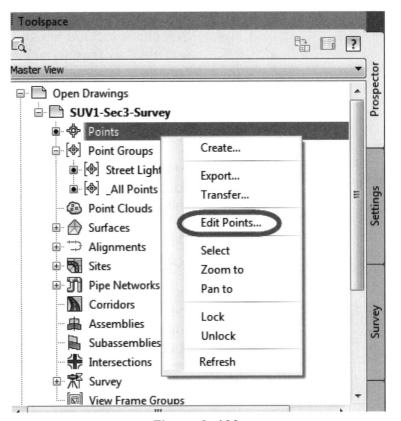

Figure 3–103

When selecting **Edit Points...**, AutoCAD Civil 3D displays the Point Editor vista inside the Panorama, as shown in Figure 3–104.

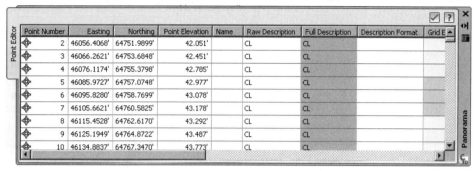

Figure 3–104

Repositioning Point Labels

Each point label style has *Dragged State* parameters. These parameters affect the label's behavior when moving the label from its original label position. Depending on the *Dragged State* parameters, a label can change completely (Stacked text) or display as it was originally defined (As composed). An example of a label is shown in Figure 3–105.

Figure 3–105

When selecting a point, it displays multiple grips. Be careful to not grip select the move point grip when your intention is to relocate the label.

A point displays four grips when selected: coordinate or relocate, rotation, drag label, and toggle sub-item. The sub-item grip relocates the individual label components. Three of the grips are shown in Figure 3–106.

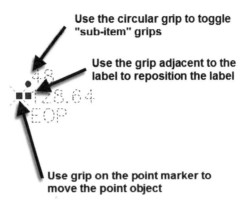

Use the circular grip to toggle "sub-item" grips

Use the grip adjacent to the label to reposition the label

Use grip on the point marker to move the point object

Figure 3–106

Each label component can be modified and the change is only for that point.

Point objects can be set to automatically rotate to match the current view through style settings. If this is not preferred, they can have a rotation assigned directly through the AutoCAD Properties dialog box.

You can reset a label to its original position by selecting the point, right-clicking, and selecting **Reset Label**.

Practice 3j | Manipulating Points

Task 1: Modify the position of the labels.

1. Continue working with the drawing from the previous practice or open the file **SUV1-Sec3-Survey.dwg** from the following folder: *C:\Civil 3D Projects\Civil3D-training\Drawings*.

2. In the *Prospector* tab, select **Points** to preview them in the *Prospector's* preview area, typically located at the bottom.

3. In the preview point list, scroll down until you see point number 10. Select it, right-click, and select **Zoom to**. This positions the point at the center of the screen.

4. In a typical drafting workflow, points can overlap, making them illegible. Since the Point Style's text height is a function of the drawing scale, changing the *Annotation Scale* changes the text size. In the Status Bar at the bottom of the window, set the *Annotation Scale* to **1:500**, as shown in Figure 3–107, to change the point size in the drawing.

Figure 3–107

5. Zoom into point 10 and select it to display its grips. Select the Drag Label grip, as shown in Figure 3–108, to relocate the label.

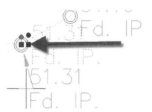

Figure 3–108

6. With the label still showing grips, right-click and select **Reset Label**.

7. With the label still showing grips, select the green circular grip, as shown in Figure 3–109, and rotate the symbol and its label.

Figure 3–109

8. Save the drawing.

3.15 Locking/Unlocking Points

AutoCAD Civil 3D has point locking that prevents its properties from edits. A locked point displays the 🔒 (Lock) icon.

To lock all points, select **Points** in the *Prospector* tab, right-click, and select **Lock**, as shown on the left in Figure 3–110. You can also lock points in a point group. To lock individual points, select the point, right-click, and select **Lock**, as shown on the right. You can also select points in a drawing and use the same right-click method to lock them.

You can select a range of points by selecting a point from the list and while holding down <Shift>, select another point from the list. This selects all points between the first and second selected points. Select individual points by holding down <Ctrl> and selecting points.

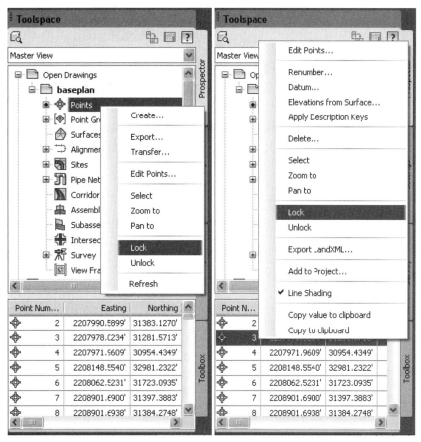

Figure 3–110

Reviewing/Editing Points

Review and/or edit points using one of the following methods: Use the tools in the *Modify* tab > Points panel; select the **Points** heading, right-click, and select **Edit Points...**; select points in a drawing, right-click, and select **Edit Points...** These commands enable you to edit all or selected points, revise the points' elevation, reassign point elevations from a surface, or renumber the points.

In the Point Editor, use <Shift> or <Ctrl> to a select a range or set of individual points. After selecting the points, right-click and select the desired editing option, as shown in Figure 3–111. You can also select points graphically and then right-click to edit the points.

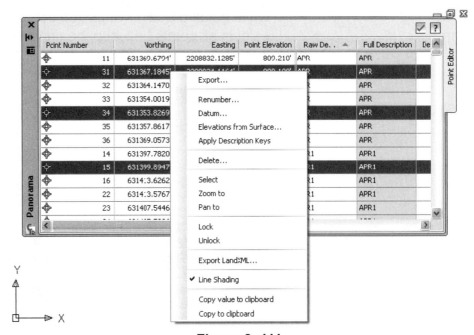

Figure 3–111

Practice 3k | Point Locking and Editing

1. Continue working with the drawing from the previous practice.

2. In the *Prospector* tab, select **Points** to display a point list in the *Prospector's* preview area at the bottom.

3. Scroll through the list, select point number **10**, right-click, and select **Zoom to**.

4. In the drawing, select point **10** and notice the move grip at its marker, as shown in Figure 3–112.

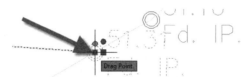

Figure 3–112

5. In the *Prospector* tab, select **Points**, right-click, and select **Lock**, as shown on the left in Figure 3–113. Notice the points in the *Prospector's* preview area now display the lock icon, as shown on the right.

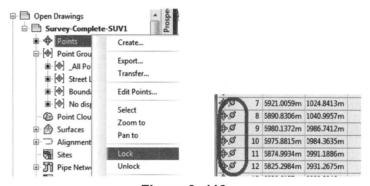

Figure 3–113

6. In the drawing, select point **10** and notice it no longer has the move grip, as shown in Figure 3–114.

Figure 3–114

7. In the *Prospector* tab, select **Points**, right-click, and select **Edit Points....**, as shown on the left in Figure 3–115. The points display the lock icon and the editor now has a gray background, as shown on the right.

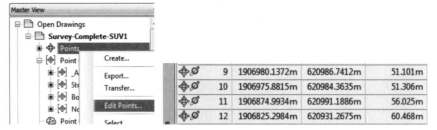

Figure 3–115

8. Select point **5** from the list of points. Scroll down the list, press <Shift> and select point **10**. With points 5 to 10 highlighted, as shown on the left in Figure 3–116, right-click, and select **Unlock**. Notice the points no longer display the lock icon and have a white background, as shown on the right. These two things indicate that the points are available for editing.

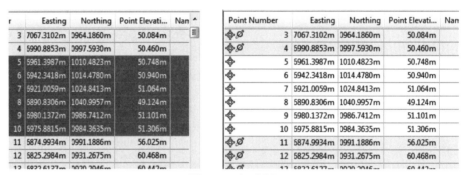

Figure 3–116

9. In the Point Editor dialog box, <double-click> on point **10**. The cell goes into edit mode now that it has been unlocked.

10. Close the Panorama by clicking ☑ in the top right corner without making any changes.

11. In the drawing, select point **10**, right-click, and review the editing options in the shortcut menu.

12. Review the commands displayed on the Ribbon. Because this is a contextual object, all entries are tools that are applicable to a point.

13. Save the drawing.

3.16 Point Reports

The surveyor needs to produce point reports. These can include a record list for the project, a checklist to find errors, reference for field crews, stakeout, etc. Incorporating survey data with an AutoCAD Civil 3D engineering project is unique in that it relies on connection and communication with third party survey equipment and software. Autodesk has collaborated with the major survey equipment vendors and they have developed applications that interface their equipment with AutoCAD Civil 3D. The following is a list of these vendors:

- TDS Survey Link
- Trimble Link
- Leica X-Change
- TOPCON Link
- Carlson Connect (Not yet available for Civil 3D 2011)

Civil 3D points can be exported and then uploaded to the survey equipment without relying on manually created lists. However, a documented point list may be desirable. There are several ways to create reports about points.

Point Reports - Reports Manager

The Civil 3D Reports Manager produces several point reports. To create reports from the Reports Manager, the *Toolbox* tab must be available in the Toolspace. To display the *Toolbox* tab, go to the *Home* tab and select **Toolbox** in the *Palettes* drop-down list. Then select the *Toolbox* tab and expand the *Reports Manager* collection to display a list of object type reports, as shown in Figure 3–117.

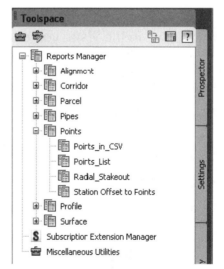

Figure 3–117

Points are easily organized into a convenient, legible list that displays the point number, northing, easting, elevation, and full description (see the example in Figure 3–118). Another point report lists the points' station and offset values relative to an alignment. Another report calculates distances and angles from an occupied and a backsight. You can transfer points to Microsoft Excel spreadsheets using a CSV report.

To create these reports, select the report's name, right-click, and select **Execute…**.

Number	Northing	Easting	Elevation	Description
1	632055.919	2208068.041	900.655	MON
2	631396.467	2207989.483	900.171	MON
3	630834.659	2207979.534	898.369	MON
4	631382.131	2207989.229	900.174	MON

Figure 3–118

Point Editor Reports

Another report method is to use the Point Editor vista. In the *Prospector* tab, select **Points**, right-click, and select **Edit…** to display the Point Editor vista, as shown in Figure 3–119.

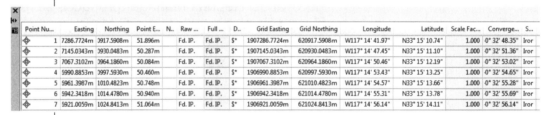

Figure 3–119

In the vista, you can select individual points using <Ctrl> or select blocks of points using <Shift>. When done selecting points, right-click and select **Copy to clipboard**. You can then paste the copied points into Excel, Notepad, or any application that accepts the points, as shown in Figure 3–120.

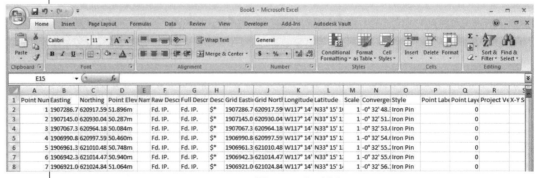

Figure 3–120

Practice 3I | Point Reports

Task 1: Create Point Reports.

1. Continue working with the drawing from the previous practice or open the file **SUV1-Sec3-Survey.dwg** from the following folder: *C:\Civil 3D Projects\Civil3D-training\Drawings*.

2. If the *Toolbox* tab is not displayed in the Toolspace, go to the *Home* tab and click the **Toolbox** icon, as shown in Figure 3–121. The Toolspace should now show the *Toolbox* tab.

Figure 3–121

3. Select the *Toolbox* tab and expand the *Reports Manager* collection to view the list of object type reports. Expand the *Points* collection to see the list of point reports, as shown in Figure 3–122.

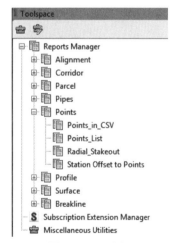

Figure 3–122

4. Select **Point List**, right-click, and select **Execute**.

5. In the Export to LandXML dialog box, click OK to generate the report. In the Save As dialog box enter a file name or accept the default **CivilReport.html**, and save the file. If the file exists, you will be asked if you want to replace it.

6. The point list is displayed in Internet Explorer. Review the report and when done, close it.

Review Questions

1. Where can you control the appearance of a point label when the point label grip is selected in the drawing and moved away from the point itself?

2. What is attached to a drawing that prevents you from having to recreate all Civil 3D styles and settings every time a new drawing is created?

3. How do you control the next point number to be used in a drawing?

4. Explain the display of the point style if the point is tagged by a Description Key Set and a Point Group?

5. Where do all points permanently reside in the drawing?

6. Can the _All Points point group be deleted?

7. Can a point group be made out of point groups?

Section 3: Civil 3D Survey Figures

3.17 Survey Figures

Survey figures consist of linework generated by coding and placed in a file that is imported into the Survey Database. A figure represents linear features (edge-of-pavement, toe-of-slopes, etc.)

A figure thus has many functions, as follows:

- A figure displays linework in a drawing.
- All preset figures in a drawing can be defined as breaklines for a surface definition with just one step.
- All preset figures in a drawing can be defined as parcel lines.
- A figure can be drawn as a pipe run. For example, a surveyor notices that only one pipe comes through a manhole. The surveyor therefore invokes a figure command to draw a survey figure that denotes the location of a pipe run. The Elevation Editor in AutoCAD Civil 3D enables you to lower each survey figure at each manhole to the distance of what was measured in the field, and what was written on the manhole field notes as the flow elevation at the invert of the pipe run. The pipe functionality can make this line represent various types of locations within the circumference of the cross-sectional pipe and convert the survey figure into an existing pipe run.
- All figures can be targets for *Width* or *Offset Targets* within a Corridor.
- All figures can be targets for *Slope* or *Elevation Targets* within a Corridor (e.g., Limits of construction for a road rehab project might be to the face of walk, which exists in the drawing as a Survey Figure, hence a target).
- The Figure Prefix database should be set up before importing any survey data to obtain the desired entities in a drawing. As point and label styles and the Description Key Set need to exist before importing points, figure styles and entries in the Figure Prefix database need to exist before importing survey data.

Drawing Settings

The Drawing Settings dialog box, as shown in Figure 3–123, sets a universal layer for figures. You can access these settings by selecting the drawing name in the *Settings* tab, right-clicking, and selecting **Edit Drawing Settings...** When selecting the *Object Layer* tab and scrolling to the bottom of the list, you see the default layer names.

Your office will likely have one or more default layers for each of the linework types. For example, edge-of-pavement, sidewalk, etc. all each have their own layers in the drawing. To accomplish this, you need to define figure styles.

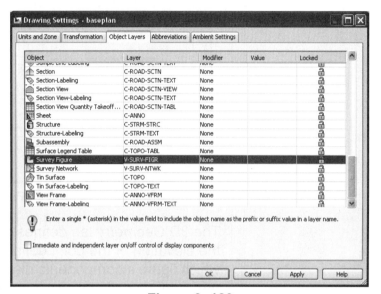

Figure 3–123

Figure Styles

Figure styles affect how survey linework appears in a drawing. They should be part of your template file. These styles are not critical, but to make figures work, you should at least define the layers they will use in the drawing.

Figure styles are tied to the Figure Prefix database. The Figure Prefix database assigns a figure style to a figure that is imported into a drawing.

A figure style includes the layers for its linework and markers. You should make these layers match the layer names in the figure styles.

A marker is a symbol placed on the figure's segment midpoints and end points. They call attention to the figure's geometry. Even though a figure style includes marker definitions, they do not need to display.

Like points, figures are three-dimensional and use the layers set in the Display tab of the Figure Style dialog box. The *Information* tab assigns the style a name. The *Plan*, *Profile*, and *Section* tabs define how the marker displays in each of these views.

The Figure Style dialog box is shown in as shown in Figure 3–124.

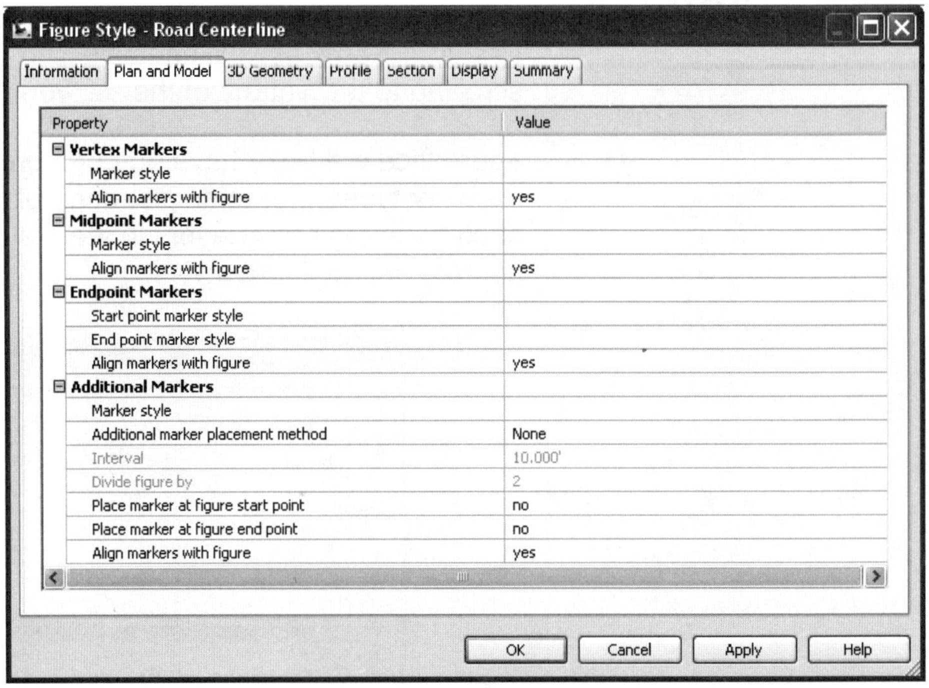

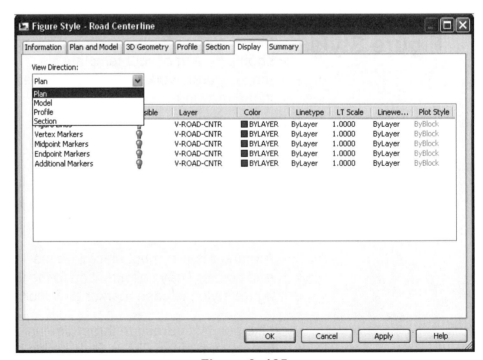

Figure 3–124

The *3D Geometry* tab defines a figure's vertical behavior. By default, the elevation of the point defines the figure. The *Display* tab defines which figure's components display and what layers they use for plan, profile, and section views, as shown in Figure 3–125.

Figure 3–125

Figure Prefix Database

The Figure Prefix database assigns the figure a style, a layer, and defines whether the figure is a surface breakline or lot line (parcel segment). If you did not define any figure styles, you should at least assign a layer to properly place the figure in the drawing. Toggling on the *Breakline* property, as shown in Figure 3–126, enables you select all tagged survey figures and assign them to a surface without having to insert or select from a drawing. Toggling on the *Lot Line* property creates a parcel segment from the figure in the drawing and if there is a closed polygon, assigns a parcel label and an entry in the survey site.

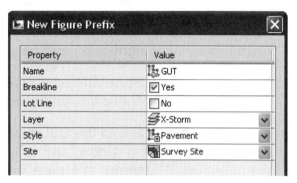

Figure 3–126

If the *Name* is **GUT**, in the example show above, then any figure starting with **GUT** uses these settings. This is similar to using a Description Key Set, except the entry in the Figure Prefix database does not need an asterisk (*). The entry GUT matches **GUT1** through **GUT100**. When inserting survey figures in the drawing, Survey looks at the Figure Prefix database for style or layer values.

Practice 3m	Creating Figure Prefixes

1. Continue working with the drawing from the previous practice or open the file **SUV1-Sec4-Survey.dwg** from the following folder:

   C:\Civil 3D Projects\Civil3D-training\Drawings

2. You might have to change the draw order to be able to view other objects. In Model Space, select the image, right-click, and select **Display Order>Send to Back**.

3. Select the *Survey* tab. Select **Figure Prefix Databases**, right-click, and select **New...** Enter **C3D Training** for the name.

4. Select the newly created **C3D training** Figure Prefix database, right-click, and select **Make Current**.

5. Select the **C3D training** Figure Prefix database again, right-click, and select **Manage Figure Prefix Database...**, as shown in Figure 3–127.

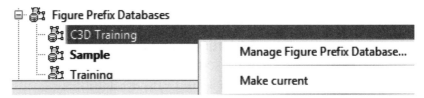

Figure 3–127

6. Click 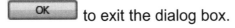 to create a new Figure definition. AutoCAD Civil 3D creates a default Figure. Change the *Name* to **Trail**, and set the *Breakline* to **Yes** and the *Style* to **Road Centerline**, as shown in Figure 3–128. Any figure starting with **Trail** will now be selectable for a surface breakline and use the style **Road Centerline**. As noted earlier, unlike the Description Key Set, an asterisk (*) is not necessary to match Trail1, Trail2, etc. Click

   OK to exit the dialog box.

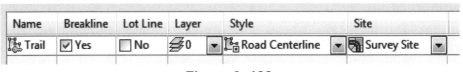

Figure 3–128

7. Click 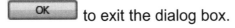 to create a new Figure definition. Change the name to **Building**, and set the *Breakline* to **No** and the *Style* to **Buildings**.

8. Save the drawing.

3.18 Importing a Field Book

To import a field book, you use the Survey's *Import Events* collection. *Import Events* provides access to an import wizard, which takes you through the steps of importing a file. To open the import wizard, select the **Import Events** in the Survey, right click, and select **Import survey data...**

The import wizard's first screen, *Specify Database*, is shown in Figure 3–129. This screen sets the survey, creates a new survey, and edits a survey's settings.

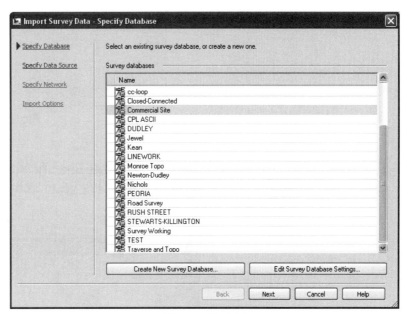

Figure 3–129

Click [Next >] . The *Specify Data Source* screen, as shown in Figure 3–130, defines the file import type, the file's path, and—if it is a coordinate file—its format.

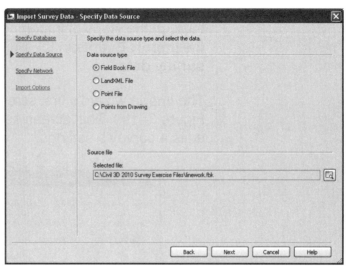

Figure 3–130

Click [Next >] . The *Specify Network* screen, as shown in Figure 3–131, enables you to change the network or create a new survey network.

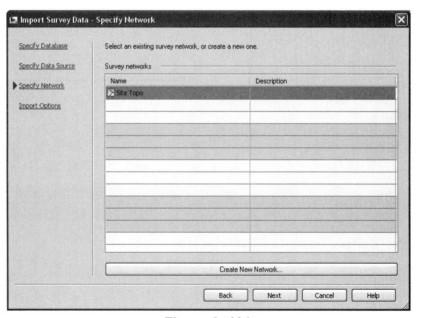

Figure 3–131

Click **Next >** . The *Import Options* screen, as shown in Figure 3–132, sets the values for the import. These settings affect what the import does and what support files it uses.

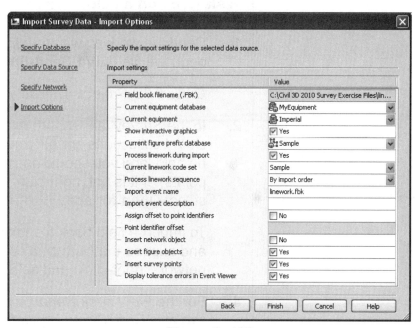

Figure 3–132

If the field book has figure coding from a conversion, you do not need to toggle on the *Process linework during import* property. This is for files with Linework Code Set commands and no CONT or END lines.

Inserting figures requires entries in the Figure Prefix database and figure styles in the drawing. This is required to point figure and linework to the correct layers in the drawing and to specify if the figure is also a breakline in a surface.

When inserting points, it is necessary to have a Description Key Set defined to assign point, point label styles, and layers, and to translate raw descriptions to full descriptions.

Practice 3n | Importing a Field Book

Task 1: Import a field book into the network.

1. Continue working with the drawing from the previous practice or open the file **SUV1-Sec4-Survey.dwg** from the following folder:

   C:\Civil 3D Projects\Civil3D-training\Drawings.

2. In the *Survey* tab, ensure that the *Survey Databases>Survey Data1* collections are expanded and set to current (the text will be bold, and you should see all the networks, figures, and survey points). If it is not, right-click on the *Survey Data1* collection and select **Open for edit**.

3. To import a field book file, expand the *Survey Data1* collection and expand the *Networks* collection. Select the **Site Topo** network, right-click, and select **Import > Import Field Book**.

4. For the *Field book filename (.FBK)*, browse to *C:\Civil 3D Projects\Civil3D-training\Data*, select **Site-Survey3.fbk**, and open it.

5. In the Re-import Field Book dialog box, set the following values, as shown in Figure 3–133: *Show interactive graphics* to **Yes**, *Process linework during import* to **No**, *Insert network object* to **Yes**, *Insert figure objects*, to **Yes**, and *Insert survey points* to

   Yes. Click [OK] to accept the changes when done.

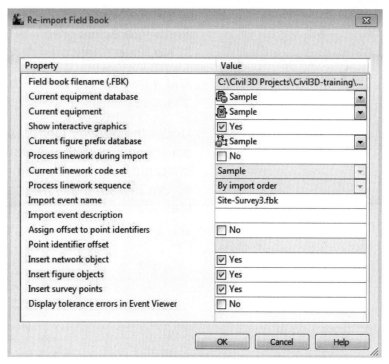

Figure 3–133

Task 2: Create a new network.

You have now imported the field book file into the existing network, Site Topo. In this task you will create a new network and import the field book file into it.

1. In the *Survey Databases>Survey Data1* collection, select **Networks**, right-click, and select **New...**, as shown in Figure 3–134.

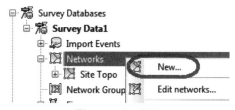

Figure 3–134

2. Enter **ExRoad** for the name.

3. To import the existing road Mission Avenue survey, select the network **ExRoad**, right-click, and select **Import>Import Field Book**.

4. For the *Field book filename (.FBK)*, browse to *C:\Civil 3D Projects\Civil3D-training\Data* and select **Road-Survey.fbk** and open it.

5. In the Re-import Field Book dialog box, set the following values: *Show interactive graphics* to **Yes**, *Process linework during import* to **No,** *Insert network object* to **Yes**, *Insert figure objects* to **Yes**, and *Insert survey points* to **Yes**. Click [OK] to accept the changes.

6. Under the *Survey Databases>Survey Data1>Import Events* collections, note that AutoCAD Civil 3D keeps a record of the imported events. You can re-import the data, as shown in Figure 3–135, if any changes are made to the original field book file.

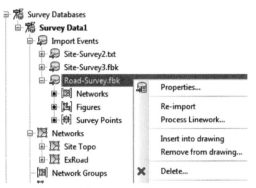

Figure 3–135

7. Save the drawing.

3.19 Working with Figures

Figures can be surface breaklines. The layer they reside on can be turned off before the final deliverable plots. A figure does not need to be inserted into a drawing to review its location. By selecting a figure from the survey's figure list, it is previewed in the drawing, as shown in Figure 3–136.

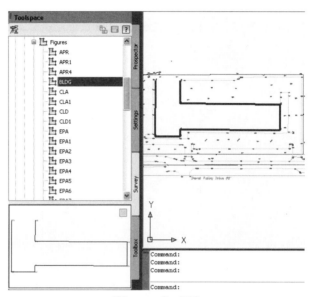

Figure 3–136

Right-click on a selected figure under the *Figures* collections to access a list of options, as shown in Figure 3–137, that enable you to remove the figure from the drawing, display its properties, insert the figure into the drawing, or insert its points into the drawing.

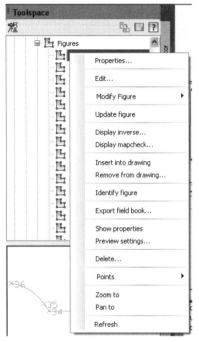

Figure 3–137

Access the Panorama's *Grading Elevation Editor* tab by selecting the figure in the drawing, right-clicking, and selecting **Elevation Edit...** Icons in the editor enable you to raise or lower its elevation for all or single vertices, as shown in Figure 3–138. You can also click in each cell and edit its elevation. The edits made in this Panorama transfer back to the survey when you select **Update Survey Data from Drawing** (select the figure and right-click to access this option).

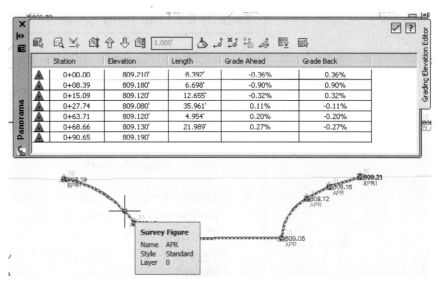

Figure 3–138

When a figure is selected in the drawing, the Ribbon displays all tools applicable to the figure. If you click the **Edit Geometry** icon on the Ribbon, you can also add or remove vertices, and offset figures to create new figures (e.g., top-face-curb from the gutter figure).

Practice 3o

Field Book Edits, Styles, and Figure Prefixes

In this practice you edit the field book and manually create a figure.

Task 1: Edit the field book.

1. Continue working with the drawing from the previous practice.

2. In the *Survey* tab, ensure that the *Survey Databases>Survey Data1* collections are expanded and set to current (the text will be bold, and you should see all the networks, figures, and survey points). If it is not, right-click on the *Survey Data1* collection and select **Open for edit**.

3. In the *Prospector* tab, expand the *Point Groups* collection and notice that the point groups are out of date. Select **Point Groups**, right-click, and select **Update**, as shown in Figure 3–139. This updates the point groups with the newly imported points.

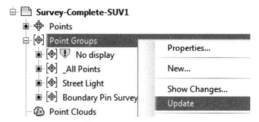

Figure 3–139

4. To zoom to and view a particular figure, in the *Survey* tab, select **Figures**. In the preview area at the bottom, as shown in Figure 3–140, select **Building1**, right-click, and select **Zoom to**, or double-click on **Building1**. In the graphics window (Model Space), you will be zoomed into the figure Building1.

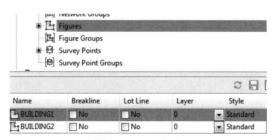

Figure 3–140

5. The survey crew in the field shot the building corners, but some minor work is still needed to close the linework in the area shown in Figure 3–141.

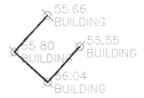

Figure 3–141

6. In the *Survey* tab, expand the *Networks* collection. Select **Site Topo**, right-click, and select **Edit Field Book**.

7. For the *Field book filename (.FBK)*, browse to *C:\Civil 3D Projects\Civil3D-training\Data* and select **Site-Survey3.fbk** and open it to display the field book in Notepad.

8. Scroll down to the line containing point number **574**. Notice that for Building1 and Building2, you have an *End* for the figure, as shown in Figure 3–142, instead of a *Close*. Change the *End* to **Close**, which will close the figure.

```
Begin Building1
NE SS 571 620894.4701 1906908.
NE SS 572 620888.7293 1906903.
NE SS 573 620883.9411 1906908.
NE SS 574 620889.5634 1906913.
End Building1 ◄━━━━━━━━
Begin Building2
NE SS 575 620834.9955 1906904.
NE SS 576 620820.588 1906904.7
NE SS 577 620820.588 1906911.(
NE SS 578 620834.9955 1906911.
End Building2 ◄━━━━━━━━

NE SS 579 620827.5755 1907112.
NE SS 580 620820.3717 1907112.
NE SS 581 620820.3717 1907105.
NE SS 582 620827.5755 1907105.
       .      .
```

```
Begin Building1
NE SS 571 620894.4701 1906908.
NE SS 572 620888.7293 1906903.
NE SS 573 620883.9411 1906908.
NE SS 574 620889.5634 1906913.
Close Building1
Begin Building2
NE SS 575 620834.9955 1906904.
NE SS 576 620820.588 1906904.;
NE SS 577 620820.588 1906911.(
NE SS 578 620834.9955 1906911.
Close Building2

NE SS 579 620827.5755 1907112.
NE SS 580 620820.3717 1907112.
NE SS 581 620820.3717 1907105.
NE SS 582 620827.5755 1907105.
                 .
```

Figure 3–142

9. Exit Notepad and when prompted, save the edits.

Task 2: Re-import the field book.

---

1. You now need to update the drawing. In the *Survey* tab, expand the *Survey Data1>Import Events* collections (if not already expanded).

2. Under the *Import Events* collection, select **Site-Survey3.fbk**, right-click, and select **Re-import**, as shown in Figure 3–143.

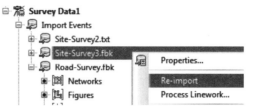

Figure 3–143

3. In the Re-import Field Book dialog box, click **OK** to reset the survey and re-import the network.

4. Select **Figures**. In the preview area at the bottom, double-click on **Building1**, then on **Building2**. As AutoCAD Civil 3D zooms into each of these figures, notice that each one is now closed.

Task 3: Create a figure manually.

---

1. In the *Prospector* tab, expand the *Point Groups* collection and select the **_All Points** point group.

2. In the preview area at the bottom, scroll to point number **579**, as shown in Figure 3–144. Select it, right-click, and select **Zoom to**.

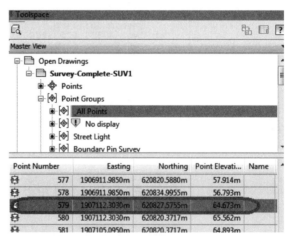

Figure 3–144

3. Using the AutoCAD **3D Polyline** command (enter **3P** at the Command Line) and the Node object snaps, draw a polyline connecting the nodes, as shown in Figure 3–145.

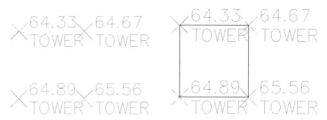

Figure 3–145

4. In the *Survey* tab, under the *Survey Databases>Survey Data1* collections, select **Figures**, right-click, and select **Create figure from object...**, as shown in Figure 3–146. In the drawing, select the polyline just drawn.

Figure 3–146

5. In the Create Figure From Object dialog box, enter **Tower** for the Name, as shown in Figure 3–147. Click [OK] to create the new figure. Press <Enter> to exit the command.

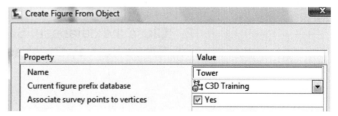

Figure 3–147

6. To update the drawing with the figure, select **Figures**, right-click, and select **Insert into drawing**, as shown in Figure 3–148.

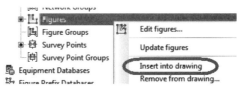

Figure 3–148

7. Review the figure's properties.

8. In the *Survey* tab, under the *Survey Databases>Survey Data1* collections, expand the *Figures* collection.

9. Select the **Tower** figure, right-click, and select **Properties**.

10. Review the figure's properties, as shown in Figure 3–149. If necessary, change the *Style* to **Buildings**. When done, click OK to exit the dialog box.

Figure 3–149

11. Save the drawing.

12. Close the database. Select **Survey Data1**, right-click, and select **Close Survey Database**. Exit the drawing.

Review Questions

1. What are some of the many functions of a survey figure in AutoCAD Civil 3D?

2. What are the three options to define a survey figure?

Module 4

Surfaces Level 1

This module introduces:

Section 1: Civil 3D Surface Overview
- ✓ **Surface Process**
- ✓ **Surface Properties**
- ✓ **Contour Data**
- ✓ **Other Surface Data**
- ✓ **Breaklines and Boundaries**
- ✓ **Surface Analysis Tools**

Section 2: Civil 3D Surface Editing
- ✓ **Surface Editing**
- ✓ **Adjusting Surfaces through Surface Properties**
- ✓ **Viewing Surfaces in 3D**

Section 3: Civil 3D Surface Labels and Analysis
- ✓ **Surface Labels**
- ✓ **Surface Volume Calculations**
- ✓ **Surface Analysis Display**

Section 1: Civil 3D Surface Overview

4.1 Surface Process

The surface building process can be divided into the following steps:

1. Assemble the data.

2. Assign the data to a surface.

3. Evaluate the resulting surface.

4. Add breaklines, assign more data, modify the data, or edit the surface as needed.

1. Assemble Data

The first step in surface building is to acquire the initial surface data. This data can be points, contours, 3D polylines, feature lines, AutoCAD objects, ASCII coordinate files, or boundaries. Each data type provides specific information about a surface.

AutoCAD Civil 3D can open approximate, non-survey grade terrain models directly from the Google Earth utility. Although rough, this DEM-based data could be useful for conceptual designs. See the *AutoCAD Civil 3D Help* documentation for more information.

2. Assign Data to a Surface

Acquired data is assigned to a surface. Once assigned, AutoCAD Civil 3D immediately processes this data and a surface object is created.

Surfaces are listed individually under the *Surfaces* collection in the *Prospector* tab. Each surface contains content information, as shown in Figure 4–1. The surface content includes *Masks, Watersheds,* and *Definition* elements. The *Definition* contains a list of all surface data that has been applied, including boundaries, breaklines, and points. The *Prospector* tab displays data for each type of surface data in the list view when one of these types is selected.

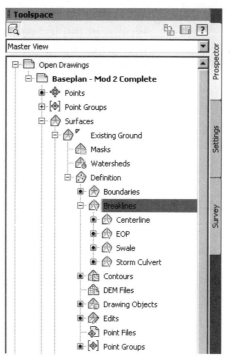

Figure 4–1

The *Definition* tab in the Surface Properties dialog box shows the allowable *Build*, *Data*, and *Edit* operations for that surface. The *Operation Type* column is a record of the surface data addition and edits. Using the checkboxes, you can toggle off individual actions in the history and view the resulting changes to the surface. The entries can be on or off no matter where they appear in the history. This helps you isolate possible errors or review features (such as surface slopes) that are greatly affected by the addition of a headwall or retaining wall.

You can change the order of items in the list of operations. Operations higher in the list are applied to the surface before items further down in the list. Open this dialog box by right-clicking on the surface name in the *Prospector* (or by selecting the surface in the drawing and right-clicking) and selecting **Surface Properties…**. The dialog box is shown in Figure 4–2.

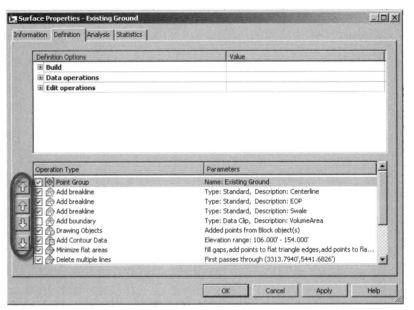

Figure 4–2

Civil 3D processes the initial data into one of two types of surfaces. The first type, the *Triangulated Irregular Network* (TIN) surface, is the most common. With triangulated surfaces, surface points are connected to adjacent points by straight lines, resulting in a triangular mesh. Surfaces generated from contour lines have surface points created at their vertices, modified by weeding and supplementing factors. An example of this type of surface is shown in Figure 4–3.

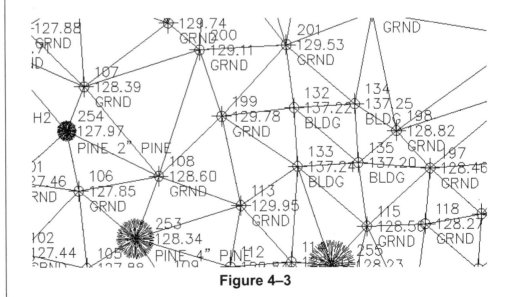

Figure 4–3

The second type of surface is a *Grid* surface. This surface interpolates and assigns an elevation from the surface data to each grid intersection. Most of the elevations at grid intersections are interpolated. *Digital Elevation Models (DEMs)* are a type of grid surface used in GIS applications. An example of this type of surface is shown in Figure 4–4.

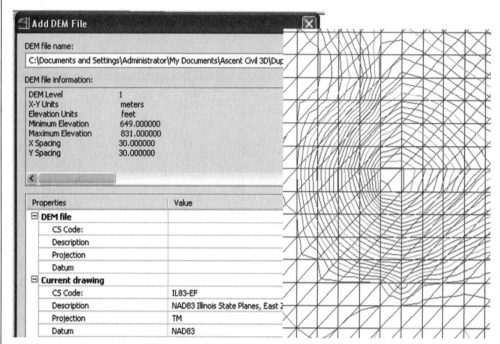

Figure 4–4

3. Evaluate the Resulting Surface

Surfaces, especially ones created from points, typically need some attention in order to represent them as accurately as possible. For any four adjacent surface points, there are two possible triangulations, as shown in Figure 4–5.

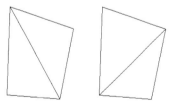

Figure 4–5

The differences can be difficult to envision when viewing the triangles from above, but these two configurations provide entirely different geometries. Take, for example, the surface shown in Figure 4–6.

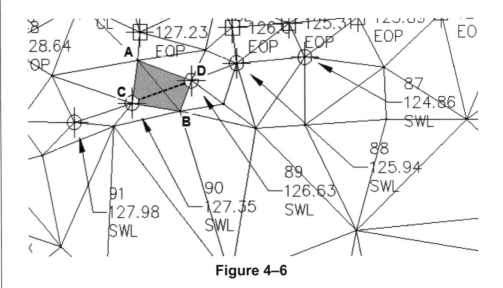

Figure 4–6

The triangulated points A, B, C, and D have a TIN line running from A to B. This configuration ignores the fact that C and D are both part of a continuous swale (SWL), shown with the dashed line. In a 3D view, this configuration would resemble the image shown on the left in Figure 4–7. However, the correct triangulation has the triangle line *following* the linear feature rather than *crossing* it, as shown on the right.

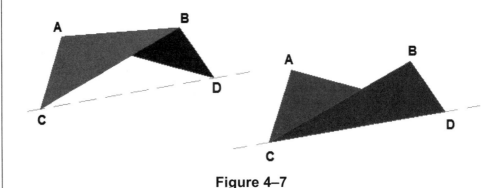

Figure 4–7

When creating surfaces, representing linear features correctly is extremely important. Examples of linear features include road center lines, edges-of-pavement, road shoulders, swales, berms, tops and bottoms of banks, and headwalls. Adding breaklines that follow linear features ensures that a terrain model is triangulated correctly along the features, rather than across them.

Other types of issues to watch out for include bad elevations (blown shots), elevations at 0 where there should be no chance of such elevation values, and points that were surveyed above or below the ground (e.g., the tops of fire hydrants). Unwanted triangles along the edges of the surface may connect points that should not be connected, which could also present problems.

In addition to the casual inspection of the triangles, surfaces can be evaluated by creating contour lines, reviewing the surface in 3D, and using the **Quick Section** command.

4. Add Breaklines, Assign More Data, Modify the Data, or Edit the Surface as needed

After you have evaluated the surface, you can add the necessary breaklines or edit the surface directly to make adjustments. If the triangulation errors are isolated, editing the surface directly might be faster than creating and applying breaklines. For example, the triangulation issue above could be addressed by "swapping" the edge that crossed the swale center line. To do this, right-click on Edits under a Surface's definition in the *Prospector* tab and select **Swap Edge**, as shown in Figure 4–8.

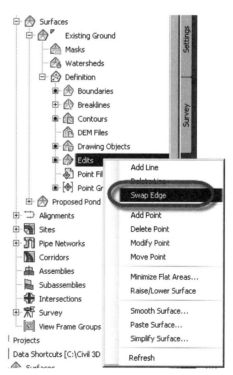

Figure 4–8

Other options enable you to add, move, modify, or remove points from the surface (but not change or erase the point object on which they were based), as well as add or remove triangle lines directly. **Minimize Flat Areas** is a group of algorithms that can be used to minimize the number of flat areas created by contour data. **Raise/Lower Surface** enables you to raise and lower the entire surface by a set amount, and a **Smooth Surface** enables you to smooth surfaces using the *Natural Neighbor* or *Kriging* method. (Contour smoothing is handled through surface styles. These techniques smooth the actual surface geometry itself.)

4.2 Surface Properties

All surfaces have properties that can be reviewed and adjusted through the Surface Properties dialog box, as shown in Figure 4–9.

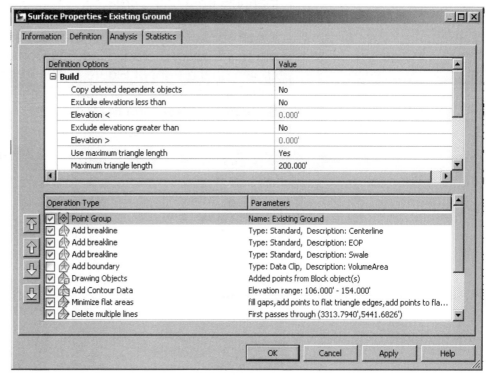

Figure 4–9

The *Information* tab enables you to rename the surface, edit the description, apply a surface object style, and render material, which controls how the surface looks in a rendered view.

The *Definition* tab enables you to review the surface's build options and the history of data added and edited. The *Data Operations* and *Edit Operations* sections enable you specify the kinds of data and edits that are permitted for this surface. By default, all are enabled for new surfaces.

The *Statistics* tab displays the current surface slope, elevation, and triangulation. It contains three sections:

- *General*: provides an overall view of the surface. The *Minimum*, *Maximum*, and *Mean* elevations are the important entries in this section and provide the first hint of bad or incorrect data.

- *Extended*: reports the *2D* and *3D* surface areas and Minimum, Maximum, and Mean slope values.

- *TIN*: reviews the number of triangles, minimum and maximum triangle areas, and leg lengths in the surface.

The areas of triangles, along with the minimum, and maximum triangle side lengths are indicators of data consistency. Generally, the longest triangles form around the perimeter of the surface. Limiting the length of triangle edges removes these types of triangles from the surface. You can delete these lines rather than try to set an optimum length, or you can create a boundary to prevent these types of triangles from being created.

When surfaces are created, they are assigned properties based on the *Build Options* area in the Edit Command Settings dialog box, as shown on the right of Figure 4–10. To access this dialog box, right-click the **CreateSurface** command and select Edit Command Settings, as shown on the left.

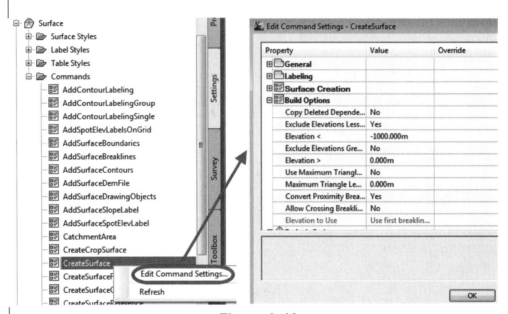

Figure 4–10

Surface Rebuilding

Some surface edits and point modifications can render a surface out of date. At that point, the surface is flagged as being out of date in the *Prospector* tab, as indicated with the drawing item modifier icon shown in Figure 4–11.

Figure 4–11

When this occurs, you can right-click on the surface in the *Prospector* tab and select **Rebuild**. This updates the surface to reflect the recent changes. Alternatively, you can right-click on the surface in the *Prospector* and select **Rebuild-Automatic**, which updates the surface automatically as necessary without input from you.

Practice 4a

Creating an Existing Ground Surface Part I

The next step in the design project is to create an existing ground terrain model. You will use this model to create existing ground contours and for reference during the design. You will begin the model with the previously created *Existing Ground* point group.

Task 1: Set up the survey database.

1. Open the file **SUF1-Sec1-Surface.dwg** from the following folder:

    C:\Civil 3D Projects\Civil3D-training\Drawings

2. At some point, you will have to incorporate survey data into the surface. To do this, you must first establish a connection to the survey database. If you have not completed the practices in the *Survey Level 1* module, create a copy of the folder *C:\Civil 3D Projects\Civil3D-training\Geomatics\Survey Data* and rename the copy to **C:\Civil 3D Projects\Civil3D-training\Geomatics\Survey Data1**.

3. If the *Survey* tab in the Toolspace is not enabled, click  in the *Home* tab > Palettes panel to toggle it on, as shown in Figure 4–12.

Figure 4–12

4. In the *Survey* tab in the Toolspace, select **Survey Databases**, right-click, and select **Set working folder**, as shown in Figure 4–13.

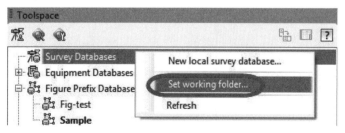

Figure 4–13

5. Select the **Civil3D-training** folder from the folder *C:\Civil 3D Projects*, as shown in Figure 4–14.

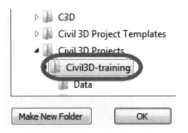

Figure 4–14

6. Select the survey database **Survey Data**, right-click, and select **Open for edit**, as shown in Figure 4–15.

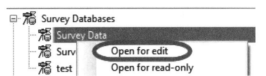

Figure 4–15

7. Save the drawing.

Task 2: Create a surface and set properties.

---

1. Open the file **SUF1-Sec1-Surface.dwg** from the following folder: C:\Civil 3D Projects\Civil3D-training\Drawings

2. In the *Prospector* tab, select **Surfaces**, right-click, and select *Create Surface*.

3. Select **TIN surface** as the surface type, enter **ExTopo** for the surface name, and select **Contours 2m and 10m (Background)** for the surface Style, as shown in Figure 4–16.

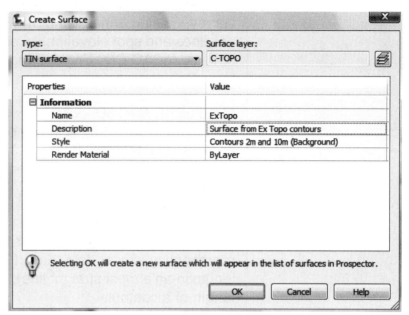

Figure 4–16

4. Click [OK] to accept the changes and close the dialog box.

5. Save the drawing.

4.3 Contour Data

Contour data is available from many sources. Large sites are often surveyed using aerial photogrammetry, which provides contour polylines and spot elevations. Contour data can also be obtained from other AutoCAD Civil Engineering applications, such as AutoCAD Land Desktop.

In AutoCAD Civil 3D, polylines with elevation are useful as custom contour objects. Whether using polylines or AutoCAD Land Desktop contour objects, AutoCAD Civil 3D builds a surface by triangulating between contours. The end of each triangle side connects to a vertex of two different contours.

When processing contours for surface data, AutoCAD Civil 3D inspects the contour vertices for two conditions: too many data points representing similar data (e.g., 10 vertices on 15 units of contour length in an almost straight line), and not enough data points over the length of a contour.

You can set the values for these conditions in the Add Contour Data dialog box, as shown in Figure 4–17, when you add contour data.

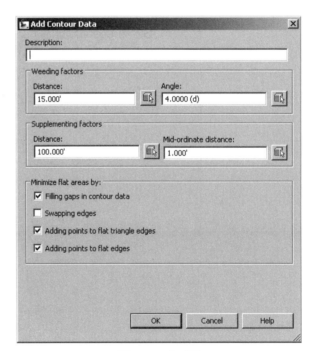

Figure 4–17

Weeding Factors

The *weeding* process removes redundant vertices from contours. The first step in the weeding process is to inspect three adjacent contour vertices, whose overall distance is shorter than a user-specified distance (e.g., three vertices in less than 15 units of contour). When encountering this situation, the weeding process asks about the change in direction between the three vertices. For example, does the direction from vertex 1 to vertex 2 change more than four degrees when going from vertex 2 to vertex 3? If not, the vertices are almost in a straight line and are too close. AutoCAD Civil 3D considers vertex 2 to be redundant and removes it from the surface data. This process repeats for the next three vertices. If the distance is under 15 units and the change of direction is less than four degrees, the next vertex 2 is removed from the data.

If a contour has three vertices in less than 15 units, and turns more than four degrees, vertex 2 is kept because the change in direction is significant. If there are more that 15 units between the three vertices, AutoCAD Civil 3D moves on to the next group.

An important feature of weeding is not what it removes from the data, but what is left over. If not enough data remains, the numbers for the weeding factors should be set to lower values.

Supplementing Factors

When AutoCAD Civil 3D inspects contour data, it uses supplementing factors to add vertices to the surface data. The first supplementing factor is the distance between contour vertices. When the distance between vertices is over 100 units, AutoCAD Civil 3D adds a vertex to the data along the course of the contour. The second supplementing factor is a mid-ordinate distance for the curve segments of a contour. If curves are distributed throughout the contour data, a setting of 0.1 is a good starting point.

- All weeding and supplementing factors are user-specified.
- Weeding and supplementing does not modify the contours or polylines in a drawing, only their data.
- There is no "correct" setting for weeding and supplementing. Varying the values creates more or less surface data.

Contour Issues

You should be aware of two issues when working with contour data: bays and peninsulas within the contours and the lack of high and low point elevations. These two issues affect triangulation and the quality of a surface.

Bays and peninsulas within contours represent gullies or isolated high points on a surface. As long as there is data to work with, AutoCAD Civil 3D builds a surface by triangulating between contours of different elevations. When AutoCAD Civil 3D cannot triangulate between different contours, the triangulation switches to connecting vertices on the same contour.

The **Minimize Flat Faces** command helps mitigate this situation by forcing the triangulation to target different contours, as shown in Figure 4–18. However, this method, similar to the edge swap method, does not correct every problem on a contour surface.

- To access the **Minimize Flat Faces** command, right-click on the *Edits* heading under the Definition collection of a surface and select the command.

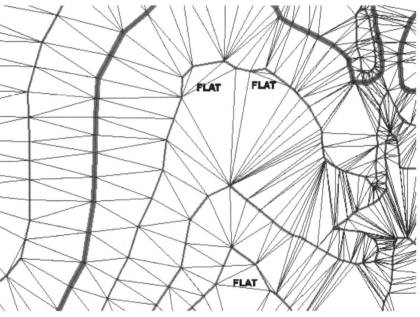

Figure 4–18

The second issue with contour data regards the loss of high and low points. Contours represent an elevation interval (120, 122, 123, etc.). However, the top of a hill could be 123.04 or 136.92 and the only contours present are for the elevations of 123 or 136. Spot elevations are needed in the surface data to help correctly resolve the high and low spots of a surface.

- Flat spots and the loss of high and low points affect the calculation of volumes for earthworks, as shown in Figure 4–19.

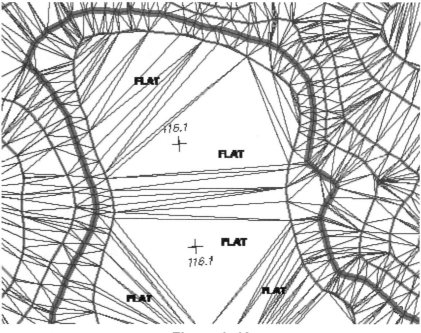

Figure 4–19

Minimizing Flat Triangle Strategies

By default, the Add Contour Data dialog box suggests using the *Minimize flat areas by:* options shown in Figure 4–20.

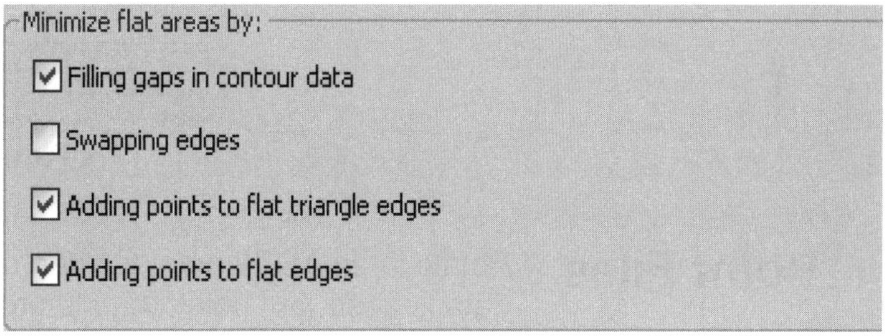

Figure 4–20

Together, these three methods attempt to detect and resolve peninsulas, bays, and other issues by adding additional points and filling in gaps based on surface trends. Generally, these provide the most expected results. The **Swapping edges** option is provided as a way of emulating how other terrain modeling software (such as AutoCAD Land Desktop) traditionally approached minimizing flat areas.

4.4 Other Surface Data

DEM Files

Digital Elevation Models (DEMs) are grid-based terrain models primarily used by GIS applications to represent large areas. Since they are large-scale and grid-based, they are generally only used in AutoCAD Civil 3D for preliminary design and other approximate tasks.

Drawing Objects

AutoCAD points, text, blocks, and other objects can be used as surface data. Individual AutoCAD Civil 3D point objects can also be selected through the **Drawing Objects** option. Selected objects need to have a valid elevation value.

*   All data added as drawing objects is considered point data.
*   You can add 3D lines and polyfaces using this method, but each end point is treated as if it were a point object. Linework is not treated as contours or breaklines. The Add Points From Drawing Objects dialog box is shown in Figure 4–21.

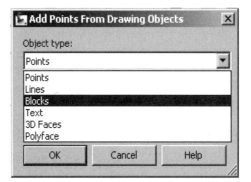

Figure 4–21

Point Files

Points in an ASCII point file can be used as surface data. The point data is used, but point objects are not created.

*   You can use any import/export file format.
*   This is an excellent way to create a large surface from a massive number of points, as it bypasses creating point objects, thereby reducing drawing overhead.

Practice 4b

Creating an Existing Ground Surface Part II

In this practice you will define the surface with surface data.

Task 1: Define surface with contour data.

1. Continue working with the drawing from the previous practice.

2. Isolate the layers **A-TOPO-MAJR** and **A-TOPO-MINR**. Use the
   AutoCAD **Isolate** 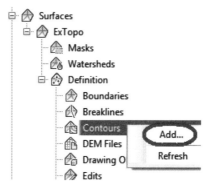 command or type **layiso** at the
   Command Line. Alternatively, you can use a saved layer state. In
   the Layer State Manager, restore the layer state **C3D-Contours
   Topo**.

3. Expand the *Surfaces* collection in the *Prospector* tab.

4. Expand the *ExTopo* surfaces collection and the *Definition*
   collection.

5. Select the **Contours** data element, right-click, and select **Add...**,
   as shown in Figure 4–22.

Figure 4–22

6. In the Add Contour Data dialog box, accept the defaults, as shown in Figure 4–23, and click [OK].

Figure 4–23

7. When prompted to select contours, use the AutoCAD *window* or *crossing* selection method to select all AutoCAD contour objects on the screen, as shown in Figure 4–24. Press <Enter> to end the command.

Figure 4–24

8. AutoCAD Civil 3D has created a surface. However, only the original two isolated contour layers are visible, so we do not see the surface. You need to restore a layer state that will display the required layers. In the *Home* tab > Layer panel, select **C3D-Contours** from the drop-down list shown in Figure 4–25.

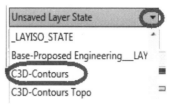

Figure 4–25

9. If you select the green surface boundary or any contour line, the contextual Ribbon tab *Tin Surface: ExTopo* will appear, as shown in Figure 4–26.

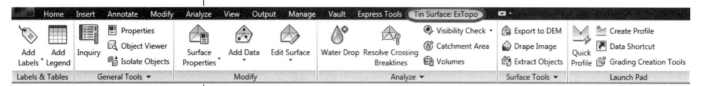

Figure 4–26

10. Save the drawing.

Task 2: Define surface with point data.

In examining the *ExTopo* surface more closely, you notice that although the internal site contours correctly reflect the surveyed point elevations, the original contours appear out of date or have missing information in the area of the existing road, **Mission Avenue**. However, you have a detailed survey of the road. Using this data, you will generate a surface.

1. Continue working with the drawing from the previous task.

2. In the *Prospector* tab, select the **Surfaces** collection, right-click, and select **Create Surface**.

3. In the Create Surface dialog box, select **TIN surface** for the surface type, enter **ExRoad** for the surface name, and enter **Contours 2m and 10m** for the style.

4. Expand the *Surfaces* collection in the *Prospector* tab and expand the *ExRoad* collection.

5. Expand the *Definition* collection, select **Point Groups**, right-click, and select **Add...**, as shown in Figure 4–27.

Figure 4–27

6. In the Point Groups dialog box, select the **ExRoad** points group, as shown in Figure 4–28. Click [OK] to accept the changes and close the dialog box.

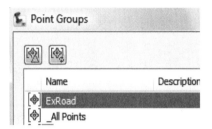

Figure 4–28

7. Save the drawing.

Task 3: Create a surface contour style.

---

1. Continue working with the drawing from the previous task.

2. Since there is very little grade change along the road, the frequency of the contours is small, making the surface difficult to see. Expand the *Surfaces* collection, right-click **ExRoad** and select **Properties**.

3. In the Surface Properties dialog box, click 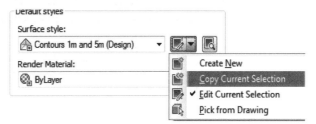 (drop-down arrow) to the right of the *Surface style* field and select **Copy Current Selection** from the drop-down list, as shown in Figure 4–29.

Figure 4–29

4. In the *Information* tab, enter **Contours 0.5m and 2.5m (Design)** for the style name, as shown in Figure 4–30.

Figure 4–30

5. In the *Contours* tab, expand the *Contour Intervals* collection and enter **0.5** for the *Minor Interval* and **2.5** for the *Major Interval*, as shown in Figure 4–31.

Figure 4–31

6. Click <u>OK</u> to accept and close the Edit Style dialog box, and click <u>OK</u> to close the Surface Properties dialog box.

7. Save the drawing.

4.5 Breaklines and Boundaries

A surface can be assigned point data through point groups. In addition, surfaces can include data from boundaries, breaklines, contours, Digital Elevation Model files (DEMs), drawing objects (AutoCAD points, individual AutoCAD Civil 3D points, lines, 3D faces, etc.), manual edits, and point files. The Boundaries collection appears above the Breaklines collection under the surface's *Definition* (*Prospector* tab), as shown in Figure 4–32. However, you should generally add boundaries after adding breaklines to a surface. However, if you use the Data Clip boundary type, any data that you add to the surface (point file, DEM file, or breakline) is added only to the area within the boundary. In that case, breaklines can be added to the surface after a Data Clip boundary type. Surface edit operations are not affected by the Data Clip boundary.

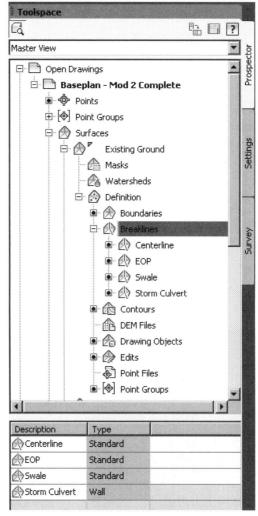

Figure 4–32

Breaklines

Breaklines affect surface triangulation and are important in point-based surfaces. They ensure that terrain models are triangulated correctly along linear features, as shown in Figure 4–33.

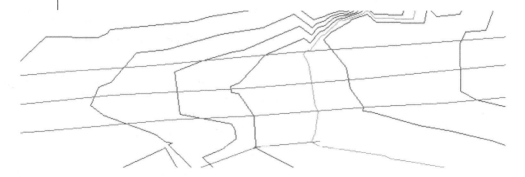

Surface before breaklines have been applied along the center line of a road.

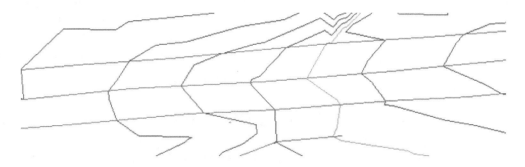

Surface after breaklines have been applied along the center line of a road.

Figure 4–33

- When adding a breakline to a surface, AutoCAD Civil 3D creates an entry under the *Breakline > Definition* collections, based on a description that you supply.
- When you define multiple breaklines at the same time, AutoCAD Civil 3D creates a single entry under the *Breaklines* collection. However, they are listed separately in the *Prospector* tab's List View.
- Breaklines can be defined as one of four types: Standard, Proximity, Wall, and Non-Destructive.

Standard Breaklines

A standard breakline is one that has valid elevations assigned at each vertex.

- Standard breaklines can be defined from 3D lines, 3D polylines, or grading feature lines.

- The number of points generated along a breakline can be reduced by specifying a *Weeding* factor or increased by specifying a *Supplementing* factor, similar to weeding and supplementing factors for contour data.

- Curves in standard breaklines are approximated through the use of a mid-ordinate distance, similar to the way curved boundaries are resolved.

- For AutoCAD Land Desktop users, tasks that you might have applied to 3D polylines in AutoCAD Land Desktop should use grading feature lines in AutoCAD Civil 3D. This is because grading feature lines are more efficient in many ways, including their support of 3D curves.

- When drafting 3D lines, polylines, or feature lines, you can use AutoCAD Civil 3D's transparent commands. For example, using the **Point Object** (**'PO**) transparent command to select a point as a vertex of a 3D polyline will tell AutoCAD Civil 3D to assign the point's elevation to the vertex of the polyline.

- Standard breaklines can also be defined from ASCII breakline data files (.FLT file extension).

Proximity Breaklines

Proximity breaklines do not need to have elevations at their vertices. A polyline at elevation 0 could be used as a proximity breakline. When a proximity breakline is defined, AutoCAD Civil 3D automatically assigns vertex elevations from the nearest TIN data point, such as a nearby point object or contour line vertex.

- AutoCAD Civil 3D can define proximity breaklines from 2D polylines or grading feature Lines.

- AutoCAD Civil 3D does not support curves in proximity breaklines. Arc segments are treated as if they were straight line segments.

- One of the default options in the surface Build section allows the conversion of all proximity (2D) breaklines into standard (3D) breaklines. After conversion, the breakline is listed as a standard breakline and has the same elevations as the point objects that are at each vertex.

Wall Breaklines

- A wall breakline can be used to represent both the top and bottom of a wall, curb, or other sheer face.

- Wall breaklines are defined by 3D lines, 3D polylines, or feature lines. When defining them from linework, the object itself is meant to define either the top or bottom of the wall.

- The other end of the wall (top or bottom) is defined interactively by entering the absolute elevations or height differences from the defining line.
- If a Wall breakline starts as a 2D polyline or feature line, it can contain curve segments.
- The number of points generated along a breakline can be reduced by specifying a *Weeding* factor or increased by specifying a *Supplementing* factor.

Boundaries

Boundaries provide interior or exterior limits to the surface triangulation. Boundaries are typically created from 2D closed polylines. There are four types of boundaries: **Outer**, **Hide**, **Show**, and **Data Clip**. An outer boundary should be one of the last items added to a surface, because adding data outside of an existing boundary extends the surface past it.

- An **Outer** boundary excludes data outside of its edge.
- A **Hide** boundary removes an interior portion of a surface to delineate features (such as water bodies and building footprints).
- A **Show** boundary displays a portion of a surface within a Hide boundary (e.g., to show an island in a pond).
- A **Data Clip** boundary acts as a filter on all data, including points, DEMs, and breaklines added to the surface after the creation of the **Data Clip** boundary.

A boundary can contain arc segments. To better represent surface elevations around an arc, AutoCAD Civil 3D uses a mid-ordinate value to calculate where the triangles interact with the boundary. The mid-ordinate value is the distance between the midpoint of the cord and the arc. The smaller the mid-ordinate value, the closer the surface data is to the original arc. An example is shown in Figure 4–34.

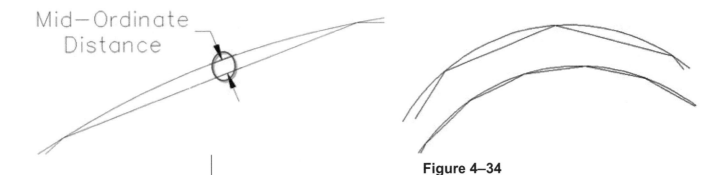

Figure 4–34

A boundary can limit a surface to the data within it. When you want to extend the triangulation exactly to a boundary line, toggle on the **Non-destructive breakline** option in the Create Boundary dialog box. A non-destructive breakline fractures triangles at their intersection with the boundary. The resulting triangles preserve, as close as possible, the original elevations of the surface at the boundary intersection.

Figure 4–35 shows the following:

1. The surface with a polyline will be used as an outer boundary.

2. The boundary is applied without the **Non-destructive breakline** option. This is typically used when the boundary polyline is approximate and not meant to represent a hard edge.

3. The boundary is applied with the **Non-destructive breakline** option. Non-destructive breaklines are often used to create a specific termination limit for the surface (such as at a parcel boundary).

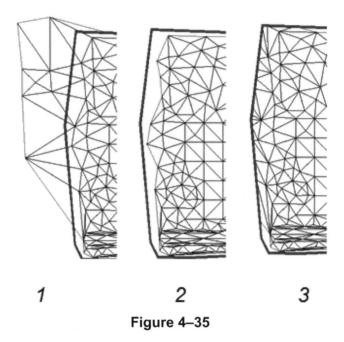

Figure 4–35

4.6 Surface Analysis Tools

**Viewing a
Surface in 3D**

AutoCAD's default view, the overhead or plan view, is not the only way to view a surface. The AutoCAD **3D Orbit** command and the AutoCAD Civil 3D **Object Viewer** tilt the coordinate space to show a 3D surface model. How the surface will be displayed is dependent upon the assigned style.

Quick Profile

Understanding the effects that breaklines and other data have on a surface is critical to generating an accurate surface. The **Analyze > Ground Data > Quick Profile** command enables you to produce an instant surface profile with minimal effort.

A *Quick Profile* is a temporary object and disappears from the drawing when you save or exit. If you are looking for a more permanent graphic, you should create an alignment and profile.

Quick Profiles can be created along lines, arcs, polylines, lot lines, feature lines, survey figures, or by selecting points. In addition to the command being found in the *Analyze* tab, you can select one of the previously mentioned objects, right-click, and select **Quick Profile**. Two examples of the Quick Profile are shown in Figure 4–36.

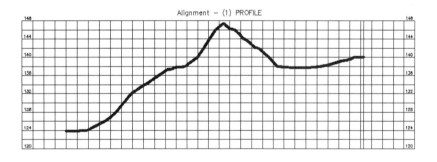

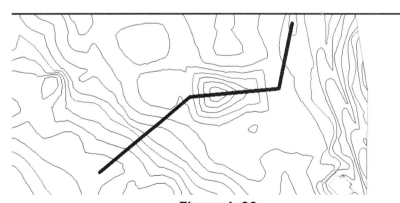

Figure 4–36

Practice 4c | Creating an Existing Ground Surface Part III

Task 1: Add surface breaklines.

TIN lines are generally created by using the shortest distance between points. To further define a surface, you may need to supplement it with breaklines of ridges, ditches, walls, etc. that accurately define the surface. These breaklines prevent the software from triangulating directly between points that are bisected by a breakline. The breakline becomes part of the triangulation between the two adjacent points.

1. Continue working with the drawing from the previous practice.

2. Select any part of the **ExTopo** surface on the screen (Model Space). The contextual Ribbon will display.

3. In the Modify panel, select **Surface Properties**, as shown in Figure 4–37. The Surface Properties dialog box opens.

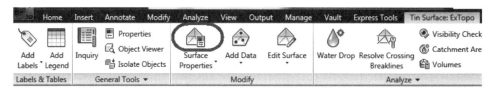

Figure 4–37

4. In the *Surface style* drop-down list, select **Contours and Triangles**, as shown in Figure 4–38. Click [OK] to close the dialog box.

Figure 4–38

Now that you can see the triangulations, you will examine how adding a feature line impacts the surface.

5. In the *View* tab > Views panel, select **C3D-Surface Breakline** in the drop-down list shown in Figure 4–39. This zooms into the breakline that is located north of the existing road.

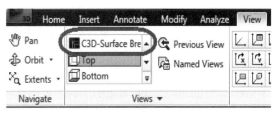

Figure 4–39

6. The triangulation crosses the breakline. Expand the *Current Drawing* collection of the *Prospector* tab, then expand the *Surfaces > ExTopo > Definition* collections. Select **Breaklines**, right-click, and select **Add**, as shown in Figure 4–40.

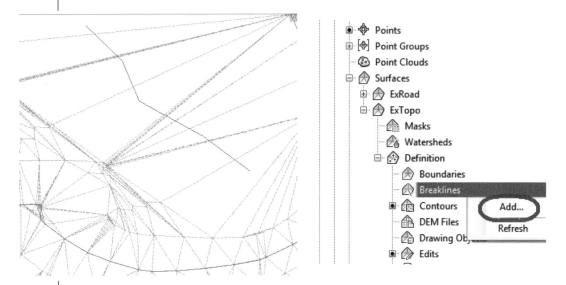

Figure 4–40

7. Enter **Ridge** in the Description field, as shown in Figure 4–41. Accept all the defaults and click OK to close the dialog box.

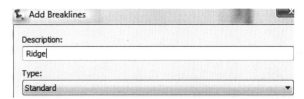

Figure 4–41

8. When prompted to select objects, select the breakline (red 3D polyline) and press <Enter> to complete the command.

9.   In the *Surfaces* collection, notice that the surface *ExTopo* is marked as out-of-date 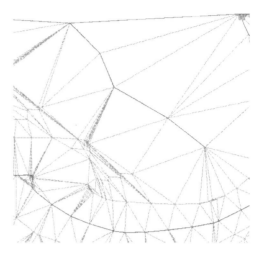 . Select the **ExTopo** surface, right-click, and select **Rebuild Automatic**. Notice that the triangulation now takes the breakline into consideration, as shown in Figure 4–42.

Figure 4–42

10. Save the drawing.

Task 2: Add field book figures as breaklines.

In the task, you will add breaklines to the surface from figures that were created when the field books were imported.

1.   Continue working with the drawing from the previous task.

2.   In the *Survey* tab, expand the *Survey Data* collection and select **Figures**. You will see the list of figures in the grid view at the bottom of the Toolspace.

3. Select the figure **Rock**, right-click, and select **Create breaklines...**, as shown in Figure 4–43.

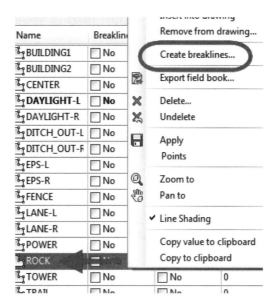

Figure 4–43

4. In the Create Breaklines dialog box, select **ExTopo** for the surface, and toggle on the **Yes** option in the *Breakline* column to create breaklines, as shown in Figure 4–44. Click OK to close the dialog box.

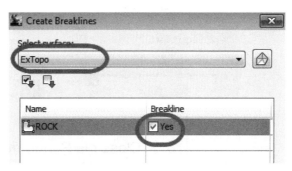

Figure 4–44

5. AutoCAD Civil 3D will zoom in to the location of the breakline, then display the Add Breaklines dialog box. Enter **Rock pile from site survey** in the Description field, and ensure that **Standard** is selected in the *Type* drop-down list, as shown in Figure 4–45. Click OK to close the dialog box.

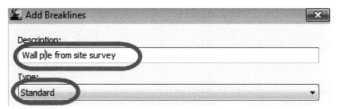

Figure 4–45

6. The Event Viewer vista in the Panorama opens. You have received a number of errors with crossing breaklines. You need to clear these errors from the event log file.

7. Click **Action** in at the top left corner of the Panorama and select **Clear All Events**, as shown in Figure 4–46.

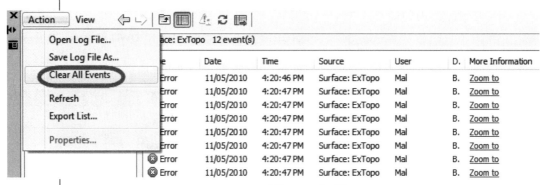

Figure 4–46

8. Close the Panorama.

9. In Model Space, select the **ExTopo** surface. The *Tin Surface: ExTopo* contextual tab displays. In the Modify panel, select **Surface Properties**, as shown in Figure 4–47.

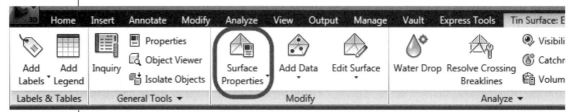

Figure 4–47

10. The Surface Properties - ExTopo dialog box opens. In the *Definition* tab, expand the *Build* collection and set the value of *Allow crossing breaklines* to **Yes**. Set the value for *Elevation to use* field to **Use last breakline elevation at intersection**, as shown in Figure 4–48. When you have finished, click ⬛ OK .

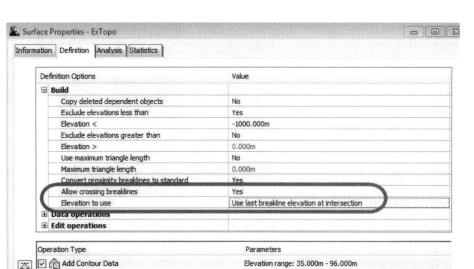

Figure 4–48

11. When prompted to *Rebuild the surface* or *Mark as out of Date*, select **Rebuild the surface**. When you review the surface contours, you will see that the surface has used the figure as a breakline.

12. Save the drawing.

Task 3: Add a Wall Breakline.

In the task, you will add a wall breakline to the surface from figures that were created when the field books were imported

1. Continue working with the drawing from the previous task.

2. In the *Survey* tab, expand the **Survey Data** collection and select **Figures**. You will see the list of figures in the grid view at the bottom of the Toolspace.

3. Select the **Wall** figure, right-click, and select **Create breaklines**.

4. In the Create Breaklines dialog box, select the **ExTopo** surface and toggle on the **Yes** option in the *Breakline* column to create breaklines. Click ⬛ OK to close the dialog box.

5. Civil 3D zooms in to the location of the breakline, then display the Add Breaklines dialog box. Enter **Rock wall from site survey** in the *Description* field, and ensure that **Wall** is selected in the *Type* drop-down list, as shown in Figure 4–49. Click 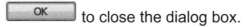 to close the dialog box.

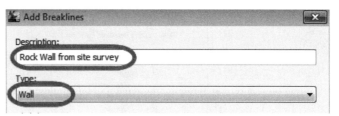

Figure 4–49

6. At the prompt to pick the offset side, select a point to the south of the wall break line, as shown in Figure 4–50.

Figure 4–50

7. When prompted to select the option for the wall height, accept the default of **All** and press <Enter> since the wall has a constant height.

8. The wall has a constant height of 0.5m from the base. When prompted for the elevation difference or elevation, type **0.5** <Enter>.

9. As in the previous task, the Event Viewer gives a warning that you have crossing breaklines. Review these warnings and then close the Event Viewer.

10. Save drawing.

Review Questions

Question 1	What are the main steps to build a surface?
Question 2	How does AutoCAD Civil 3D display surface information?
Question 3	How do you set the lowest and highest acceptable elevations for a surface?
Question 4	What is a Standard breakline and what is it used for?
Question 5	What happens to a Quick Profile when you save or exit a drawing?
Question 6	What does the weeding process remove?

Section 2: Civil 3D Surface Editing

4.7 Surface Editing

There are three ways of adjusting surfaces graphically: using lines, points, and area edit tools, such as **Minimize Flat Areas** and **Smooth Surface**. All of these tools are available by right-clicking on the *Edits* heading under a surface's *Definition* area (*Prospector*), as shown in Figure 4–51.

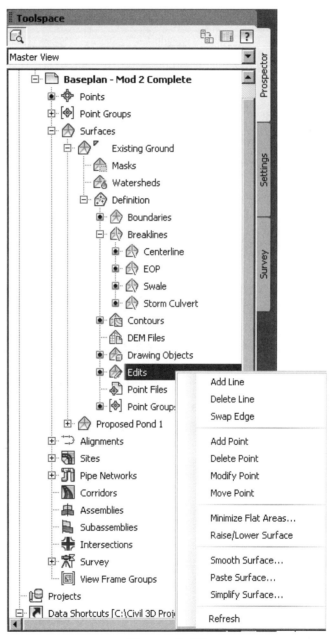

Figure 4–51

*   AutoCAD Civil 3D considers each graphical surface edit to be additional data that can later be removed.

- Most surface edits apply immediately. If you see the drawing item modifier icon (shown in Figure 4–52), then an edit has rendered the surface out of date. When this happens, a surface should be rebuilt by right-clicking on the surface name in the *Prospector* tab and selecting **Rebuild**.

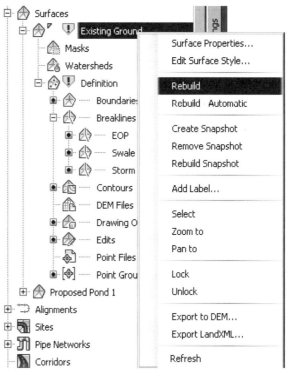

Figure 4–52

- To have a surface automatically rebuild as needed, right-click on the surface name in the *Prospector* tab and select **Rebuild-Automatic**.

- To delete an edit from a surface permanently, remove it from the *Edits* list in *Prospector's* preview area or from the *Operations Type* list in the *Definition* tab of the Surface Properties dialog box.

Line Edits

The line editing commands include **Add Line**, **Delete Line**, and **Swap Edge**. As their names suggest, the **Add Line** and **Delete Line** commands add or remove triangle lines. The **Delete Line** command is often only applied around the outside edge of a surface to remove unwanted edge triangulation. Deleting lines in the interior of a surface causes both of the triangles next to the removed line to be deleted, leaving a hole in the surface that will need to be repaired by adding another line.

If you are considering deleting a line only to replace it with the opposite diagonal, such as the central line shown in Figure 4–53, you may find using the **Swap Line** command easier instead.

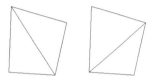

Figure 4–53

Adding an interior line that crosses many existing triangles swaps them where possible to adhere to the geometry represented by the added line. This method can be a good way of swapping multiple edges at once.

Point Edits

The Point editing commands can **Add**, **Delete**, **Modify**, or **Move** surface points. These commands do not affect point objects in the drawing, but rather the surface points created from them. Surface points can be adjusted or deleted as needed. Edits to surface points have no affect on the original AutoCAD Civil 3D point objects on which these surface points are based.

When an AutoCAD Civil 3D point object is adjusted (e.g., moved), the surface containing that point data might not be identified as being out-of-date nor update automatically. In this situation, you should rebuild the surface.

Simplify Surface

As the collection methods of surface data continue to evolve, yielding significantly larger data sets, drawing file size will increase in proportion to the surface data contained in the drawing. AutoCAD Civil 3D has a limit of 2.5 million vertices for a surface. Once it exceeds this limit, the software prompts you to store surface data to an external file with an .mms extension. These resulting external surface files can be quite large. To avoid this, you can simplify your surface using the *Simplify Surface wizard*. Extra points can be removed from a surface without compromising its accuracy. Points you may want to remove include points that are in an external point file or database, or redundant points in areas of high data concentration where the value of this extra information is minimal. There are two simplification methods available.

- *Edge Contraction*: This method simplifies the surface by using existing triangle edges. It contracts triangle edges to single points by removing one point. The location of the point to which an edge is contracted is selected so that the change to the surface is minimal.
- *Point Removal*: This method simplifies the surface by removing existing surface points. More points are removed from denser areas of the surface.

When you simplify a surface, you specify which regions of the surface the operation should address. The region options include using the existing surface border, or specifying a window or polygon. The **Pick in Drawing** icon lets you select the region from the drawing. If a closed line exists in the drawing that you would like to use as the region boundary, you can select the **Select objects** option, then use the **Pick in Drawing** icon to select the boundary. Curves in the boundary are approximated by line segments. The line segment generation is governed by a *Mid Ordinate Distance* value that you determine.

Once you've selected the region, the dialog box displays the *Total Points Selected In Region* value. You can refine the surface reduction options by setting a percentage of points to remove, the maximum change in elevation, or the maximum edge contraction error.

Smooth Contours

Although not a true surface edit, AutoCAD Civil 3D surface contours can be smoothed to reduce their jagged appearance using the Surface Object Style settings. There are two approaches to this: the *Add Vertices* method and the *Spline Curve* method. The *Add Vertices* method enables you to select a relative smoothness from the slider bar at the bottom of the Surface Style dialog box, as shown in Figure 4–54.

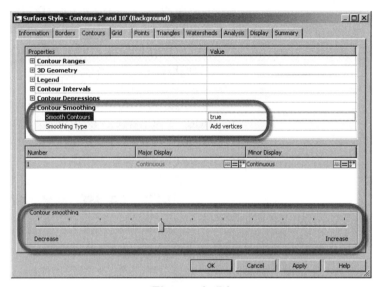

Figure 4–54

The *Spline Curve* method generates very smooth contours; however, the contours are more liberally interpolated and might overlap where surface points are close together. This approach is best applied to surfaces with relatively few data points or in areas of low relief, as shown in Figure 4–55.

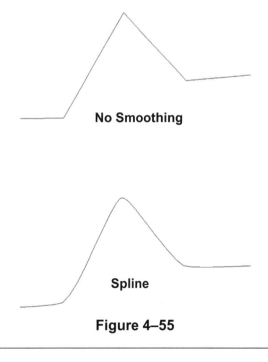

No Smoothing

Spline

Figure 4–55

Smooth Surface

The Smooth Surface edit introduces new, interpolated elevations between surface data. It is used to create a more realistic-looking terrain model, though not necessarily a more accurate one. Generally, surface smoothing works best with point-based surface data.

AutoCAD Civil 3D has two smoothing methods: *Natural Neighbor* and *Kriging*.

*   *Natural Neighbor* interpolates a grid of additional data points that produce a smoother overall terrain model.
*   *Kriging* reads surface trends to add additional data in sparse areas.

Surface smoothing is applied by right-clicking on the *Edits* collection under a surface's *Definition* and selecting **Smooth Surface**. The Smooth Surface dialog box and example of surface smoothing are shown in Figure 4–56.

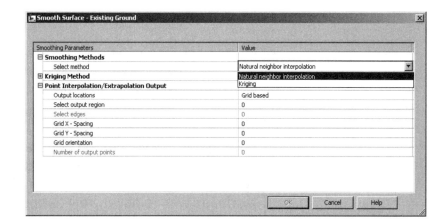

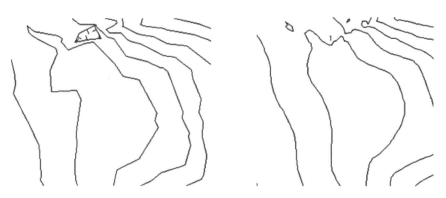

Before Smoothing   After Smoothing

Figure 4–56

Copy Surface

AutoCAD Civil 3D does not have a copy surface command, but surface objects can be copied using the AutoCAD **Copy** command (**Modify > Copy**). When copying surface objects, select the same base and second point to make sure the surface is not moved during the copy. After a copy, a duplicate surface is created and is visible in the *Prospector* tab. The copy has the same name as the original followed with a number in parenthesis, such as (1). These copied surfaces can be renamed as needed. Surface copies are independent of each other and can be edited.

Surface Paste

The **Surface Paste** command enables AutoCAD Civil 3D to combine multiple surfaces into a single surface. You may want to paste into a copy of a surface if you want to keep the original unmodified. For example, a finished condition surface is needed that includes a proposed surface (*Proposed*) along with the existing ground (*EG*) around its periphery. In this situation, you would first make a copy of the EG surface and name this new surface *Finished Ground*. In the *Surfaces* collection of the *Prospector* tab, right-click on the *Finished Ground* surface's *Edit* collection and select **Paste** to merge in the *Proposed* surface. Once the command has executed, the surface's *EG* and *Proposed* surfaces are left unchanged, and the *Finished Ground* surface represents a combination of the two. If you did not create the *Finished Ground* surface, but pasted the *Proposed* surface into the *EG* surface, you would not have the original *EG* surface for reference in profiles and other places.

Surfaces remain dynamically linked after pasting. Therefore, if the *Proposed* surface changes, the *Finished Ground* surface updates to show the change. You can use this feature to create a dynamic copy of a surface by creating a new surface and pasting another into it.

Raise/Lower Surface

The **Raise/Lower Surface** command adds or subtracts a specified elevation value. This adjustment is applied to the entire surface. It is useful for modeling soil removal and changing a surface's datum elevation.

4.8 Adjusting Surfaces through Surface Properties

In addition to the graphical edit methods, you can adjust surfaces by changing their surface properties. Surface property adjustments include setting a *Maximum triangle length* or *Exclude elevations* greater or less than certain values. You can also enable or disable the effects of certain surface data (such as breaklines and boundaries) by disabling them in the dialog box.

To locate these options, as shown in Figure 4–57, right-click on a surface in the *Prospector* tab and select **Surface Properties**.

Definition Options	Value
Build	
Copy deleted dependent objects	No
Exclude elevations less than	No
Elevation <	0.000'
Exclude elevations greater than	No
Elevation >	0.000'
Use maximum triangle length	No
Maximum triangle length	0.000'
Convert proximity breaklines to standard	Yes
Allow crossing breaklines	No
Elevation to use	Use average breakline elevation at intersection
Data operations	
Edit operations	

Figure 4–57

4.9 Viewing Surfaces in 3D

You can view a surface in 3D using the *Object Viewer* or directly in the drawing window using the **3D Orbit** command. Both have similar navigation controls, but the *Object Viewer* enables you to review your surface in 3D without changing your current view.

Both methods can display a wireframe (3D Wireframe and 3D Hidden), conceptual, or realistic view. By default, a *Conceptual* display shows a cartoon-like rendering without edge lines, while a *Realistic* display shows material styles with edge lines. Both viewing methods use the AutoCAD *ViewCube*, which uses labels along with a compass to indicate the direction from which you are viewing a model.

The Object Viewer method is shown in Figure 4–58.

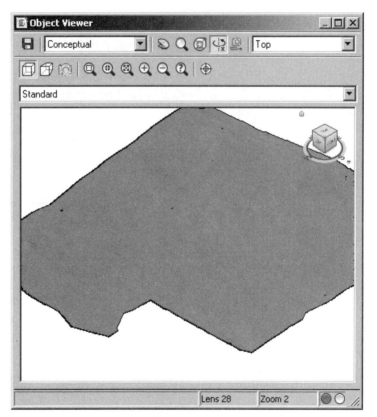

Figure 4–58

Practice 4d | Surface Edits

In this practice you will refine a previously created surface. The **ExTopo** surface has some triangulations that are not valid. You will eliminate these TIN lines using three methods: you will set the maximum triangle edge length, delete TIN lines (triangle edges), and add a boundary to the surface. Each of these methods has its advantages and disadvantages and should be used appropriately.

Task 1: Set the maximum triangle length.

---

1. Continue working with the drawing from the previous practice or open the file **SUF1-Sec2-Surface.dwg** from the following folder:

    C:\Civil 3D Projects\Civil3D-training\Drawings

2. Ensure that the ExTopo surface is using the **Contours and Triangles** surface style.

3. In the *View* tab > Views panel, select the preset view **C3D-Surface Edits**, as shown in Figure 4–59.

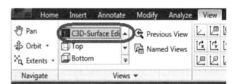

Figure 4–59

4. Notice the long TIN lines, as shown in Figure 4–60.

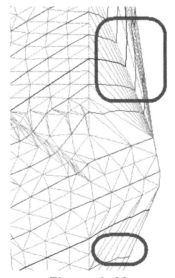

Figure 4–60

5. In the graphics screen (Model Space), select the **ExTopo** surface. The *Tin Surface ExTopo* contextual Ribbon will display. In the *Modify* panel, select **Surface Properties**, as shown in Figure 4–61.

Figure 4–61

6. The Surface Properties dialog box opens. Select the *Definition* tab and expand the *Build* options in the *Definition Options* section.

7. Set the *Use maximum triangle length* value to **Yes** and the *Maximum triangle length* value to **100**, as shown in Figure 4–62. Although there are invalid triangle lengths less than 100 in this area, entering a smaller number may remove some valid

    triangles within the site. Click [OK] to close the dialog box and accept the changes.

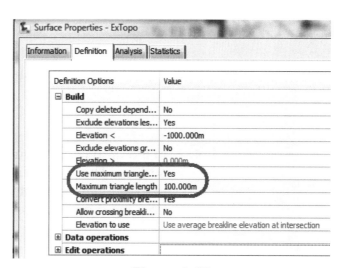

Figure 4–62

8. When prompted to *Rebuild the surface* or *Mark the surface as out-of-date*, select **Rebuild the surface**. All triangles that have edge lengths greater than 100m are removed from the surface.

9. Save the drawing.

Task 2: Delete lines.

Although you have eliminated triangle edge lengths greater than 100m, you still have some triangles that you will remove using a scalpel (i.e., deleting selected lines).

1. Continue working with the drawing from the previous task.

2. If you are not still in the drawing view from the previous task, select the *View* tab > Views panel, select the preset view **C3D-Surface Edits**.

3. Delete the TIN lines shown in Figure 4–63.

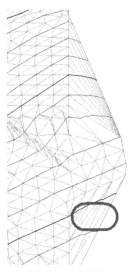

Figure 4–63

4. In the graphics screen (Model Space), select the **ExTopo** surface. The *Tin Surface ExTopo* contextual Ribbon will display. In the *Modify* panel, select **Edit Surface** and select **Delete Line** from the drop-down list, as shown in Figure 4–64.

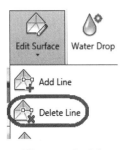

Figure 4–64

5. Select each of the required TIN lines in Model Space, as shown in Figure 4–65. When you have finished, press <Enter> to end the command.

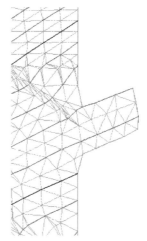

Figure 4–65

6. Save the drawing.

Task 3: Add a boundary.

The **Delete Line** command can be effective, but might not efficiently clean up the edges of large surfaces. A surface boundary may be useful if you have a well-defined boundary. The *Data Clip Boundary* helps ensure that new information you add to the surface does not ignore the surface boundary and model outside of it.

1. Continue working with the drawing from the previous task.

2. If you are not still in the drawing view from the previous task, then in the *View tab* > Views panel, select the preset view **C3D-Surface Edits**.

3. In the graphics screen (Model Space), select the **ExTopo** surface. The *Tin Surface ExTopo* contextual Ribbon will display. In the *Modify* panel, select **Add Data** and select **Boundaries** from the drop-down list, as shown in Figure 4–66.

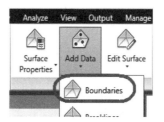

Figure 4–66

4. The Add Boundaries dialog box opens, as shown Figure 4–67. Enter **EG Outside** in the *Name* field, and select **Outer** in the *Type* drop-down list. Do not select the **Non-destructive breakline** option, since you do not want to trim to this polyline shape. Instead, the dialog box options selected will erase all triangle lines that cross or are beyond the boundary. Click

   OK to accept the changes and close the dialog box.

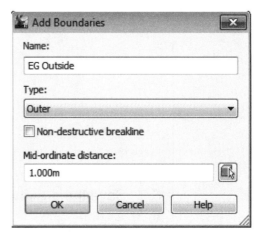

Figure 4–67

5. When prompted to select an object, select the red polyline that represents the boundary (you may have to regen the screen to see the boundary), as shown Figure 4–68.

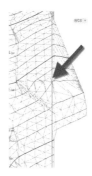

Figure 4–68

6. Examine how this boundary affected the surface. The boundary excluded all data that crossed or fell beyond it. This boundary is a dynamic part of the *ExTopo* surface.

7. (Optional) Select the boundary line and move the grips. Notice how the surface expands or contracts to the match the change in the boundary. Undo the changes.

8. Save the drawing.

Task 4: Set the elevation range.

In reviewing the drawing, you need to address an error within the site. The original topographical contour file contains an invalid piece of data that has transferred to the surface.

1. Continue working with the drawing from the previous task.

2. If you are not still in the drawing view from the previous task, then in the *View* tab >Views panel, select the preset view **C3D-Surface Elev Edit**.

3. In the graphics screen (Model Space), as shown on the left in Figure 4–69, select the **ExTopo** surface, right-click, and select **Object Viewer**.

4. In the *Object Viewer*, click and drag the view, as shown on the right in Figure 4–69, to rotate the 3D view to identify the issue.

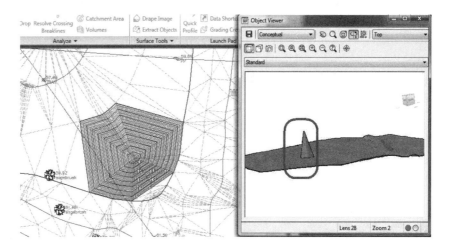

Figure 4–69

5. Close the *Object Viewer* by selecting the **X** in the top right corner of the dialog box.

6. In the graphics screen (Model Space), select the **ExTopo** surface. The *Tin Surface ExTopo* contextual Ribbon will display. In the Modify panel, select **Surface Properties**, as shown Figure 4–70. The Surface Properties dialog box opens.

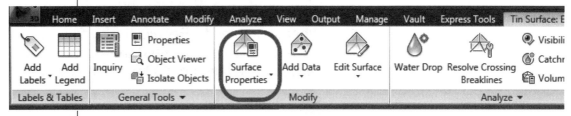

Figure 4–70

7. Select the *Statistics* tab and expand the value list in the *General* section.

8. When you review the site conditions, you see that the site ranges from an elevation of roughly 30m to 100m. However, the statistics show that the surface ranges from an elevation of 35m to 150m, as shown Figure 4–71.

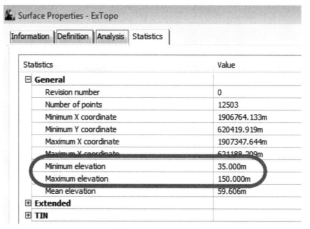

Figure 4–71

9. To correct the surface, select the *Definition* tab. Expand the *Build* properties and set the *Exclude elevation less than* value to **Yes**. Set the *Elevation* < value to **30**, the *Exclude elevation greater than* value to **Yes**, and the *Elevation* > value to **100**, as shown Figure 4–72.

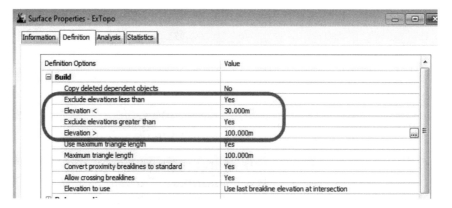

Figure 4–72

10. Click [OK] to accept the changes and close the dialog box.

11. When prompted to *Rebuild the surface* or *Mark the surface as out-of-date*, select **Rebuild the Surface**. All points that are above an elevation of 100m are removed and the error is fixed.

12. Save the drawing.

Task 5: Review edits in the Prospector tab and the Surface Properties dialog box.

The history of all changes made to a surface is saved in the drawing. You can apply and remove these changes selectively to the surface.

1. Continue working with the drawing from the previous task.

2. In the *Prospector* tab, expand the *Surfaces* collection and select the **ExTopo** surface. Right-click and select **Surface Properties**. In the Surface Properties dialog box, the bottom area in the *Definition* tab lists the history of operations applied to the surface. You can clear any operation to review its impact on the surface. You can also change the order in which these operations are applied by highlighting an operation and clicking the arrows to the left, as shown in Figure 4–73. Clear the **Add boundary** *Operation Type* and click ⬛ Apply .

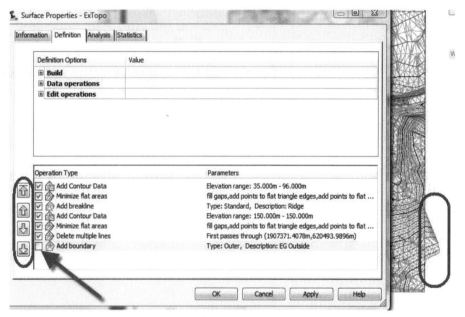

Figure 4–73

3. When prompted, select **Rebuild the Surface** in the Warning dialog box that opens. The boundary is ignored.

4. Select the **Add boundary** *Operation Type* and click ⬛ Apply . When prompted, select **Rebuild the Surface** in the Warning dialog box that opens. The boundary is once again used in the surface definition.

5. Save the drawing.

Task 6: Create a composite surface.

In the preceding tasks, you created a surface from available contour data. However, the data around the existing road, Mission Avenue, was inaccurate, so you surveyed the road and created a surface. You need to create a composite surface that represents the site condition combined with the road.

1. Continue working with the drawing from the previous task.

2. In the *Prospector* tab, right-click on the *Surfaces* collection and select **Create Surface**.

3. Select **TIN surface** for the surface *Type*. Enter **Existing-Site** for the surface name and **composite surface of ExTopo and ExRoad** for the *Description*. Select **Contours 2m and 10m**

    (Background) for the surface *Style*. Then click [OK] to close the dialog box and create a surface.

4. Expand the *Surfaces* collection in the *Prospector* tab and select the **ExRoad** surface. Right-click and select **Surface Properties**.

    Set the surface style to **_No Display**, then click [OK] to accept the changes and close the dialog box.

5. Expand the *Surfaces* collection in the *Prospector* tab and select the **ExTopo** surface. Right-click and select **Surface Properties**.

    Set the surface style to **_No Display**, then click [OK] to accept the changes and close the dialog box.

6. In the *Prospector* tab, expand the *Surfaces > Existing-Site > Definition* collections for that surface and select **Edits**. Right-click and select **Paste Surface...**, as shown in Figure 4–74.

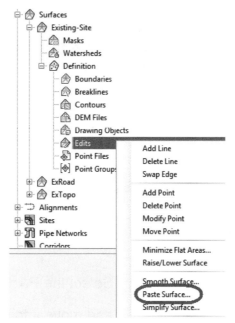

Figure 4–74

7. In the Select Surface to Paste dialog box, select the **ExTopo** and **ExRoad** surfaces, as shown in Figure 4–75. To select both surfaces, hold down the <Ctrl> key when selecting the second surface. Once selected, click ⌷ OK ⌷ to close the dialog box.

Figure 4–75

8. On closer examination, notice that the *ExRoad* surface was pasted first, followed by the *ExTopo* surface. In the area of overlap along the road, the *ExTopo* surface data will take precedence. This is not the desired result.

9. In Model Space, select the **Existing-Site** surface from the surfaces listed in the *Surfaces* collection of the *Prospector* tab. The contextual Ribbon for the surface object will display. Select **Surface Properties** in the Ribbon panel. The Surface Properties - Existing Site dialog box opens. In the *Definition* tab, notice the order of the paste operations, as shown in Figure 4–76.

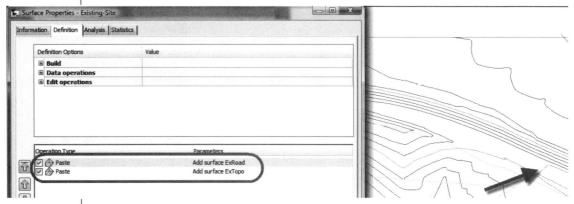

Figure 4–76

10. Select the Paste operation with the value **Add surface ExTopo** and move it to the top of the list by clicking ⬆, as shown in Figure 4–77.

Figure 4–77

11. Click **Apply**. When prompted to *Rebuild the surface* or *Mark the surface as out-of-date*, select **Rebuild the Surface**.

12. Click **OK** to exit the dialog box.

13. As a consequence of AutoCAD Civil 3D's dynamic abilities, any changes to either the *ExTopo* or *ExRoad* surface will be reflected in the *Existing-Site* surface.

14. Save the drawing.

Review Questions

Question 1 | What does the size of triangles indicate about the data?

Question 2 | How do you delete an edit from a surface permanently?

Question 3 | What does the **Raise/Lower Surface** command do?

Question 4 | Why would you use a *Data Clip* boundary type over an *Outer* boundary type?

Section 3: Civil 3D Surface Labels and Analysis

4.10 Surface Labels

Surface labels can be used to label contour elevations, slope values, spot elevations, and watershed delineations. Label values update if the surface changes.

To create surface labels, in the *Annotate* tab > Labels & Tables panel, select **Add Labels > Surface** to access the surface label flyout menu, as shown in Figure 4–78.

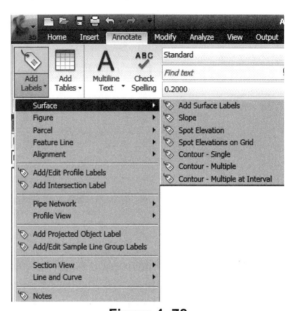

Figure 4–78

You can also select **Add Labels > Notes**, as shown on the left in Figure 4–79, to open the *Add Labels* dialog box. This dialog box enables you to select the feature and label type while being able to control the label style on the fly, as shown on the right.

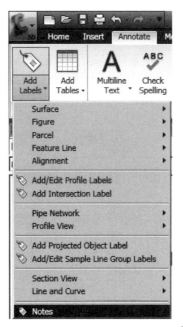 

Figure 4–79

Contour Labels

Contour labels can be created individually, as multiples along a linear path, or as multiples along a linear path with repeated labels at a set interval. Multiple contours are aligned along an object called a *Contour Label Line*, which can be repositioned as needed, and in turn updates the position of its labels. These label lines have a selectable property that can make them visible only when an attached label is selected. If they are left visible, they should be placed on a non-plotting layer.

Spot and Slope Labels

Spot elevation and slope labels can be created as needed to annotate a surface. These are dynamic surface labels and not point objects, although they may look similar to points. Slopes can be measured at a single point or be averaged between two points.

4.11 Surface Volume Calculations

You can generate volume calculations in AutoCAD Civil 3D in many ways. Surface-to-surface calculations are often used to compare an existing ground surface to a proposed surface to determine cut and fill quantities. In AutoCAD Civil 3D, quantities can be adjusted by an expansion (cut) or a compaction (fill) factor. Surfaces representing different soil strata can be compared to each other to determine the volume between the soil layers. There are multiple ways of comparing surfaces to each other in AutoCAD Civil 3D, described below.

Composite Volumes vista

In the *Analyze* tab > Volumes and Materials panel, select **Volumes > Volumes**, as shown in Figure 4–80.

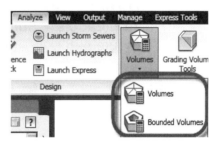

Figure 4–80

The composite method calculates volumes based on a graphical subtraction of one surface from the other, as shown in Figure 4–81.

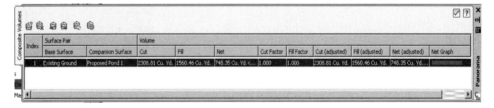

Figure 4–81

The *Net Graph* color displays in red if the surface difference results in a net cut, and green if it is a net fill. You can have multiple volume entries listed if you are comparing multiple surfaces. If any surfaces change, return to this vista and click ![icon] (Recompute Volumes) to update the calculations. Alternatively, you can add another volume entry. Select the same two surfaces and compare before and after volume calculations..

Bounded Volumes

In the *Analyze* tab > Volumes and Materials panel, select **Volumes > Bounded Volumes**. This method is similar to the composite method, but can be limited to the area defined by a defined polyline, polygon, or parcel.

Grid Volume or TIN Volume Surface

This method enables you to assign the surfaces you want to compare as object properties of a volume surface. The volume between the surfaces is calculated and included in the volume surface object properties. The TIN surface calculation is the same one conducted in the Composite Volumes vista. The Grid surface calculation is based on a grid of points interpolated from both surfaces, rather than all of the surface points of both. Grid surfaces tend to be less accurate, but faster to calculate and easier to prove by manual methods.

Grid of spot elevation labels that list the elevation differences between two surfaces can be generated from either a Grid Volume surface or TIN Volume surface. Once the volume surface is created, you can create the labels. In the *Annotate* tab > Labels & Tables panel, select **Add Labels > Surface > Spot Elevations on Grid**, as shown in Figure 4–82.

Figure 4–82

4.12 Surface Analysis Display

AutoCAD Civil 3D can calculate and display many different surface analyses, including:

- *Contours*: This analysis can display contours differently based on their elevation ranges.
- *Directions*: This analysis can render surface triangles differently depending on which direction they face.
- *Elevations*: This analysis can render surface triangles differently depending on their elevation ranges.
- *Slopes*: This analysis can render surface triangles differently depending on their slope ranges.
- *Slope Arrows*: This analysis creates a dynamic slope arrow that points downslope for each triangle, colorized by slope range.
- *User-Defined Contours*: This analysis can display user-defined contours differently based on their elevation ranges.
- *Watersheds*: This analysis can calculate watershed areas, and render them according to area type. AutoCAD Civil 3D's watershed analysis usually results in a very large number of individual watersheds. Although a **Catchment Areas** command is available to assist in drawing the catchment areas, it is still up to the engineers to draw their own conclusions on how these should be merged together into catchment areas.

The above analyses are calculated on demand for each surface and their results are stored under the surface's Surface Properties.

In addition, the following separate utilities may be helpful when analyzing surfaces:

- **Check for Contour Problems** is used to locate problems with the contour data, including crossing or overlapping contours. To access this command, in the *Surface* tab > expanded Analyze panel, select **Check for Contour Problems**, as shown in Figure 4–83.

Figure 4–83

- **Water Drop** draws a 2D or 3D polyline indicating the expected flow path of water across the surface from a given starting point. To access this command, in the *Surface* tab > Analyze panel, select **Water Drop**, as shown in Figure 4–84.

Figure 4–84

- **Catchment Area** draws a 2D or 3D polyline indicating the catchment boundary and catchment point marker for a surface drainage area. To access this command, in the *Surface* tab > Analyze panel, select **Catchment Area**, as shown in Figure 4–85. You should use this command in conjunction with the **Water Drop** command to determine an accurate placement of catchment regions and points.

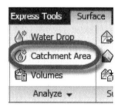

Figure 4–85

Analysis Settings

You apply a surface analysis through the *Analysis* tab in the Surface Properties dialog box. In this tab, you can select the number of ranges and a legend table to be used. All of the remaining analysis settings are located in the *Surface Object* style, including whether to display in 2D or 3D, the color scheme, elevations, range groupings, etc. If you want to change the number of ranges or the range values, use the settings in this tab at any time.

Analysis Data Display

Overall visibility, layer, linetype, and related controls for analysis elements are managed through the *Display* tab in the Object Style dialog box, as shown in Figure 4–86. You can see component entries for *Slopes, Slope Arrows, Watersheds*, and so on. These can be set to display different settings and combinations of elements in 2D and 3D.

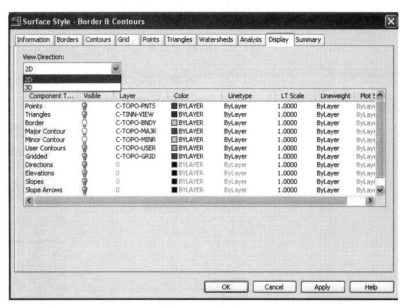

Figure 4–86

Practice 4e | Surface Labeling and Analysis

Task 1: Add surface labels.

1. Continue working with the drawing from the previous practice or open the file **SUF1-Sec3-Surface.dwg** from the following folder:

    C:\Civil 3D Projects\Civil3D-training\Drawings

2. In the *View* tab > Views panel, select the preset view **C3D-Surface Label**.

3. Select the **Existing-Site** surface in the graphics screen (Model Space). The contextual Ribbon for the surface object will display. In the Labels & Tables panel, select **Add Labels** and select the **Contour - Multiple** from the drop-down list, as shown in Figure 4–87.

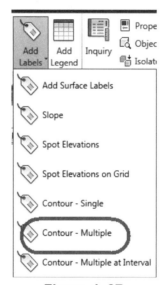

Figure 4–87

4. When prompted to select the first point and second point, specify any two points. When prompted for the next point, select a third point that creates a line intersecting all of the contours you want to label, as shown in Figure 4–88. Press <Enter> when done.

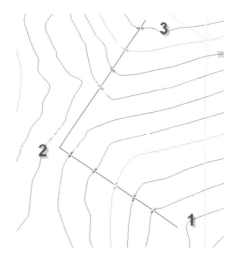

Figure 4–88

5. Move and reorient the contour label line. The labels update.

6. The *Display Contour Label Line* property can be set to be visible only when contour labels are selected. To change the visibility property, select the line in Model Space and select **Properties** in the contextual Ribbon. Then, in the Properties dialog box, set the *Display Contour Label Line* property to **False as** shown in Figure 4–89.

Figure 4–89

7. Close the Properties dialog box and press <Esc> to cancel your selection. Once the grips disappear, the line is no longer visible. Select a contour label to have the contour label line temporarily reappear for editing.

8. To have all future contour label lines behave this way in this drawing, select the *Settings* tab in the Toolspace. Select **Surface**, right-click, and select **Edit Feature Settings...**,as shown in Figure 4–90, to edit the surface.

Figure 4–90

9. In the Edit Feature Settings dialog box, expand *Contour Labeling Defaults* and set the *Display Contour Label Line* property to

False, as shown in Figure 4–91. Click [OK] to accept the changes and close the dialog box.

Figure 4–91

10. Select the **Existing-Site** surface again in the graphics screen (Model Space). The contextual Ribbon for the surface object will display. In the Labels & Tables panel, select **Add Labels** and select **Contour - Multiple** in the drop-down list.

11. Select two points that will draw a line across some contours and press <Enter> when done. The contour label line now does not display.

12. Select the **Existing-Site** surface in the graphics screen (Model Space). The contextual Ribbon for the surface object will display. In the Labels & Tables panel, select **Add Labels** and select **Slope** in the drop-down list.

13. To accept the prompt for the default One-point label, press <Enter>, then select a point in Model Space within the surface boundary. AutoCAD Civil 3D will place the slope value at that point. When you finish placing the labels, press <Enter> to exit the command.

14. (Optional) Using the same process as in steps 10 and 11 above, experiment with labeling the surface with spot elevations and two point slopes. Note that you will be able to copy a label and place it at a different location. As the labels are dynamic, the values will change to reflect the surface information at the location of the label.

Task 2: Perform a slope analysis.

1. Continue working with the drawing from the previous task.

2. In the *View* tab > Views panel, select the preset view **C3D-Surface**.

3. Select the **Existing-Site** surface in the graphics screen (Model Space). The contextual Ribbon for the surface object will display. In the Modify panel, select **Surface Properties**.

4. In the *Information* tab in the Surface Properties dialog box, select **Slope Banding (2D)** as the surface style.

5. In the *Analysis* tab, select **Slopes** for the *Analysis type* and select **5** for the number of ranges to use. Then click 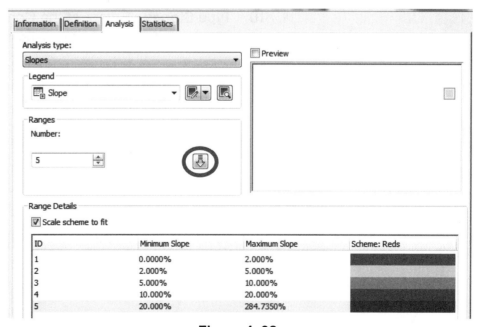 (Run Analysis). AutoCAD Civil 3D calculates a range of values to fit within the specified number of ranges. Change the range values for Range1 to 0-2%, Range2 to 2-5%, Range3 to 5-10% Range4 to 10-20%, and Range5 to 20-70000%, as shown in Figure 4–92.

Figure 4–92

6. Change the range of colors for the slope range. To change the color, click on the color and in the Select Color dialog box, as shown in Figure 4–93, select the desired color. Assign color **51** for the the *slope range 1* and color **1** for *slope range 5*.

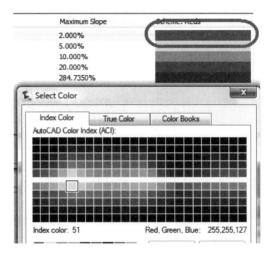

Figure 4–93

7. Click [OK] to close the dialog box and apply the changes.

8. Review the area you want to develop. The slope ranges will be an issue.

9. You need to create a slope values table. Select the **Existing-Site** surface in the graphics screen (Model Space). The contextual Ribbon for the surface object will display. In the Labels & Tables panel, select **Add Legend**.

10. Type **Slopes** <Enter> at the Command Line. Accept the default for a dynamic table by pressing <Enter>.

11. When prompted for the top corner of the table (top left), select a location in an open area to the right of the surface, as shown in Figure 4–94.

Slopes Table				
Number	Minimum Slope	Maximum Slope	Area	Color
1	0.00%	2.00%	44592.80	
2	2.00%	5.00%	88686.61	
3	5.00%	10.00%	138515.84	
4	10.00%	20.00%	165142.36	
5	20.00%	284.74%	33325.20	

Figure 4–94

12. Because this table is dynamic, any changes made to the surface or to the ranges in the analysis will update the table automatically.

13. (Optional) Open the Surface Properties dialog box (steps 3-7) and change the number of slope ranges or the values. The Model Space Legend table will be updated.

14. Save the drawing.

Review Questions

Question 1 What do surface labels do?

Question 2 Which is more accurate, a composite or grid volume calculation?

Question 3 After a surface analysis has been completed, how do you change the number of ranges or range limits?

Question 4 What determines how a style enables an object to be displayed when viewed from above or from another vantage point?

Module 5

Alignments Level 1

This module introduces:

Section 1: Civil 3D Alignments

✓ **Roadway Design Overview**

✓ **AutoCAD Civil 3D Sites**

✓ **Alignments**

✓ **Alignment Properties**

✓ **Labels and Tables**

Section 1: Civil 3D Alignments

5.1 Roadway Design Overview

Alignments and Profiles are used in nearly every civil engineering project to help lay out roads, railways, runways, and walking and bike trails—any kind of linear design feature. In these types of applications, alignments are used to represent center lines, lane boundaries, shoulders, right-of-ways, construction baselines, and similar features. In addition, many other kinds of projects can benefit from alignments, such as swales, waterways, utilities, and even some types of earthwork (such as levee, dam, and landfill designs). In this Student Guide, alignments, profiles, and corridors are referred to as the *road design system* for convenience.

Roads are typically designed through multiple 2D views: plan (top view), profile (side view), and cross-section (left to right view). The result of this approach is a set of documents showing the alignment as a plan, a profile as part of a profile view, and a series of cross-sections. AutoCAD Civil 3D uses these views, resulting in a 3D roadway model called a corridor. An example is shown in Figure 5–1.

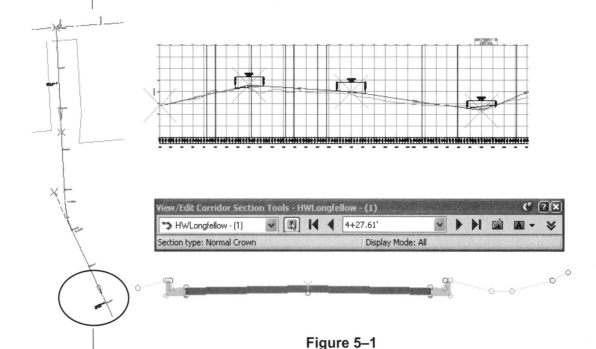

Figure 5–1

5.2 AutoCAD Civil 3D Sites

Alignments, profiles, cross-sections, feature lines, grading groups, and parcels can be organized into containers referred to as *sites* in AutoCAD Civil 3D. A site serves as a logical grouping of design data, such as:

- A particular phase of a project.
- A named geographic area within a larger project.
- A design alternative.

Sites are managed through a collection in the *Prospector* tab. A drawing can have any number of sites, as shown in Figure 5–2, or none at all.

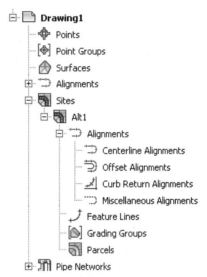

Figure 5–2

Profiles and cross-section data are displayed in the *Prospector* tree below the alignment on which they are based. Corridors are stored in their own collection in the *Prospector*, separate from the site's collection.

Parcel lines only interact with other parcels and alignments in the same site, enabling multiple parcel and road alternatives to be present in the same drawing at the same time.

Alignments and their profiles and cross-sections might exist in a drawing without being part of a particular site. Those that are not can be found in the separate Alignment collection below Surfaces in the *Prospector* tree. This enables alignments to exist in the drawing and not interact with any parcels, or to create a parcel if the alignment closes on itself (e.g., the bulb of a cul-de-sac).

5.3 Alignments

An AutoCAD Civil 3D alignment is a custom object that resembles an AutoCAD polyline. Alignments have rule-based constraints that make them very powerful design tools. Alignments can contain tangents (line segments), circular curves, and spirals.

The appearance and annotation of alignments are controlled by object and label styles. These styles are flexible, and have an extensive list of label properties and control layer assignments for objects and their labels.

AutoCAD Civil 3D alignments can be created in the following ways:

- If previously defined, alignments can be imported from Autodesk LandXML or directly from an AutoCAD Land Desktop project.
- A polyline can be converted directly to an alignment. Converted polylines follow the direction of the original polyline object. Use the **Alignments > Reverse Alignment Direction** option to change the direction of an alignment, if necessary.
- An alignment can be created interactively using the Alignment Layout toolbar (similar to creating a polyline).
- Individual AutoCAD lines and arcs can be converted to alignments through the Layout toolbar as well.

When creating new alignments, remember that you can use transparent commands to draw line segments by Angle and Distance, Bearing and Distance, Azimuth and Distance, and Deflection distance. These commands are available in the Transparent Commands toolbar, as shown in Figure 5–3.

Figure 5–3

Criteria-Based Design

Default or custom standards can be used in AutoCAD Civil 3D to evaluate alignment and profile designs. The Design Criteria Editor enables you to view, edit, or create criteria files (such as AASHTO tables). When you create a new alignment, the Create Alignment dialog box appears, as shown in Figure 5–4. You can tell the software what type of alignment you are creating to make intersection design easier later. The dialog box includes a *Design Criteria* tab that enables you to type the starting design speed, use criteria-based design, use a design criteria file, or use a design check set.

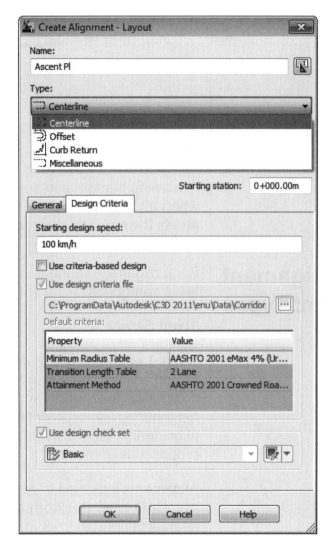

Figure 5–4

When an entity does not meet the criteria in the file, it is displayed with a warning marker. Hover over the marker to see which criteria the entity violates, as shown in Figure 5–5.

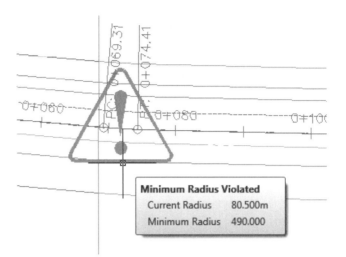

Figure 5–5

A warning marker also appears in the sub-entity and grid view editors when a violation occurs. This marker disappears when the value meets the required criteria.

Alignment Segment Types

Each alignment tangent, circular curve, and spiral falls into one of three categories:

Fixed Segment

A **fixed segment** is one defined by certain criteria that have only a limited ability to be dynamically updated. Fixed curves hold their initial constraints (like length and radius) and might not remain tangent if a neighboring line segment is adjusted. You should avoid fixed curves in alignments that you might want to dynamically update (such as proposed alignments).

Alignments imported from Autodesk LandXML (and directly from AutoCAD Land Desktop) contain all fixed segments. Alignment segments created from individual lines and arcs are also created as fixed segments. These fixed curves can be deleted and replaced with other types as needed.

Floating Element

A **floating element** is one that depends entirely on the object before it in the alignment. If a preceding object is moved, stretched, or otherwise adjusted, a floating element (and everything following it) translates accordingly while holding all of the initial constraints (length, radius, pass-through-points, etc.).

For example, the alignment shown in Figure 5–6 begins with a fixed line followed by a series of floating curves and a floating line that together define a cul-de-sac. Changing the end point of the fixed line causes all of the floating elements to translate while maintaining the original length of the floating line, as well as the original length, radius, and direction of the following curves.

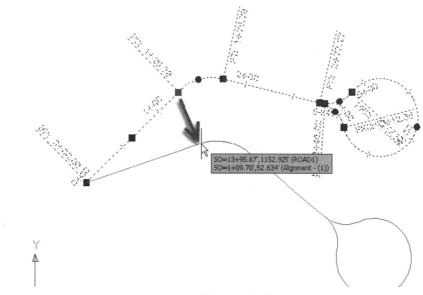

Figure 5–6

Free Segment

A **free segment** is one that is adjusted if the geometry of either neighboring segment is changed. Free segments always adjust to remain tangent to adjacent segments. For example, the free line shown in Figure 5–7 was drawn connected to two fixed arcs. If either of the arcs were assigned a different property (such as a new radius), the line would be completely redrawn to remain tangent to both.

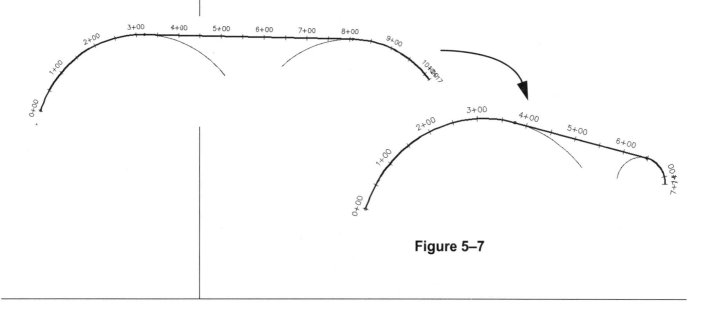

Figure 5–7

Alignments created by layout and polyline are made of fixed lines and free curves and spirals. These tend to be the most flexible types of alignments.

Because of their flexibility and ability to remain tangent through changes, free and floating elements are more useful in alignments that are subject to change, such as those for proposed roadway center lines.

Alignment Layout Tools

Alignments are created and edited through the Alignment Layout toolbar, which can be opened from the *Home* tab > Create Design panel. Select **Alignment > Alignment Creation Tools**, as shown in Figure 5–8.

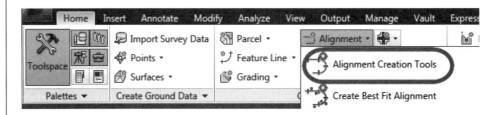

Figure 5–8

To create or add to an alignment interactively by locating new Points of Intersection (PIs), select one of the first two options in the Draw Tangents drop-down list, as shown in Figure 5–9.

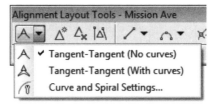

Figure 5–9

These two methods (with or without curves) are similar to drawing an AutoCAD polyline. If the **With Curves** option is selected, default curve information can be assigned in the Curve and Spiral Settings dialog box, as shown in Figure 5–10.

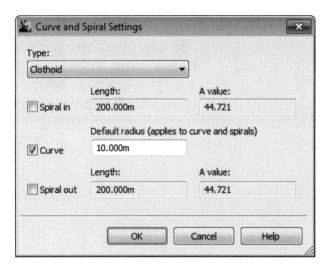

Figure 5–10

The Layout toolbar also includes tools that enable you to:

	Create new Points of Intersection (PIs).
	Delete PIs (and associated curves).
	Break apart PI.
	Convert AutoCAD lines and arcs to alignment segments.
	Delete a line, circular curve, or spiral segment.
	Edit best-fit data for all entities.
	Select an individual segment for editing in the Sub-Entity Editor.
	Review and adjust alignment properties (length, radius, etc.) in the Alignment Entities Vista.
	Undo a recent alignment edit.
	Redo a recent alignment edit.

Most of the other tools in the Layout toolbar are intended for creating segments with various constraints.

Alignment Editing

In addition to the Edit tools available in the Alignment Layout toolbar, alignments can be edited through the AutoCAD Modify commands, such as **Move** and **Stretch**. Alignment entities can also be grip-edited into new positions. You can delete an alignment with the AutoCAD **Erase** command, or by right-clicking on the name of the alignment in the *Prospector* tab and selecting **Delete**. To open the Alignment Layout toolbar, select **Alignments > Edit Alignment Geometry**.

Practice 5a | Creating and Modifying Alignments

In this practice you will create horizontal alignments using three methods. First, you create an alignment from an existing polyline that defines a road center line alignment. Second, you create an alignment from a xref file that defines a proposed center line alignment. Third, you create a free form alignment, based on some design parameters.

Task 1: Create Alignment from a Polyline.

1. Open the file **ALN1-Sec1-Alignment.dwg** from the following folder:

   C:\Civil 3D Projects\Civil3D-training\Drawings

   In the drawing, the red polyline running east-west represents the existing center line alignment of Mission Avenue, as shown in Figure 5–11.

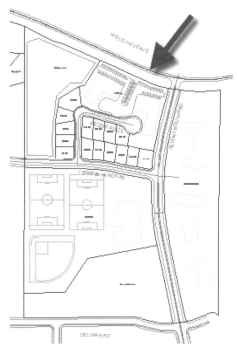

Figure 5–11

2. In the *Home* tab > Create Design panel, select **Alignment > Create Alignment from Objects**, as shown in Figure 5–12, and select the **Mission Ave polyline** (shown above). Be sure to select the west end of the polyline and press <Enter>. Selecting the west end of the polyline identifies the start direction of the alignment.

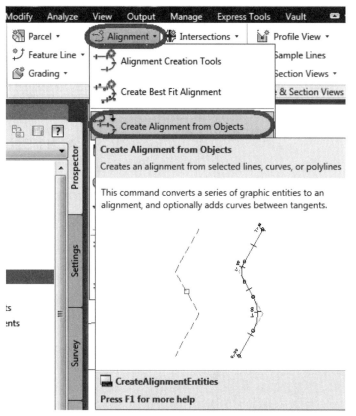

Figure 5–12

3. Confirm the alignment direction arrow is pointing East and press <Enter> to accept the alignment direction. At this point, if you wanted to reverse the direction of the alignment, you would have to type **R**. However, you can still reverse the direction of the alignment at a later time.

4.   In the Create Alignment from Objects dialog box, assign the
     values shown in Figure 5–13 to define the properties of this
     alignment:

   •   Alignment name: **Mission Ave**

   •   Type: Leave as **Centerline**

   •   Description: Enter a description if desired

   •   Starting station: **0**

   •   Site (*General* tab): **None**

   Note: The difference between having an alignment within a site
   or not, is that if an alignment is in a site, any parcels in that same
   site will be divided by the alignment that bisects the parcel.

   Accept the remaining default values.

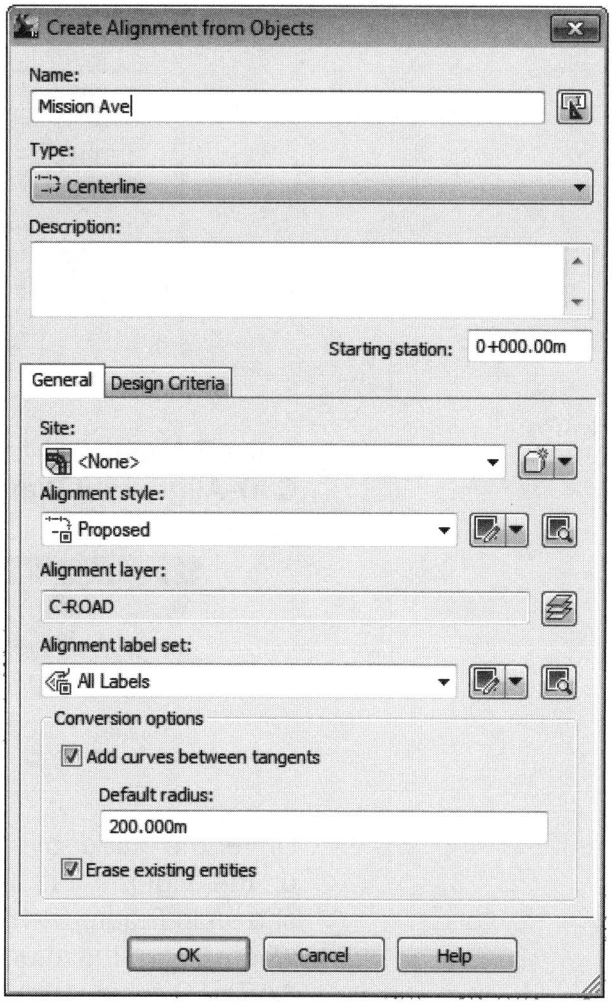

Figure 5–13

5. Select the *Design Criteria* tab. Ensure that the design speed is set to **100Km/h**, and that both the **Use criteria-based design** and **Use design criteria file** options are selected. This means that AutoCAD Civil 3D will reference the design criteria file **_Autodesk Civil 3D Metric Roadway Design Standards.xml**.

6. Enter the remaining values shown Figure 5–14, and click

   [OK]. An AutoCAD Civil 3D alignment is automatically created complete with labeling.

Figure 5–14

7. In the Ribbon *View* tab > Views panel, select the preset view **C3D-Alignment Warning**, as shown in Figure 5–15.

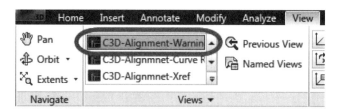

Figure 5–15

8. Hover the cursor over the exclamation mark at the station 0+580 on the alignment to see which design check was violated, as shown in Figure 5–16. In this case, notice that the radius is 315, whereas the minimum radius for a 100km/hr road based on the AASHTO table must be greater than 490. In the following task, you will fix the design.

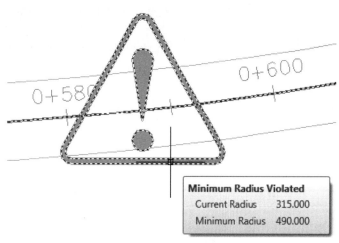

Figure 5–16

Task 2: Create an Alignment by Object (Xref).

---

1. In the *View* ta b> Views panel, double-click on the preset view **C3D-Alignment Xref**.

2. In the *Home* tab > Create Design panel, select **Alignment > Create Alignment from Objects**. When prompted to select an object, enter **Xref** <Enter>. You will then be prompted to select a Xref object. Select the **Jeffries Ranch Rd** center line, as shown in Figure 5–17. Be sure to select the west end of the polyline and press **<Enter>.** Selecting the west end of the xref line identifies the start direction of the alignment.

Figure 5–17

3. In the Create Alignment from Objects dialog box, enter **Jeffries Ranch Rd** for the alignment name and accept all the default values. For this alignment, you will not be using design criteria. In the *Design Criteria* tab, ensure that the **Use criteria-based design** option is not selected, as shown in Figure 5–18.

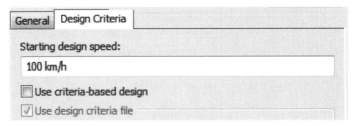

Figure 5–18

4. Click [OK] to close the dialog box and create the alignment.

Task 3: Create an Alignment by Layout.

---

1. In the *View* tab > Views panel, double-click on the preset view **C3D-Alignment-Create**.

2. You will create an alignment for Ascent Place based on existing design data, as shown in Figure 5–19. According to this data, the street right-of-way extends north at an azimuth of 1d18'04.79" and then east at an azimuth of 104d41'28.44", and that the north center line leg is 107.65m and the east leg is 116.41m. In addition, the center line of Ascent Place intersects Jeffries Ranch road at sta 0+176.52.

Figure 5–19

3. Before proceeding, you need to turn off the xref center line layer. The reason for this is that you will be prompted to select the alignment in a later step. Since the alignment object and the xref center line occupy the same location in space, you cannot select the alignment object. Pressing <shift> + <space> to cycle through overlaid objects does not work while within a transparent command. In the Ribbon *Home* tab > Layer panel, start the **Freeze object layer** command and select the center line, as shown in Figure 5–20.

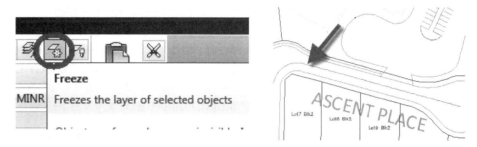

Figure 5–20

4. In the *Home* tab > Create Design panel, select **Alignment > Creation Tools**.

5. In the Create Alignment Layout dialog box, enter **Ascent PI** for the alignment name and accept all the default values. For this alignment, you will not be using design criteria. In the *Design Criteria* tab, ensure that the **Use criteria-based design** option is not selected. Click ⬜ OK ⬜ to close the dialog box and create the alignment.

6. A number of tools are available to help create and edit a horizontal geometry alignment. Click the first tool icon and select **Curve and Spiral Settings**, as shown in Figure 5–21.

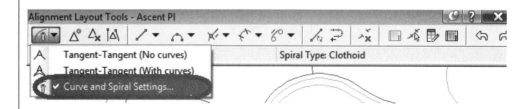

Figure 5–21

7. For the curve settings, clear the **spiral** option and select the **curve** option. Set the curve radius to **10.00**, and click ⬜ OK ⬜ to close the Curve and Spiral Settings dialog box.

8. Click the first tool icon and select the **Tangent-Tangent (With curves)** to start creating the horizontal alignment.

9. You want to start the alignment at a reference station to Jeffries Ranch Rd. When prompted for the start of the alignment, click the **transparent command station and offset** icon, as shown in Figure 5–22.

Figure 5–22

10. When prompted for an alignment, select **Jeffries Ranch Rd**. When prompted for a station, enter **176.52** <Enter>, and when prompted for the offset, enter **0** <Enter>. Press <Esc> to exit the transparent command. AutoCAD Civil 3D has now established the starting location of the alignment by converting the station/offset to a x,y value.

11. You now need to specify the next point; you will do this by using the transparent command to enter an azimuth and a distance. Click the **Azimuth Distance transparent** icon, as shown in Figure 5–23.

Figure 5–23

12. Enter an azimuth of **1d18'04.79"**<Enter> and a distance of **107.65**<Enter>. Press <Esc> to exit the transparent command.

13. You now need to specify the next point; you will do this by using the transparent command to enter a turned angle and a distance. Click the **Angle Distance transparent** icon, as shown in Figure 5–24.

Figure 5–24

14. As you will be entering a counter-clockwise include angle, enter **C**<Enter>, enter the include angle of **76d35'36.34"**<Enter>, and for the distance enter **116.41**<Enter>.

15. Press <Esc> to exit the transparent command and press <Enter> to complete the horizontal alignment.

Task 4: Edit Alignments.

1. Save the drawing before continuing (recommended).

2. Activate a saved named view. In the *View* tab > Views panel, start the **Named views** command and select **C3D-Alignment radius-Curve Radius** as the active view.

3. Select the alignment **Ascent PI**. In the contextual Ribbon > Modify panel, select **Geometry Editor**, as shown in Figure 5–25.

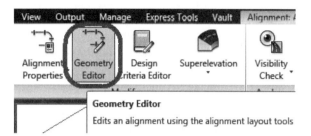

Figure 5–25

4. Select and edit a sub-entity on the alignment to revise the radius. In the alignment Tool Layout toolbar, click the **Sub-entity editor** and the **Pick Sub-entity** icons, as shown in Figure 5–26.

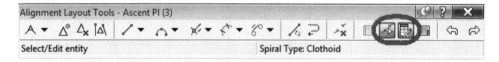

Figure 5–26

5. When prompted to select the sub-entity, select the curve shown on the left side in Figure 5–27. Change the radius to **15.25** <Enter>. Notice the radius dynamically changes in the graphics view. Click on the **X** in the Alignment Layout Tools dialog box to close both dialog boxes.

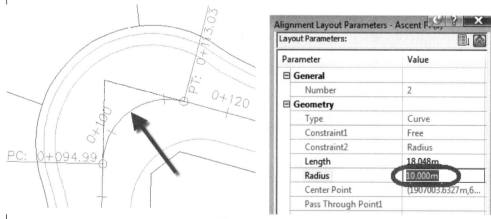

Figure 5–27

6.   Select the alignment **Ascent PI**. In the contextual Ribbon >
     Modify panel, select **Geometry Editor > Delete Sub-entity** in
     the Alignment Layout toolbar, as shown in Figure 5–28. Select
     the curve and press <Enter> to exit the command.

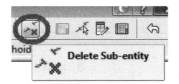

Figure 5–28

7.   Add a curve between two tangents. In the Alignment Layout
     toolbar, select **Free Curve Fillet (between two entities, radius)**
     from the icon pull-down shown in Figure 5–29.

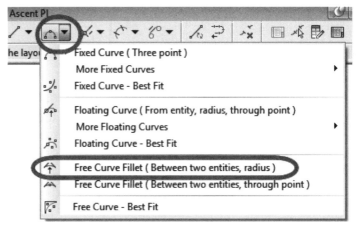

Figure 5–29

8.   Select the two tangents and press <Enter> to accept that the
     angle is less than 180deg, as shown on the left side in
     Figure 5–30. For the radius, enter **15.25** <Enter> and press
     <Enter> again to complete the command, as shown on the right.

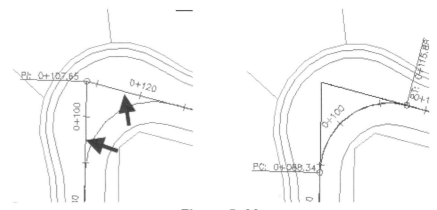

Figure 5–30

9.   Close the Alignment Layout toolbar and save the drawing.

5.4 Alignment Properties

The Alignment Properties dialog box (found by right-clicking on the alignment name in the *Prospector* tab and selecting **Properties**) controls stationing, station equations, references to the alignment by profiles and profile views, design speeds, superelevation settings, and related controls.

Station Control Tab

The *Station Control* tab sets the beginning station of the alignment. All labeling referencing the alignment dynamically updates its values when any change occurs to the alignment.

The *Station Equation* section of the panel adds and deletes equations from the alignment. A station equation is a point along the alignment where the stationing changes. The equation can represent the meeting of two stationing systems or the change in authority over the center line.

When adding an equation, AutoCAD Civil 3D displays a station jig reporting its station at the cursor. You set the station by selecting a point along the center line or entering a specific station value. After identifying the station equation point, set the station ahead value and whether the stationing increases or decreases. This is done after the location of the equation is defined.

- You can select a station in the drawing and refine its value in the *Station Control* tab in the Alignment Properties dialog box.

Design Criteria Tab

Each roadway can have multiple design speeds that reflect the conditions, design, and type of roadway surface. Design speeds affect the amount of superelevation and other safety concerns (stopping sight distance, passing sight distance, etc.) surrounding the roadway design.

When working with superelevations and vertical curves, the design speed of the roadway is critical for computing the correct parameters for the road design. When setting design speeds, AutoCAD Civil 3D displays a station selection jig and prompts for a station at the Command Line. After setting the station for the speed, you set the speed and enter any comments. You set the station in the drawing and refine its value in the *Design Speeds* tab of the Alignment Properties dialog box.

The option to **Use criteria-based design** is also found here, as shown in Figure 5–31. Select this option, and then decide whether you plan to use a design criteria file or design checks that you have created yourself.

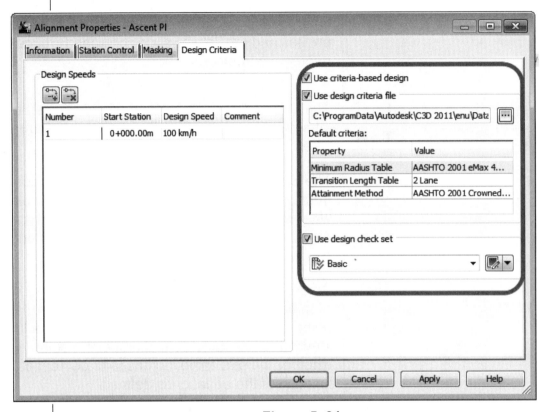

Figure 5–31

5.5 Labels and Tables

Alignment labels fall into two general categories: those controlled as a group through the **Edit Alignment Labels** command (referred to here as *Alignment Point Labels*), and those managed individually (referred to here as *Independent Alignment Labels*). Alignment labels of both types can be selected, repositioned, and erased separate from the alignment object itself.

Alignment Point Labels

Alignment point labels are organized into five categories, each of which is controlled by specific label styles:

* Major and Minor Stations
* (Horizontal) Geometry Points, such as Points of Curvature (PCs)
* Station Equations
* Design Speeds
* Profile Geometry Points, such as Points of Vertical Curvature (PVCs)
* Superelevation Critical Points

AutoCAD Civil 3D enables you to organize various alignment point labels into *Alignment Label Sets*, as shown in Figure 5–32, to simplify adding a group of them at the same time.

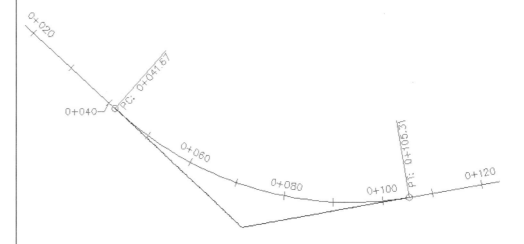

Figure 5–32

Alignment point labels are organized into *label groups*, so that when one is selected, all similar labels on the alignment are also selected, as shown in Figure 5–33. This enables you to change their properties (through the AutoCAD Properties dialog box, for example), or erase them all at once.

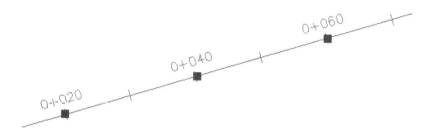

Figure 5–33

If you only want to select one of these labels (for example, to erase one of them), hold down <Ctrl> when selecting.

If you select an alignment and a large number of grips highlight, you have most likely selected an alignment station label group, as shown in Figure 5–34. If you want to select the alignment itself (rather than the labels), press <Esc>, zoom in, and try again.

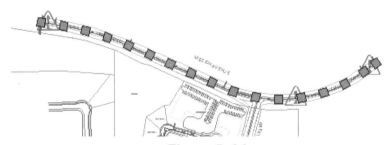

Figure 5–34

Alignment point labels can be selected when the alignment is defined and can later be managed by right-clicking on an alignment and selecting **Edit Alignment Labels**.

Independent Alignment Labels

Independent Alignment Labels can be used to add labels to alignment segments, as well as station and offset labels. They can be added through the Add Labels dialog box, which can be opened from the *Annotate* tab > Add Labels panel. Select **Alignment > Add Alignment Labels...**, as shown in Figure 5–35.

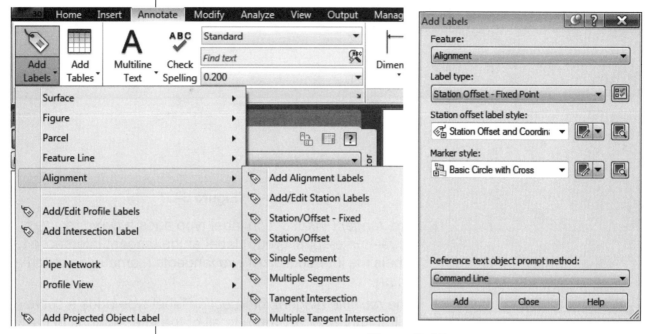

Figure 5–35

These labels include:

- The *station and offset* label type (as shown in Figure 5–36), which moves with the alignment if it changes to maintain the same station and offset.

- The *station and offset – fixed point* label type does not move if the alignment changes, and its station and offset values update to reflect the alignment edit.

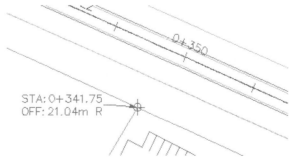

Figure 5–36

- The *single segment* label type adds a single line, curve, or spiral label to one alignment segment.

- The *multiple segment* label type adds a single line, curve, or spiral label to each alignment segment at the same time, as shown in Figure 5–37.

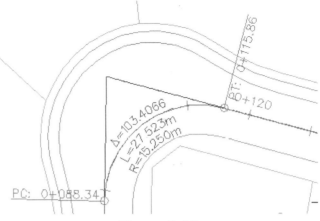

Figure 5–37

- The *tangent intersection* label type adds a curve (or spiral-curve-spiral group) label at the tangent intersection, and labels the intersection of two tangents (sometimes called an *angle point*).
- The *multiple tangent intersection* label type adds a curve (or spiral-curve-spiral group) to all of the intersections in the alignment.

Alignment Table Styles

If desired, alignment segments can be given *tag* labels (such as **C1** shown in Figure 5–38) and the segment data can be tabulated. For more information, see the topic *Setting Up Label Styles To Be Used as Tags* in the AutoCAD Civil 3D 2010 Help System.

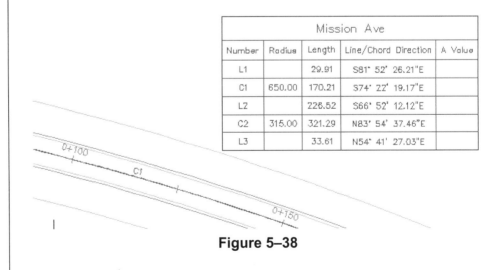

Mission Ave				
Number	Radius	Length	Line/Chord Direction	A Value
L1		29.91	S81° 52' 26.21"E	
C1	650.00	170.21	S74° 22' 19.17"E	
L2		226.52	S66° 52' 12.12"E	
C2	315.00	321.29	N83° 54' 37.46"E	
L3		33.61	N54° 41' 27.03"E	

Figure 5–38

Practice 5b | Alignment Properties and Labels

Task 1: Edit Alignment Properties.

1. Continue working with the drawing from the previous practice or open the file **ALN1-Sec2-Alignment-Complete.dwg** from the following folder:

   C:\Civil 3D Projects\Civil3D-training\Drawings

2. Activate a saved named view. In the *View* tab > Views panel, select **C3D-Alignment-Warning** as the active view.

3. When you created this alignment, you entered 100km/hr as the speed. You can see that, based on the design criteria, the radius is below the minimum. The warning is displayed both on the graphics screen and in the Panorama view, as shown in Figure 5–39.

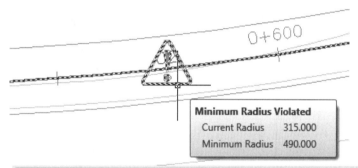

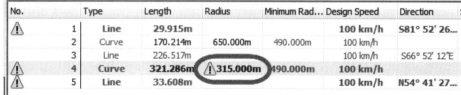

No.		Type	Length	Radius	Minimum Rad...	Design Speed	Direction	
⚠	1	Line	29.915m			100 km/h	S81° 52' 26...	
	2	Curve	170.214m	650.000m	490.000m	100 km/h		
	3	Line	226.517m			100 km/h	S66° 52' 12"E	
⚠	4	Curve	321.286m	⚠315.000m	490.000m	100 km/h		
⚠	5	Line	33.608m			100 km/h	N54° 41' 27...	

Figure 5–39

You need to fix the properties of this alignment to reflect the correct speed.

4. Select the alignment **Mission Ave**. In the contextual Ribbon > Modify panel, select **Alignment Properties**.

Alternatively, in the *Prospector* tab, right-click on the alignment *Mission Ave* (under the *Alignments > Centerline Alignments* collections), as shown in Figure 5–40, and select **Properties**.

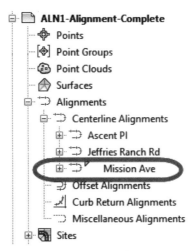

Figure 5–40

5. In the *Design Criteria* tab, change the *Design Speed* to **80km/h**, as shown in Figure 5–41, and click [OK] to exit.

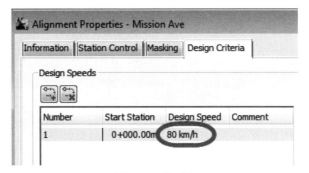

Figure 5–41

Now that you have the correct design speed, the radius is within the minimum requirements.

Task 2: Add and change alignment labels.

1. Currently, the station label intervals are every 20m. Change it to show station labels at every 25m. Select the alignment **Mission Ave**, right click, and select **Edit Alignment Labels**, as shown in Figure 5–42.

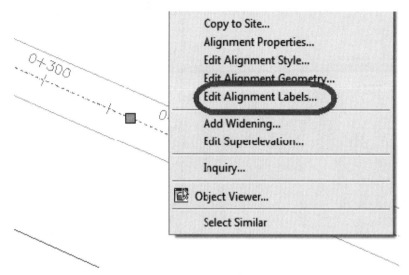

Figure 5–42

2. In the Alignment Labels dialog box, change the *Increment* for the Major labels to **50** and the Minor labels to **25**, as shown in Figure 5–43. Click [OK] to close the dialog box and apply the changes.

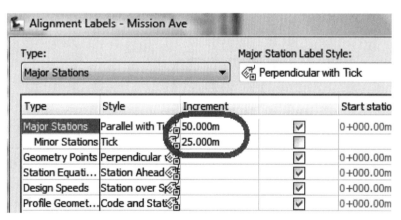

Figure 5–43

3. With the alignment still selected, select **Add Labels > Multiple Segment** in the Labels & Tables panel, as shown in Figure 5–44.

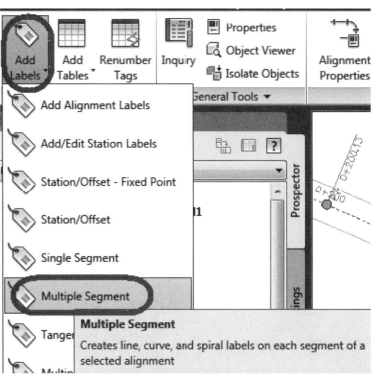

Figure 5–44

4. When prompted to select the alignment, select the **Mission Ave** alignment again, as shown in Figure 5–45, and press <Enter> to complete and exit the command.

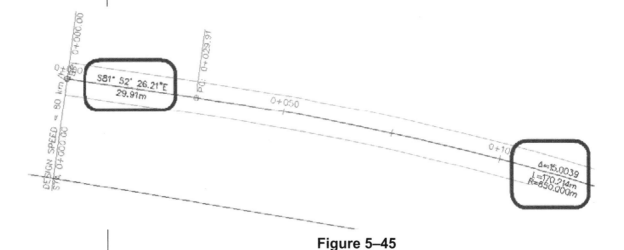

Figure 5–45

5. Activate a saved named view. In the *View* tab > Views panel, start the **Named views** command and select **C3D-Alignment-Label** as the active view. Switch back to the contextual *Alignment: Mission Ave* tab or reselect the alignment in Model Space to activate the contextual Ribbon.

6. To create a Table listing the segments, select **Add Tables > Add Segments** in the Labels & Tables panel, as shown in Figure 5–46.

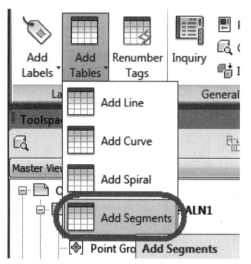

Figure 5–46

7. In the Alignment table creation dialog box, set the options as shown in Figure 5–47 and click [OK] when done.

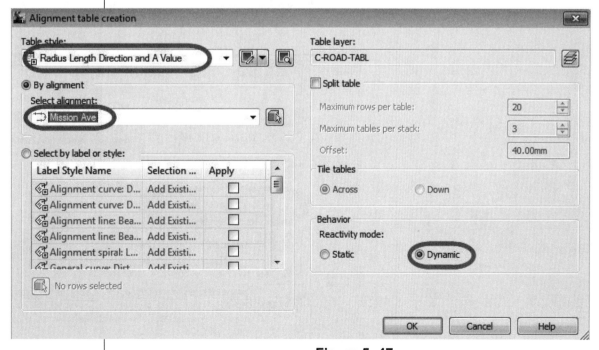

Figure 5–47

8. AutoCAD Civil 3D will convert the labels to tags. Select a point on the graphics screen to set the location of the table, as shown in Figure 5–48.

Mission Ave				
Number	Radius	Length	Line/Chord Direction	A Value
L1		29.91	S81° 52' 26.21"E	
C1	650.00	170.21	S74° 22' 19.17"E	
L2		226.52	S66° 52' 12.12"E	
C2	315.00	321.29	N83° 54' 37.46"E	
L3		33.61	N54° 41' 27.03"E	

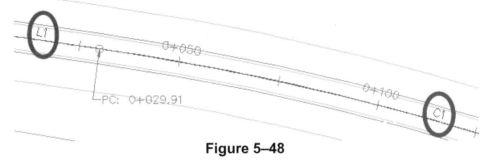

Figure 5–48

9. Activate a saved named view. In the *View* tab > Views panel, start the **Named views** command and select **C3D-Alignment-Sta Label** as the active view.

10. Select the **Jeffries Ranch Rd** alignment and in the contextual Ribbon, select **Add Labels > Station/Offset - Fixed Point** in the Labels & Tables panel, as shown in Figure 5–49.

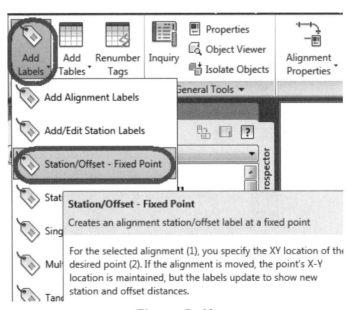

Figure 5–49

11. Select the end point where the Ascent Pl alignment intersects with Jeffries Ranch Rd, as shown on the left side in Figure 5–50. Select the label and move to a location to avoid clutter, as shown on the right.

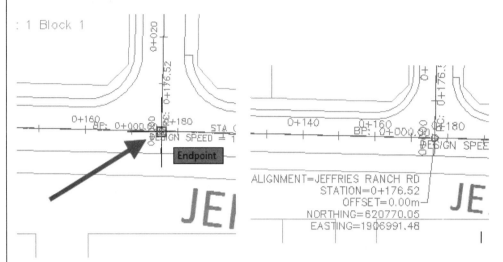

Figure 5–50

12. Save the drawing.

Review Questions

Question 1 | When can an alignment subdivide parcels?

Question 2 | How do you open the Alignment Layout toolbar for an existing alignment?

Question 3 | How do you select an individual alignment point label for deletion?

Question 4 | How do you apply a design check to an alignment?

Module 6

Data Sharing Level 1

This module introduces:

Section 1: Data Sharing Overview
- ✓ **AutoCAD Civil 3D Projects**
- ✓ **Sharing Data**

Section 2: Data Shortcuts
- ✓ **Data Shortcuts**

Section 3: Vault
- ✓ **Vault Overview**
- ✓ **Using the Vault Client**

Section 1: Data Sharing Overview

6.1 AutoCAD Civil 3D Projects

There are multiple ways of organizing AutoCAD Civil 3D project drawings. Three of the most common approaches are:

Single-Design Drawing Projects

Since AutoCAD Civil 3D surfaces, alignments, and other AEC objects can be entirely drawing-based, you can have a single drawing file act as the repository for all design data. Realistically, this might only be feasible with the smallest of projects and/or those worked on by only one person. The only external data would be survey databases, and possibly drawings containing plotting layouts that XREF the single design drawing.

Multiple Drawings Sharing Data through Shortcuts

This approach permits multiple survey and design drawings that share data. For example, a surface could exist in one drawing and an alignment in another. A third could contain a surface profile based on the alignment and terrain model, and all could be kept in sync with each other through Data Shortcuts. This approach is usually preferable to the single-drawing approach, because it permits more than one user to work on the project at the same time (in the different design drawings). This approach does not create any external project data other than survey databases and XML data files used to share data between drawings.

Shortcuts tend to be efficient for projects with a small number of drawings and project team members. Since the XML data files that connect drawings must be managed manually, keeping a large number of drawings and/or people in sync with shortcuts can be cumbersome. It is highly recommended that you establish procedures to ensure that data is not unintentionally deleted or changed. You will also want to document these procedures very carefully.

Multiple Drawings Sharing Data with Autodesk Vault

Vault is Autodesk's data and document management system (ADMS). It is used in conjunction with several Autodesk applications in many different industries. When working with Vault, all project drawings, survey databases, and references are managed by Vault and stored inside an SQL-managed database. Vault consists of user-level access permissions, drawing check-in/check-out, project templates, automated backups, data versioning, and more. These significant benefits are offset by the additional time required to manage and administer the database, and in some cases purchasing additional hardware and software. If you work on large projects with multiple design drawings or have many team members (more than 10 of either), you might find Vault is the best way to keep those projects organized.

6.2 Sharing Data

In the AutoCAD Civil 3D workflow, you can use two main methods of project collaboration or the sharing of intelligent Civil 3D design data: Data Shortcuts and Vault references.

Vault and Data Shortcuts can be used to share design data between drawing files in the same project, such as alignment definitions, profiles, surfaces, pipe networks, and View Frames. They do not permit the sharing of profile views, assemblies, corridors, sample line groups, or other AutoCAD Civil 3D objects. Drawing sets utilizing shortcuts typically make use of XREFs, as well as reference other line work and annotations between drawings. Whether using Vault Shortcuts or Data Shortcuts, the process is similar.

Figure 6–1 demonstrates the sharing of data in a project collaboration environment. The data is broken down into three distinctive levels. Using either Data Shortcuts or Vault, these levels can be accessed and contributed to, either on a local or remote server.

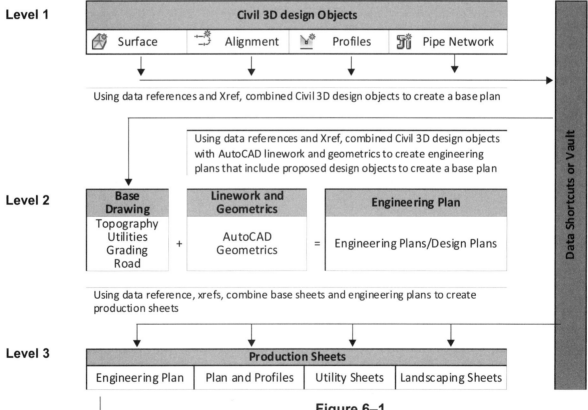

Figure 6–1

Review Questions

Question 1	In the AutoCAD Civil 3D workflow, what are the two main methods of project collaboration (or the sharing of intelligent Civil 3D design data)?
Question 2	Why would you want to use Vault references over Data Shortcuts?
Question 3	There are multiple ways of organizing AutoCAD Civil 3D project drawings. What are three of the most common methods?
Question 4	When sharing data in a project collaboration environment, what is the recommended number of levels into which the data should be broken?

Section 2: Data Shortcuts

6.3 Data Shortcuts

Data Shortcuts can be used to share design data between drawing files through the use of XML files. Using Data Shortcuts is similar to using Vault, but does not provide the protection of your data or the tracking of versions the way that Vault does.

Data Shortcuts are managed through the Prospector tab in the Toolspace under the Data Shortcuts collection, as shown in Figure 6–2. The shortcuts are stored in XML files within one or more working folders that you create. They can use the same folder structure as Vault. This method simplifies the transition to using Vault at a future time.

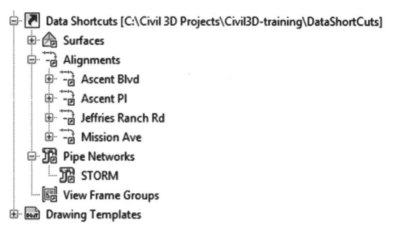

Figure 6–2

Whether using Vault or Data Shortcuts, the intelligent Civil 3D object design data can be consumed and utilized on different levels. However, this referenced data only can be edited in the drawing that contains the original object. As referenced data can be assigned a different style than those in the source drawing, you have the ability to separate the design phase (where drawing presentation is not critical) from the drafting phase (where drawing presentation is paramount). What this means is that after the styles are applied at the drafting phase, any changes to the design will have minimal visual impact to the completed drawings.

Changing the name of a drawing file that provides Data Shortcuts or the shortcut XML file itself will invalidate the shortcut. Although the Data Shortcuts Editor outside of AutoCAD Civil 3D permits re-pathing if a source drawing moves, shortcuts might not resolve if the source drawing file name has changed.

Update Notification

If the shortcut objects are modified and the source drawing is saved, any drawings that reference those objects are updated when opened. If the drawings consuming the data referenced in the shortcuts were open at the time of the edit, a balloon message appears to warn you of the changes, as shown in Figure 6–3.

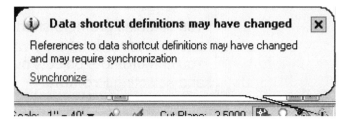

Figure 6–3

The modifier icons shown below help you determine the state of many AutoCAD Civil 3D objects.

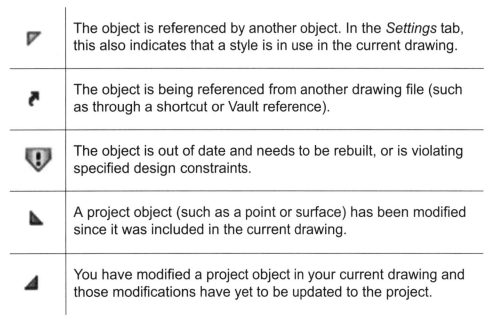

▽	The object is referenced by another object. In the *Settings* tab, this also indicates that a style is in use in the current drawing.
↗	The object is being referenced from another drawing file (such as through a shortcut or Vault reference).
⊙	The object is out of date and needs to be rebuilt, or is violating specified design constraints.
◣	A project object (such as a point or surface) has been modified since it was included in the current drawing.
◢	You have modified a project object in your current drawing and those modifications have yet to be updated to the project.

The example in Figure 6–4 shows how the modifier icons are used with a Civil 3D object as it appears in the *Prospector* tab.

Figure 6–4

To update the shortcut data, select **Synchronize** in the balloon message or right-click on the object in the *Prospector* and select **Synchronize**.

Removing and Promoting Shortcuts

Shortcut data can be removed from the Shortcut tree in the *Prospector* by right-clicking on it and selecting **Remove**, but this does not remove the data from the drawing. To do so, right-click on the object in the *Prospector* and select **Delete**. This removes the shortcut data from the current list, so that the item is not included if a Data Shortcut XML file is exported from the current drawing.

You can also promote shortcuts, which converts the referenced shortcut into a local copy with no further connection to the original. You can promote objects by right-clicking on them in the *Prospector* and selecting **Promote**.

eTransmit Data References

Projects that use Data Shortcuts can be packaged and sent to reviewers, clients, and other consultants using the AutoCAD **eTransmit** command. With the **eTransmit** command, all of the related dependent files (such as XML files, XREFs, and text fonts) are automatically included in the package. This reduces the possibility of errors and ensures that the recipient can use the files you send them. A report file can be included in the package that explains what must be done with drawing-dependent files (e.g., XML, XREFs) so that they are usable with the included files. The Create Transmittal dialog box is shown in Figure 6–5.

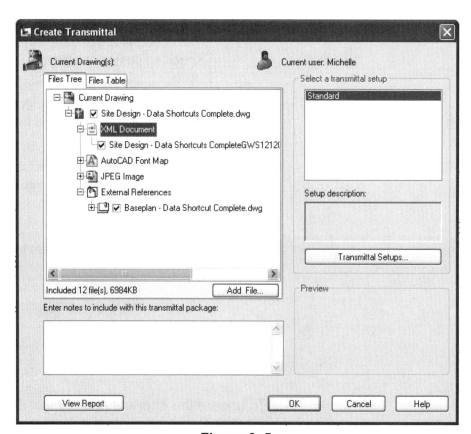

Figure 6–5

Data Shortcut Workflow

1. In the *Prospector* tab, right-click on *Data Shortcuts* and select **Set the Working Folder….**

2. In the *Prospector* tab, right-click on *Data Shortcuts* and select **New Data Shortcuts Folder...** to create a new project folder for all your drawings.

3. Create or import the data you want to share in the source drawing and save it in the current working folder under the correct project folder.

4. In the *Prospector* tab, right-click on *Data Shortcuts* and select **Create Data Shortcuts**.

5. Select all items you want to share, such as surfaces, alignments, or profiles, and then click OK .

6. Save the source drawing (and close as needed).

7. Open, create and save the drawing to receive the shortcut data. Expand the *Data Shortcuts* collection and relevant object trees (*Surfaces*, *Alignments*, *Pipe Networks*, or *View Frame Groups*).

8. Highlight an item to be referenced, right-click and select **Create Reference…**. Repeat for all objects as needed. You are prompted for the styles and other settings that are required to display the object in the current drawing.

9. You might also want to add an XREF to the source drawing if there is additional AutoCAD line work you would like to show in the downstream drawing.

10. AutoCAD Civil 3D tools for Data Shortcuts are located in the Manage tab, as shown in Figure 6–6, and in the *Prospector* tab.

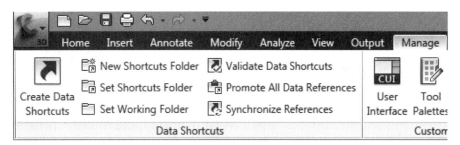

Figure 6–6

Workflow Details

1. **Set Working Folder**: This option sets a new working folder as the location to store the Data Shortcut project. The default working folder for Data Shortcut projects is *C:\Civil 3D Projects*. The default working folder is also used for Autodesk Vault projects and local (non-Vault) Survey projects. If you work with Autodesk Vault, local Survey, and Data Shortcut projects, you should have separate working folders for each project type for ease of management.

2. **New Shortcuts Folder**: This option creates a new folder for storing a set of related project drawings and Data Shortcuts.

3. **Create Data Shortcuts**: This option creates Data Shortcuts from the active drawing.

Data Shortcuts are stored in the *Shortcuts* folder for the active project, and used to create data references to source objects in other drawings. Each Data Shortcut is stored in a separate XML file.

Advantages of Data Shortcuts

- Data Shortcuts provide a simple mechanism for sharing object data, without the added system administration needs of Autodesk Vault.
- Data Shortcuts offer access to an object's intelligent data while ensuring that this referenced data can only be changed in the source drawing.
- Referenced objects can have styles and labels that differ from the source drawing.
- When you open a drawing that has revised referenced data, the referenced objects are automatically updated.
- During a drawing session, if the referenced data has been revised, you are notified both in the *Communication Center* and the *Prospector* tab in Toolspace.

Limitations of Data Shortcuts

- Data Shortcuts cannot provide data versioning.
- Data Shortcuts provide no security or data integrity controls.
- Unlike Autodesk Vault, Data Shortcuts do not provide a secure mechanism for sharing point data or survey data.
- Maintaining links between references and their source objects requires fairly stable names and locations on the shared file system. However, most broken references can easily be repaired with tools provided within AutoCAD Civil 3D.

Practice 6a | Data Shortcuts Part I

In this practice you will walk through the steps of creating a project-based Data Shortcuts folders.

Task 1: Set the Working folder.

In this task, you set up a new working folder as the location to store Data Shortcut projects. The default working folder for Data Shortcut projects is *C:\Civil 3D Projects*.

1. Create a new drawing, as shown in Figure 6–7, using the **C3D Training.dwt** template in the following folder:

    C:\Civil 3D Projects\Civil3D-training\Drawings

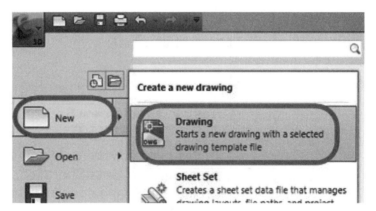

Figure 6–7

2. In the *Manage* tab > Data Shortcuts panel, select **Set Working Folder**, as shown in Figure 6–8.

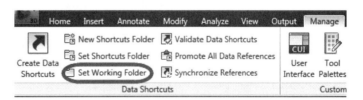

Figure 6–8

3. In the Browse For Folder dialog box, select the Civil 3D Projects folder and click **Make New Folder**, as shown on the left in Figure 6–9. Enter **Training Data Shortcuts** as the folder name and click **OK** to close the dialog box, as shown as shown on the right.

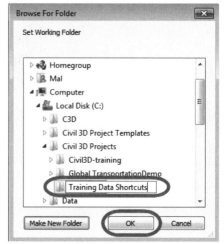

Figure 6–9

Task 2: Create new Shortcuts folders.

In this task, you create a new folder for storing a set of related project drawings and Data Shortcuts. Create a folder name that reflects the project name and specify whether or not to use a project template to organize your data.

1. Continue working with the drawing from the previous task.

2. In the *Manage* tab > Data Shortcuts panel, select **New Shortcuts Folder**, as shown in Figure 6–10.

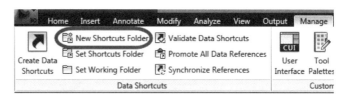

Figure 6–10

3. In the New Data Shortcut Folder dialog box, enter Ascent Phase 1 for the name and select the Use project template option. The template is found in the default folder *C:\Civil 3D Templates*, as shown in Figure 6–11. Civil 3D will replicate this template folder structure in the Data Shortcuts project folder. Click **OK** to close the dialog box.

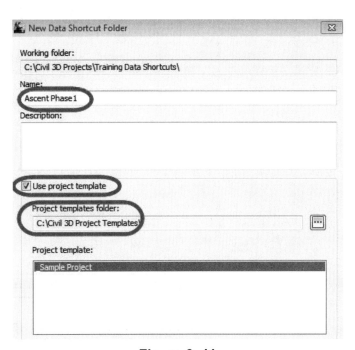

Figure 6–11

4. In the *Prospector* tab, you should now see a Data Shortcut folder in *C:\Civil 3D Projects\Training Data Shortcuts\Ascent Phase1*. If you view Windows File Explorer, you will see the folder structure Civil 3D has created for this project, as shown in Figure 6–12.

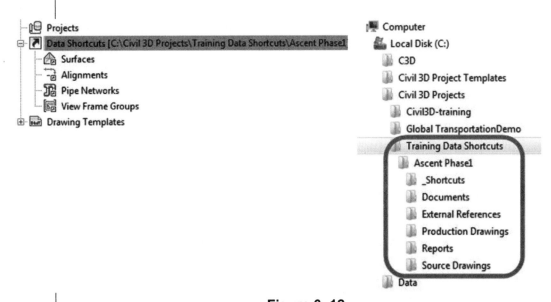

Figure 6–12

5. Create a new shortcuts folder. In the *Manage* tab > Data Shortcuts panel, select **New Shortcuts Folder**.

6. In the New Data Shortcut Folder dialog box, enter **Ascent Phase 2** for the name and select the **Use project template** option. Click OK to close the dialog box.

7. You now have two projects in the working folder: *Ascent Phase 1* and *Ascent Phase 2*, as shown in Figure 6–13.

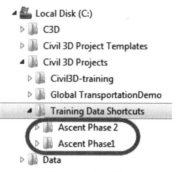

Figure 6–13

Task 3: Set up Shortcuts folder.

Setting the shortcut folder specifies the project path for Data Shortcuts. The path to the current Data Shortcuts folder (also known as the project folder) is specified on the *Prospector* tab in the Toolspace, under the *Data Shortcuts* collection. The project folder typically contains both Data Shortcuts and source objects for data references.

1. Continue working with the drawing from the previous task.

2. In the *Manage* tab > Data Shortcuts panel, select **Set Shortcuts Folder**.

3. The current Data Shortcut folder is signified by a green circle with a check mark. Select **Ascent Phase1** to make it current and click OK , as shown in Figure 6–14.

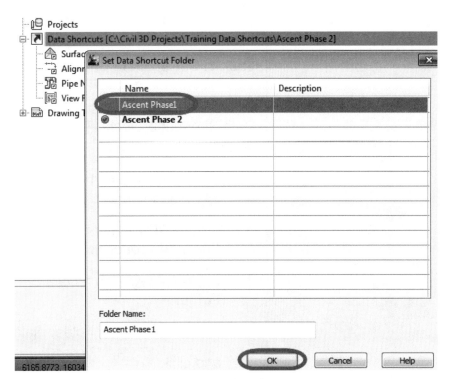

Figure 6–14

Practice 6b | Data Shortcuts Part II

In this practice you will walk through the steps of creating project-based Data Shortcuts folders.

Task 1: Set up Data Shortcuts folders.

In this task, you set up a new working folder as the location to store Data Shortcut projects. The default working folder for Data Shortcut projects is *C:\Civil 3D Projects*.

1. Open the file **DAT1-DataSharing-surface.dwg** from the following folder:

    C:\Civil 3D Projects\Civil3D-training\Training Shortcuts\Ascent Phase1\Production Drawings

2. In the *Manage* tab > Data Shortcuts panel, select **Set Working Folder**.

3. In the Browse For Folder dialog box, select **Training Shortcuts** and click ⌐OK¬ to close the dialog box, as shown in Figure 6–15.

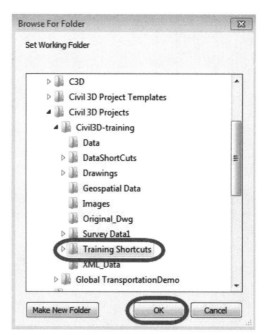

Figure 6–15

4. In the *Manage* tab > Data Shortcuts panel, select **Set Shortcuts Folder**.

5. In the Set Data Shortcut Folder dialog box, select **Ascent Phase1** and click ⬚ OK ⬚ to close the dialog box.

Task 2: Create Data Shortcuts.

1. Continue working with the drawing from the previous task or open the file **DAT1-DataSharing-surface.dwg** from the following folder:

    C:\Civil 3D Projects\Civil3D-training\Training Shortcuts\Ascent Phase1\Production Drawings

2. In the *Prospector* tab, ensure that the Data Shortcuts point to the following folder, as shown in Figure 6–16:

    C:\Civil 3D Projects\Civil3D-training\Training Shortcuts\Ascent Phase1

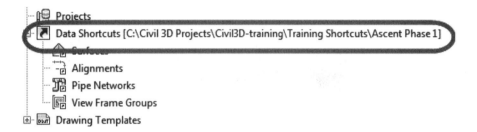

Figure 6–16

3. This drawing contains some surfaces for which you want to create Data Shortcuts. In the *Manage* tab > Data Shortcuts panel, select **Create Data Shortcuts**, as shown in Figure 6–17.

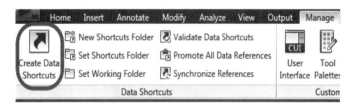

Figure 6–17

4. If you receive a message that the drawing has not yet been saved, click ⬚ OK ⬚. Save the drawing and start the **Create Data Shortcuts** command again.

5. In the Create Data Shortcuts dialog box, you will see a list of all objects that are available for use in shortcuts. Select **Surfaces**, as shown in Figure 6–18, and click 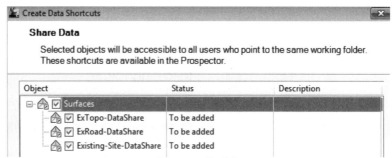.

Figure 6–18

6. Save and close the drawing. To close, select **DAT1-DataSharing-Surface**, right-click, and select **Close**, as shown in Figure 6–19.

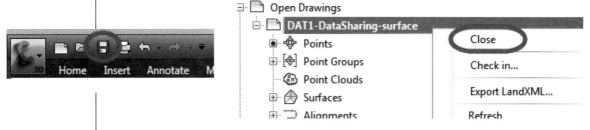

Figure 6–19

7. Notice in the *Prospector* tab, under the *Data Shortcuts* and *Surfaces* collections, you now have access to all surfaces. In the list view below, you can see the source file name and source path, as shown in Figure 6–20.

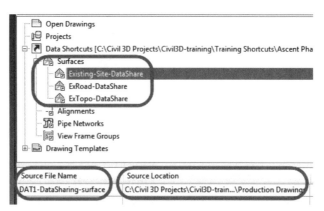

Figure 6–20

8. Open the file **DAT1-DataSharing-Alignment.dwg** from the following folder:

   C:\Civil 3D Projects\Civil3D-training\Training Shortcuts\Ascent Phase1\Production Drawings

9. In the *Manage* tab > Data Shortcuts panel, select **Create Data Shortcuts**.

10. If you receive a message that the drawing has not yet been saved, click OK. Save the drawing and start the **Create Data Shortcuts** command again. In the Create Data Shortcuts dialog box, you will see a list of all objects that are available for use in shortcuts. At the bottom left corner of the dialog box, click (Pick in drawing).

11. In Model Space, select the three alignments, as shown on the left in Figure 6–21. Then press <Enter>. Notice in the Create Data Shortcuts dialog box, the three alignments are selected, as shown on the right. Click OK to close the dialog box.

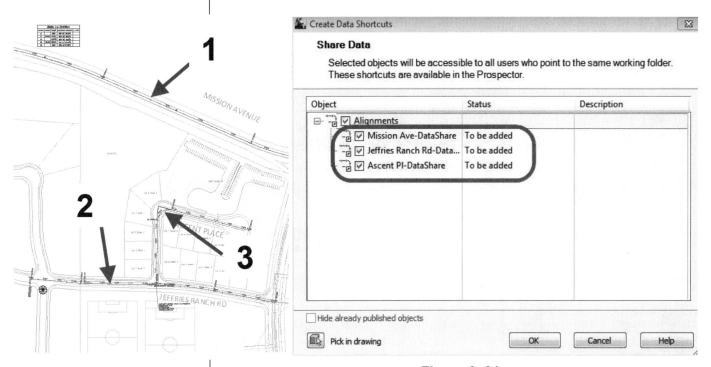

Figure 6–21

12. You have now created shortcuts for the alignments. This means that if the shortcuts are in a shared network folder, anyone on the network has access to these Civil 3D objects.

13. Save the drawing, but do not close it.

Task 3: Data-reference Data Shortcuts.

1. Open the file **DAT1-DataSharing.dwg** from the following folder:

    C:\Civil 3D Projects\Civil3D-training\Training Shortcuts\Ascent Phase1\Production Drawings

2. In the *Prospector* tab, ensure that the Data Shortcuts point to the following folder:

    C:\Civil 3D Projects\Civil3D-training\Training Shortcuts\Ascent Phase1

3. In the *Prospector* tab, under the *Data Shortcuts* collection, expand the *Surfaces* collection (if not already expanded) and expand the *Alignments* collection, as shown in Figure 6–22.

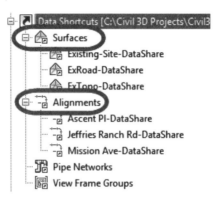

Figure 6–22

4. Under the *Surfaces* collection, select the surface **Existing-Site-DataShare**, right-click, and select **Create Reference**, as shown in Figure 6–23.

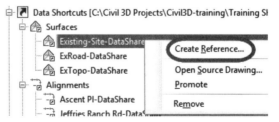

Figure 6–23

5. In the Create Surface Reference dialog box, you can rename the reference surface and assign a different surface and render style. Enter **ExSurface** for the *Name*, enter **Data referenced surface** for the *Description*, and enter **Contours 5m and 25m (Background)** for the *Style*, as shown in Figure 6–24. Click OK to close the dialog box.

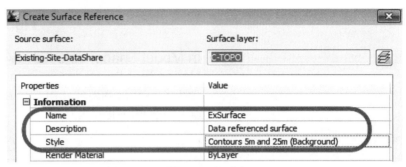

Figure 6–24

6. In this step, you will create a data reference to the alignment. In the *Alignments* collection, select **Ascent PI-DataShare**, right-click, and select **Create Reference**.

7. In the Create Alignment Reference dialog box, accept the default for the *Name*. Enter **Data referenced alignment** for the *Description*. Set the *Alignment style* to **Layout** and set the *Alignment label set* to **Major and Minor only**. Click OK when done, as shown in Figure 6–25.

Figure 6–25

8. In the *View* tab > Views panel, select the preset view **C3D-DataSharing-Alignment**, as shown in Figure 6–26.

Figure 6–26

9. In Model Space, select the **Ascent PI** referenced alignment. Notice that there are no grips; you are not able to geographically redefine this alignment. However, you can add labels using the contextual Ribbon.

10. In the contextual Ribbon > Labels & Tables panel, select **Add Labels > Station/Offset - Fixed Point**, as shown in Figure 6–27.

Figure 6–27

11. When prompted to select a point, select the center of the bulb of the cul-de-sac, as shown on the left in Figure 6–28. Select the label and move its location so that it is easier to read, as shown on the right. Note the station is 0+212.96.

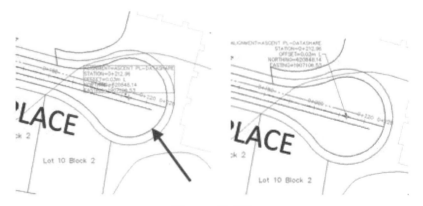

Figure 6–28

12. In the *Prospector* tab, expand the *Surfaces* and the *ExSurface* collections, as shown on the left in Figure 6–29. Notice that it does not contain the definition elements that you might otherwise see in a surface that is not data-referenced, as shown on the right. What this means is that you are not able to edit or make design changes to a referenced surface.

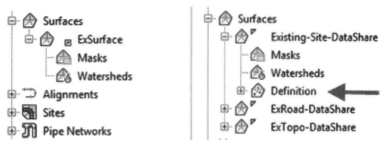

Figure 6–29

13. Save the drawing but do not close it.

Task 4: Revise original referenced object.

---

1. Continue working with the drawing from the previous task or open the file **DAT1-DataSharing-Alignment.dwg** from the following folder:

   C:\Civil 3D Projects\Civil3D-training\Training Shortcuts\Ascent Phase1\Production Drawings

2. In the *Prospector* tab, ensure that the Data Shortcuts point to the following folder: *C:\Civil 3D Projects\Civil3D-training\Training Shortcuts\Ascent Phase1*.

3. If you are continuing with the previous session, ensure that the **Master View** is enabled in the Toolspace so that you can see all the drawings that are loaded. Select **Dat1-DataSharing-Alignment**, right-click, and select **Switch to**, as shown in Figure 6–30. **Dat1-DataSharing.dwg** is now the current drawing.

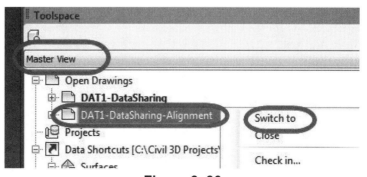

Figure 6–30

4. In the *View* tab > Views panel, select the preset view **C3D-DataSharing-Alignment**.

5. You will now change the length of this alignment. In Model Space, select the alignment, then select the grip that signifies the end of the alignment, and move it to the center of the cul-de-sac bulb, as shown in Figure 6–31.

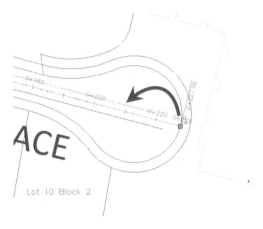

Figure 6–31

6. From the contextual Ribbon > Modify panel, select **Alignment Properties**, as shown in Figure 6–32.

Figure 6–32

7. In the *Station Control* tab of the Alignment Properties - Ascent Pl-DataShare dialog box, set the reference point Station to **100**, as shown in Figure 6–33. You receive a warning that changing the station will affect objects and data already created. Click

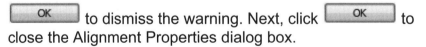 to dismiss the warning. Next, click 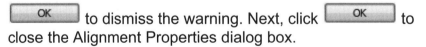 to close the Alignment Properties dialog box.

Figure 6–33

8. Save the drawing. This will cause the Data Shortcut to update.

9. If you are continuing with the drawing from the previous session, ensure that the Master view is enabled in the Toolspace so that you can see all the drawings that are loaded. Select **Dat1-DataSharing**, right-click, and select **Switch to**. **Dat1-DataSharing.dwg** is now the current drawing.

10. If you closed the drawing in the previous step, open the drawing **DAT1-DataSharing-Alignment.dwg** (see step 13).

11. At the bottom right corner of the application window, you receive a message that data shortcut definitions may have been changed. To synchronize your current drawing, select the **Synchronize** link in the balloon notification, as shown in Figure 6–34.

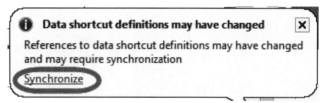

Figure 6–34

12. Alternatively, in the *Prospector* tab, select the alignment **Ascent PI-DataShare** from the *Alignments* collection. Right-click and select **Synchronize**, as shown in Figure 6–35.

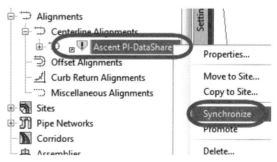

Figure 6–35

13. Complete this step only if the drawing is not open. Open the file **DAT1-DataSharing-Alignment.dwg** from the following folder:

    C:\Civil 3D Projects\Civil3D-training\Training Shortcuts\Ascent Phase1\Production Drawings

14. Notice that the alignment has updated geographic information, as shown in Figure 6–36. The end of alignment is at the center of the cul-de-sac bulb, and the station label is updated to reflect the change to the original alignment design.

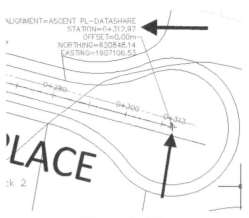

ALIGNMENT=ASCENT PL–DATASHARE
STATION=0+312.97
OFFSET=0.00m
NORTHING=620848.14
EASTING=1907106.53

Figure 6–36

15. Save and close the drawing.

Practice 6c	# Data Shortcuts Part III

In this practice you will create a transmittal package to send to other design professionals on the project team.

1. Open the file **DAT1-DataSharing.dwg** from the following folder:

    C:\Civil 3D Projects\Civil3D-training\Training Shortcuts\Ascent Phase1\Production Drawings

2. Select **Application Menu**  **> Send > eTransmit**, as shown in Figure 6–37. If a Warning dialog box appears stating that the current drawing is not saved, click [Yes] to save it.

Figure 6–37

3. In the eTransmit dialog box, click 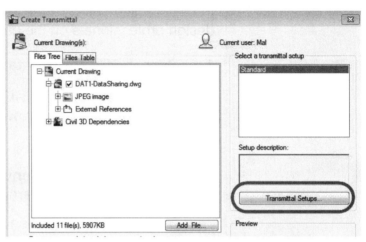, as shown in Figure 6–38.

Figure 6–38

4. In the Transmittal Setups dialog box, select the **Standard** setup and click 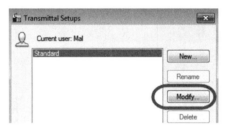, as shown in Figure 6–39.

Figure 6–39

5. In the Modify Transmittal Setup dialog box, accept the *Transmittal file folder.* Select **Prompt for a filename** from the *Transmittal file name* drop-down list and select the **Keep files and folders as is** option. In the *Include options* section, select all of the options, as shown in Figure 6–40. Accept the remaining defaults and click OK to close the dialog box.

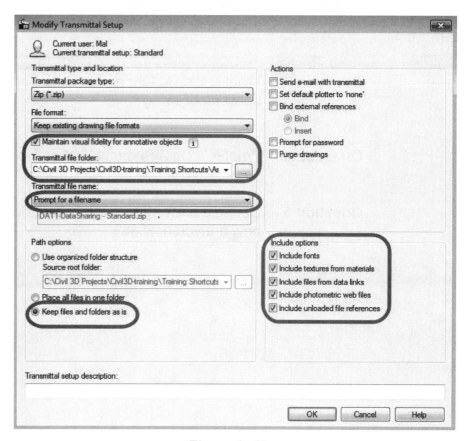

Figure 6–40

6. Close the Transmittal Setups dialog box.

7. Click OK to close the Create Transmittal dialog box and create the transmittal.

8. When prompted for the file name for the transmittal file, accept the default and save it. AutoCAD Civil 3D will proceed to create a compressed file of all the relevant data.

Review Questions

Question 1   How can you edit an object referenced through Data Shortcuts?

Question 2   Using Data Shortcuts is similar to using Vault, but what are the two things that Vault does that Data Shortcuts do not?

Question 3   What is the file format that Data Shortcuts use to share design data between drawing files?

Question 4   What is a Data Shortcut Update Notification?

Question 5   During a drawing session, if the referenced data has been revised, how are you notified?

Section 3: Vault

6.4 Vault Overview

Autodesk Vault is a flexible data management application integrated with your Autodesk software that optimizes your investment in design data. Autodesk Vault helps design teams organize and reuse designs by consolidating project information and reducing the need to recreate designs from scratch. Users can store and search both CAD data (such as AutoCAD drawings and Autodesk DWF files) and non-CAD data (such as Microsoft Word and Excel files, as well as image files). When files are added to the vault, a copy is made of each file and included in the vault. These files become the "master" and the original files on your local machine become copies of the master files maintained by the vault. In addition, when files are added, information (also referred to as metadata) about the files is saved in the Microsoft SQL Server database and the physical files are copied to the vault file store.

The Autodesk Vault file store saves the files in a semi-proprietary format. Each time you check in a new version, a version of that file is saved to the file store. This enables Autodesk Vault to maintain a version history of changes.

Vault has two components: 1) the Autodesk Data Management Server (ADMS) and 2) the Vault Client. The Vault Client is the component that is used to access information stored in the ADMS. Vault will protect data as well as track changes that are made throughout the design process.

Key Terms

The following table describes some key terms in Autodesk Vault.

Data Management	A means of organizing and tracking files through the design process.
Autodesk Data Management Server (ADMS)	Server component that manages the database and file store of Autodesk Vault.
Clients	Applications that access the Autodesk Data Management Server. These include the Autodesk Vault Client, the Civil 3D Add-in, and the Microsoft Office Add-in.

Autodesk Vault Explorer	Standalone client for Autodesk Vault used to organize vaulted information. Can also be used to manage any file in the Vault.
Microsoft® Internet Information Services (IIS)	A Microsoft® Web server necessary for the Autodesk Data Management Server to communicate with the client systems.
Vault	The combination of a database and a file store. Each installation of the ADMS can manage several independent vaults. A single user can have connections to several vaults, but not simultaneously.
Vault Manager	Application used by administrators for creating vaults, backing up and restoring data, and adding users and controlling their permissions.

Vault Architecture

The *Autodesk Data Management Server* and the *Vault Client* make up the primary components of Autodesk Vault. Figure 6–41 illustrates a basic setup of the vault. You can have two types of configurations: Single Site or Multiple Sites. The configuration used will depend on the type of requirements and the structure of the design team.

Single Site

You can configure Autodesk Vault for a single office site, as shown in Figure 6–41.

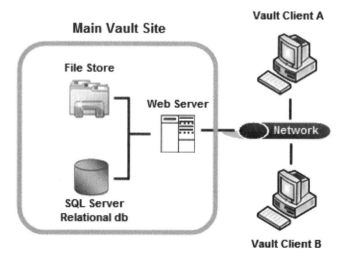

Figure 6–41

The simplest way to organize your projects with Autodesk Vault is to use a single vault to store all projects and their information. All team members have access to this one location; you set up access control and user names only once. A single vault keeps project data centralized and easier to manage.

Multiple Sites

Autodesk Vault can also manage project data for users at multiple sites as if they were all working in the same office, as shown in Figure 6–42. This capability is provided by a multi-site option, available with Autodesk Vault at an extra cost.

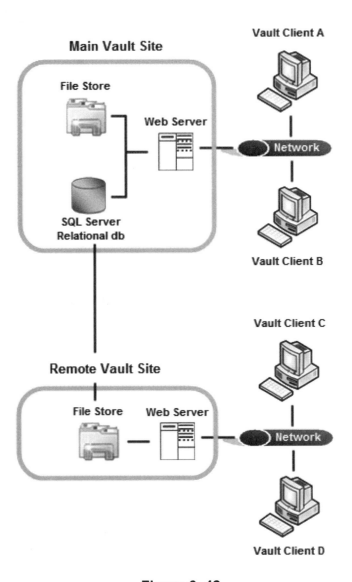

Figure 6–42

Autodesk Vault has the ability to create and manage multiple vaults. A vault is a separate storage repository, similar to having multiple hard drives on a computer. Using multiple vaults right from the beginning is recommended for large organizations with several departments that use AutoCAD Civil 3D independently. Each department-such as the survey, site, or highway departments-has its own vault. This structure makes it easier to separately manage departmental permissions and project access.

Each vault can have a separate system administrator, and users can be granted access to only one vault, if necessary. If some users need access to multiple vaults, you must configure their permissions separately for each vault. Also note that users cannot log into more than one vault at a time.

Benefits of Using Multiple Vaults

The following are some of the benefits of using more than one vault:

- One of the best reasons for multiple vaults is to provide training areas where users can feel free to experiment without interfering with the production or main vault. You can even create a new vault for each user for training purposes, deleting them when they are finished.
- For companies that specialize in engineering consulting, it might be useful to create a separate vault for each customer you work with. This enables you to keep templates, standards, and project information separate and isolated.
- You can support different departments within your group. If you have multiple teams that work on separate projects and do not need to share data, multiple vaults might help.

Disadvantage of Using Multiple Vaults

The most important thing to remember when working with multiple vaults is that the data is completely separate and can never be merged. The only way to combine two or more vaults is to remove data from one vault and manually add it to the other, resolving any conflicts that might occur.

Sharing Vault Projects

Vault projects can be packaged and shared with other project team members who do not have access to your vault. Multiple options are available for sharing files. One way is through the **Pack and Go** feature in the Vault Explorer. Another way is by creating a ZIP file through the *Prospector* tab within AutoCAD Civil 3D. With a ZIP file, the project can be imported into another vault. Projects that used Data Shortcuts can also be imported into a vault project. Any broken references are detected and resolved after all drawings have been added to the vault.

Working Folders

When working on a project using Vault, a copy of the file is saved in the working folder. This is where AutoCAD Civil 3D will make changes to the data. When changes and updates are completed, the user has to push the data up to Vault to ensure that Vault has the most current data. This working folder is essentially a scratch pad that is used when working with the files.

You can use one of three workflows, each with its pros and cons, to specify where this scratch pad or working folder exists. The three workflows are *Local Working Folder, Individual Network Working Folder* and *Shared Network Working Folder*.

Local Working Folder: With this workflow, the working folder resides on the local machine. This process allows team members to work offline outside of the network connection. Once changes are completed, the user can connect to the network and push the updated files to Vault. This setup also minimizes network traffic. However, network traffic occurs only when files are checked in or checked out. The disadvantage is that local workstations are seldom on a company backup process. This means that the user must be diligent in ensuring that important data is pushed back up to Vault, as it is on a regular backup plan.

Figure 6–43 illustrates the Local Working Folder workflow.

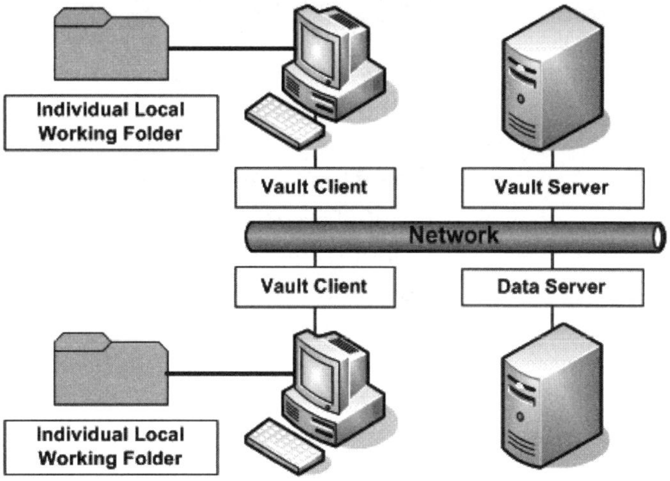

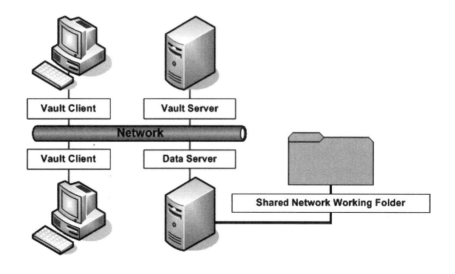

Figure 6–43

Shared Network Working Folder: With this workflow, multiple users share a single working folder on the network. This setup is similar to the current configurations within most companies. Drawing and other data files are saved on a shared network drive. As the shared working folder is on the network, it is also on a regular backup plan. Another benefit to this type of configuration is that drawings with data references or external references are notified and updated every time they are saved, rather than only when they are checked back into the vault, as with the Local Working Folder option. As the working folder is a replication of the project files, accidental changes can occur more easily when users work with files in the same set of folders.

Figure 6–44 illustrates the Shared Network Working Folder workflow.

Figure 6–44

Individual Network Working Folder: This is a hybrid of the two previous configurations. A working folder is set up on the network for each user. By maintaining individual working folders on the server, you protect each user's work-in-progress from changes by other users. Locating these folders on the server allows for nightly backup of the data.

The disadvantage to having individual working folders on the server is the increase in network traffic. Additionally, backups of the user working folders will have a lot more data than you really need, because you may back up multiple copies of the same files in each folder. Vault also contains a master updated copy of all the data. Figure 6–45 illustrates the Individual Network Working Folder workflow.

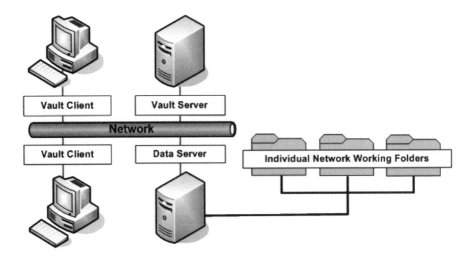

Figure 6–45

6.5 Using the Vault Client

Vault Shortcuts are managed through the Master View in the Prospector tab in the Toolspace under the Projects tree. The shortcuts are stored in the Autodesk Data Management System (ADMS) within a folder structure that you create. This enables you to use the same folder structure that you have been using in Land Desktop or other project-oriented programs.

Status Symbols in Civil 3D Toolspace

Once you have logged into Vault, you see something similar to Figure 6–46. If you are not sure of the status of the files, you can hover your cursor over the icon and AutoCAD Civil 3D will display a tool tip indicating the status of the file.

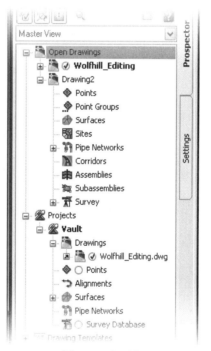

Figure 6–46

Autodesk Vault uses icons to indicate the status of files in the vault. The icons indicate if a file is checked out to another user, if you have a local copy, if your local copy is up to date, and so on. A circular icon always indicates that a local copy of the file is on your computer. The following table describes the icons in the Autodesk Vault browser.

	If no icon is displayed, the drawing is not currently in an vault project.
	File has attachments. Expand to see what files are attached.

(White "I")	One or more referenced objects are out of date and need to be synchronized with the project.
(White Circle)	File is in the vault and available to be checked out. The version in your working folder is the same as in the vault. Also referred to as the Latest Version.
(Green Circle)	File is in the vault and available to be checked out, but the local version is newer than the latest version in the vault. This typically means the local file was changed without checking it out. If you want to save these changes, check the file out with the Get Latest Version option not selected.
(Red Circle)	File is in the vault and available to be checked out, but the local copy is out of date. Get the latest version from the vault.
(White Circle)	File is checked out to you and the local version is the same as in the vault. Also referred to as the Latest Version.
(Green Circle)	File is checked out to you and the local copy is newer than the latest version in the vault. This typically means that you made changes to the file since it was checked out but have not checked it back in.
(Red Circle)	File is checked out to you and the local copy is older than the latest version in the vault. This typically means that you started with a version that was older than the latest version, and then checked it out to promote it to the latest.
No Icon	File is not present in the vault and needs to be added.
(White Circle)	File is checked out by someone else and the local copy is the same as in the vault. Also referred to as the Latest Version. This typically happens if the other user did not check changes back into the vault.
(Green Circle)	File is checked out to someone else, but the local copy is newer than the latest version in the vault. This typically happens if the other user checked changes into the vault, but kept the file checked out.
(Red Circle)	File is checked out to someone else, but the local copy is older than the latest version in the vault.

Vault Workflow

1. In the Master view of the Prospector tab, right-click on *Projects* and select **Set the Working Folder...**.

2. In the *Prospector* tab, right-click on *Projects* and select **Log-In to Vault**. Click **Log In** if a second screen is displayed. Type your user name and password and set the *Server* and *Database*, as shown in Figure 6–47.

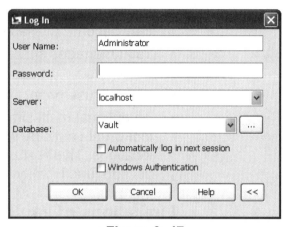

Figure 6–47

3. In the *Prospector* tab, right-click on *Projects* again and select **New...** to create a new project.

4. Create or import the data you want to share in the source drawing and save it in the current working folder under the correct project folder.

5. In the *Prospector* tab, right-click on the drawing name and select **Add to Project**.

6. Select all of the items you want to share, such as surfaces, alignments, or profiles, and click ⌷ OK ⌷.

7. Save the source drawing (and close as needed).

8. Open or create the drawing to receive the data in the vault. Expand the Project tree and relevant object trees (*Surfaces, Alignments, Pipe Networks,* or *View Frame Groups*).

9. Select an item to be referenced, right-click, and select **Create Reference...**. Repeat for all objects as needed. You are prompted for the styles and other settings that are required to display the object in the current drawing.

10. You might also want to add an XREF to the source drawing if you want to show additional AutoCAD linework in the downstream drawing.

Advantages of Vault

- This robust database management system provides user security, data integrity protection, version control, and backup and restore functionality.
- Vault facilitates design collaboration among large teams and it is scalable when a team grows.
- Vault incorporates new features from Autodesk and Microsoft as they become available with software upgrades.
- Vault manages shared objects when checking a drawing into the database.
- You can use project templates when creating projects in Vault.
- An optional multi-site Vault feature supports the sharing of individual vaults by workgroups in separate geographical locations. This feature supports the same data management and backup functionality that Vault provides on a local network.

Limitations of Vault

- Vault requires at least double the disk space needed by other project management systems, because all files exist both in the Vault file store and in one or more external working folders.
- It requires ongoing server administration activities.

Practice 6d | Vault Client

In this practice you will begin by logging into the vault client.

Task 1: Log into the Vault Client.

---

1. Create a new drawing, as shown in Figure 6–48, using the **C3D Training.dwt** template from the following folder:

   C:\Civil 3D Projects\Civil3D-training\Drawings

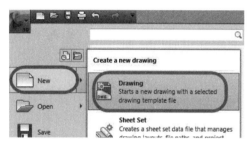

Figure 6–48

2. In the *Prospector* tab, select **Projects**, right-click, and select **Log In to Vault**, as shown in Figure 6–49.

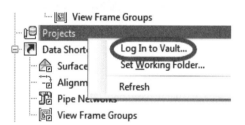

Figure 6–49

3. On the *Welcome* screen, click Log In , as shown in Figure 6–50. If you do not get this screen, skip this step.

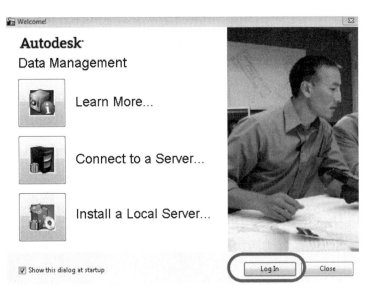

Figure 6–50

4. If you are logging into a training vault server, enter the information provided to you by the instructor. If you are logging into a local vault, enter **Administrator** for the *User Name*. There is no password. The *Server* is **localhost** and the *Database* is **Vault**, as shown in Figure 6–51.

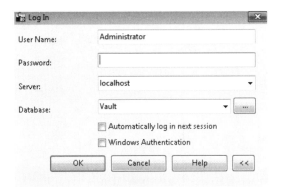

Figure 6–51

5. At the Command Line, you will see the following message: *User 'Administrator' has successfully logged into the Vault.*

Practice 6e	# Setting up the Vault - Part I

In this practice you will learn the steps of creating project-based data Vault folders.

Task 1: Set up the Vault Working folder.

By setting a new working folder, you are setting the location to store Vault projects. The default working folder for Vault projects is *C:\Civil 3D Projects*.

1. Create a new drawing, as shown in Figure 6–52, using the **C3D Training.dwt** template from the following folder:

   C:\Civil 3D Projects\Civil3D-training\Drawings

Figure 6–52

2. In the *Prospector* tab, right-click on *Projects* and select **Set Working Folder...**, as shown in Figure 6–53.

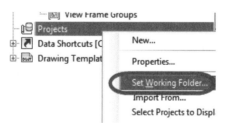

Figure 6–53

3. In the Browse For Folder dialog box, select the **Civil 3D Projects** folder and click Make New Folder , as shown on the left in Figure 6–54. Enter Training Vault as the folder name and click OK , as shown on the right, to close the dialog box.

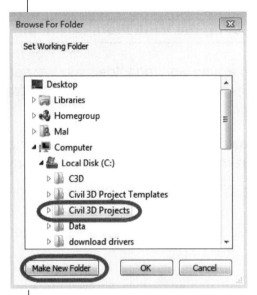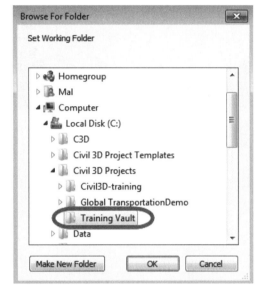

Figure 6–54

Task 2: Set up new vault project folders.

In this task you will create two new folders for storing a set of related project drawings and Vault references. Create a folder name that reflects the project name, and specify whether or not to use a project template to organize your data.

1. Continue working with the drawing from the previous task.

2. In the *Prospector* tab, right-click on *Projects* and select **New...**, as shown in Figure 6–55.

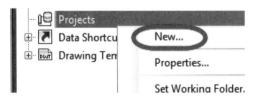

Figure 6–55

3. In the New Project dialog box, set the *Name* to **Ascent Phase 1** and select the **Use project template** option, as shown in Figure 6–56. The template is in the default folder *C:\Civil 3D Templates*. Civil 3D will replicate this template folder structure in the Vault project folder. Click [OK] to close the dialog box.

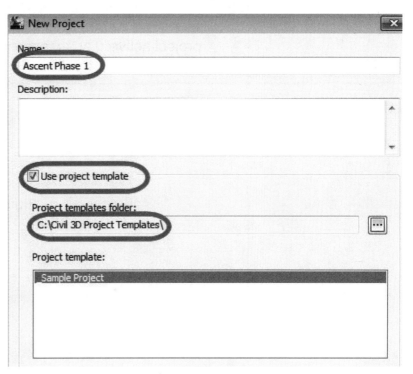

Figure 6–56

4. Create another new Project. In the *Prospector* tab, right-click on *Projects* and select **New**.

5. In the New Project dialog box, set the *Name* to **Ascent Phase 2** and select the **Use project template** option. Click [OK] to close the dialog box.

6. You now have two projects in the working folder, as shown in Figure 6–57, as well as in the vault.

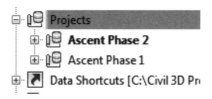

Figure 6–57

Task 3: Set the active project.

In this task you will set the active project for vault.

1. Continue working with the drawing from the previous task.

2. In the *Prospector* tab, right-click on project *Ascent Phase 1* and select **Set Active**, as shown in Figure 6–58. This makes the project active. The active project will be in bold lettering.

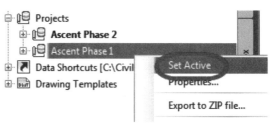

Figure 6–58

Practice 6f

Working with Vault - Part II

In this practice you will walk through steps of creating a project-based Vault workflow.

Task 1: Set up Vault project.

Set a new working folder as the location to store Vault projects. The default working folder for Vault projects is *C:\Civil 3D Projects*.

1. Open the file **DAT1-DataSharing-surface.dwg** from the following folder:

   C:\Civil 3D Projects\Civil3D-training\Training Vault Drawing

2. If not already logged in, log into the vault server (see *Vault Client - Task 1 - Logging into Vault*).

3. If not already set, set the working folder. In the *Prospector* tab, select **Project**, right-click, and select **Set Working Folder**. Set the working folder to *C:\Civil 3D Projects\Training Vault*.

4. If the **Ascent Phase 1** project is not already active, set it as the active project. In the *Prospector* tab, expand the *Projects* collection, select the project **Ascent Phase 1**, right-click, and select **Set active**.

Task 2: Check data into the Vault.

1. Continue working with the drawing from the previous task or open the file **DAT1-DataSharing-surface.dwg** from the following folder:

   C:\Civil 3D Projects\Civil3D-training\Training Vault Drawing

2. In the *Prospector* tab, you will notice the **?** symbol, which indicates that this drawing has not been checked into the vault. Select the drawing, right-click, and select **Check in**, as shown in Figure 6–59.

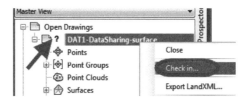

Figure 6–59

3. In the Add To Project dialog box, select **Ascent Phase 1**, as shown in Figure 6–60, and click 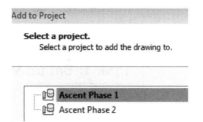 .

Figure 6–60

4. On the *Select a drawing location* screen, select the **Production Drawings** folder, as shown in Figure 6–61, and click Next > .

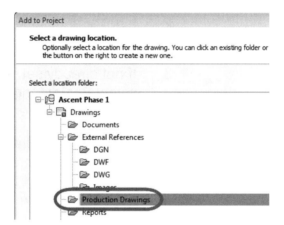

Figure 6–61

5. On the *Drawing file dependencies* screen, clear the **Keep files checked out** option, since you want to close this drawing as soon as you check it into the vault. Set the *DWF publishing options* to **Do not create**, as shown in Figure 6–62. In the *Project Files* section, select all of the files and click <u>Next ></u> .

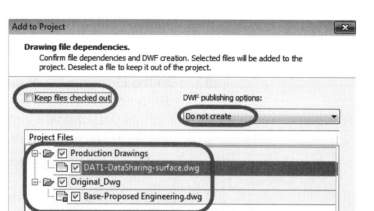

Figure 6–62

6. On the *Share data* screen, select all of the listed surfaces, as shown in Figure 6–63, so that all surfaces are accessible to the project team. Click <u>Finish</u> to complete the process and close the dialog box.

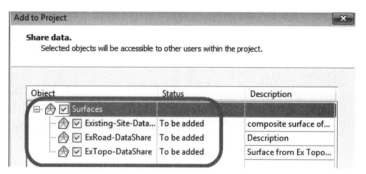

Figure 6–63

7. A number of things have happened. The drawing has been checked into the vault using the appropriate folder structure, surfaces have been checked into the vault, and you have exited the drawing.

8. Open the file **DAT1-DataSharing-Alignment.dwg** from the following folder:

   C:\Civil 3D Projects\Civil3D-training\Training Vault Drawing

9. As in steps 2 through 7 above, you will check in this drawing as well as the alignments.

10. In the *Prospector* tab, notice the **?** symbol, which indicates that this drawing has not been checked into the vault. Select the drawing, right-click, and select the **Check in**.

11. In the Add To Project dialog box, select **Ascent Phase 1** and click Next >.

12. On the *Select a drawing location* screen, select **Production Drawings** and click Next >.

13. On the *Drawing file dependencies* screen, clear the **Keep files checked out** option, since you want to close this drawing as soon as you check it into the Vault. Set the *DWF publishing options* to **Do not create**. In the *Project Files* section, select all of the files and click Next >.

14. On the *Share data* screen, select all of the listed alignments so that all alignments are accessible to the project team. Click Finish to complete the process and close the dialog box.

Task 3: Check data out of the Vault.

---

1. This session assumes that you have completed *Task 1 - Set up Vault Project* and *Task 2 - Check data into the Vault*.

2. Open the file **DAT1-DataSharing.dwg** from the following folder:

   C:\Civil 3D Projects\Civil3D-training\Training Vault Drawing

3. In the *Prospector* tab, expand the *Projects* collection, expand the *Ascent Phase 1* collection, and expand the *Alignments and Surfaces* collections, as shown in Figure 6–64.

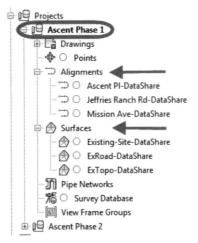

Figure 6–64

4. Under the *Surfaces* collection, the ○ symbol (hollow circle) indicates that the surface is available to be checked out. Right-click on the surface *Existing-Site-DataShare* and select **Create Reference...**, as shown in Figure 6–65.

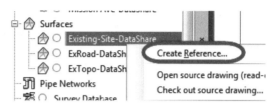

Figure 6–65

5. In the Create Surface Reference dialog box, you can give the reference surface a different name and assign a different style. Enter **ExSurface** for the *Name*, enter **Vault Data referenced surface** for the *Description*, and enter **Contours 5m and 25m (Background)** for the *Style*, as shown in Figure 6–66. Click

   [OK] to close the dialog box.

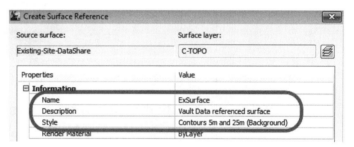

Figure 6–66

6. In this step, you will create a data reference to the alignment. In the Alignments collection, right-click on *Ascent PI-DataShare* and select **Create Reference...**.

7. In the Create Alignment Reference dialog box, accept the default value in the *Name* field. Enter **Data referenced alignment** for the *Description*. Set the *Alignment style* to **Layout**, and set the *Alignment label set* to **Major and Minor only**, as shown in Figure 6–67. Click [OK] when you are finished.

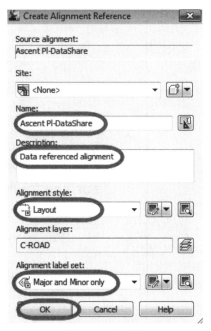

Figure 6–67

8. In the *View* tab > Views panel, select the preset view **C3D-DataSharing-Alignment**, as shown in Figure 6–68.

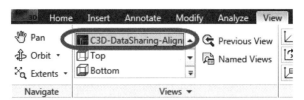

Figure 6–68

9. In Model Space, select the **Ascent PI** referenced alignment. Notice that there are no grips. You are not able to geographically redefine this alignment. However, you can add labels in the contextual Ribbon.

10. In the contextual Ribbon > Labels & Tables panel, select **Add Labels > Station/Offset - Fixed Point**, as shown in Figure 6–69.

Figure 6–69

11. When prompted to select a point, select the center of the bulb of the cul-de-sac, as shown on the left in Figure 6–70. Select the label and move its location so that it is easier to read, as shown on the right. Note the station value is 0+212.96.

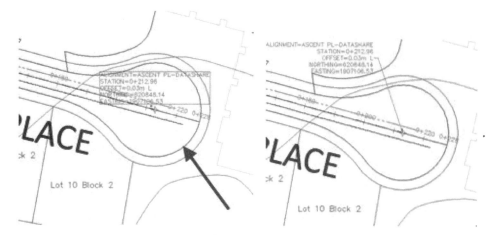

Figure 6–70

12. In the *Prospector* tab, expand the *Surfaces* collection, and expand the *ExSurface* collection, as shown on the left in Figure 6–71. Notice that it does not contain the definition collection that you might otherwise see in a surface that is not data-referenced, as shown on the right. This means that you are not able to edit or make design changes to a referenced surface.

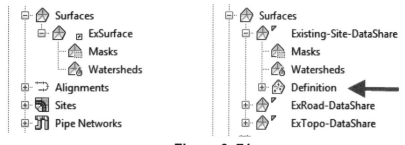

Figure 6–71

13. You can check this drawing back into the vault (see *Task 2 - Check in data into Vault, steps 2-7*). If you do check the drawing back into the vault, remember to keep the drawing checked out.

14. Alternatively, you can save the drawing, but do not close it.

Task 4: Revise original referenced object.

In this task, you continue from the previous session and make edits to the alignment. If you closed the drawing, you will first have to check out the drawing.

1. In Task 2 - Check data into the Vault, step 8, you opened the drawing **DAT1-DataSharing-Alignment.dwg**. if this drawing is now closed, you will have to open the drawing as described in step 2 below.

2. You can use one of two methods to open the source drawing to make edits to the shared object data. Use either method (a) or method (b), but not both.

    *   (a) In the *Prospector* tab, under the project *Ascent Phase 1*, in the *Alignments* collection, select **Ascent PI-DataShare**, right-click, and select **Check out source drawing...**, as shown in Figure 6–72.

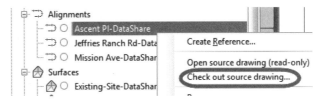

Figure 6–72

    *   (b) In the *Prospector* tab, under the project *Ascent Phase 1*, in the *Drawings* collection, then in the *Production Drawings* collection, select **DAT1-DataSharing-Alignment**, right-click, and select **Check out...**, as shown in Figure 6–73.

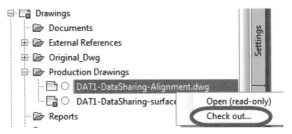

Figure 6–73

3.   In the Check Out Drawing dialog box, select the **Include file dependencies** and **Get latest version** options. In the *Enter version comments* section, enter **Update Alignment start station and end station location**, as shown in Figure 6–74.

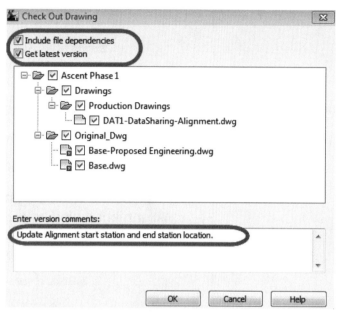

Figure 6–74

4.   In the *View* tab > Views panel, select the preset view **C3D-DataSharing-Alignment**.

5.   You will now change the length of this alignment. In Model Space, select the alignment, then select the grip that signifies the end of the alignment. Move it to the center of the bulb of the cul-de-sac, as shown in Figure 6–75.

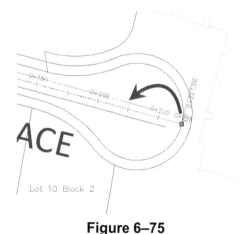

Figure 6–75

6.   In the contextual Ribbon > Modify panel, select **Alignment Properties**, as shown in Figure 6–76.

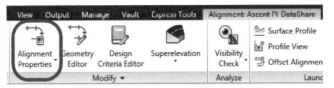

Figure 6–76

7.   In the Alignment Properties - Ascent PI-DataShare dialog box, enter **100** as the reference point in the *Station* field, as shown in Figure 6–77. You receive a warning that changing the station will affect objects and data already created. Click OK to dismiss the warning, and then click OK to close the Alignment dialog box.

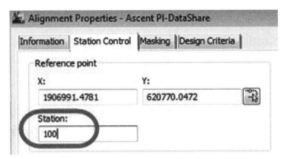

Figure 6–77

8.   Save the drawing. Just saving the drawing does not send the revised data to the vault. When exiting the drawing, you will receive the message: *Do you want to check in your changes?*

9.   The correct way to exit a Vault drawing session is to check in the changes, and then exit the drawing. In the *Prospector* tab, select the drawing **Dat1-DataSharing-Alignment**, right-click, and select **Check in...**, as shown in Figure 6–78.

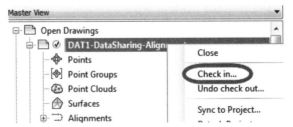

Figure 6–78

10. In the Check In Drawing dialog box, clear the **Keep files checked out** option on the *Drawing file dependencies* screen, as shown in Figure 6–79. You want to close this drawing as soon as you check it into the vault. Set the *DWF publishing options*: to **Do not create**. In the *Project files* section, select all of the files.

    Once you've made the changes, click [Finish].

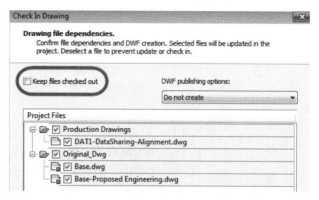

Figure 6–79

11. If you are continuing with the previous session, ensure that the Master view is enabled in the *Prospector* tab of the Toolspace, so that you can see all drawings that are open. Select **Dat1-DataSharing.dwg**, right-click, and select **Switch to**. **Dat1-DataSharing.dwg** is now the current drawing.

12. Near the bottom right corner of the application window, in the *Status* section, you will see a message that data shortcut definitions may have changed. To synchronize your current drawing, select the **Synchronize** link in the balloon message, as shown in Figure 6–80.

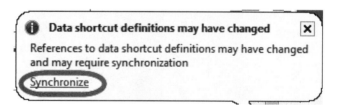

Figure 6–80

13. Alternatively, you can expand the *Alignments* collection in the *Prospector* tab. Select **Ascent PI-DataShare**, right-click, and select the **Synchronize**, as shown in Figure 6–81.

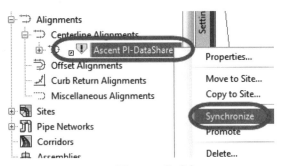

Figure 6–81

14. The alignment has the updated geographic information, as shown in Figure 6–82, with the end of the alignment now at the center of the cul-de-sac bulb. The station label has been updated to reflect this change to the original alignment design.

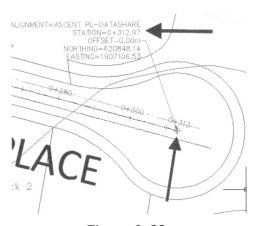

Figure 6–82

15. Save and close the drawing.

Review Questions

Question 1 | What are the two components of Vault?

Question 2 | What are the two types of configurations in Vault Architecture?

Question 3 | What is a working folder?

Question 4 | How many different types of configurations for working folder locations are there, and what are the names of the configurations?

Module 7

Profiles Level 1

This module introduces:

Section 1: Civil 3D Profiles

✓ **Profiles Overview**

✓ **Create Profiles from Surface**

✓ **Create Profile View Wizard**

✓ **Finished Ground Profiles**

✓ **Create and Edit Profiles**

Section 1: Civil 3D Profiles

7.1 Profiles Overview

A profile is the second plane of a roadway design. It is a view of the alignment from one side of the center line showing elevations along the alignment. An AutoCAD Civil 3D profile is a combination of a *profile view* and any number of *profiles* displayed in the view, as shown in Figure 7–1.

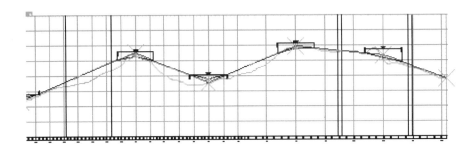

Figure 7–1

- A *profile view* consists of a profile grid and its annotation. The view's vertical lines represent alignment stationing and the horizontal lines represent elevations.
- A *profile* represents a surface or roadway vertical design. A typical road design profile view contains two profiles: the existing ground and a proposed vertical design. The existing ground profile represents elevations along the path of the alignment, usually from a sampled surface. The proposed vertical defines elevations along the path of the proposed roadway. You can have any number of existing and proposed vertical alignments displayed in the same profile view at the same time.

AutoCAD Civil 3D Profiles are managed by:

- **Profile View Properties:** Control settings specific to individual profiles, such as datum elevation and maximum height.
- **Profile View Styles:** Affect how the grid and its annotation are displayed.
- **Profile Styles:** Control how the profile linework is displayed.

- **Bands:** Control optional, additional annotation that can be displayed across the top or bottom of a profile view. Bands are grouped into Band Sets to make it easier to apply multiple, related bands at once. An example of a profile band is the elevation and station data shown in Figure 7–2.

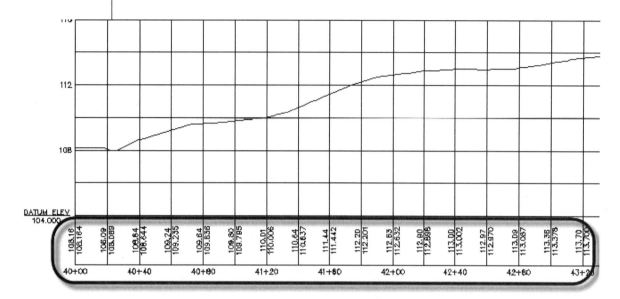

Figure 7–2

Repositioning and Deleting Profile Views

AutoCAD Civil 3D Profile Views are safe to reposition as needed with the AutoCAD **Move** command, and copy with the AutoCAD **Copy** command. They can also be erased with the AutoCAD **Erase** command. Erasing a profile view also erases the design profile grade line that is attached; however, if the profile grade line exists in another profile view, the profile grade line data is saved.

7.2 Create Profiles from Surface

Most profile views display at least one profile based on a surface, such as from an existing ground terrain model. To create a profile from a surface, use the following steps:

1. In the *Home* tab > Create Design panel, select **Profile > Create Surface Profile**.

2. In the Create Profile from Surface dialog box, as shown in Figure 7–3, select the desired alignment and surface (or surfaces if you want to sample more than one).

3. Enter a desired station range.

4. Click **Add>>** to sample each surface based on these settings.

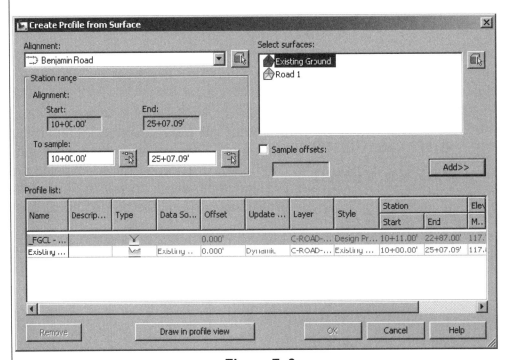

Figure 7–3

This creates a profile along the alignment itself. If you want to sample at an offset from the alignment, select the **Sample Offsets** option, enter an offset value (negative for left), and click **Add>>** . You can sample multiple offsets by entering values one at a time and clicking **Add>>** after each.

There are two ways to exit this dialog box (other than clicking
[Cancel]):

- If you do not have a profile view of this alignment in the drawing,
  click [Draw in profile view]. This launches the Create Profile View
  dialog box.

- If you already have a profile view of this alignment click [OK]
  and any new profiles are added to the existing view. If you clicked
  [OK] accidentally without having a view in which to display
  the profile, go to the *Home* tab > Profile and Section Views panel,
  and select **Profile View > Create Profile View**.

7.3 Create Profile View Wizard

You can create a profile view at any time using the **Profile View >**

Create Profile View command. Clicking Draw in profile view in the Create Profile from Surface dialog box takes you to the same wizard. All of the settings selected in the wizard can be reassigned later through Profile View Properties (except for the alignment they are based on).

The *General* page in the Create Profile View wizard enables you to select the alignment you want to work with and assign the profile view a name, description, view style, and layer. The **Show offset profiles by vertically stacking profile views** option, shown in Figure 7–4, enables you to display offset profiles in a different view from the center line profile without overlapping.

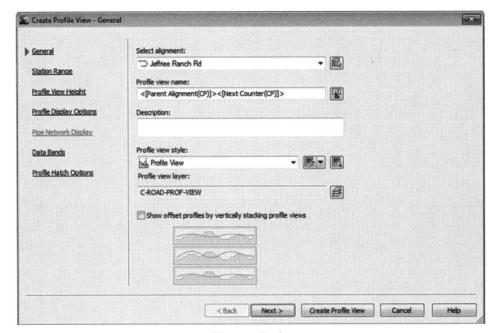

Figure 7–4

The *Station Range* page, as shown in Figure 7–5, enables you to select the station range you want to work with. The **Automatic** option includes the entire alignment's length.

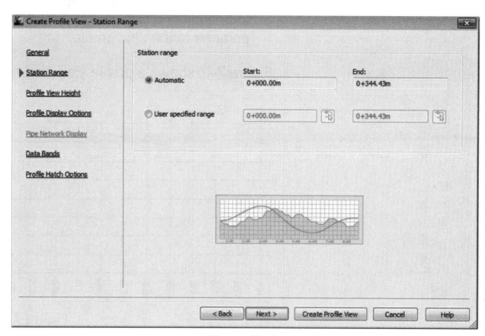

Figure 7–5

The *Profile View Height* page, as shown in Figure 7–6, enables you to select the desired height of the profile grid.

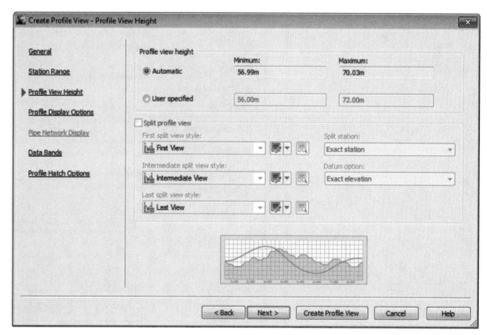

Figure 7–6

- The **Automatic** option creates a profile view that is sized to avoid having to be split.

- The **User Specified** option enables you to assign specific minimum and maximum heights to the profile view. If a profile in one of these views had an elevation below or above the specified values the profile view is split to accommodate it. If a profile needs to be split you can assign different styles to control the different portions of the split profile.

Figure 7–7 shows a profile view that has been split.

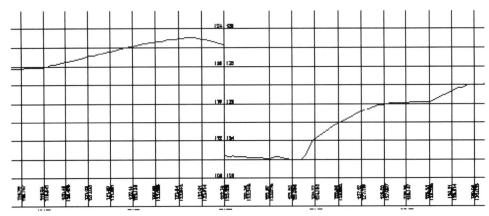

Figure 7–7

The *Stacked Profile* page, as shown in Figure 7–8, enables you to set the number of stacked views, the gap between those views, and the styles for each one.

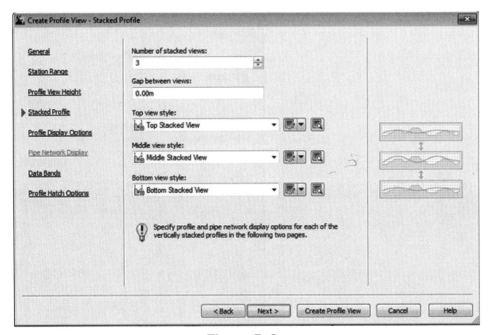

Figure 7–8

The *Profile Display Options* page, as shown in Figure 7–9, enables you to apply specific controls to profiles that are displayed in the views.

Some of the most important options include:

- **Draw:** Disabling this option prevents the profile from being displayed in the view.
- **Style:** Sets the profile style to show in the profile.
- **Labels:** Sets the profile label set to shown in the profile.

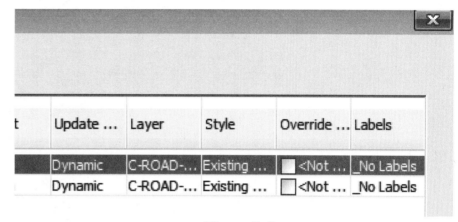

Figure 7–9

The *Data Bands* page, as shown in Figure 7–10, enables you to select the bands you want to include. Bands are additional profile information that can be included along the top or bottom of a profile. Bands are applied in this dialog box by selecting a Band Set.

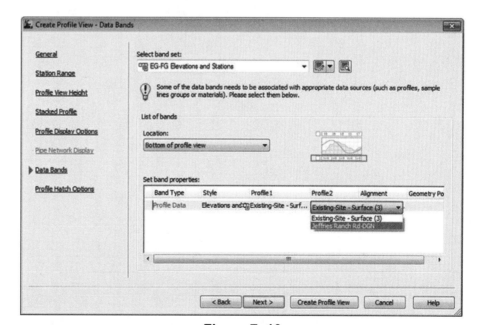

Figure 7–10

Profile Hatch option, as shown in Figure 7–11. You can hatch the profile according to the *Cut Area*, *Fill Area*, *Multiple boundaries*, or *From criteria* that you import. If you select one of these options, the software will allow you to specify the upper and lower boundaries for the hatch area.

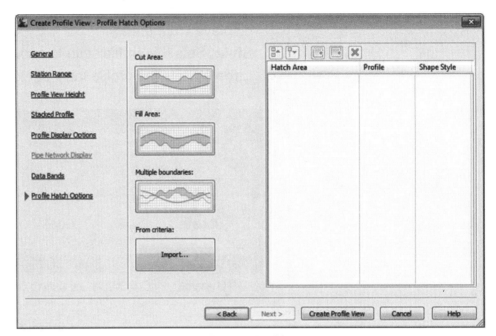

Figure 7–11

When satisfied, click **Create Profile View** to create the profile view. After the profile view is created these settings can be reviewed and adjusted through Profile View Properties. To open this dialog box, select the profile view, right-click and select **Profile View Properties**.

Practice 7a

Working with Profiles Part I

Task 1: Create reference to object data.

1. Open the file **PRF1-Sec1-Profile.dwg** from the following folder:

   C:\Civil 3D Projects\Civil3D-training\Drawings

2. To import the data, you must first ensure that data shortcut paths have been set. If this has not already been done, you will have to set the working folder to point to the data shortcuts.

3. Right-click on the Data shortcuts collection in the Toolspace, *Prospector* tab, and select **Set Working Folder**, as shown on the left in Figure 7–12. Then select the **Civil3D-training** folder.

   Click [OK] to exit and apply the selection.

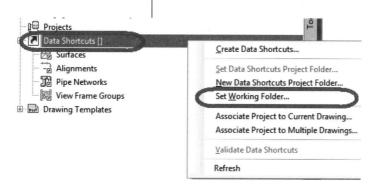
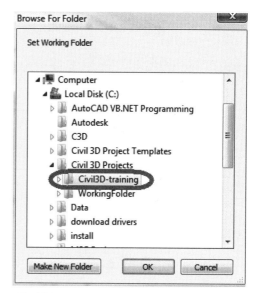

Figure 7–12

The other method is to go to the *Manage* tab > Data Shortcuts panel and select **Working Folder**, as shown in Figure 7–13.

Figure 7–13

4. Right-click on the Data shortcuts collection and select **Data Shortcuts Project Folder**, as shown on the left in Figure 7–14. Select **DataShortCuts** as the project.

Figure 7–14

5. Once you have established the Data shortcuts project, you can reference the data. Expand both the Surface and the Alignment collections by clicking on the "+" sign, as shown in Figure 7–15.

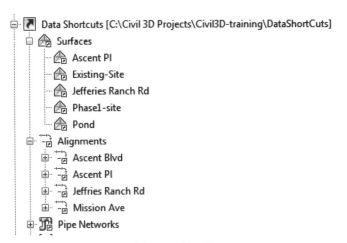

Figure 7–15

6. In the Surfaces collection, select the **Existing-Site** surface, right-click, and select **Create Reference**, as shown on the left in Figure 7–16. In the create Surface Reference dialog box, accept the defaults, as shown on the right. Click ⌐ OK ⌐ to complete the reference to the surface. The surface based on the style selected now appears in the graphics screen.

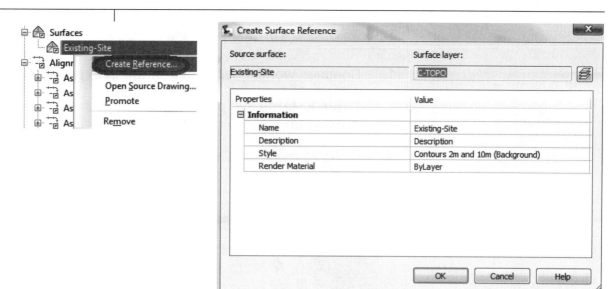

Figure 7–16

7. In the Alignment collection, select the **Ascent Blvd** alignment, right-click, and select **Create Reference**, as shown on the left in Figure 7–17. In the Create Alignment Reference dialog box,

    accept the defaults, as shown on the right. Click [OK] to complete the reference to the alignment. The alignment based on the style selected now appears in the graphics screen.

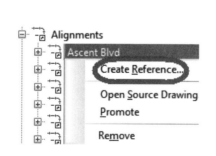

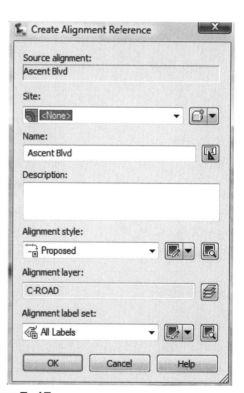

Figure 7–17

8. Repeat step 7 for alignments **Ascent Pl**, **Jeffries Ranch Rd**, and **Mission Blvd**.

Task 2: Create surface profiles.

1. Continue working with the drawing from the previous task

2. **Zoom Extents** and pan the drawing so that you have some open drawing area to the right in which to create profiles.

3. In the *Home* tab > Create Design panel, select **Profile – Create Surface Profile**, as shown in Figure 7–18.

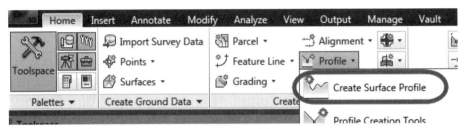

Figure 7–18

4. In the dialog box, select the **Jeffries Ranch Rd** alignment, highlight the **Existing-Site** surface and click [Add>>], as shown in Figure 7–19. This samples an existing ground profile along the center line, the entire length of Jeffries Ranch Rd.

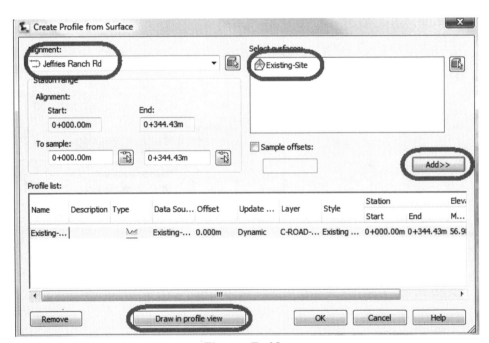

Figure 7–19

Note: If you want to sample the left and right of the center alignment, select the **Sample offsets** option. Enter a positive (+) value to sample the right side and a negative(-) value to sample the left side of the alignment. The information will be added to the Profile list window.

You can also select the **Sample offsets** option and enter all three profile offsets at once, as shown in Figure 7–20. Then set the *Profile Style* as required.

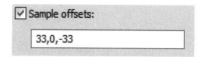

Figure 7–20

5. Click ⬛ Draw in profile view . (If you clicked ⬛ OK instead, select **Profile View > Create Profile View** in the *Home* tab > Profile & Section Views panel).

6. In the Create Profile View wizard, *General* page, confirm **Jeffries Ranch Rd** as the alignment and set the *Profile view style* to **Profile View**, as shown in Figure 7–21, and click ⬛ Next > .

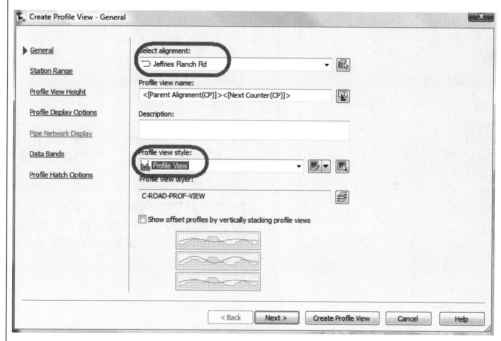

Figure 7–21

7. Accept the defaults on the *Station Range* page and click Next >.

8. Accept the defaults on the *Profile View Height* page and click Next >.

9. Accept the defaults on the *Profile Display Options* page and click Next >.

10. On the *Data Bands* page, accept the default band, ensure that the style is **EG-FG Elevations and Stations**, and click Next >.

11. On the *Profile Hatch Options* page, accept the default of no hatching and click Create Profile View, as shown in Figure 7–22.

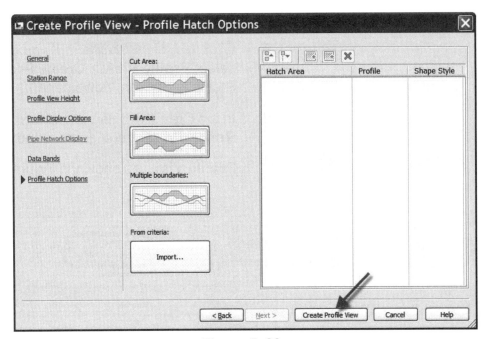

Figure 7–22

12. If the event viewer is visible, close it by clicking the check mark located in the top right corner. When prompted for a location for the profile, click a point to the right of the plan view to define the lower left corner of the Profile View, as shown in Figure 7–23.

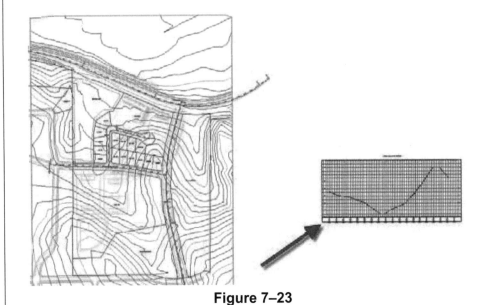

Figure 7–23

13. Repeat steps 3 – 12 for the alignment **Ascent Pl**.

14. Save the drawing.

Task 3: Adjust the Profile View.

1. On occasion, you may be required to modify some of the choices you made in the Create Profile View Wizard—in particular, the datum elevation or grid height.

   Select the **Ascent Pl** profile view, right-click, and select **Profile View Properties**, as shown on the left in Figure 7–24.

   You can also go to the *Prospector* tab and expand *Alignments > Centerline Alignments > Ascent Pl > Profile Views*. Right-click on *Ascent Pl2* and select **Properties**, as shown on the right in Figure 7–24.

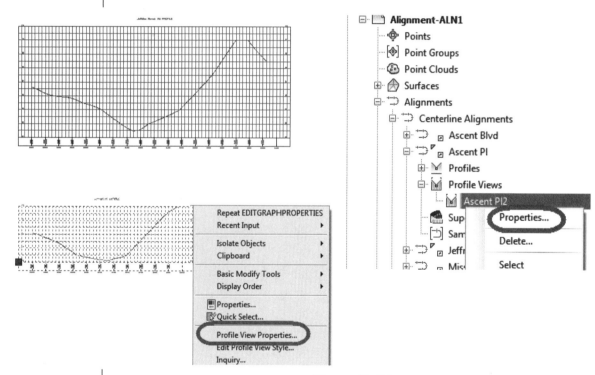

Figure 7–24

2. In the *Elevations* tab, select the **User specified height** option. Enter a *Minimum* of **50** and a *Maximum* of **65**, as shown in Figure 7–25. Click [OK].

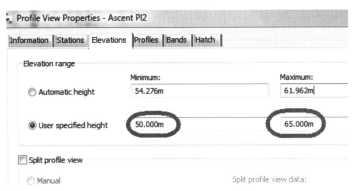

Figure 7–25

3. Save the drawing.

7.4 Finished Ground Profiles

Finished ground profiles (also referred to as proposed profiles or proposed vertical alignments) are often created interactively through the Profile Layout Tools toolbar, as shown in Figure 7–26. This is similar to how alignments are created by layout. The toolbar can be opened by going to the *Home* tab > Create Design panel and selecting **Profile > Profile Creation Tools**.

Figure 7–26

- Vertical curves transition a vehicle from one tangent grade to another and occur in two situations: *Crest* (top of a hill) and *Sag* (valley).

- There are four types of vertical curves to transition between changing the tangent grades of a crest or sag: **Circular**, **Parabolic**, **Asymmetric Parabolic**, and **Best Fit**. Roadways almost always use parabolic (equal length) curves. Asymmetric parabolic curves are usually only used if layout constraints do not permit an equal-length curve. True circular curves are used in some parts of the world for low-speed rail design; generally, they should *never* be used for roadways (which could lead to vehicle vaulting or bottoming out). Best fit curves follow the most likely path through a series of points.

- In the *Settings* tab, Profile heading, the Edit Features Settings sets the default curve type, styles, and command settings.

Most vertical designs have regulations affecting the minimum and maximum values for tangent slopes, distances along tangents between vertical curves, and safety design parameters for passing sight and stopping sight distances. Refer to local design manuals for more information on these design constraints.

The points connecting tangents in a finished ground profile are referred to as a *Point of Vertical Intersection* (PVI).

7.5 Create and Edit Profiles

Similar to the Alignments Layout toolbar, the Profile Layout Tools toolbar contains an overall vista (Profile Grid View) and Profile Layout Parameters (segment data viewer). These vistas enable you to review and edit the vertical design. The settings used when creating a finished ground profile can be selected in the **Draw Tangents** flyout menu of the toolbar, as shown in Figure 7–27. This toolbar is used to edit any kind of profile, including profiles created from surfaces.

Figure 7–27

Other toolbar commands, shown in Figure 7–28, enable you to **Add**, **Delete**, or **Move** individual tangents, PVIs, or vertical curve segments.

- When editing a profile in the layout parameters or grid view, editable parameters appear in black.
- You can graphically edit a design profile using grips. As soon as you select the profile, a new tab appears in the Ribbon that is specific to that profile.

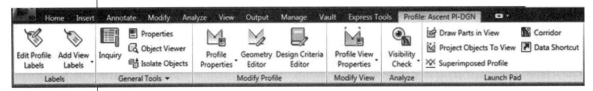

Figure 7–28

- When graphically editing a vertical alignment, the tangents, PVIs, and vertical curves display grips that represent specific editing functions, as shown in Figure 7–29.

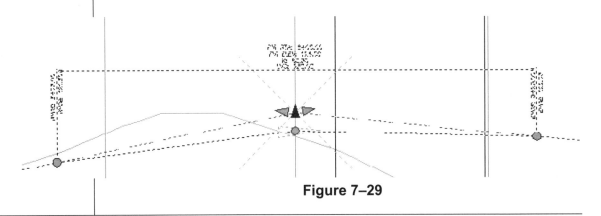

Figure 7–29

- The red triangular grip moves the PVI to a new station and/or elevation.
- The cyan triangles extend the selected tangent, hold its grade, and modify the grade of the opposite tangent to relocate the PVI.
- The middle or end circular grips lengthen or shorten the vertical curve without affecting the location of the PVI.
- When you move the cursor to the original location of the grip, the cursor snaps to that location.

Transparent Commands

AutoCAD Civil 3D has several transparent commands that can be extremely helpful when creating or editing a finished ground profile. They are listed below in the order shown in the Transparent Commands toolbar (from left to right), as shown in Figure 7–30:

Figure 7–30

- **Profile Station from Plan:** When creating or adjusting a PVI, this command enables you to pick a point in plan view next to the base alignment. AutoCAD Civil 3D then calculates the station value automatically and prompts you for the elevation to use at that station.
- **Profile Station and (surface) Elevation from Plan:** This command is similar, except that it enables you to determine elevation from a surface.
- **Profile Station and Elevation from COGO Point:** This command enables you to determine station and elevation values for a PVI based on the location of a point object.
- **Profile Station Elevation:** By default, when adding a PVI you are prompted for a drawing X,Y location. If you would rather enter a station value and elevation, use this command.
- **Profile Grade Station:** This command enables you to locate a PVI based on a grade and an ending station value.
- **Profile Grade Elevation:** This command enables you to locate a PVI based on a grade and an ending elevation value.
- **Profile Grade Length:** This command enables you to locate a PVI based on a grade and tangent length.

Assigning Profile Band Elevations

Profile band elevations are assigned through Profile View Properties, in the *Bands* tab. When you create a profile view, you should review the band settings and make sure each profile band is assigned the correct profile in the *Profile1* and *Profile2* fields, as shown in Figure 7–31. AutoCAD Civil 3D does not make any assumptions about which profile to use in either field.

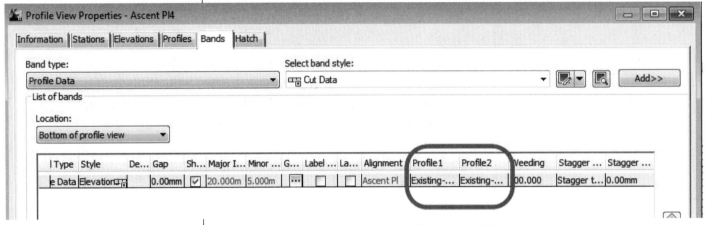

Figure 7–31

Using the styles supplied with the AutoCAD Civil 3D templates, the existing ground surface would be assigned the *Profile1* field, and the finished ground profile would be assigned the *Profile2* field.

Profile Segment Types

Profile segments created by layout (tangent lines, parabolas, and circular curves) can be created as fixed, free, or floating.

Profile Labels

Profiles have dynamic labels that are organized into two categories:

- *Profile* labels include labels for Major and Minor Stations, Horizontal Geometry Points, Profile Grade Breaks, Lines, and Crest and Sag curves. These can be selected when the profile is created and managed later through right-clicking on a profile and selecting **Edit Labels**.

- *Profile View* labels include a Station & Elevation label type and a Depth label type. These are created by going to the *Annotate* tab > Labels & Tables panel and selecting **Add Labels > Profile View > Add Profile View Labels**, as shown in Figure 7–32. They can be removed with the AutoCAD **Erase** command.

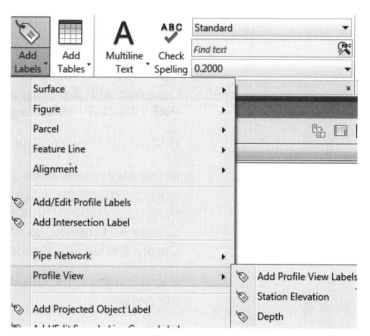

Figure 7–32

Practice 7b

Working with Profiles Part II

Task 1: Gather design criteria.

Before starting any type of design, you need to obtain all of the constraints. In this task, you create a reference to the design grade lines for **Ascent Blvd** and **Mission Ave**.

1. Continue with the previous drawing or open the file **PRF1-Sec2-Profile.dwg** from the following folder:

   C:\Civil 3D Projects\Civil3D-training\Drawings

2. In the Alignments collection under Data Shortcuts, click the "+" sign to expand the Ascent Blvd alignment collection. Expand the Profiles collection, right-click on Ascent Blvd-DGN, and select **Create Reference**, as shown on the left of Figure 7–33. In the Create Profile Reference dialog box, accept the defaults, as shown on the right. Click ▭ OK ▭ to complete the reference to the profile.

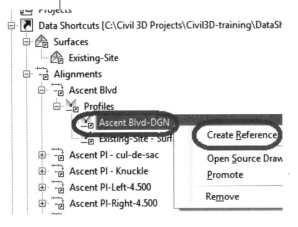

Figure 7–33

3. Repeat the previous step for the **Mission Ave** alignment, **Mission Ave-DGN** profile.

4. To create profile view, in the *Home* tab > Create Design panel, select **Profile > Create Surface Profile** to create the profile view.

5. In the dialog box, select the **Ascent Blvd** alignment. Note that the design grade for this alignment is already in the profile list, but you still need to include the Existing-Site profile data in this profile view. Highlight the **Existing-Site** surface and click

   Add>> , as shown in Figure 7–34.

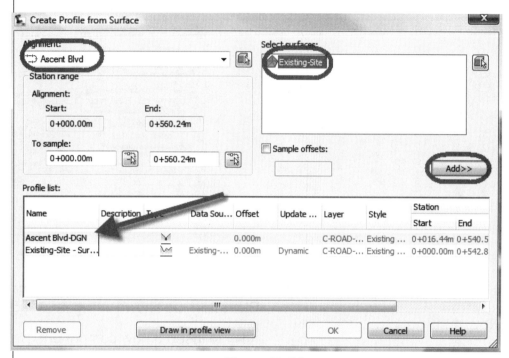

Figure 7–34

6. Complete the steps to create the profile view and to insert it into the graphic view (refer to Working with Profiles Part 1 in the previous exercise on how to create a profile view).

7. Repeat steps 4-6 for the alignment **Mission Ave**.

8. In these next steps, you will create a style to display the design street elevations at key points.

9. Activate a saved named view. In the contextual Ribbon tab > Views panel, select **Named views** > **C3D-Profile Intersection1** as the active view.

10. In the *Annotate* tab > Labels & Tables panel, select **Add Labels**.

11. In the Add Labels dialog box, set the *Feature* to **Alignment**, the *Label type* to **Station Offset – Fixed Point**, and the *Station offset label style* to **Station and Offset**. Click the adjacent drop-down arrow and select **Copy current selection**, as shown Figure 7–35.

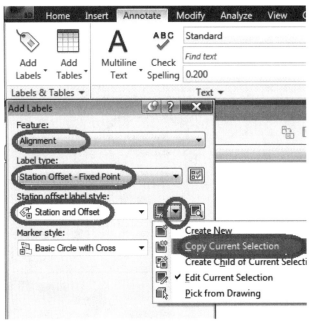

Figure 7–35

12. In the Label Style Composer, set the *Name* to **Station and Elevation**, as shown in Figure 7–36. In the *Layout* tab, click

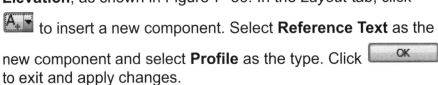 to insert a new component. Select **Reference Text** as the

new component and select **Profile** as the type. Click [OK] to exit and apply changes.

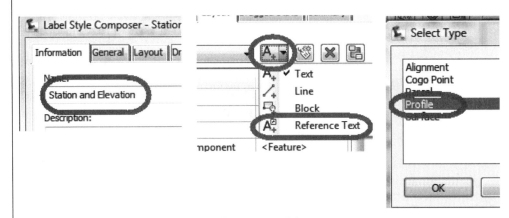

Figure 7–36

13. In the Label Style Composer, change the *Name* to **Elevation** and click ⬚ (ellipsis), as shown in Figure 7–37, to open the text Component Editor.

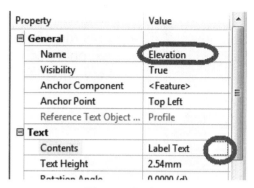

Figure 7–37

14. In the Text Component Editor, select the **Label Text** in the window on the right and change it to **Elev=**.

In the window on the left, click the drop-down arrow and select **Profile Elevation**, as indicated in Figure 7–38. Click the arrow icon, as indicated in Figure 7–38, to paste the code in the window on the right. Click ⟦ OK ⟧ twice to close the Text Component Editor and the Label Style Composer.

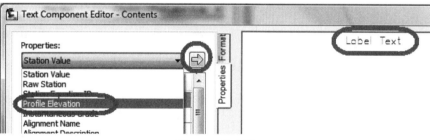

Figure 7–38

15. With the Add Labels dialog box still open, click [Add]. When prompted to select an alignment, select **Ascent Boulevard**. When prompted to select a point, select the intersection point of the two alignments **Ascent Blvd** and **Jeffries Ranch Rd**, as shown on the left in Figure 7–39. When prompted for the profile, press the <Spacebar> and select **Ascent Blvd-DGN**. For the next point, select the property line adjacent to the cul-de-sac, as shown on the right in Figure 7–39.

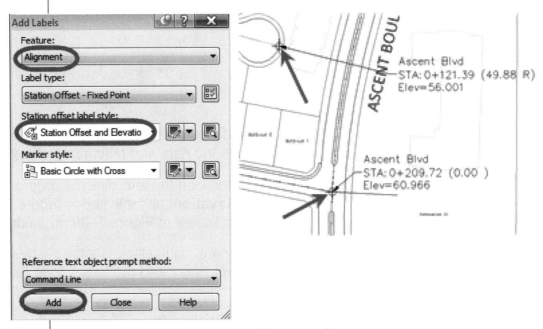

Figure 7–39

16. Close the Add Labels dialog box.

17. You now know that the tie in elevation for Jeffries Rd at the east end is 60.966. You also know that based on survey data that the tie in elevation at the west end at sta 0+001.88 is 63.334, with an existing grade of approximately 3.79%. The cul-de-sac will be based on the grade of Jeffries Ranch Rd and an adjacent grade at Ascent Blvd. The low point overflow drainage in the Knuckle will be addressed by an overland gutter to the pond.

Figure 7–40 roughly shows the type of street drainage you want to establish.

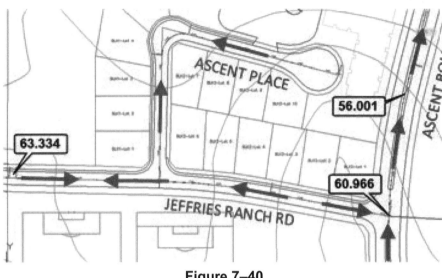

Figure 7–40

Task 2: Create the Finished Ground Profile.

---

1. Continue with the previous drawing.

2. Zoom to the Jeffries Ranch Rd profile view. In the *Home* tab > Create Design panel, select **Profile > Profile Creation Tools**. When prompted to select a profile view, select the **Jeffries Ranch Rd** profile view

   Alternatively, select the **Jeffries Ranch Rd** profile view and in the contextual Ribbon tab > Launch Pad panel, select **Profile Creation Tools**, as shown in Figure 7–41.

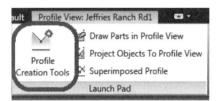

Figure 7–41

3. In the Create Profile dialog box that appears, enter **DGN** for the *Name*, as shown in Figure 7–42. Set the *Profile style* to **Design Profile** and the *Profile label set* to **Complete Label Set**. Then click  .

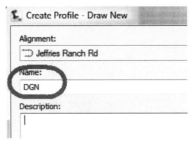

Figure 7–42

4. Locate the Transparent Commands toolbar, as shown in Figure 7–43.

Figure 7–43

5. In the drop-down menu in the Profile Layout Tools toolbar, select **Draw Tangents**, as shown in Figure 7–44. AutoCAD Civil 3D prompts you for a start point, which indicates the location of the road's first PVI.

Figure 7–44

6. In the Transparent Commands toolbar, click 🔡 (Profile Station Elevation).

7. When prompted, select any part of the Jeffries Ranch Rd profile view, enter the starting station of **1.88** <Enter>, and then enter **63.334** <Enter> for the starting elevation. The routine prompts you for another station and elevation value. As you want to enter another method of setting the next point, press <Esc> to exit this transparent command.

8. You want to set the next point based on a grade to a given station, so you will use the transparent command **Profile Grade Station**. Click 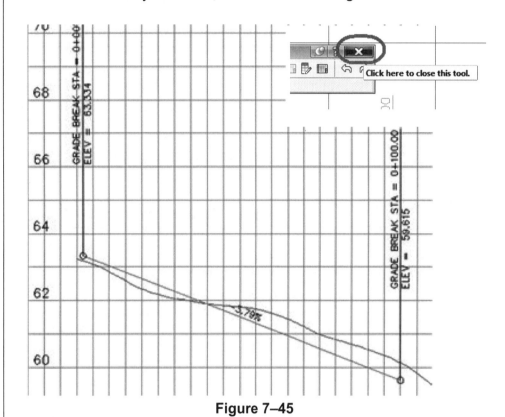 to enter a grade followed by a station. When prompted, enter **-3.79** <Enter> for the slope (to indicate -3.79%) and **100** <Enter> for the station. Press <Esc> to end the transparent command and <Esc> again to end the layout command. The profile is shown on the left in Figure 7–45. Close the Profile Layout Tools, as shown on the right.

Figure 7–45

9. At any time, you can continue to edit a profile by selecting it, right-clicking, and selecting Edit Profile Geometry. In the Jeffries Ranch Rd profile view, select the **DGN** grade line drawn in the previous step, and in the contextual Ribbon tab > Modify Profile panel, select **Geometry Editor** to edit it.

10. To continue adding PVIs, return to the Profile Layout Tools toolbar and click ⊠▾ > **Draw Tangents**. Start by snapping to the end point of the last segment you drew (i.e., sta=0+100.00 elev=59.615).

11. In the Transparent Commands toolbar, click ↗ (Profile Grade Length) and select the **Jeffries Ranch Rd** profile view. Enter **0.8** <Enter> for the slope and **147** <Enter> for the length. Press <Esc> to exit the command.

12. To tie back to the final design point, click 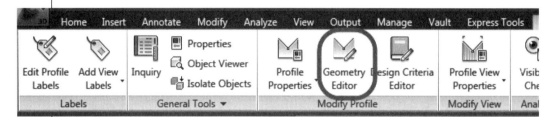 (Profile Station Elevation) in the Transparent Commands toolbar. Enter the end alignment station **of 344.43** <Enter> and the tie in elevation of **60.966** <Enter>.

13. Press <Esc> to exit the transparent command and <Enter> to exit the Draw Tangent command.

14. In the Profile Layout Tools toolbar, click on the **X** to close it.

Task 3: Adjust the FG Profile.

1. Select the **DGN** profile you just drew (Task 2 step 9) and notice the grips that appear. You are able to graphically revise your design by repositioning the PVI through the grips.

2. In the contextual ribbon tab, in the Modify Profile panel, select the **Geometry Editor**, as shown in Figure 7–46.

Figure 7–46

3. The PVIs do not have any vertical curves yet. You will add them to the design using the Free Vertical Curve (Parameter) option, as shown in Figure 7–47. You could have also done this at the initial stage of the design using the Draw Tangent with Curves tool rather than the Draw Tangent tool.

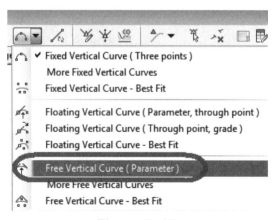

Figure 7–47

4. Click 🔼 ▾ **Free Vertical Curve (Parameter)** and when prompted to select the first entity, select the incoming grade (1) then select the outgoing grade (2), as shown in Figure 7–48. Enter **30** for the length of vertical curve.

5. Do the same for the second vertical curve. Select the entities labeled 3 and 4 in Figure 7–48 and enter **30** for the length of the vertical curve. Press <Enter> to exit the command.

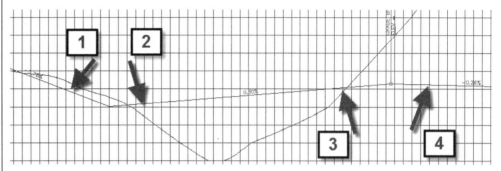

Figure 7–48

6. In the Profile Layout Tools toolbar, click 🖼 (Profile Grid View). The Profile Entities vista should appear in the Panorama.

7. The *Grade In* elevation at the station is -0.18%. This is less than minimum, so you need to change it to 0.8% while maintaining both PVI stations. However, the elevation at sta 0+247.00 will be revised. Select the *Grade In* elevation and change -0.18 to **-0.8**, as shown in Figure 7–49.

No.	PVI Station	PVI Elevation	Grade In	Grade Out
1	0+001.88m	63.334m		-3.79%
2	0+100.00m	59.615m	-3.79%	0.80%
3	0+247.00m	60.791m	0.80%	0.18%
4	0+344.43m	60.966m	0.18%	

Figure 7–49

8. You will change the *Grade In* elevation at sta 0+247.00 to also be 0.80%. Select the *Grade In* elevation and change 1.45 to **0.8**, as shown in. Figure 7–50. This affects the elevation at sta 0+100.

No.	PVI Station	PVI Elevation	Grade In	Grade Out
1	0+001.88m	63.334m		-3.79%
2	0+100.00m	59.615m	-3.79%	1.45%
3	0+247.00m	61.745m	1.45%	-0.80%
4	0+344.43m	60.966m	-0.80%	

Figure 7–50

9. At this point, the as built grade from sta 0+001.88 is no longer 3.79%; however, from a simple calculation you know that if you move the PVI from sta 0+100.00, elevation 60.569 to sta 0+079.26, elevation 60.40, you will be able to preserve the 3.79% grade as well as the 0.8% minimum grade. There are two methods to accomplish this:

Simply edit the station and elevation in the grid view, as shown in Figure 7–51.

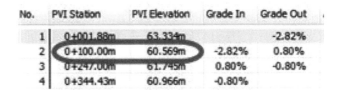

No.	PVI Station	PVI Elevation	Grade In	Grade Out
1	0+001.88m	63.334m		-2.82%
2	0+100.00m	60.569m	-2.82%	0.80%
3	0+247.00m	61.745m	0.80%	-0.80%
4	0+344.43m	60.966m	-0.80%	

Figure 7–51

Alternatively, in the graphics view, move the PVI to a station and elevation. For training proposes, perform the more complex process of the two.

10. In the graphic view, select the **DGN** grade line to display its grips.

11. At the 0+100 PVI station, select the PVI grip for the new location, click ⊞ (Station and Elevation).

12. When prompted for the profile view, select one of the grid lines of the Jeffries Ranch Rd profile view.

13. Enter a sta value of **79.26** <Enter> and an elevation value of **60.40** <Enter>.

14. The grid view should have the values shown in Figure 7–52. Click on the **X** on the Profile Layout Tools toolbar to close both the grid view and the toolbar.

No.	PVI Station	PVI Elevation	Grade In	Grade Out
1	0+001.88m	63.334m		-3.79%
2	0+079.26m	60.400m	-3.79%	0.80%
3	0+247.00m	61.745m	0.80%	-0.80%
4	0+344.43m	60.966m	-0.80%	

Figure 7–52

Task 4: Create a second FG Profile.

In this task, you will create a design grade for Ascent Place. To do this, you first establish the tie in elevation at Jeffries Ranch Rd. Once you have this elevation, you can create the design. Design requirements include PVI at sta 0+115.05 elev 57.07 and a slope of 0.8% to the end station of 0+212.96.

If you are not able to complete this task on your own, use the following steps.

1. Continue with the drawing from the previous task.

2. You need to obtain the tie in elevation at Jeffries Ranch Rd. Activate a saved named view. In the *View* tab > Views panel, select **Named views** and select **C3D-Profile Intersection2** as the active view.

3. In the *Annotate* tab > Labels & Tables panel, select **Add Labels**, as shown on the left in Figure 7–53. In the Add Labels dialog box, set the *Feature* to **Alignment**, the *Label type* to **Station Offset – Fixed Point**, and *Station offset label style* to **Station and Elevation**, as shown on the right in Figure 7–53.

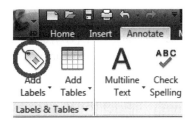
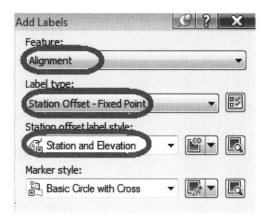

Figure 7–53

4. Click [Add] and when prompted, select the center line intersection of **Jeffries Ranch Rd** and **Ascent Pl**, as shown in Figure 7–54. When prompted for the profile, press the <Spacebar> and select **DGN** as the profile grade. Cllck [OK] to accept the selection.

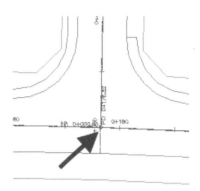

Figure 7–54

5. Press <Enter> to exit the Add label command and click **Close** in the Add labels dialog box.

6. Move the station and elevation label so that there is no clutter. Notice the tie in elevation is 61.180.

7. Zoom into the **Ascent Pl** profile view. In the *Home* tab > Create Design panel, select **Profile > Profile Creation Tools**. When prompted to select a profile view, select the **Ascent Pl** profile view.

   Alternatively, select the **Ascent Pl** profile view and in the contextual Ribbon tab > Launch Pad panel, select **Profile Creation Tools**, as shown in Figure 7–55.

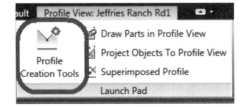

Figure 7–55

8. In the Create Profile dialog box that appears, enter **DGN** for the *Name*, as shown in Figure 7–56. Set the *Profile style* to **Design Profile** and the *Profile label set* to **Complete Label Set**. Then click  .

Figure 7–56

9. Locate the Transparent Commands toolbar, as shown in Figure 7–57.

Figure 7–57

10. In the drop-down menu in the Profile Layout Tools toolbar, select **Curve Settings**, as shown in Figure 7–58.

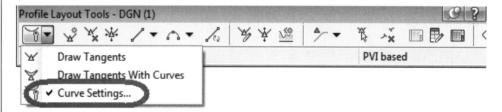

Figure 7–58

11. In the Vertical Curve Settings dialog box, set the curve type to **Parabolic** for both the Crest and Sag curves. Select the **Length** option and enter **30** as the length for both curves. Click

    OK to close dialog box.

12. Click Y ▾ > **Draw Tangent with Curves**.

13. AutoCAD Civil 3D prompts you for a start point, which indicates the location of the road's first PVI. In the Transparent Commands toolbar, click ⊡ (Profile Station Elevation). When prompted for a profile view, select the **Ascent PI** profile view.

14. AutoCAD Civil 3D will prompt for the station and elevation. Enter a starting station of **0** <Enter>, and then enter **61.180** <Enter> for the starting elevation. For the next station, enter **115.05** <Enter> and **57.07** <Enter> for the elevation type. The routine prompts you for another station and elevation value. As you want to enter another method of setting the next point, press <Esc> to exit this transparent command.

15. In the Transparent Commands toolbar, click ⌂ (Profile Grade Station). Enter **0.80** <Enter> for the grade and **212.96** <Enter> for the station.

16. Press <Esc> to exit the transparent command and <Enter> to exit the Profile Draw command. Click on the **X** to close the Profile Layout Tools toolbar.

Task 5: Update profile bands.

The profile views display existing ground elevations in both the existing and proposed slots of the profile bands, as shown in Figure 7–59.

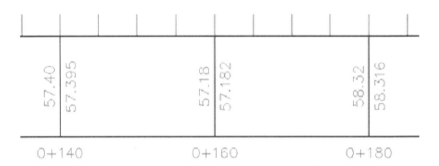

Figure 7–59

1. To update, select the **Jeffries Ranch Rd** profile view, right-click, and select **Profile View Properties**. In the *Bands* tab, assign Profile2 to reference **DGN**, as shown in Figure 7–60. Click OK to close the dialog box.

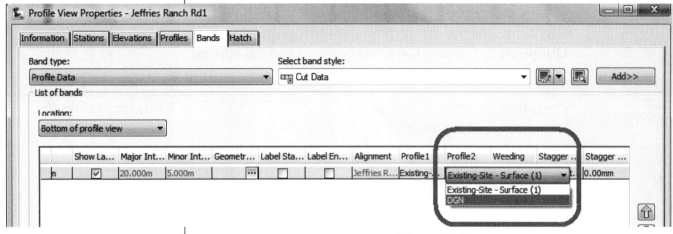

Figure 7–60

2. The profile band now displays the existing ground elevations on the left side and the design elevations on the right side, as shown in Figure 7–61.

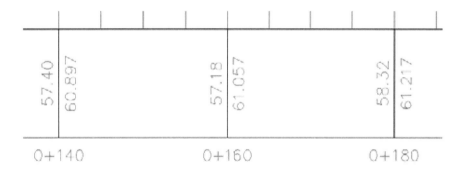

Figure 7–61

3. Save the drawing.

Review Questions

Question 1   Can you safely relocate profile views in AutoCAD Civil 3D using the AutoCAD **Move** command?

Question 2   Name the three types of vertical curves.

Question 3   Which grip do you use to move the PVI to a new station and/or elevation?

Question 4   What do Profiles 1 and 2 annotate in profile bands?

Module 8

Corridors Level 1

This module introduces:

Section 1: Civil 3D Assemblies
- ✓ **Assembly Overview**
- ✓ **Modifying Assemblies**

Section 2: Civil 3D Corridors
- ✓ **Creating a Corridor**
- ✓ **Corridor Properties**
- ✓ **Corridor Surfaces**
- ✓ **Corridor Section Review and Edit**

Section 1: Civil 3D Assemblies

8.1 Assembly Overview

Assemblies

An *assembly* defines the attachment point of a roadway cross-section to the horizontal and vertical alignments. This attachment point occurs at the midpoint of the assembly marker, as shown in Figure 8–1. The 3D progression of the attachment point along the corridor is also sometimes referred to as the *profile grade line*. Assemblies are typically placed at the center line of two-lane crowned roadways.

Figure 8–1

Assemblies can be placed anywhere in a drawing. Assembly styles only affect the display of the marker itself (color, layer, etc.).

Subassemblies

Assemblies are assigned *subassemblies*, which represent individual components of the proposed cross-section (such as lane or curb subassemblies). Subassemblies attach to the left or right side of an assembly's attachment point. When building an assembly, you build from the middle out to the left or right edges.

- The library of stock subassemblies supplied with AutoCAD Civil 3D makes use of a wide array of dynamic parameters (e.g., dimensions like lane width and slope). If these values change, the road model can automatically update. Custom dynamic subassemblies can also be created using the .net programming language.
- You can create static subassemblies (without dynamic parameters) from polylines.
- Each point (vertex) of a subassembly can be assigned a name or *point code* for reference later. A point is a potential location for offset and elevation annotation. It is also a connection point for an adjacent subassembly. For example, points are commonly assigned at edge-of-travelways, back-of-curbs, gutters, etc. Marker styles define the properties for points and their labels.

- Corridors can generate *feature lines* at every location that is assigned a point code. These linear 3D objects can be used as input for surfaces and grading solutions.

- Lines shown in subassemblies are referred to as *links*. A link can be automatically given a slope or grade label in the cross-sections as needed. Links can also be used as surface data. Link styles define the properties of a link and its labels.

- A subassembly *shape* is an area enclosed by links. Shapes are typically assigned material types and can be used to calculate quantities. Shape styles define the display properties of a shape.

- Marker styles, feature line styles, and link and shape styles are all assigned based on a Code Set Style. The Code Set Style assigns the styles to be applied based on the codes assigned to these objects. Code Sets and each of these styles are all configured under the *Multipurpose Styles* collection in the *Settings* tab.

The example in Figure 8–2 shows an assembly containing lane, curb, and daylight subassemblies. This assembly has been assigned to display an offset and elevation marker (point) label at the edge of the lane, a pavement slope (link) label, and shape labels displaying the area of the sub-base.

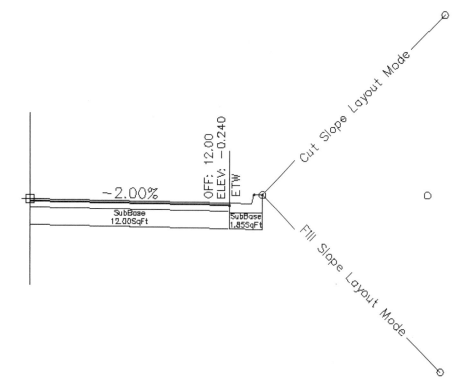

Figure 8–2

- Each subassembly attaches to the assembly connection point or to a point on an adjacent subassembly. OSNAPs are not necessary.

- You should assign each assembly, and the subassemblies that comprise it, a logical, unique name after creation.
- AutoCAD Civil 3D Help contains extensive documentation for each subassembly.

The *Prospector* tab lists each assembly and subassembly, but does not explain how they are grouped together, as shown in Figure 8–3.

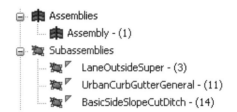

Figure 8–3

To review their interconnections and parameters, select the assembly, right-click, and select **Assembly Properties**. The Assembly Properties dialog box appears as shown in Figure 8–4.

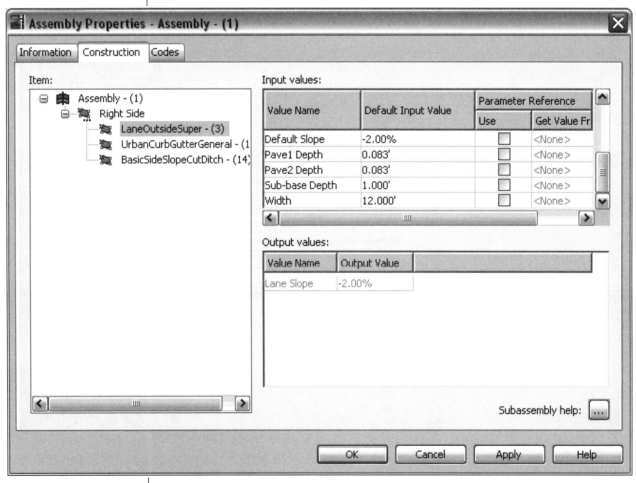

Figure 8–4

8.2 Modifying Assemblies

Attaching Subassemblies

The easiest way to add an AutoCAD Civil 3D subassembly to an assembly is through the Tool Palettes. You can open the Tool Palettes using the  icon in the *View* tab > Palettes panel, as shown in Figure 8–5, or the *Home* tab > Palettes panel. You can also use the keyboard shortcut <Ctrl> + <3>.

Figure 8–5

AutoCAD Civil 3D provides a number of stock subassembly tool palettes, as shown on the left in Figure 8–6. In addition, it is continually updating and adding new subassemblies with every release. The help file is an invaluable resource for an updated list, as well as information in regards to specific attributes and properties of each subassembly, as shown on the right in Figure 8–6.

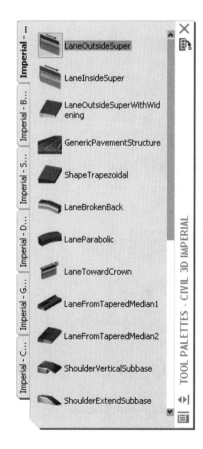
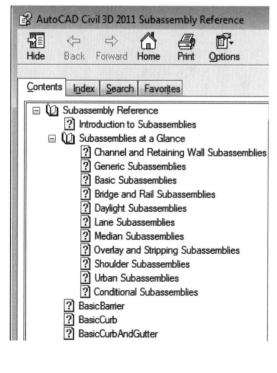

Figure 8–6

Additional subassemblies can be accessed through the Corridor Modeling catalogs. Open the catalog by selecting an assembly or subassembly from the drawing. In the *Assembly/Subassembly* tab > Launch Pad panel, select **Catalog**, as shown in Figure 8–7.

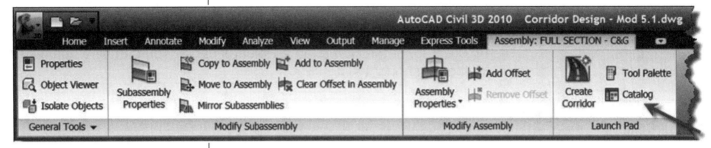

Figure 8–7

You can drag and drop the catalog onto a tool palette, if needed. When working with the tool palettes and Properties palette, you might find it helpful to turn off the **Allow Docking** option to prevent them from docking on the sides of the screen. Right-click on the palette title bar to set the option, as shown in Figure 8–8.

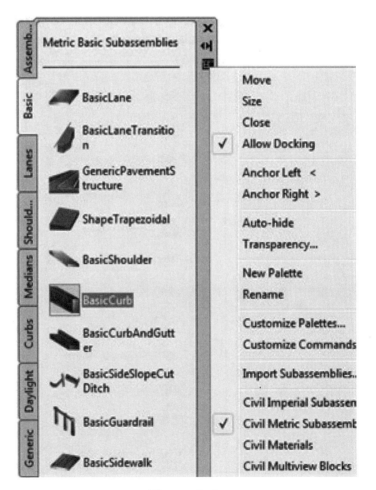

Figure 8–8

Detaching Subassemblies

Individual subassemblies can be deleted directly from an assembly with the AutoCAD **Erase** command or through Assembly Properties. Assemblies can also be deleted with the **Erase** command.

Copying Assemblies

Assemblies can be copied with the AutoCAD **Copy** command. Copying an assembly creates an independent assembly with no relationship to the original. Select the assembly by clicking on the Assembly Baseline.

Mirroring Assemblies

In AutoCAD Civil 3D, assemblies can be mirrored by selecting the subassemblies, right-clicking, and selecting **Mirror**. This enables you to create one side of the roadway and make a duplicate image for the other side in one step.

Sharing Assemblies

Assemblies can be shared with AutoCAD Civil 3D in three ways:

- Assemblies can be dragged from the drawing area to a tool palette. The tool palette can then be shared.
- The Content Browser can be used to add assemblies to a catalog.
- Assemblies can be placed in their own drawing files, and then shared by dragging the assembly drawing into the destination drawing file. If this method is used, the assembly drawing must only contain the assemblies that you want to share.

Getting More Information on Subassemblies

Many subassemblies have a large number of parameters. If you want to read the documentation on a subassembly, right-click on its tool icon in a tool palette and select **Help**. You can also find out more from Subassembly Properties and Assembly Properties using the **Subassembly help** icon, as shown in Figure 8–9.

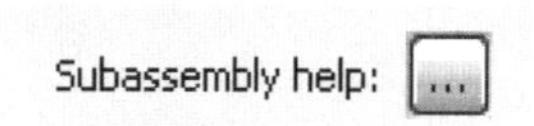

Subassembly help: [...]

Figure 8–9

Practice 8a | Creating Assemblies

In this practice you will create two assemblies: one for Jeffries Ranch Rd, and the second for the existing Mission Ave that contains day lighting.

Task 1: Create the assembly containing daylighting.

A typical x-section of the existing Mission Avenue is shown in Figure 8–10.

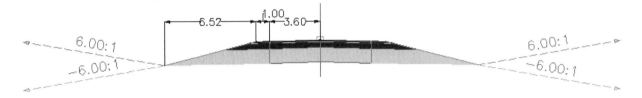

Figure 8–10

1. Open **COR1-Sec1-Corridor.dwg** from the following folder:

   C:\Civil 3D Projects\Civil3D-training\Drawings

2. In the *Home* tab > Create Design panel, select **Assembly > Create Assembly**.

3. In the Create Assembly dialog box, name the new assembly **Ex-Mission**. Leave the other settings at their defaults, as shown in Figure 8–11, and click OK.

Figure 8–11

4. When prompted, locate the assembly baseline to the left of the profile view Mission Ave in the current drawing. Once selected, AutoCAD Civil 3D will change the view to zoom into the assembly baseline location, as shown in Figure 8–12.

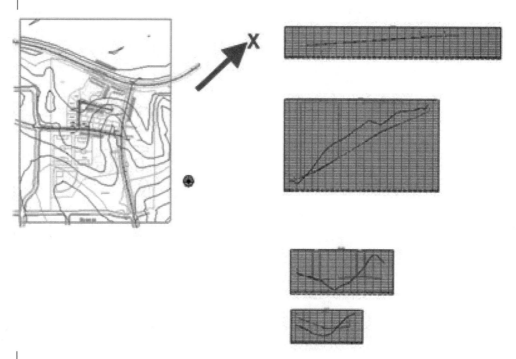

Figure 8–12

5. Open the Tool Palettes window by clicking in the *View* tab > Palettes panel.

6. Ensure that the Civil Metric Subassemblies tool palette is open. This is displayed as a label at the top of the tool palette. To select a different tool palette, right-click in the blank space of the tool palette and select the appropriate one from the list, as shown in Figure 8–13.

Figure 8–13

7. The Help files on subassemblies are a critical source of information in the understanding of AutoCAD Civil 3D stock subassemblies. Right-click on a subassembly in the tool palette, select **Properties**, and click the **Help** button to open the Help file.

8. To close the Help file, click on the **X** to close the Tool Properties dialog box and click OK .

9. In the Lanes tool palette, select the **LaneInsideSuper** subassembly to add it to your assembly, as shown on the right in Figure 8–14. The AutoCAD Properties window appears. The stock subassemblies with "Super" in their names indicate that they can be superelevated, if necessary.

10. Review the parameters shown in the *Advanced* area of the Properties window, as shown on the left in Figure 8–14. Confirm that the *side* is set to **Right**, the *Crown Point on Inside* is set to **Yes,** the *Width* is set to **3.6**, and the *Default Slope* is set to **-2%**. To add the Right lane subassembly, click on the **assembly baseline** object.

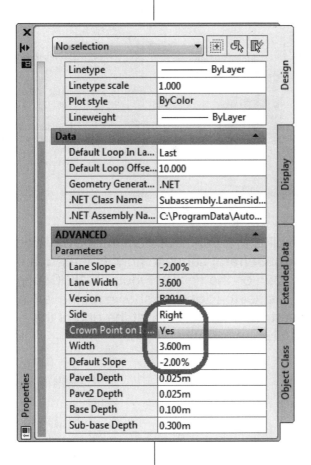
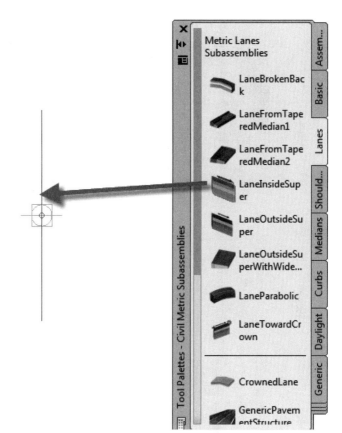

Figure 8–14

11. In the Subassemblies tool palette, select the *Shoulders* tab and select the **ShoulderExtendAll** subassembly, as shown on the right in Figure 8–15. In the Advanced Properties, ensure that the *side* is set to **Right** and the *Shoulder width* is set to **1.00**, as shown on the left in Figure 8–15. Insert the subassembly at the end of the LaneInsideSuper subassembly.

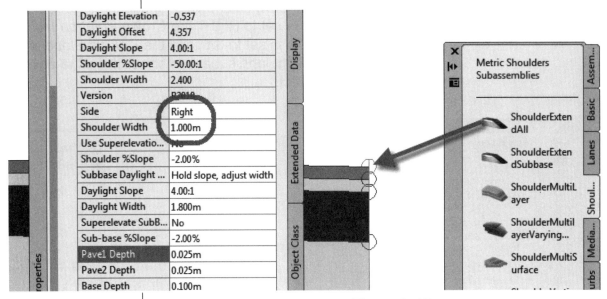

Figure 8–15

12. In the Subassemblies tool palette, select the *Daylighting* tab and select the **DaylightGeneral** subassembly. In the Advanced Properties, as shown on the right in Figure 8–16. Confirm that the *Side* property is set to **Right**, as shown on the left in Figure 8–16. Insert the subassembly at the end of the ShoulderExtendAll subassembly.

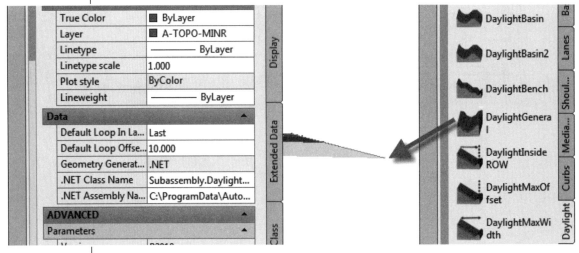

Figure 8–16

13. Select the three subassemblies that you just created on the right side (not the assembly baseline), right-click, and select **Mirror**. At the prompt, *Select marker point within assembly:*, select the assembly baseline (the red vertical line), as shown in Figure 8–17, which represents the road center line.

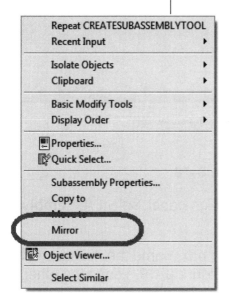

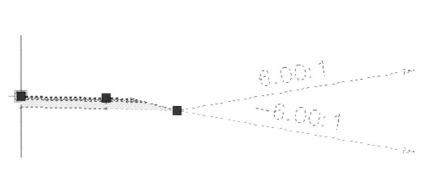

Figure 8–17

14. Save the drawing.

Task 2: Create the Collector Road subassembly.

A typical x-section of Jeffries Ranch Road is shown in Figure 8–18 (See Appendix A for design criterla).

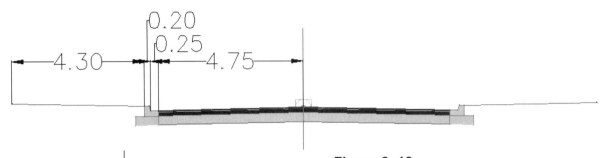

Figure 8–18

1. In the *Home* tab > Create Design panel, select **Assembly > Create Assembly**.

2. In the Create Assembly dialog box, name the new assembly **Collector-Full**, as shown in Figure 8–19. Leave the other settings at their defaults and click [OK].

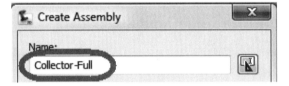

Figure 8–19

3. When prompted, locate the assembly baseline to the left of the profile view of Jeffries Ranch Rd in the current drawing. Once selected, AutoCAD will zoom into the assembly baseline location.

4. In the Lanes tool palette, select the **LaneInsideSuper** subassembly to add it to your assembly.

5. Review the parameters shown in the *Advanced* section of the Properties window. Confirm that the *side* is set to **Right**, the *Crown Point on Inside* is set to **Yes,** the *width* is set to **4.75**, and the *slope* is set to **-2%**. To add the Right lane subassembly, click on the assembly baseline object, as shown in Figure 8–20.

Figure 8–20

6. In the Subassemblies tool palette, select the *Curbs* tab and select the **UrbanCurbGutterGeneral** subassembly. In the Advanced Properties, ensure that the *side* is set to **Right** and *Dimension B* is set to **250**. Insert the subassembly at the end of the LaneInsideSuper subassembly, as shown in Figure 8–21.

Figure 8–21

7. You will now create a subassembly that links the back of curb to property line. In the Subassemblies tool palette, select the *Generic* tab and select the **LinkWidthAndSlope** subassembly. In the Advanced Properties, ensure that the *side parameter* is set to **Right** and the *width* is set to **4.30**. Insert the subassembly at the end of the UrbanCurbGutterGeneral subassembly, as shown in Figure 8–22.

Figure 8–22

8. Select the three sub-assemblies that you just created on the right side (not the assembly baseline), right-click, and select **Mirror**. At the prompt, *select marker point within assembly:*, select the assembly baseline (the red vertical line), as shown in Figure 8–23, which represents the road center line.

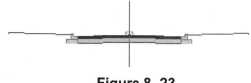

Figure 8–23

Task 3: Create the Residential Road subassembly.

A typical x-section of Ascent Pl Road is shown in Figure 8–24 (See Appendix A for design criteria).

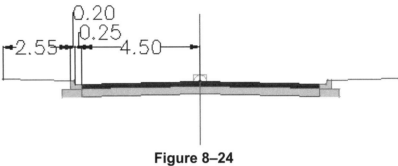

Figure 8–24

1. In the *Home* tab > Create Design panel, select **Assembly > Create Assembly**.

2. In the Create Assembly dialog box, name the new assembly **Residential-Full**. Leave the other settings at their defaults and click OK.

3. Follow the same steps in Task 2, steps 4-9 to create the residential subassembly. For this subassembly, set the pavement LaneInsideSuper *width* to **4.50** and the LinkWidthAndSlope *width* to **2.55**.

Task 4: Copy and modify an assembly.

Copying an assembly can be helpful if you need another, similar assembly for other design purposes. In this task, you will create assemblies appropriate for the intersection area of Jeffries Ranch Rd and Ascent Place.

1. Start the AutoCAD **Copy** command. Copy the **Collector-Full** assembly to a location just below the original, as shown in Figure 8–25.

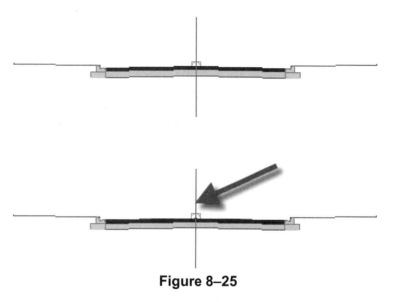

Figure 8–25

2. Select the bottom assembly baseline, right-click, and select **Assembly Properties**.

3. In the *Information* tab, change the *Name* to **Collector - Part Curb RT**.

4. Start the AutoCAD **Erase** command and erase the left **UrbanCurbGutterGeneral** and the left **LinkWidthAndSlope**, as shown in Figure 8–26.

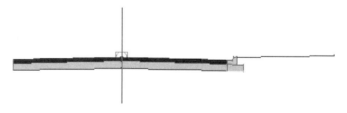

Figure 8–26

Task 5: Create the subassemblies required for the intersection.

In the previous task, you created all the Jeffries Ranch Rd subassemblies that were required for the intersection. In this task, you will create all the required Ascent Place subassemblies.

1. Start the AutoCAD **Copy** command. Copy the **Residential -Full** assembly to two locations below the original, as shown in Figure 8–27.

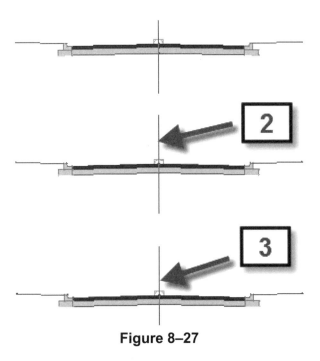

Figure 8–27

2. Select the second assembly baseline, right-click, and select **Assembly Properties**. In the *Information* tab, change the *Name* to **Residential - Half Curb LT**.

3. Start the AutoCAD **Erase** command and erase the right **LaneInsideSuper**, the right **UrbanCurbGutterGeneral**, and the right **LinkWidthAndSlope**.

4. Select the third assembly baseline, right-click, and select **Assembly Properties**. In the *Information* tab, change the *Name* to **Residential - Half Curb RT**.

5. Start the AutoCAD **Erase** command and erase the left **LaneInsideSuper**, the left **UrbanCurbGutterGeneral**, and the left **LinkWidthAndSlope**, as shown in Figure 8–28.

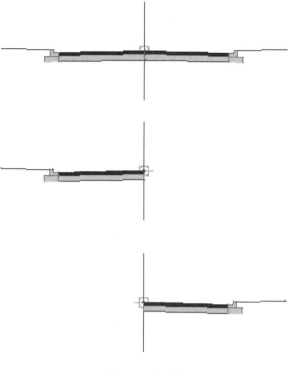

Figure 8–28

Task 6: Create a Curb Return assembly.

To include the intersection in the corridor model, you need another assembly to go around the curb returns This assembly will have the assembly baseline at the edge of pavement or flange of the curb and gutter.

1. In the *Home* tab > Create Design panel, select **Assembly > Create Assembly**.

2. In the Create Assembly dialog box, name the new assembly **Residential - Curb LT**, as shown in Figure 8–29. Leave the

    other settings at their defaults and click ![OK].

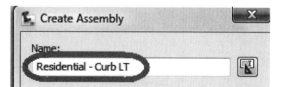

Figure 8–29

3. When prompted, locate the assembly baseline below and to the left of the other three assemblies in the current drawing.

4. In the Curbs tool palette, select the **UrbanCurbGutterGeneral** subassembly to add it to your assembly.

5. Confirm that the *side* is set to **Left** and *Dimensions B* is set to **250**. Select the assembly baseline to add the curb and gutter, as shown in Figure 8–30.

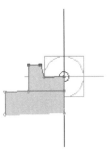

Figure 8–30

6. In the Lanes tool palette, select the **LaneInsideSuper** subassembly to add it to your assembly. Confirm that the *side* is set to **Right**, the *width* is set to **4.5**, and the *slope* is set to **+2%**. To add the Right lane subassembly, click on the assembly baseline object.

Task 7: Create a subassembly to link the back of curb to the property line.

---

1. You will now create a subassembly that links the back of curb to the property line. In the Subassemblies tool palette, select the *Generic* tab and select the **LinkWidthAndSlope** subassembly. In the Advanced Properties, ensure that the *side* is set to **Left** and the *width* is set to **2.55**. Insert the subassembly at the end of the UrbanCurbGutterGeneral subassembly, as shown in Figure 8–31.

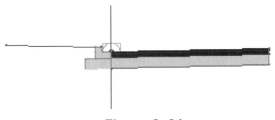

Figure 8–31

To create the left side subassemblies, you will use the AutoCAD **Copy** command and change the subassemblies' properties.

2. Start the AutoCAD **Copy** command. Copy the **Residential - Curb LT** assembly to a location right of the original, as shown in Figure 8–32.

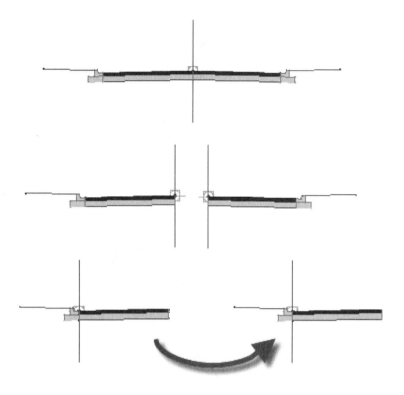

Figure 8–32

3. Select the newly copied assembly. On the contextual Ribbon, in the Modify Assembly panel, click (Assembly Properties), not the label.

4. In the *Information* tab, enter **Residential – Curb RT** for the name, as shown in Figure 8–33.

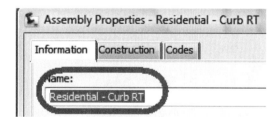

Figure 8–33

5. Select the *Construction* tab. If the groups are not already expanded, expand all the collections by clicking the + (plus) sign. Select **UrbanCurbGutterGeneral** and in the *Input values* pane, change the *Side* to **Right**, as shown in Figure 8–34.

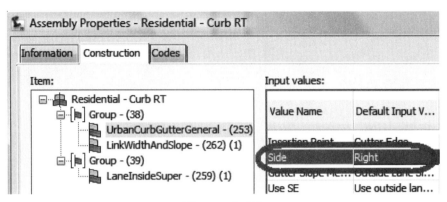

Figure 8–34

6. Select **LinkWidthAndSlope** and in the *Input values* pane, change the *Side* to **Right**.

7. Select **LaneInsideSuper** and in the *Input values* pane, change the *Side* to **Left**.

8. Save the drawing.

Section 2: Civil 3D Corridors

8.3 Creating a Corridor

A corridor is a 3D model of a proposed design based on alignments, profiles, and assemblies. Corridors can be used to create terrain models (such as a finished ground terrain model) and generate section data. Corridors appear as complex drawing objects made up of individual cross-sections, feature lines that connect marker points (locations where point codes are assigned), and other related data, as shown in Figure 8–35.

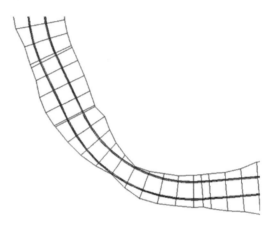

Figure 8–35

Corridors can be used to represent an individual alignment, profile, and assembly (such as for a single road) or can contain multiples of each. When modeling intersections, it is often easiest to have all intersecting roads as part of the same corridor object. However, it might not be practical to include all proposed roads in a single corridor on large projects. You can have any number of corridors present in the same drawing file.

Two commands can be used to create a corridor:

*   For small, fairly simple corridors based on only one alignment, profile, and assembly, **Corridors > Create Simple Corridor** is sufficient.
*   For corridors with more than one of each, consider using **Corridors > Create Corridor** instead.

Both commands create the same kind of corridor object, and all corridors are adjusted similarly through **Corridor Properties**. Corridors created using the **Create Simple** command might have additional data added to them later on.Either method requires you to select at least one alignment, profile, and assembly. A dialog box also appears where you can enter a description, as well as select a corridor style and layer.

Target Mapping

Either method enables you to assign Target Mapping objects. Target Mapping is where you assign a surface to which daylight subassemblies are graded.

Many stock subassemblies also include transitional components, such as the lanes you added to the 2 Lane Road assembly. These lanes are able to have their outside edge-of-pavement (EOP) controlled by other alignments, feature lines, survey figures, and 3D polylines as needed, which can be used to specify widening and contraction of the lanes. These lanes also include profile controls at the EOP points. These types of controls are all assigned through Target Mapping.

In the Target Mapping dialog box shown in Figure 8–36, the subassembly name and assembly groups are listed. Giving these items logical names is important, as you did in previous practices. Otherwise, it would be difficult to tell them apart in this dialog box.

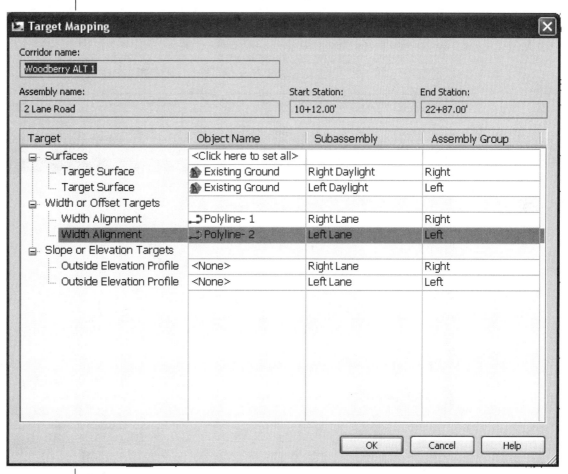

Figure 8–36

8.4 Corridor Properties

Once created, corridors are adjusted in the Corridor Properties dialog box.

Information Tab

The *Information* tab enables you to name the corridor (recommended), add a description, and select a corridor style.

Parameters Tab

The *Parameters* tab enables you to review and adjust corridor parameters, including which alignments, profiles, and assemblies are being used. Each unique road center line is listed here as a *baseline*. Within each baseline is at least one *region*. Each region is an area over which a particular assembly is applied. You can have multiple baselines and multiple regions within the same baseline as needed. The *Parameters* tab is shown in Figure 8–37.

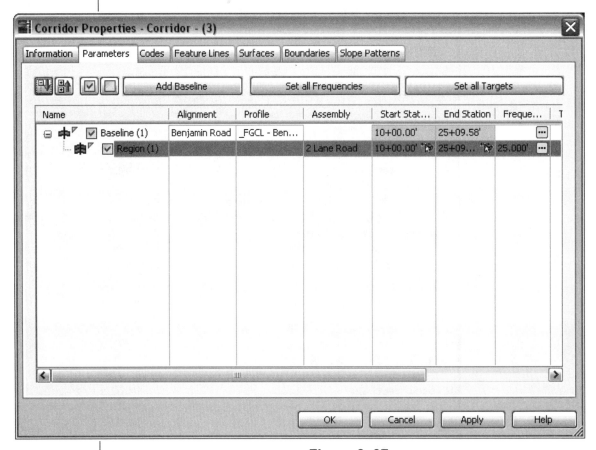

Figure 8–37

Each region has controls that enable you to review the Target Mapping, as well as the *Frequency* at which corridor sections should be created. If the corridor has had overrides applied through the Corridor Section Editor (select the corridor > *Corridor* tab > Modify panel), then those can be reviewed here as well.

At the top of the dialog box are two important icons: **Set all Frequencies** and **Set all Targets**. These commands can be used to assign frequencies and targets to all corridor regions. Otherwise, these properties can be adjusted for individual regions using ⊡ (Ellipsis), which is available in the *Frequency* and *Targets* columns.

Codes

The *Codes* tab lists all codes available in the corridor based on the subassemblies in the assembly, as shown in Figure 8–38. These codes are available for section labels and quantity take-off.

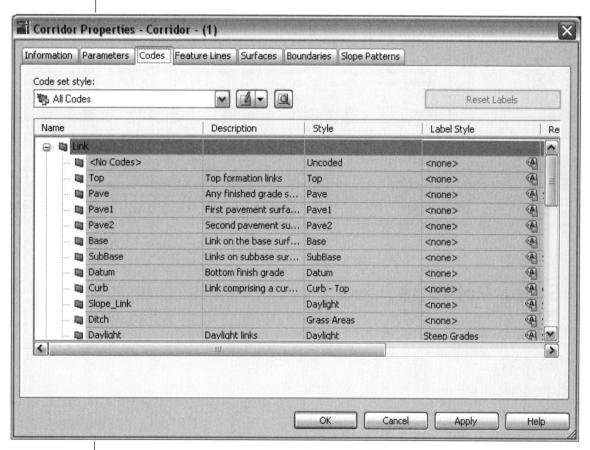

Figure 8–38

Feature Lines

Feature lines are named 3D linework that connect marker points (locations assigned point codes) in your assemblies, as shown in Figure 8–39. From any feature line listed in the *Feature Lines* tab, you can export a polyline or feature line (such as for grading purposes).

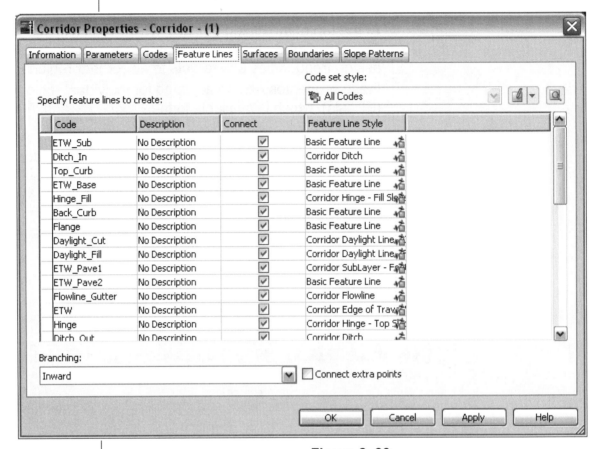

Figure 8–39

Slope Patterns

Slope patterns can be used to indicate if an area of side slope is a cut or fill.

Practice 8b

Working with Corridors Part I

Task 1: Create a simple corridor.

In this task, you will use an assembly to create a simple corridor for Mission Avenue.

1. Open the file **COR1-Sec2-Corridor.dwg** from the following folder:

    C:\Civil 3D Projects\Civil3D-training\Drawings

2. In the *Home* tab > Create Design panel, select **Corridors > Create Simple Corridor**.

3. In the Create Simple Corridor dialog box, enter **Mission Ave** for the name of the corridor, accept the remaining defaults, and click .

4. When prompted for an alignment to use, select the **Mission Ave** alignment in plan view, or press <Enter> and select **Mission Ave** from the list.

5. When prompted for a profile, press <Enter>and select **Mission Ave-DGN** from the list, or select it visually by panning to the profile view and selecting it.

6. When prompted to select a subassembly, press <Enter> and select **Ex Mission Ave** or select it visually from the screen in Model Space.

7. In the Target Mapping dialog box, select **<click here to set all>** and set the target surface for daylighting to the **Existing-Site** surface, as shown in Figure 8–40. Click [OK] to apply the changes.

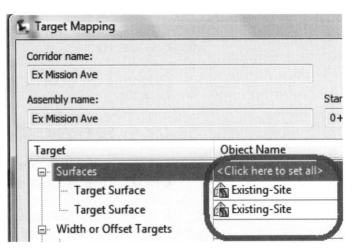

Figure 8–40

The Event viewer displays a number of warnings. All of these warnings address the issue that at the west end, the alignment and corridor extends outside of the surface boundary; as a result, Civil 3D cannot daylight. The other issue is at the east end, where the design profile does not extend the entire length of the horizontal alignment.

8. In the Events viewer, select **Action > Clear All events**, as shown in Figure 8–41. Click on the **X** to close the Events viewer.

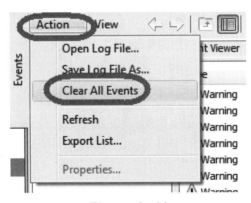

Figure 8–41

9. To fix the warnings, select the corridor and in the contextual Ribbon, in the Modify Corridor panel, start the **Corridor Properties** command, as shown in Figure 8–42.

Figure 8–42

10. In the Corridor Properties dialog box, change the *Start Station* to **51** to match the design ground profile and enter **600** for the *End Station* of the profile alignment. Click ⌷ OK ⌷ to accept the changes. The dialog box is shown in Figure 8–43.

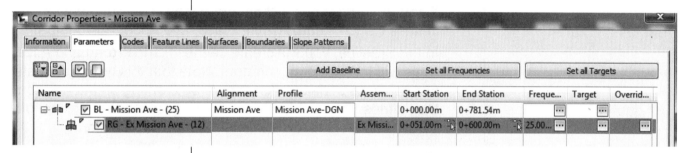

Figure 8–43

Notice that the style for this corridor shows cut areas as red. The fill areas, if any, will be displayed in green. You can experiment with the dynamic capabilities of Civil 3D.

11. In the Mission Ave profile view, select the design grade profile. Use grip edit and make revisions to the grades, or use **Edit Profile Geometry** and edit the grades in the grid view.

12. If Rebuild Automatic is not set you will get the out-of-date symbol (▶ Ex Mission Ave). To set this option, right-click on the Ex Mission Ave Corridor and select **Rebuild Automatic**.

Task 2: Create a corridor with regions.

In this task, you will use the assemblies to create a corridor for both Jeffries Ranch Rd and Ascent Place.

1. In the *Home* tab > Create Design panel, select **Corridors > Create Corridor**.

2. When prompted for an alignment to use, select the **Jeffries Ranch Rd** alignment in plan view, or press <Enter> and select **Jeffries Ranch Rd** from the list.

3. When prompted for a profile, press <Enter> and select **Jeffries Ranch Rd-DGN** from the list, or select it visually by panning to the profile view and selecting it.

4. When prompted to select a subassembly, press <Enter> and select **Collector-Full** or select it visually from the screen in Model Space.

5. Since you selected **Create Corridor** instead of **Create Simple Corridor** as you did in the previous task, the Create Corridor dialog box appears. The options available here are the same as those in the *Parameters* tab of the Corridor Properties dialog box.

   In the *Corridor Name* field, name the corridor **Jeffries Ranch Road**. A corridor can include more than one alignment (such as Jeffries Ranch Road, Ascent Place, and Ascent Blvd, etc.).

   In this practice, you will create Jeffries Ranch Road and Ascent Pl as two independent corridors. Note that this will also create two separate surfaces. As you will be creating an intersection in the Jeffries Ranch Rd, you will have to create two regions: one before the intersection and one after the intersection.

6. The dialog box identifies the Baseline (BL) as *BL-Jeffries Ranch Road*. This baseline currently has one Region (RG). Change the region name to **Before Intersection** and adjust the start stations to **0+001.88**, as shown in Figure 8–44.

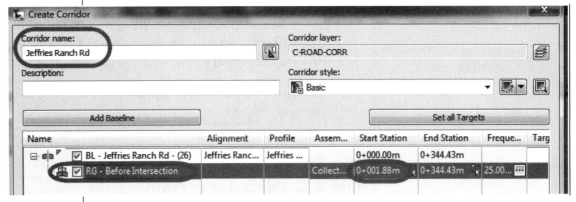

Figure 8–44

7. To split the region for the intersection, right-click on RG-Before Intersection and select **insert region after**. Enter **RG-After Intersection** for the *Region name* and **Collector – Full** for the *Assembly*, and click OK. The Create Corridor Region dialog box is shown in Figure 8–45.

Figure 8–45

8. You now need to enter the start and end stations for the regions. You have already entered **1.88** for the start station for the RG-Before Intersection. Enter the following values, as shown in Figure 8–46.

    *   RG-Before Intersection End station: **160.27**

    *   RG-After Intersection Start station: **192.25**

    *   RG-After Intersection End station: **315.75**

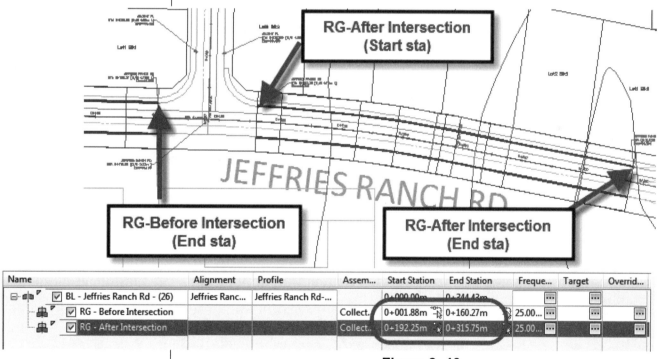

Figure 8–46

9. Save the drawing.

Task 3: Create a corridor.

In this task, you will use the assemblies to create a corridor, applying the Residential-Full subassembly from station to station. The steps to accomplish this are similar to Task 1 in this practice.

1. Continue working with the drawing from the previous task.

2. In the *Home* tab > Create Design panel, select **Corridors > Create Corridor**.

3. When prompted for an alignment to use, you can select the **Ascent PI** alignment in plan view, or press <Enter> and select **Ascent PI** from the list.

4. When prompted for a profile, press <Enter> and select **Ascent PI-DGN** from the list, or select it visually by panning to the profile view and selecting it.

5. When prompted to select a subassembly, press <Enter> and select **Residential-Full** or select it visually from the screen in Model Space.

6. In the Create Corridor dialog box, enter **Ascent PI** as the name of the corridor.

7. The dialog box identifies the Baseline (BL) as *BL-Ascent PI*. This baseline currently has one Region, which is assigned the Residential - Full Assembly. Rename the region to **RG – Start**. Adjust the *Start Station* for **RG-Start** to **0+016.50** and the *End Station* to **0+080.92**, as shown in Figure 8–47.

Name		Alignm...	Profile	Assem...	Start Station	End Station
☐ ☑ BL - Ascent Pl - (20)		Ascent Pl	Ascent ...		0+000.00m	0+212.96m
☑ RG - Start				Residen.	0+016.50m	0+080.92m

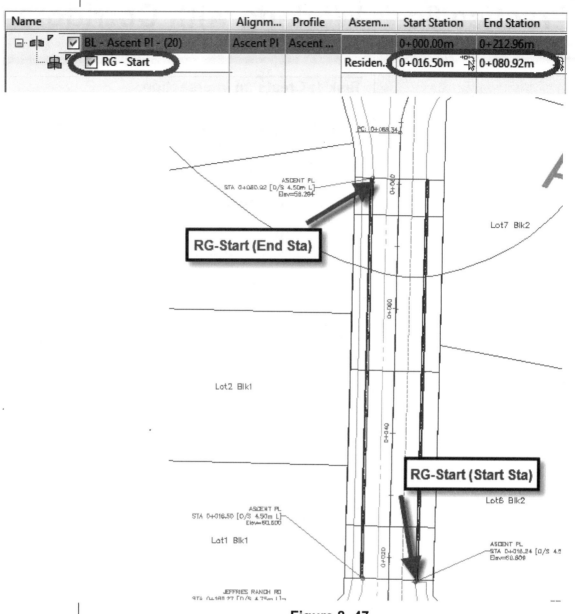

Figure 8–47

8. Click [OK] to create the corridor.

9. Save the drawing.

Practice 8c | Working with Corridors Part II

Task 1: Create an intersection.

In this task, you will create an intersection at Jeffries Ranch Rd and Ascent Pl. This intersection will fill in the gap you left in the Jeffries Ranch Rd corridor by setting regions.

1. Open the file **COR1-Sec3-Corridor.dwg** from the following folder:

    C:\Civil 3D Projects\Civil3D-training\Drawings

2. In the *View* tab > Views panel, double-click on the preset view **C3D-Corridor-Intersection1**, as shown in Figure 8–48.

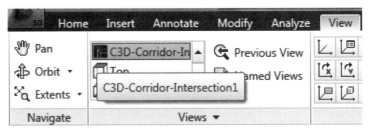

Figure 8–48

3. The default intersection settings are in the Intersection command settings. In the *Toolspace Settings* tab, expand the *Intersection* and then *Commands* collections. Select **CreateIntersection**, right-click, and select **Edit Command Settings...**, as shown in Figure 8–49.

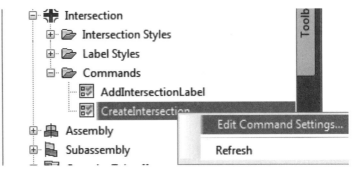

Figure 8–49

4. In the dialog box, review the settings. You will not make any changes for this practice. Click   Cancel to close the dialog box, as shown in Figure 8–50.

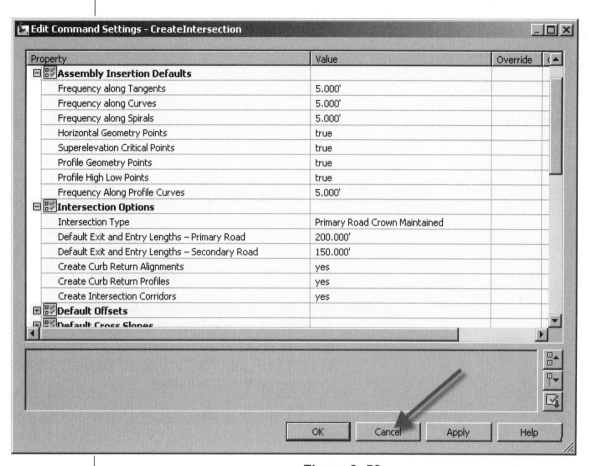

Figure 8–50

5. In the *Home* tab > Create Design panel, select **Create Intersection**, as shown in Figure 8–51.

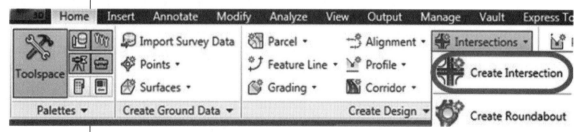

Figure 8–51

6. AutoCAD Civil 3D sets an Intersection OSNAP and prompts you to *Select Intersection Point*.

7. Select the intersection of the Jeffries Ranch Rd and Ascent Pl alignments, as shown on the left in Figure 8–52. Zoom in to ensure you are snapping to the correct intersection point, as shown on the right.

Figure 8–52

8. If you are having problems selecting the intersection point, press the <Esc> key to exit the **Intersection** command. In Model Space, select the two alignments **Jeffries Ranch Rd** and **Ascent Pl**, right-click, and select **Display order>Bring to front**. Then create the intersection.

If this were a four-way intersection, you would be prompted to select the Primary road. In this case, Civil 3D assumes Jeffries Ranch Rd is the primary road.

9. Position the Create Intersection wizard so that you can also see the intersection in the drawing. On the *General* page, enter **Intersection–(Jefferies Ranch & Ascent Pl)** as the *Intersection Name*, and accept the *Intersection Marker Style* and *Intersection Label Style* defaults. Confirm the *Intersection Corridor Type* is

    Primary Road Crown Maintained and click Next >, as shown in Figure 8–53.

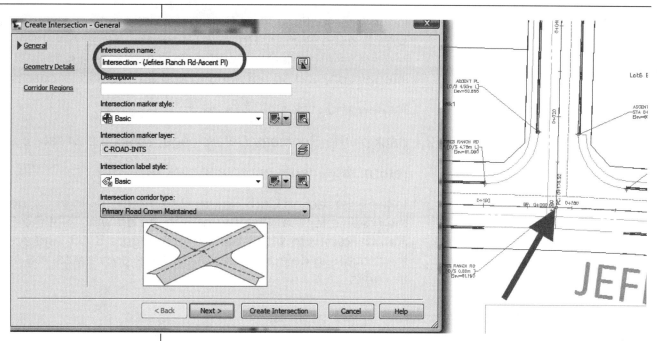

Figure 8–53

10. On the *Geometry Details* page, the alignments, intersection stations, and profiles to be used are listed. The profile can be changed here if required. In the *Offset and curb returns* section, select the **Create or specify offset alignments** option and click

    Offset Parameters , as shown in Figure 8–54.

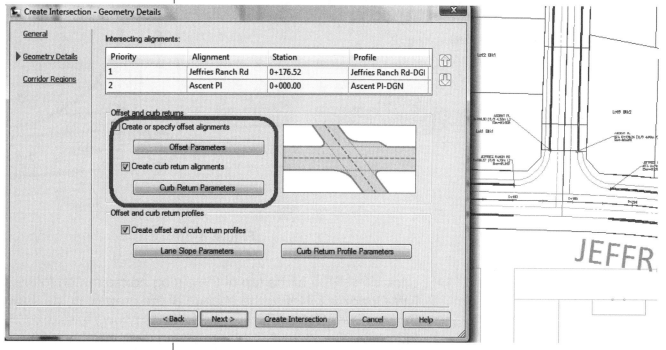

Figure 8–54

11. In the Intersection Offset Parameters dialog box, notice that the selection the Primary Road or Secondary Road highlights the respective alignment in the drawing. As this is a simple intersection, you do not need to add any additional offsets.

   Review and click ▭ OK ▭.

12. Back on the *Geometry Details* page, select the **Create curb return alignments** option and click ▭ Curb Return Parameters ▭.

13. In the Intersection Curb Return Parameters dialog box, notice the graphic for the **NE-Quadrant** in the drawing. Set the *Curb Return Radius* to **11.75**, as shown in Figure 8–55, and accept the remaining default values. Notice the preview as you make the edits.

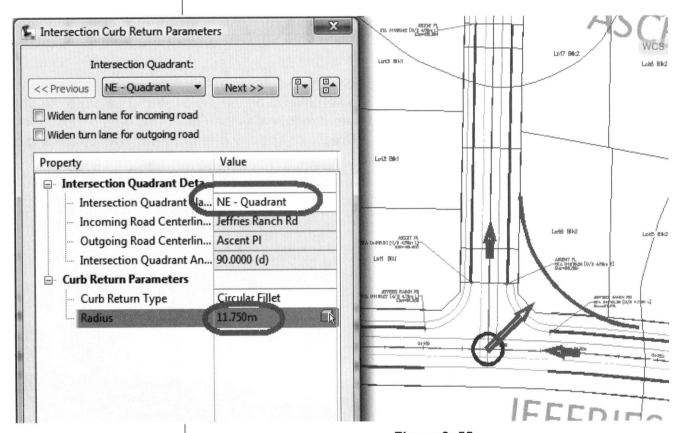

Figure 8–55

14. Click ▭ Next >> ▭ at the top of the dialog box to switch to the **NW-Quadrant**. Notice the change of the graphic in the drawing. Set the *Curb Return Radius* to **11.75**, as shown in Figure 8–56, and accept the remaining default values. Click ▭ OK ▭ to return to the *Geometry Details* page.

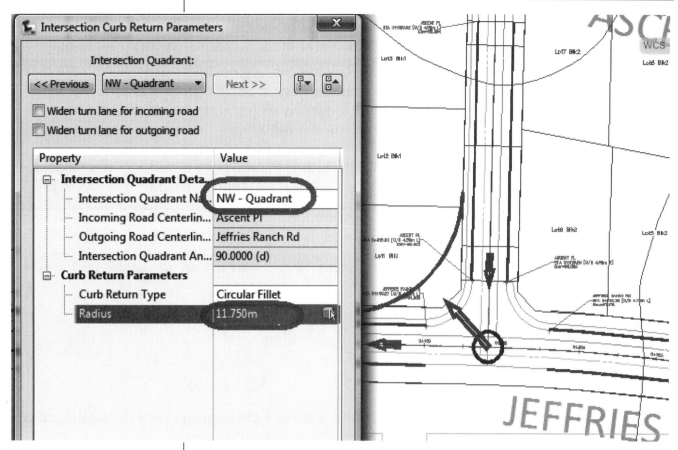

Figure 8–56

15. To automatically create curb return profiles, in the *Offset and curb return profiles* section, select the **Create offset and curb return profiles** option. Accept the defaults for the *Lane Slope* and *Curb Return* parameters and click [Next >].

16. On the *Corridor Regions* page, you have the option to create a new corridor or add this intersection to an existing corridor. Select the **Create corridors in the intersection area** option and select the **Create a new corridor** option, as shown in Figure 8–57.

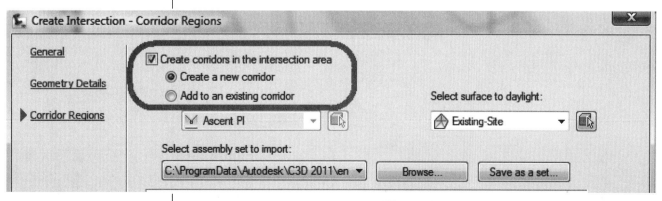

Figure 8–57

17. Some assembly sets ship with Civil 3D and you find them using
Browse... . By default, a metric assembly set displays

various assemblies that are set in the window. You will click [...]
for each Corridor Region Section Type and select the
appropriate assembly as required. As you do so, notice the
previews below the window.

18. For the **Curb Return Fillets**, right-click on [...] and select the
Residential – Curb RT assembly, as shown in Figure 8–58.
Click OK .

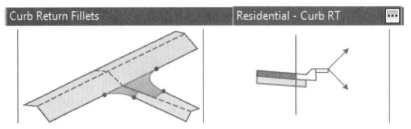

Figure 8–58

19. For the **Primary Road Full Section** select the **Collector - Full**
assembly, as shown in Figure 8–59.

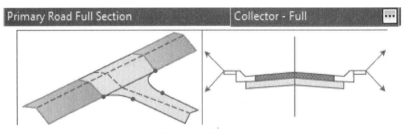

Figure 8–59

20. For the **Primary Road Part Section – Daylight Left** leave the
default value, as shown in Figure 8–60, as this is not applicable
to your intersection.

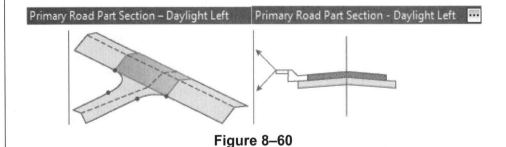

Figure 8–60

21. For the **Primary Road Part Section – Daylight Right** select the **Collector – Part Curb RT** assembly, as shown in Figure 8–61.

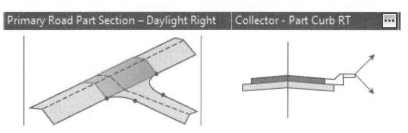

Figure 8–61

22. For the **Secondary Road Full Section** select the **Residential – Full** assembly, as shown in Figure 8–62.

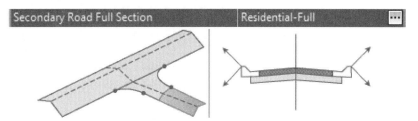

Figure 8–62

23. For the **Secondary Road Half Section – Daylight Left** select the **Residential - Half Curb LT** assembly, as shown in Figure 8–63.

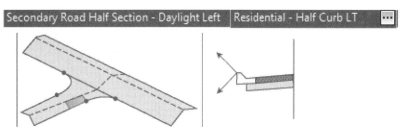

Figure 8–63

24. For the **Secondary Road Half Section – Daylight Right** select the **Residential - Half Curb RT** assembly, as shown in Figure 8–64.

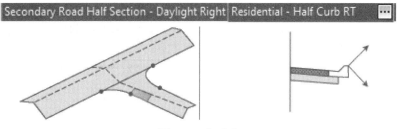

Figure 8–64

25. When finished, click **Create Intersection**. You may have to perform a **REGEN** to see the newly created Intersection Corridor.

26. In the Events viewer, select **Action > Clear All Events**, as shown in Figure 8–65. Click on the **X** to close the Events viewer.

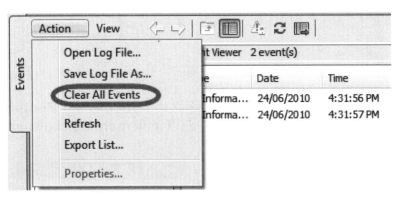

Figure 8–65

27. Save the drawing.

Task 2: Edit corridor targets.

You will notice that at the curb returns, the Intersection wizard may be targeting the wrong portion of the alignment, as shown in Figure 8–66. In this task you will explore how to edit and fix this issue.

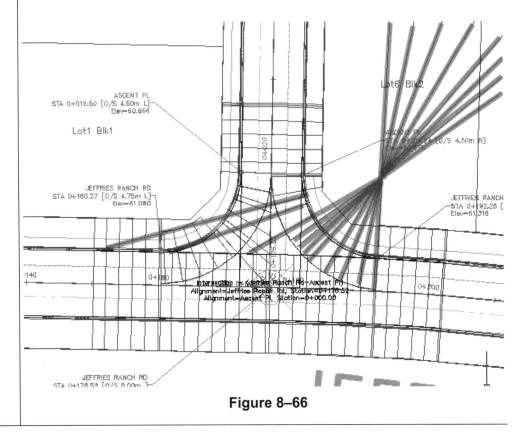

Figure 8–66

1. Continue working with the drawing from the previous task.

2. In Model Space, select the Intersection corridor. In the contextual Ribbon tab > Modify Corridor panel, select **Corridor Properties**, as shown in Figure 8–67.

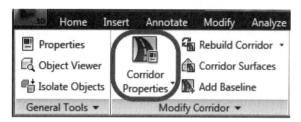

Figure 8–67

3. In the Corridor Properties dialog box, select the *Parameters* tab. In the Intersection NE Quadrant, select the **RG – Residential – Curb RT** region. Notice that in Model Space, the appropriate corridor region is highlighted, as shown in Figure 8–68.

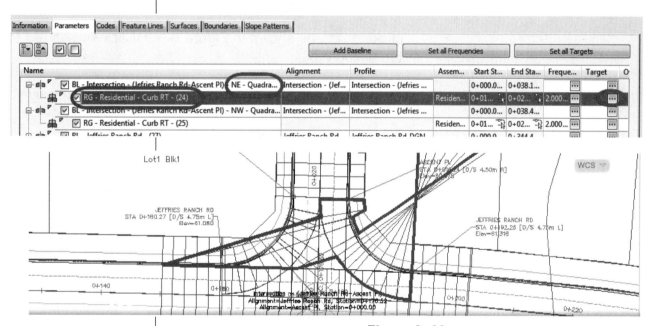

Figure 8–68

4. For this baseline, the **NE Quadrant**, and the **RG – Residential – Curb RT** region, click ⋯ in the *Target* column.

5. In the Target mapping dialog box, under *Width or Offset Targets*, click in the cell beside *Target Alignment*, as shown in Figure 8–69.

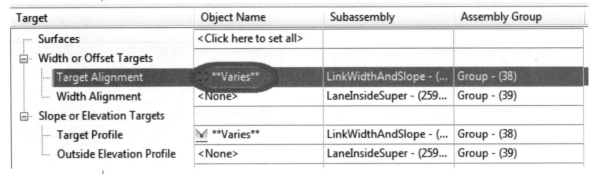

Target	Object Name	Subassembly	Assembly Group
Surfaces	\<Click here to set all\>		
Width or Offset Targets			
Target Alignment	**Varies**	LinkWidthAndSlope - (...	Group - (38)
Width Alignment	\<None\>	LaneInsideSuper - (259...	Group - (39)
Slope or Elevation Targets			
Target Profile	**Varies**	LinkWidthAndSlope - (...	Group - (38)
Outside Elevation Profile	\<None\>	LaneInsideSuper - (259...	Group - (39)

Figure 8–69

6. Because the Intersection wizard targeted the wrong alignments, you will first remove the targets and then add new targets. In the Set Width Or Offset Target dialog box, in the *Selected entities to target* section, select each of the targets and remove them by clicking ☒, as shown in Figure 8–70. Click OK to close the dialog box.

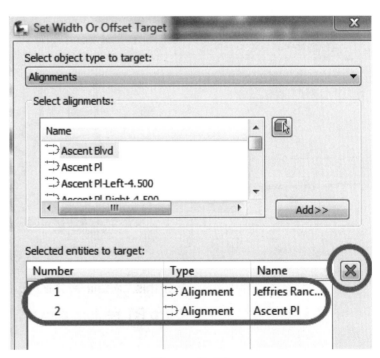

Figure 8–70

7. Now you will add the correct targeting. In the Target mapping dialog box, under *Width or Offset Targets*, click in the cell beside *Width Alignment*, as shown in Figure 8–71.

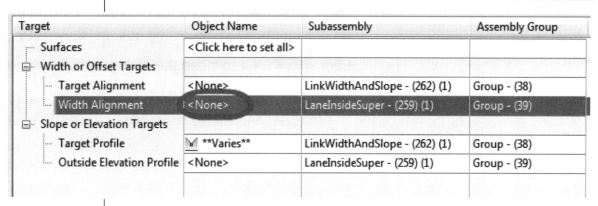

Figure 8–71

8. In the Set Width Or Offset Target dialog box, click ![icon] to select the object from the drawing, as shown in Figure 8–72.

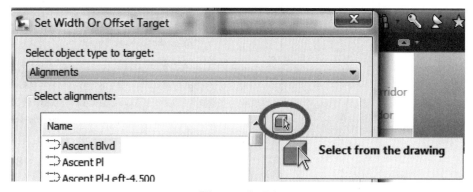

Figure 8–72

9. In Model Space, select the Ascent Pl alignment and the Jeffries Ranch Rd offset alignment, as shown in Figure 8–73.

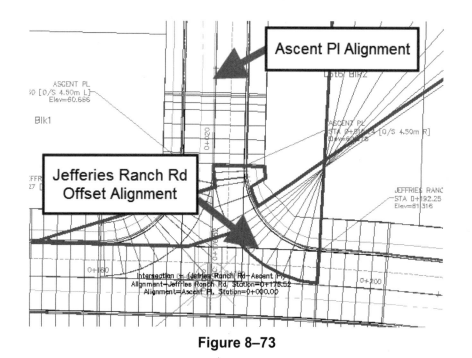

Figure 8–73

10. Alternatively, you could have selected the alignments from the list of alignments in the dialog box, as shown in Figure 8–74.

Click [OK] to close the dialog box.

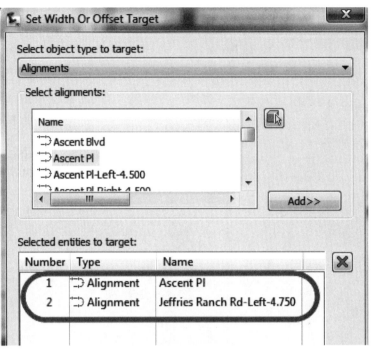

Figure 8–74

11. Click [OK] to close the Target mapping dialog box for the NE curb return.

12. Do the same for the NW curb return. While still in the *Parameters* tab, in the Intersection NW Quadrant, select the **RG – Residential – Curb RT** region, as shown in Figure 8–75. Notice that in Model Space the appropriate corridor region is highlighted.

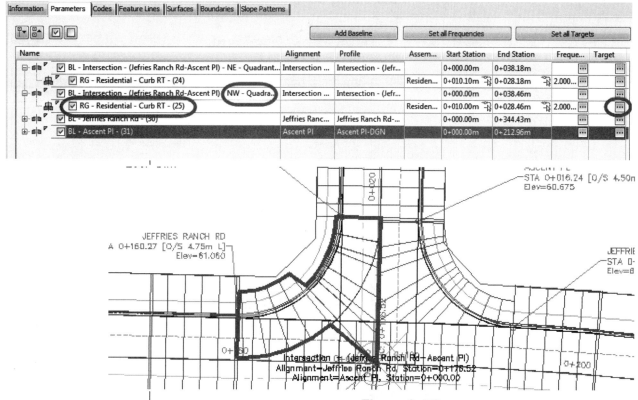

Figure 8–75

13. For this baseline, the **NW Quadrant**, and the **RG – Residential – Curb RT** region, click 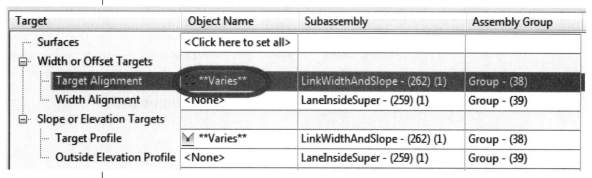 in the *Target* column.

14. In the Target mapping dialog box, under *Width or Offset Targets*, click in the cell beside *Target Alignment*, as shown in Figure 8–76.

Target	Object Name	Subassembly	Assembly Group
Surfaces	<Click here to set all>		
Width or Offset Targets			
Target Alignment	**Varies**	LinkWidthAndSlope - (262) (1)	Group - (38)
Width Alignment	<None>	LaneInsideSuper - (259) (1)	Group - (39)
Slope or Elevation Targets			
Target Profile	**Varies**	LinkWidthAndSlope - (262) (1)	Group - (38)
Outside Elevation Profile	<None>	LaneInsideSuper - (259) (1)	Group - (39)

Figure 8–76

15. Because the Intersection wizard targeted the wrong alignments, you will first remove the targets and then add new targets. In the Set Width Or Offset Target dialog box, in the *Selected entities to target* section, select each of the targets and remove them by clicking ✖, as shown in Figure 8–77. Click [OK] to close the dialog box.

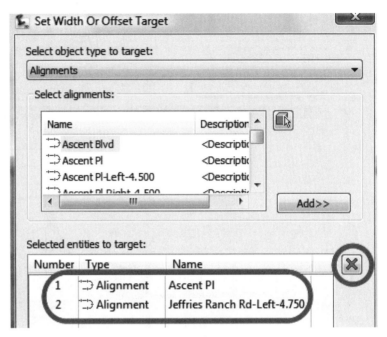

Figure 8–77

16. Now you will add the correct targeting. In the Target mapping dialog box, under *Width or Offset Targets* click in the cell beside *Width Alignment*, as shown in Figure 8–78.

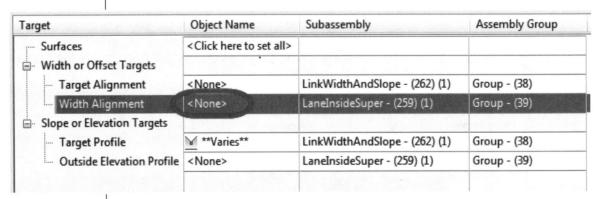

Figure 8–78

17. In the Set Width Or Offset Target dialog box, click 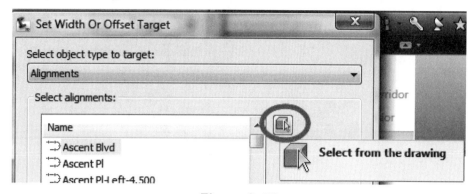 to select the object from the drawing, as shown in Figure 8–79.

Figure 8–79

18. In Model Space, select the Ascent Pl alignment and the Jeffries Ranch Rd offset alignment, as shown in Figure 8–80.

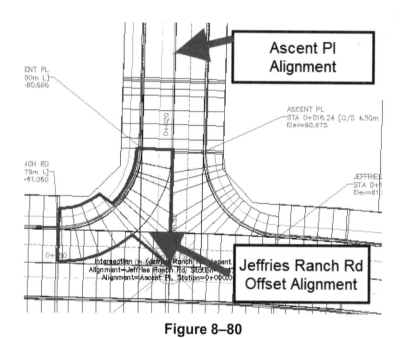

Figure 8–80

19. Alternatively, you could have selected the alignments from the list of alignments in the dialog box, as shown in Figure 8–81.

    Click [OK] the close the dialog box.

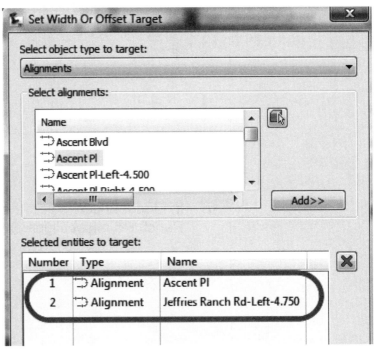

Figure 8–81

20. Click [OK] to close the Target mapping dialog box for the NW curb return.

21. Save the drawing.

8.5 Corridor Surfaces

The *Surfaces* tab of the Corridor Properties dialog box enables you to build the proposed surfaces based on corridor geometry. You can create these surfaces from corridor links, and/or from features lines based on marker points (point codes). As the corridor changes, its surfaces automatically update.

The two most common types of corridor surfaces are Top and Datum surfaces.

- **Top** surfaces follow the uppermost geometry of the corridor. These are useful for many purposes, such as in the display of finished ground contours and as a way of determining rim elevations of proposed utility structures.
- **Datum** surfaces generally follow the bottommost corridor geometry. These can be used in both Surface-to-Surface volume calculations and Section-based Earthworks calculations to determine site cut and fill totals (when compared to existing ground).
- **Corridor** surfaces, as with all AutoCAD Civil 3D surfaces, cannot contain vertical elements. Be sure to include slight offsets so that vertical curbing and similar geometry are not absolutely vertical.

Overhang Correction

In some configurations, some AutoCAD Civil 3D assemblies might have top or datum points, or links in locations that might lead to incorrect surfaces, such as the datum surface represented by the heavy line in Figure 8–82.

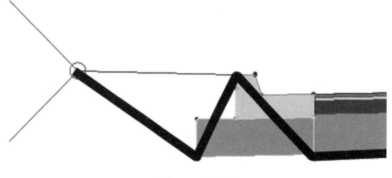

Figure 8–82

In cases like these, the **Overhang Correction** option forces these surfaces to follow either the top or bottom of the corridor geometry, as shown in Figure 8–83. This setting is typically only needed for datum surfaces.

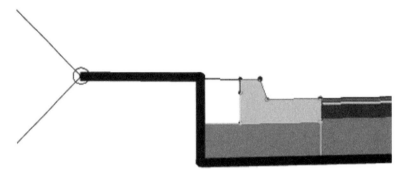

Figure 8–83

Surface Boundaries

Corridor surfaces, as with all AutoCAD Civil 3D surfaces, often benefit from a boundary to remove unwanted interpolation between points. The *Boundaries* tab of the Corridor Surfaces dialog box enables you to add these boundaries in a number of ways—selecting a closed polyline or interactively tracing the boundary through a jig.

When working with a corridor that has a single baseline and daylight components, often the best option is to "automatically" add a boundary that follows the daylight feature lines on both sides. This can be done in Civil 3D 2011 using the new **Create Boundary from Corridor Extents** command.

8.6 Corridor Section Review and Edit

Creating complex corridors can be greatly simplified through the **View/Edit Corridor Section** command. It is accessed through the shortcut menu after selecting a corridor, as shown in Figure 8–84.

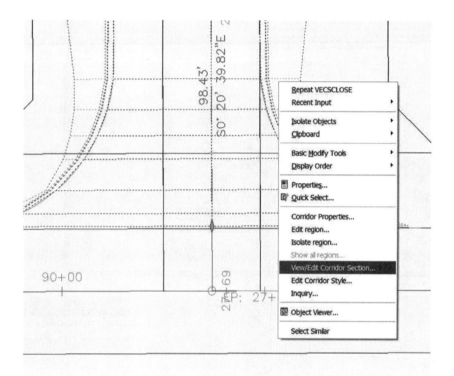

Figure 8–84

This command launches the *Section Editor* contextual tab in the Ribbon, which enables you to review and edit sections interactively using the appropriate panels. The **Parameter Editor**, as shown in Figure 8–85, enables you to review and change most subassembly parameters.

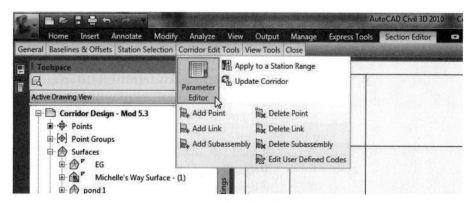

Figure 8–85

The editor enables you to modify those sections that need special attention, such as different daylight slopes. The editor also enables you to add and remove some subassemblies or links directly to and from a section. These parameter changes, additions, and deletions can be done for a single section or for a range of sections. An example is shown in Figure 8–86.

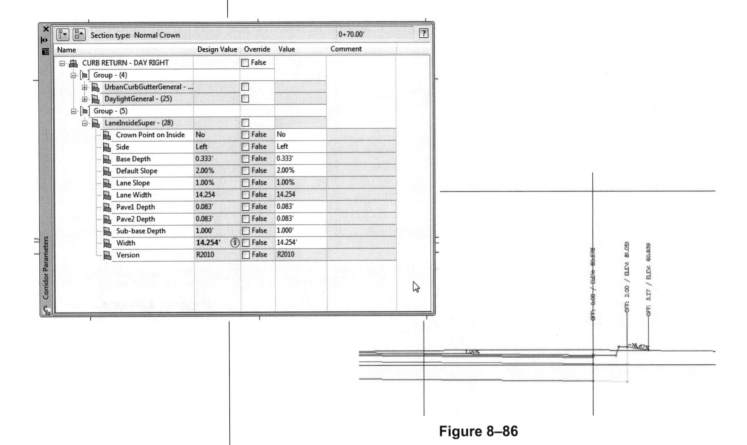

Figure 8–86

To more easily see the modifications that are taking place on the corridor section, you can work in three different zoom modes within the **View/Edit Corridor Section** command:

- **Zoom To Extents** ensures that the full assembly is in view when you navigate to another station after zooming in.
- **Zoom to A Subassembly** ensures that a subassembly that you select remains at the center of the view when you navigate to another station. The zoom level is also maintained.
- **Zoom To An Offset And Elevation** ensures that the current zoom level is maintained when you navigate to another station after a zoom.

If you set up multiple viewports in Model Space before you start the **View/Edit Corridor Section** command, a Station Tracker indicates, with a vertical line, the current section in both the plan view and any associated profile views.

Practice 8d | Working with Corridors Part II

Task 1: Create corridor surfaces.

1. Continue working with the drawing from the previous practice.

2. In the AutoCAD Model Space window, select the **Jeffries Ranch Rd corridor** and click **Corridor Properties**.

3. In the *Surfaces* tab, click 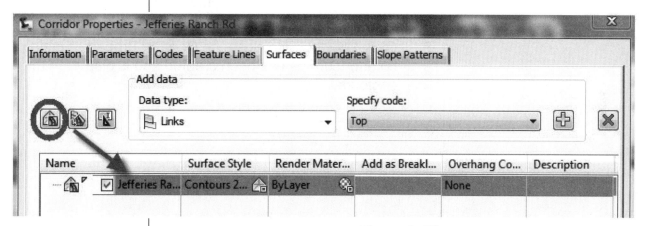 (Create a Corridor Surface), as shown in Figure 8–87.

Figure 8–87

4. The surface appears in the dialog box with the default name Jeffries Ranch Rd Surface - (1). Rename it to **Road 1** by clicking on the current name.

5. The default surface style **Contours 2m and 10m (Design)** works well for this task, so leave that it as the default.

6. In the *Add Data* section, confirm the *Data type* is set to **Links** and the *code* is set to **Top**, and then click  (Add Surface Item), as shown in Figure 8–88.

Figure 8–88

7. Select the *Boundaries* tab. Right-click on the corridor surface name and select **Add Automatically > P2**, as shown in Figure 8–89. This automatically adds a boundary that follows the corridor extents (in this case, the daylight lines) on both sides.

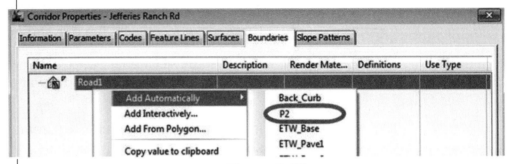

Figure 8–89

8. Click [OK] to close the Corridor Properties dialog box. The corridor surface has been created and is displayed through contours.

Review Questions

Question 1 How does an assembly define the attachment point of a roadway cross-section?

Question 2 How does each subassembly attach to the assembly?

Question 3 What does the subassembly Tool Palette contain?

Question 4 Which parameters does each subassembly contain and what do they control?

Question 5 What does a corridor model represent?

Question 6 Which command is used to create corridors in small and uncomplicated subdivisions and roads?

Question 7 Name the seven tabs in the Corridor Properties dialog box.

Question 8 What are feature lines?

Question 9 What does the View/Edit Corridor Section Editor enable you to do?

Module 9

Grading Level 1

This module introduces:

Section 1: Grading Overview

✓ **Grading Overview**

✓ **Configuring AutoCAD Civil 3D Grading**

Section 1: Grading Overview

9.1 Grading Overview

AutoCAD Civil 3D grading makes use of objects called *feature lines* and *grading groups*.

- *Feature lines* are complex, linear 3D objects that define a string of known elevations, such as the perimeter of a proposed pond. Feature lines can be created by converting AutoCAD lines, arcs, or polylines. Grading feature lines can also be exported from Corridors through the *Modify* tab > Corridor panel > **Feature Lines from Corridor** command.

- Parcel lines double as feature lines, and can be edited directly through the feature line elevation editor. Parcel lines that exist within the extents of a grading group are also automatically added to the surface, even if they are at elevation 0. (You can avoid this by locating feature lines and parcels in separate sites.)

- In AutoCAD Civil 3D, feature lines can be created from an alignment. They can also be dynamically linked to the alignment or corridor model from which they are created.

- AutoCAD Civil 3D can calculate the position of one feature line based on another, such as a pond bottom calculated at a certain slope and elevation below the perimeter. Distance, slope, and surface parameters used in solutions are assigned through *grading criteria*.

- *Grading groups* are collections of these solutions that form a contiguous whole, such as the detention pond shown in Figure 9–1.

Figure 9–1

- Grading groups can be used to automatically generate AutoCAD Civil 3D surfaces. Tools are also available for calculating grading group volume, and adjusting grading groups to help balance cut and fill.

- Surfaces created from grading groups (as well as corridor surfaces) appear in the *Prospector* and can be adjusted through normal surface editing tools, such as **Add** or **Delete Surface Point** or **Swap Edge**. These edits are maintained and dynamically reapplied if the grading group is adjusted.

- Feature lines and grading groups are organized by site, so that any feature lines added within the perimeter of a grading group (in the same site) are automatically added to the grading group.

Feature Line Contextual Tab

The *Feature Line* contextual tab, as shown in Figure 9–2, contains commands to edit and modify feature lines. These commands include tools to edit feature line elevations and feature line geometry, such as **Break**, **Trim**, **Extend**, and **Fillet** (which creates a true, three-dimensional curve).

Figure 9–2

The **Create Feature Lines from Objects** command is available through the *Home* tab > Create Design panel > **Feature Line** command, as shown in Figure 9–3.

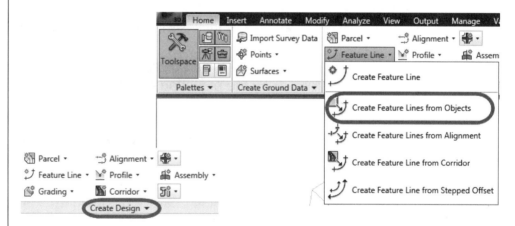

Figure 9–3

Elevation Editor

The Grading Elevation Editor vista, as shown in Figure 9–4, enables you to add, modify, or vary the elevations of a feature line. The feature line data is organized into rows, where one row lists the data for a particular vertex.

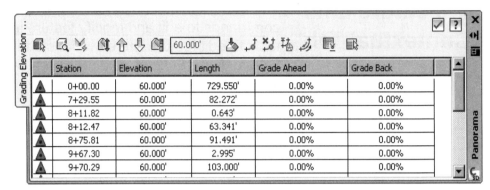

Station	Elevation	Length	Grade Ahead	Grade Back
0+00.00	60.000'	729.550'	0.00%	0.00%
7+29.55	60.000'	82.272'	0.00%	0.00%
8+11.82	60.000'	0.643'	0.00%	0.00%
8+12.47	60.000'	63.341'	0.00%	0.00%
8+75.81	60.000'	91.491'	0.00%	0.00%
9+67.30	60.000'	2.995'	0.00%	0.00%
9+70.29	60.000'	103.000'	0.00%	0.00%

Figure 9–4

- (Select a Feature Line Or Lot Line): Enables you to change the feature line that you are editing.

- (Zoom to): Enables you to zoom in to a highlighted vertex.

- (Quick Profile): Creates a quick profile along the feature line.

- (Raise/Lower): Raises or lowers all of the feature line vertices by the elevation entered in the edit field on the right side.

- (Raise/Lower Incrementally): Raises or lowers the elevations by the elevation increment entered (the default is 1).

- (Set Increment): Enables you to set the increment value.

- (Flatten Grade or Elevations): Enables you to flatten selected vertices to a specified grade or single elevation.

- Green (Insert Elevation Point): Adds an elevation control to the feature line. Elevation points provide an elevation control without creating a whole new vertex. These points are Z-controls without X- or Y-components.

- Red (Delete Elevation Point): Removes elevation points.

- (Elevations from Surface): Takes the elevations of all the vertices from the surface if no rows are selected. If a row is selected, it takes the surface elevation for just that vertex.

-  (Reverse the direction): Changes the direction of the feature line by reversing the order of its points.

- (Show Grade breaks only): Only shows rows for vertices where there is a change is grade.

- (Unselect All Rows): Clears any selected vertices. With no rows selected, the **Raise/Lower** commands apply to all of the rows.

You can edit the elevations of a feature or parcel line before or after it becomes part of a grading group.

Grading Creation Tools Toolbar

Grading groups are created and edited through the Grading Creation Tools toolbar, as shown in Figure 9–5, which is accessed through the *Grading* tab > Create Grading panel.

Grading Creation Tools

Grade to Surface

Group: Style Management. rface:

Figure 9–5

Some of the more commonly used tools include:

- (Set the Grading Group): Enables you to consolidate grading objects into a single collection in order to generate a grading group surface for volume computations.

- Grade to Surface ▼ (Criteria drop-down list): Enables you to select particular criteria within a given criteria set.

- (Create Grading): Generates a grading solution from the currently selected criteria.

- (Edit Grading): Enables you to change the grading parameters after a solution has been generated.

- (Grading Volume Tools): Opens the Grading Volume Tools toolbar, which provides cut and fill information about the grading group, as well as adjustment tools.

9.2 Configuring AutoCAD Civil 3D Grading

Grading Styles

A grading style defines how the grading solution appears on the screen. The components of a grading style include the grading marker (for selecting the grading solution), slope patterns, and the solution's layers and their properties.

Feature Line Labels

Feature lines have their own family of labels, which can be accessed through the *Annotate* tab > Add Labels panel > **Feature Line > Add Feature Line Labels** command (e.g., a label indicating grade and distance).

Grading Criteria

Grading methods (to a surface, at a certain distance and slope, etc.) are organized inside AutoCAD Civil 3D drawings as grading criteria. Criteria include the grading method, slope projection, and conflict resolution properties. The Grading Criteria dialog box is shown in Figure 9–6.

- The *Grading Method* properties define what you want to grade to. Targets can include a *Surface*, *Elevation*, *Relative Elevations*, or a *Distance*. If the method uses a distance, you have to specify a default distance. If the method is to a surface, you can specify whether it is only for cut or fill, for both cut and fill, or for a distance. Each setting changes the information the Grading Method needs to complete its task.
- The *Slope Projection* properties assign the format of the slope (e.g., slope or grade) and the default values when using the command.
- The *Conflict Resolution* properties define how to resolve problem areas such as internal corners that overlap.

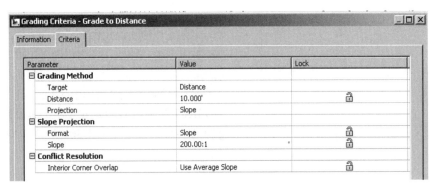

Figure 9–6

Grading Criteria Set

Criteria sets are collections of grading criteria that are helpful to group together for a specific task. For example, you could create different sets for residential or commercial site grading, and so on. These sets (and the criteria within them) can be found in the *Settings* tab under the *Grading* collection.

In this course, you work only with the **Basic** criteria set provided in the default AutoCAD Civil 3D templates.

Grading Volumes

The Grading Volumes Tools toolbar, as shown in Figure 9–7, displays the volume for all or selected grading solutions in a group. One tool raises or lowers all of the members of a grading group by an incremental value. The icon at the far right forces the group or selected grading solution to determine which elevations it needs for balance. Balance is a design that creates as much excavation material as needed to fill in depressions in the design area.

- The volumes in the Grading Volume Tools toolbar are dynamically linked to the grading objects.
- Grading volumes change when editing one or all of the grading group objects.

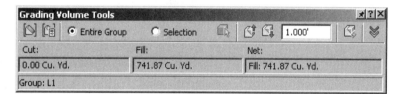

Figure 9–7

Practice 9a

Pond Grading Part I - Create Existing Site Conditions

The first step in grading is to establish existing site conditions. In this practice you will define the perimeter of the pond using three methods to define a feature line:

- Feature line from Existing Surface
- Feature line based on design data
- Feature line from Corridor

Task 1: Create a feature line from surface.

The north boundary of the site is defined by Mission Avenue and the west boundary is defined by an existing subdivision. To establish a design control line for the north and west perimeters of the site, you will create a feature line that extracts elevations from the existing surface.

1. Open the file **GRD1-Sec1-Grading.dwg** from the following folder:

    C:\Civil 3D Projects\Civil3D-training\Drawings

2. In the *View* tab > Views panel, select the preset view **C3D-Grading-Feature2**. You should see a red polyline that runs along the north and west property lines; you may have to type **Regen** at the Command Line to regenerate the graphics.

3. In the *Home* tab > Create Design panel, select **Feature Line > Create Feature Lines from Objects**, as shown in Figure 9–8.

Figure 9–8

4. When prompted to *select the object*, select the red polyline and press <Enter> when done

5. In the Create Feature Lines dialog box, select **Site 1** for the site and select the **Erase existing entities**, **Assign elevations**, and **Weed Points** options in the *Conversion options* section, as shown in Figure 9–9. Accept all other defaults and click  when done.

Figure 9–9

6. In the Assign Elevations dialog box, select the **From surface** option and select **Existing -Site** from the drop-down list, as shown in Figure 9–10. Click OK to accept the changes and close the dialog box.

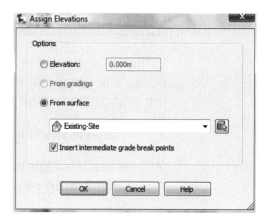

Figure 9–10

7. In the Weed Vertices dialog box, accept the defaults and click
   [OK], as shown in Figure 9–11.

Figure 9–11

8. A feature line has been created for the north and west property lines of the site, with elevations matching the existing ground surface. Save the drawing.

Task 2: Create a feature based on design elevations.

In this task you will create a feature line of the east perimeter of the pond. The grades at the east perimeter of the pond are governed by the rear grades of the lots or parcels.

1. Continue working with the drawing from the previous task.

2. In the *View* tab > Views panel, select the preset view **C3D-Grading-Feature3**.

3. Based on the street grades and types of lots that are required (Walkout Basements), elevations for the east property line have been roughly calculated. The last *pt7* ties into the existing ground elevation that is controlled by Mission Avenue, as shown in Figure 9–12.

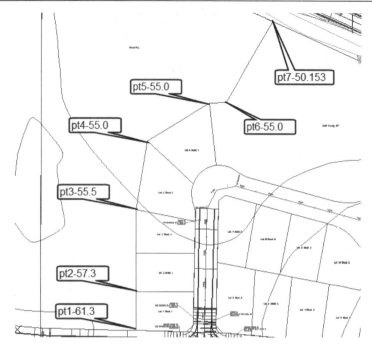

Figure 9–12

4. In the *Home* tab > Create Design panel, select **Feature Line** > **Create Feature Line**, as shown in Figure 9–13.

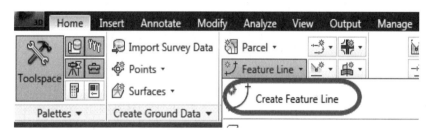

Figure 9–13

5. In the Create Feature Lines dialog box, select **Site 1** and accept all other defaults. Click [OK] to close the dialog box and start creating the feature line.

6. When prompted for the feature line points, select the end point **Pt1**, shown in Figure 9–12 above. When prompted to *Specify elevation or [surface] <0.000>:* type **61.3** <Enter>.

7. When prompted for the next point, select end point **Pt2**, shown in Figure 9–12 above.

8. You are prompted to *Specify grade or [SLope/Elevation/Difference/SUrface/Transition] <0.00>:*. If the option is not set to accept elevations, type **E** <Enter> to set the default as the elevation.

9. Once the option is set to accept elevations, you are prompted to *Specify elevation or [Grade/SLope/Difference/SUrface/Transition] <61.300>*. Type **57.3** <Enter>. Continue this process of selecting the end point and entering the elevation for all points as shown in Figure 9–12 above. When done entering the elevation for the last point, pt7, press <Enter> to exit the command.

10. In Model Space, select the feature line and in the contextual Ribbon > Modify panel, select **Edit Elevations** to toggle on the Edit Elevations panel, then select **Elevation Editor**, as shown in Figure 9–14.

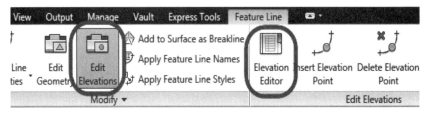

Figure 9–14

11. In the Grading Elevation Editor vista, as shown in Figure 9–15, you are able to make changes to feature line design.

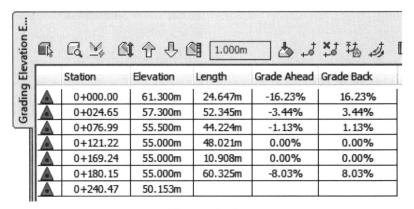

Station	Elevation	Length	Grade Ahead	Grade Back
0+000.00	61.300m	24.647m	-16.23%	16.23%
0+024.65	57.300m	52.345m	-3.44%	3.44%
0+076.99	55.500m	44.224m	-1.13%	1.13%
0+121.22	55.000m	48.021m	0.00%	0.00%
0+169.24	55.000m	10.908m	0.00%	0.00%
0+180.15	55.000m	60.325m	-8.03%	8.03%
0+240.47	50.153m			

Figure 9–15

12. Due to the grade difference between Jeffries Ranch Rd and the adjacent lot grade, the start of the feature line must be adjusted to show a 1:1 slope.

13. With the feature still selected and the contextual Ribbon enabled, select **Edit Elevations** in the Modify panel to toggle on the Edit Elevations panel, then select **Insert Elevation Point**, as shown in Figure 9–16. If the contextual Ribbon is not enabled for the feature line, you will have to reselect the feature line in Model Space.

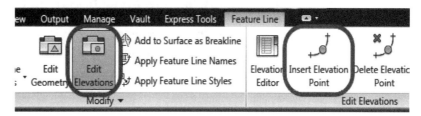

Figure 9–16

14. When prompted for a point, type **D** <Enter> at the Command Line (for Distance).

15. As you will be grading down at a 1:1 slope from 61.3 to 57.3, type **4** <Enter> at the Command Line for the Distance value. Type **57.3** <Enter> for the Elevation value.

16. Press <Enter> to exit and complete the command.

17. If you did not close the Grading Elevation Editor vista, you will see the new station, as shown in Figure 9–17. To reactivate the vista if is not visible, in the contextual Ribbon > Modify panel, select **Edit Elevations** to toggle on the Edit Elevations panel, then select **Elevation Editor**.

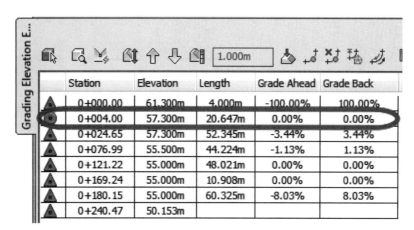

Figure 9–17

18. Save the drawing.

Task 3: Create a feature line from Corridor.

The grades at the south end of the pond are controlled by Jeffries Ranch Rd. In this task you will extract a feature from the corridor to establish the elevation of the south property line.

1. Continue working with the drawing from the previous task.

2. In the *View* tab > Views panel, select the preset view **C3D-Grading-Feature1**, as shown in Figure 9–18.

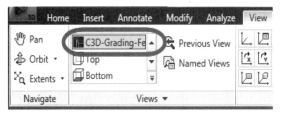

Figure 9–18

3. In Model Space, select the Jeffries Ranch Rd corridor object, right-click, and select **Display Order > Bring to Front**.

4. In Model Space, select the Jeffries Ranch Rd corridor object again and in the contextual Ribbon > Launch Pad panel, select **Feature Lines from Corridor**, as shown in Figure 9–19.

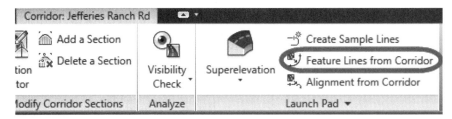

Figure 9–19

5. Depending on the sequence of selection of the corridor objects, AutoCAD Civil 3D may first prompt you for the feature line followed by the Create Feature Line from Corridor dialog box. Or, it may reverse the order and provide you with the dialog box followed by the selection of the feature line. In either case, steps 6 and 7 are required, but not necessarily in that order.

6. When prompted to select the corridor feature line, select the **north property** (green) line, as shown in Figure 9–20.

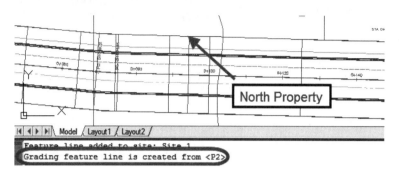

Figure 9–20

7. In the Create Feature Line from Corridor dialog box, select **Site 1** in the *Site* drop-down list and clear the **Create dynamic link to the corridor** option, as shown in Figure 9–21. Accept the remaining defaults and click [OK] to accept and close the dialog box.

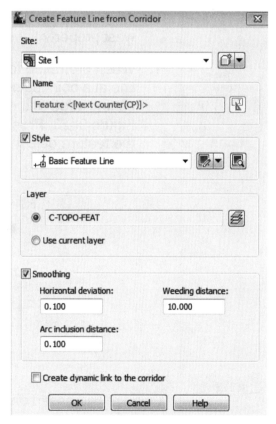

Figure 9–21

8. You will see a message at the Command Line that a feature line from <P2> has been created. Press <Enter> to exit the command

9. In Model Space, select the newly created feature line, as shown in Figure 9–22. In the contextual Ribbon > Modify panel, select **Edit Geometry**, and then in the Edit Geometry panel, select the **Trim** command.

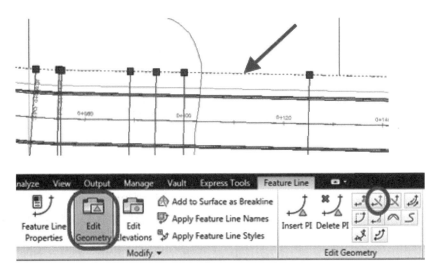

Figure 9–22

10. When prompted to select the cutting edge, select the east and west property lines of the pond and press <Enter> when done.

11. When prompted to select the object to trim, select the feature line at a point outside of the pond property lines, west of the west cutting edge and east of the east cutting edge, as shown in Figure 9–23. Press <Enter> when done and press <Esc> to exit the feature object selection.

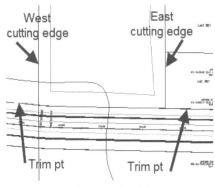

Figure 9–23

A feature line based on the corridor road design has now been created.

12. In the *View* tab > Views panel, select the preset view **C3D-Grading-Feature2**.

13. To join the three feature lines you created, select the feature line at the west side of the pond (in Model Space).

14. In the contextual Ribbon > Modify panel, select **Edit Geometry** to toggle on the Edit Geometry panel, then select the **Join** command, as shown in Figure 9–24.

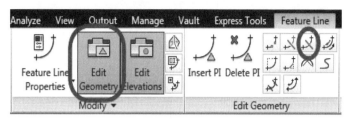

Figure 9–24

15. When prompted to select the feature line to the south, select the feature line to the east. Press <Enter> to end the command and press <Esc> to exit the feature line selection.

16. Save the drawing.

Practice 9b | Pond Grading Part II

In this practice you will grade a pond based on the design criteria shown in the cross-section in Figure 9–25.

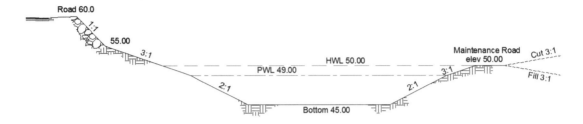

Figure 9–25

Each side of the pond requires different grading criteria:

At the **South end** of the pond site is Jeffries Ranch Rd, which is designed at an elevation of 60m. The road is elevated at an average of 6m above the adjacent parcels. As a result, you will use a 1:1 grade from the road so that you can drop to a workable pond base elevation of 55m.

At the **North end**, you designed a maintenance access road that is elevated 1m above the Permanent Water Level (PWL).

At the time of this guides publication (June 2010), AutoCAD Civil 3D was unable to use stacked grading based on different stations.

To grade the pond as shown in the cross-section, you must establish a base feature line to which a common grading criteria can be applied. This involves the following:

- Creating a base feature line to the South (1:1 to elev 55.00m).
- Creating a base feature line to the North (3:1 to elev 50.00m).
- Joining the trimmed east and west feature lines to the north and south control feature lines.
- Grading the pond based on this new combined feature line.

Task 1: Establish control feature lines (south end).

---

1. Open the file **GRD1-Sec2-Grading.dwg** from the following folder:

    C:\Civil 3D Projects\Civil3D-training\Drawings

2. In the *View* tab > Views panel, select the preset view
    C3D-Grading-Feature3.

3. In the *Home* tab > Create Design panel, select **Grading** >
    Grading Creation Tools, as shown in Figure 9–26.

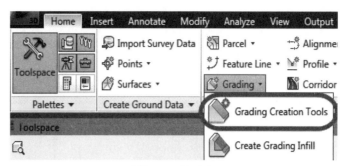

Figure 9–26

4. In the Grading Creation Tools toolbar, click 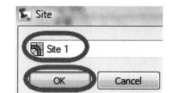 (Set the
    Grading Group). Accept the default **Site 1** for the site and click

    OK , as shown in Figure 9–27.

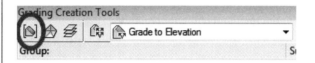

Figure 9–27

5. You will create a temporary grading object in which you can create pre-design information. In the Create Grading Group dialog box, enter **Temp** as the name, as shown in Figure 9–28.

Accept all the other defaults and click [OK].

Figure 9–28

6. Establish a feature line with a 1:1 slope to an elevation of 55. In the Grading Creation Tools toolbar, set the criteria to **Grade to Elevation** and click [icon] (Create Grading), as shown in Figure 9–29.

Figure 9–29

7. When prompted to select a feature, select the green pond boundary feature line that defines the perimeter pond site. When prompted to weed the feature line, select **Continue grading without feature line weeding**, as shown in Figure 9–30.

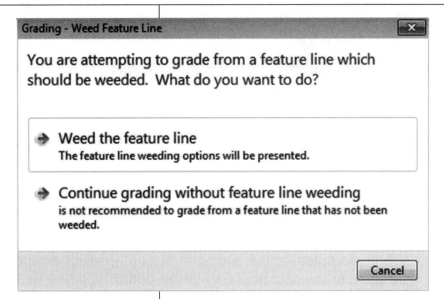

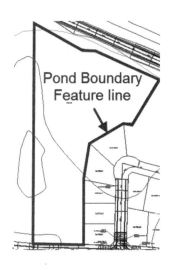

Pond Boundary
Feature line

Figure 9–30

8. When prompted for the side to grade, select a point inside of the pond. Enter **No** when prompted to *Apply to the entire length*.

9. When prompted for the start point, select any point adjacent to the west boundary of the pond. Type **373** at the Command Line for the starting station and press <Enter>.

10. When prompted for the end point or length, select any point adjacent to the south boundary of the pond. Type **485** for the ending station and press <Enter>.

11. When prompted for the elevation, type **55.00** and press <Enter>.

12. When prompted for cut format, type **Slope** <Enter> followed by **1** <Enter> to indicate a cut slope of 1:1.

13. When prompted for the fill format, enter **Slope** <Enter> followed by **1** <Enter> to indicate a fill slope of 1:1.

14. This defines the 1:1 slope from the road, as shown in Figure 9–31.

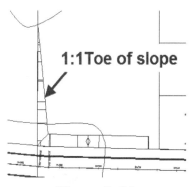

1:1 Toe of slope

Figure 9–31

15. Next we need to determine where the 3:1 slope from the parcels to the east will intersect the 1:1 slope of the pond.

16. When prompted to select a feature line, select the pond boundary feature line, the green line that defines the outer perimeter of the pond site.

17. When prompted for the grading side, select a point inside of the pond. Enter **No** if prompted to *Apply to the entire length*.

18. When prompted for the start point, select any point adjacent to the east boundary of the pond. Type **495** at the Command Line for the starting station and press <Enter>.

19. When prompted for the end point or length, select any point adjacent to the east boundary of the pond. Type **510** for the ending station and press <Enter>.

20. When prompted for the elevation, type **50.00** <Enter>.

21. When prompted for cut format, type **Slope** <Enter> followed by **3** <Enter> for a cut slope of 3:1.

22. When prompted for the fill format, type **Slope** <Enter> followed by **3** <Enter> for a fill slope of 3:1.

23. Press <Esc> to end the feature line selection and click on the **X** in the Grading Creation Tools toolbar to close the dialog box.

24. In order to use the toe of slope for further grading, the feature line that represents the toe of slope must be extracted from the grading object. In Model Space, select the toe of slope feature line, right-click, and select **Move to Site...**, as shown in Figure 9–32.

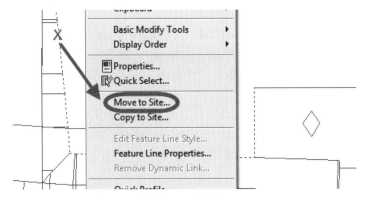

Figure 9–32

25. In the Move to Site dialog box, select **Storm Pond** in the *Destination site* drop-down list, as shown in Figure 9–33, and click ⬜ OK ⬜.

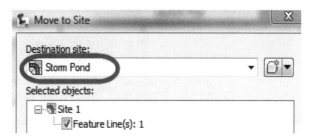

Figure 9–33

26. By moving the feature line to a different site, the grading object is deleted, leaving just the toe of slope. At the time of the publication of this Student Guide, AutoCAD Civil 3D does not finish creating the feature line; therefore, you are not able to edit the elevations. To fix this, you have to move the feature line back to Site 1.

27. Select the feature line, right click, select **Move to Site**. Select **Site 1** as the destination site.

28. In Model Space, select the feature line and in the contextual Ribbon > Modify panel, select **Feature Line Properties**, as shown in Figure 9–34.

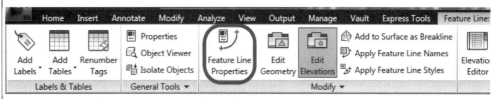

Figure 9–34

29. In the Feature Line Properties dialog box, select the **Name** option and enter **Toe of slope** in the field, as shown in Figure 9–35. Click ⬜ OK ⬜ to close the dialog box.

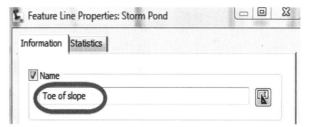

Figure 9–35

30. In Model Space, select the toe of slope feature line. In the contextual Ribbon > Modify panel, select **Edit Elevations**, and then in the Edit Elevations panel, select **Elevation Editor**, as shown in Figure 9–36.

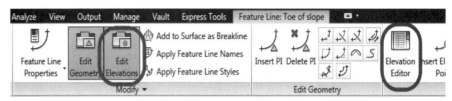

Figure 9–36

31. In the Grading Elevation Editor vista, the elevation shown for station 0+085.19 is 52.50, as shown in Figure 9–37. The correct elevation is 55.00 so will have to be changed.

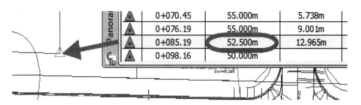

Figure 9–37

32. Click in the elevation cell for station 0+085.19 and change it to **55.00**.

33. Close the Grading Elevation Editor vista by clicking the check mark or the **X**.

34. Save the drawing.

Task 2: Establish control feature lines (North End).

In this task you will determine the location of the Pond maintenance access road, based on a 3:1 grade from the existing boundary.

1. Continue working with the drawing from the previous task.

2. In the *View* tab > Views panel, select the preset view **C3D-Grading-Feature2**.

3. In the *Home* tab > Create Design panel, select **Grading** > **Grading Creation Tools**.

4. In the Grading Creation Tools dialog box, set the Grading Group name to **Temp** (if not already set) and ensure the grading criteria is **Grade to Elevation**.

5. Click , as shown in Figure 9–38, and select the Pond boundary feature line, the green line that represents the perimeter of the pond site.

Figure 9–38

6. When prompted to weed the feature line, select **Continue grading without feature line weeding**.

7. When prompted for the side to grade, select a point inside of the pond. Enter **No** when prompted to *Apply to the entire length*.

8. When prompted for the start point, select any point adjacent to the north boundary of the pond. Type **0** at the Command Line for the starting station and press <Enter>.

9. When prompted for the end point or length, select any point adjacent to the west boundary of the pond. Type **190** for the ending station and press <Enter>.

10. When prompted for the elevation, type **50.00** <Enter>.

11. When prompted for cut format, type **Slope** <Enter> followed by **3** <Enter> for a cut slope of 3:1.

12. When prompted for the fill format, type **Slope** <Enter> followed by **3** <Enter> for a fill slope of 3:1.

13. Press <Esc> to exit the feature line selection. Click on the **X** in the Grading Creation Tools toolbar to close the dialog box.

14. This grading object defines a 3:1 slope from the existing boundary and establishes the approximate location of the maintenance road. To save time, the access road has already been designed, as shown in Figure 9–39. To view the access road, in the *View* Tab > Views panel, select the preset view **C3D-Grading-MaintenanceRoad**. You may have to type **Regen** at the Command Line to refresh the screen.

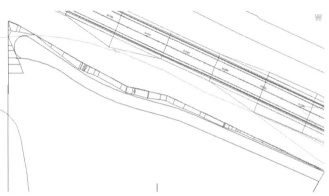

Figure 9–39

15. Based on the 3:1 cut and fill slope to an elevation of 50.00m, you now have a feature line representing the access road. This access road will have a maximum side slope of 3:1 to existing ground on the north side of the road. On the south side of the road, you will continue to grade based on the design criteria for the pond.

16. You no longer require the grading 3:1 maximum slope, so you can erase it. In Model Space, select the grading object and select the AutoCAD **Erase** command.

17. Save the drawing.

Practice 9c | Grading the Proposed Pond

In this practice you will create a stormwater detention pond with feature lines and grading tools. Now that a common base of control feature lines have been established, you can continue to grade the storm pond.

In the previous practice, the following control feature lines were created:

- A feature line defining the existing conditions along the entire pond site boundary.
- A feature line defining the Access road at the North end.
- A feature line defining the toe of 1:1 slope at the South end.
- To save time, the east and west feature lines have already been created. These two feature lines were created by copying the feature line from step 1 above, and were trimmed at the tie in points of the feature lines from steps 2 and 3.

In this practice you will join these feature lines, creating a base feature line, which will enable you to use the grading tools to grade the pond.

Task 1: Create a pond outside of the rim feature line.

1. Open the file **GRD1-Sec3-Grading.dwg** from the following folder:

    C:\Civil 3D Projects\Civil3D-training\Drawings

2. In the *View* tab > Views panel, select the preset view **C3D-Grading-Pond Control**.

3. In the *Prospector* tab, expand the *Sites* collection and expand the *Storm Pond* collection. Select **Feature lines** and notice the grid view usually at the bottom of the pane. This list displays the names of the feature lines, the style, layer, and 2D length.

4. Select one of the feature lines from the list, right-click, and select **Select**, as shown in Figure 9–40. AutoCAD Civil 3D will highlight the appropriate feature line.

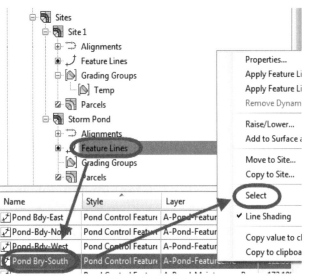

Figure 9–40

5. Select the un-named feature line representing the Access road, right-click, and select **Properties**. In the Feature Line Properties dialog box, enter **Pond Access Rd-North** for the name and set the *Style* to **Corridor Lane Break**, as shown in Figure 9–41.

   Click [OK]. Notice the style of the feature line in Model Space.

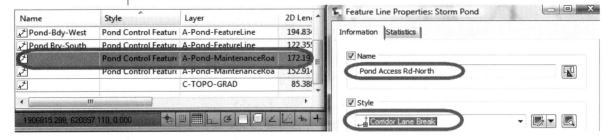

Figure 9–41

6. In the *View* tab > Views panel, select the preset view **C3D-Grading-1to1 slope**.

7. To join the toe of slope feature line to the east pond boundary, select the toe of slope feature line, then select the last NE grip, and drag to connect it to the end point of the Pond-Bdy East feature line, as shown in Figure 9–42.

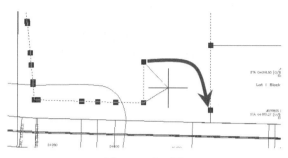

Figure 9–42

8. In the contextual Ribbon > Modify panel, select **Feature Line Properties**, as shown in Figure 9–43.

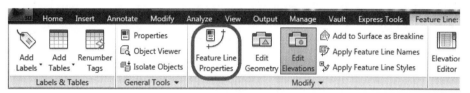

Figure 9–43

9. In the Feature Line Properties dialog box, change the *Name* from Toe of slope to **Pond-Bdy-Control** and set the *Style* to **Pond Control Feature Line**, as shown in Figure 9–44. Click 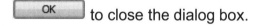 to close the dialog box.

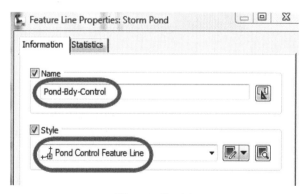

Figure 9–44

10. In the *View* tab > Views panel, select the preset view **C3D-Grading-Pond Control**.

11. To join all feature lines, first select the feature line
    Pond-Bdy-Control. In the contextual Ribbon > Modify panel,
    select **Edit Geometry**, and then in the Edit Geometry panel, click

    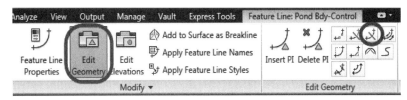 , as shown in Figure 9–45.

Figure 9–45

12. When prompted to select the connecting feature lines, select the
    feature line **Pond-Bdy-East** (2), **Pond-Bdy-North** (3), and
    finally **Pond-Bdy-West** (4), as shown in Figure 9–46.

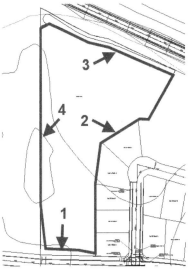

Figure 9–46

13. Press <Esc> to exit the feature line selection.

14. In the grid view list of feature lines (see step 3 above), note that
    only four feature lines now exist, as shown in Figure 9–47.

Name	Style	Layer	2D Length
Pond Access Rd-N	Corridor Lane Break	A-Pond-MaintenanceRoa	172.199m
Pond-Bdy-North	Pond Control Feature	A-Pond-FeatureLine	186.597m
Pond Bdy-Control	Pond Control Feature	C-TOPO-FEAT	685.898m
Pond Bry-South	Pond Control Feature	A-Pond-FeatureLine	122.355m

Figure 9–47

15. Save the drawing.

Task 2: Create pond grading.

With the pond boundary established, the rest of the pond can now be graded to the criteria set out in the cross-section.

1. Continue working with the drawing from the previous task or open the file **GRD1-Sec4-Grading.dwg** from the following folder:

    C:\Civil 3D Projects\Civil3D-training\Drawings

2. In the *View* tab > Views panel, select the preset view **C3D-Grading-Pond Control**.

3. In the *Home* tab > Create Design panel, select **Grading** > **Grading Creation Tools**, as shown in Figure 9–48.

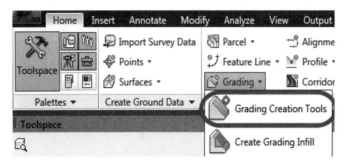

Figure 9–48

4. In the Grading Creation Tools toolbar, click , as shown in Figure 9–49.

Figure 9–49

5. In the Select Grading Group dialog box, set the *Site name* to **Storm Pond**, as shown on the left in Figure 9–50. To create a new group, click (Create a Grading Group). In the Create Grading Group dialog box, enter **Pond** for the name and select the **Automatic surface creation** option, as shown on the right. Click ` OK ` to close the dialog box.

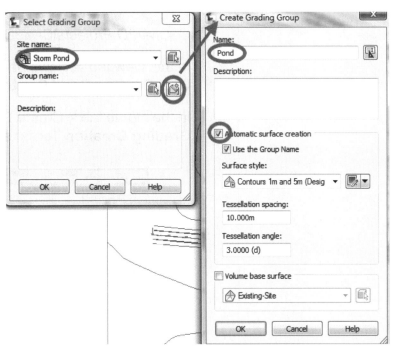

Figure 9–50

6. In the Create Surface dialog box, accept the defaults and click ` OK `.

7. In the Select Grading Group dialog box, click ` OK ` to close the dialog box.

8. You now have the new grading group Pond in the site Storm Pond. You can proceed to grade the pond. In the Grading Creation Tools toolbar, set the grading criteria to **Grade to Elevation** and click (Create a Grading Group), as shown in Figure 9–51. The first step is to grade to the Permanent water level of 49.00 at a slope of 3:1.

Figure 9–51

9. When prompted to select the feature line, select the Pond-Bry-Control feature line.

10. When prompted to weed feature line select **Continue grading without weeding**.

11. When prompted to select the side to grade, select the inside of the pond. Enter **Yes** when prompted to *Apply to entire length*.

12. Enter **49.00** for the elevation.

13. When prompted for the Cut format, type **Slope** <Enter> and then type **3** <Enter> for the slope value to signify a 3:1 slope.

14. When prompted for the Fill format, type **Slope** <Enter> and then type **3** <Enter> for the slope value to signify a 3:1 slope.

15. You now need to grade to the bottom of the pond, which is 4m deep at a slope of 2:1.

16. In the Grading Creation Tools toolbar, change the criteria to **Grade to Relative Elevation**, as shown in Figure 9–52.

Figure 9–52

17. When prompted to select the feature line, select the inside of pond feature line created by the last grading object, as shown in Figure 9–53. Enter **Yes** when prompted to *Apply to entire length*.

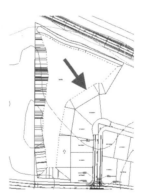

Figure 9–53

18. If prompted to select the side to grade, select the inside of the pond.

19. When prompted for the relative elevation, type **4** <Enter>.

20. When prompted for the format, type **Slope** <Enter> and then type **2** <Enter> for the slope value to signify a 2:1 slope.

21. In the Grading Creation Tools toolbar, click the drop-down arrow next to 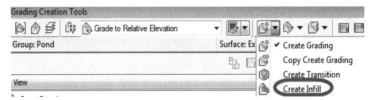 (Create a Grading Group) and select **Create Infill**, as shown in Figure 9–54. When prompted to select an area to infill, select the center of the pond, and press <Esc> to exit the command.

Figure 9–54

22. To view the pond grading in 3D, select the surface in Model Space, right-click, and select **Object Viewer**. Looking at the model or at the contours, notice that there is an error. The 2:1 slope that is supposed to project down to the bottom of the pond was mistakenly projected up. In step 19, a negative value should have been entered to indicate the slope projection as downwards (i.e., -4 instead of +4). Close the Object Viewer by clicking on the **X** in the right top corner of the dialog box, as shown in Figure 9–55.

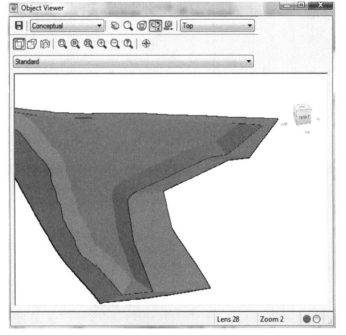

Figure 9–55

23. In the *Modify* tab > Design panel, select **Grading** to display the contextual *Grading* tab, as shown in Figure 9–56.

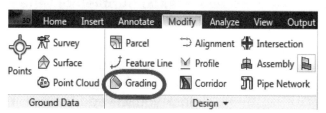

Figure 9–56

24. In the *Grading* tab > Modify panel, select **Grading Editor**, as shown in Figure 9–57.

Figure 9–57

25. When prompted to select a point in the grading or site, select a point in the second grading object (the 2:1 slope closest to the pond bottom), as shown in Figure 9–58.

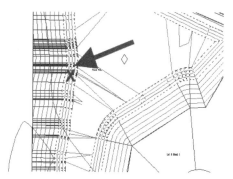

Figure 9–58

26. In the Grading Editor vista, under *Grading Method*, change the *Relative Elevation* to **-4**, as shown in Figure 9–59.

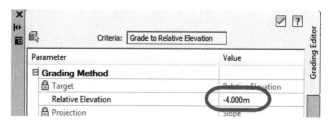

Figure 9–59

27. Close the Grading Editor vista by clicking on the **X** in the top right corner of the dialog box.

28. Save the drawing.

Task 3: Supplement the surface with feature lines.

Add feature lines to represent critical grade breaks and other important elevation breaklines on the surface. These lines will accentuate the geometry and make the surface more accurate. In this task you will add feature lines at the north and south ends of the site.

1. Continue working with the drawing from the previous task.

2. In the *View* tab > Views panel, select the preset view **C3D-Grading-Pond Control**.

3. In the *Prospector* tab, expand the *Sites* collection, expand the site *Storm Pond* collection, and select **Feature Lines**. In the grid view at the bottom, select the three feature lines **Pond-Bdy-North**, **Pond-Bdy-South**, and **Pond-Access Rd-North** using the <Ctrl> key. Right-click and select **Select**, as shown in Figure 9–60.

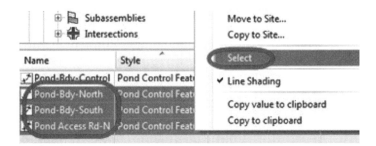

Figure 9–60

4. Once selected, the feature lines can be added to the surface as breaklines.

5. In the *Prospector* tab, expand the *Surfaces > Pond > Definition* collections for the point, and select **Breaklines**. Right-click and select **Add**, as shown in Figure 9–61.

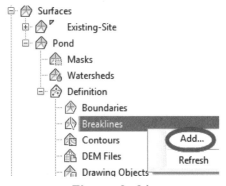

Figure 9–61

6. In the Add Breaklines dialog box, accept all the defaults and click .

7. You now have a pond surface that matches the proposed design of the parcels on the east side and Jeffries Ranch Road on the south side. The north and west sides of the pond have been graded to match the existing ground.

8. Save the drawing.

Review Questions

Question 1   What does the combination of feature lines and their grading solutions do?

Question 2   How do you raise or lower feature line vertices?

Question 3   What is the function of a grading group?

Module 10

Pipe Networks Level 1

This module introduces:

Section 1: Pipe Networks Overview
- ✓ **Pipes Overview**
- ✓ **Pipes Configuration**
- ✓ **The Network Layout Toolbar**
- ✓ **Creating Networks from Objects**

Section 2: Pipe Networks Editing and Annotation
- ✓ **Network Editing**
- ✓ **Annotating Pipe Networks**

Section 1: Pipe Networks Overview

10.1 Pipes Overview

AutoCAD Civil 3D's utility design system is often referred to as *AutoCAD Civil 3D Pipes*.

- You can create pipe networks in AutoCAD Civil 3D drawings to represent storm sewers, sanitary sewers, and more. Unlike AutoCAD Land Desktop, AutoCAD Civil 3D networks can model multiple, connected trunk lines and laterals as part of the same system.

- In AutoCAD Civil 3D, pipes are geared for gravity flow systems (sewers). Pressurized flow systems, electrical ducts, and similar types of conduit can also be modeled, but require special attention.

- Pipes are created in plan view interactively or by converting other linework into pipes (including 2D and 3D polylines and feature lines). Pipes can also be imported directly from AutoCAD Land Desktop projects and through Autodesk LandXML.

- Pipe networks can be created from customized part lists, styles, and rules that can help lay them out (and display them) appropriately.

- Once created, pipe networks can be displayed in profile and section views. Pipes can be edited in plan or profile, and through layout tools like the Grid View Vista (a spreadsheet-like view of pipe network pipes and structures). Changes made in plan, profile, or Grid View automatically update all other displays.

- AutoCAD Civil 3D includes an interference check utility to search for possible conflicts between pipe networks.

- AutoCAD Civil 3D includes hydrology or hydraulic (H&H) calculators with the Hydraflow Express, the Hydraflow Hydrographs, and the Hydraflow Storm Sewer applications available in the Analyze tab on the Ribbon. Without these applications, the system is set up to automate the drafting of utility systems, but not to analyze them or suggest pipe sizes.

> **Note:** These extensions are not taught in the Civil 3D Fundamentals course. Talk to a Value Added Reseller or Autodesk Authorized Training Center for information regarding hydrology or hydraulic courses.

- Many 3rd party H&H applications also support the Autodesk LandXML transfer of networks configured in AutoCAD Civil 3D. Therefore, a conceptual layout could be created in AutoCAD Civil 3D, exported for analysis and adjustment, and then reinserted into AutoCAD Civil 3D using Autodesk LandXML.

10.2 Pipes Configuration

The *Settings* tab contains values and styles affecting pipe networks. The *Parts Lists* and *Pipe Rules* are the most important settings. Parts Lists contain typical pipes and structures for a type of utility. Pipe Rules trigger error messages if pipes or structures are not created in accordance with predefined design constraints, such as the maximum pipe length of a slope.

Edit Drawing Settings

The Edit Drawing Settings dialog box contains values affecting the pipe layout layers (e.g., pipe networks, profiles, and section views).

Pipe Network Feature Settings

The Pipe Network Edit Feature Settings dialog box contains values that assign styles, set the pipe network naming convention, set the default pipe and structure rules, and set the default location for pipe and structure labels.

* To access the Edit Feature Settings dialog box, right-click on Settings under the Pipe Network collection, and select **Edit Feature Settings**. The dialog box is shown in Figure 10–1.

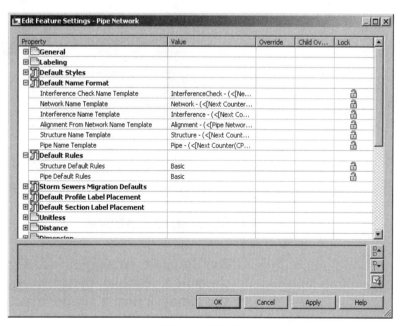

Figure 10–1

Pipe Catalog

AutoCAD Civil 3D includes standard catalogs in both Imperial and Metric units. Catalog specifications define the size and shape of the underground structures and pipes for sanitary or storm gravity systems.

- The *US Imperial Pipes* folder contains the **US Imperial Pipes.htm** file, which displays the components of the Pipe catalog.
- You can view the contents of these libraries by clicking on this file and viewing it in Internet Explorer.
- The Pipe catalog includes circular, egg, elliptical, and rectangular shapes. For each pipe shape, the catalog includes inner and outer pipe diameters and wall thicknesses.

Pipe catalog components can be edited by selecting **Modify > Pipe network > Parts List > Part Builder**. The catalog in Internet Explorer is shown in Figure 10–2.

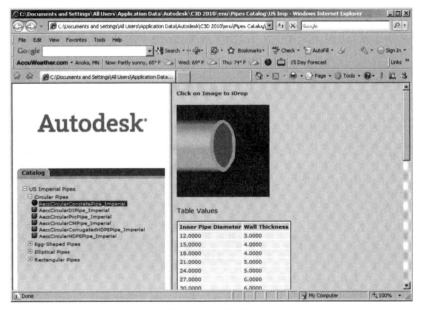

Figure 10–2

Structure Catalog

The Structure catalog includes specifications for inlets, junction structures, (circular, rectangular, or eccentric) with or without frames, and simple junction shapes (rectangular or circular).

- The Structure catalog consists of tables and lists that define allowable sizes, thicknesses, and heights.
- The *US Imperial Structure* folder contains the **US Imperial Structure.htm** file that is the Structure catalog.

- You can view the files and their contents by clicking on a file and viewing it in Internet Explorer, as shown in Figure 10–3.

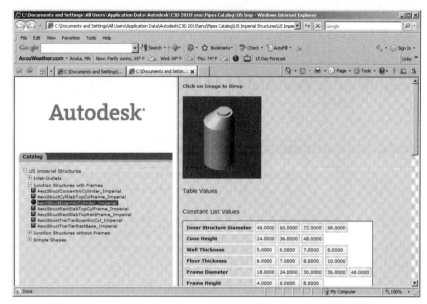

Figure 10–3

Pipe Network Parts Lists

While the catalogs listed above are shared between multiple projects (and multiple users), each AutoCAD Civil 3D drawing can contain any number of Part Lists that are specific to that drawing.

Part Lists are populated with pipes and structures from the catalog, and are organized for a specific task (such as Sanitary Sewer and Drain).

- Parts Lists are in the Settings tab under the Pipe Network collection, as shown in Figure 10–4.
- To access a parts list, right-click on the list's name and select **Edit…**.

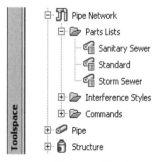

Figure 10–4

The parts list has typical pipe sizes in the *Pipes* tab and typical structures in the *Structure* tab, as shown in Figure 10–5. If needed, you can change a pipe or structure size list, or add a new part type.

Two important settings for each tab are Rules and Render Material. Render Material affects how the pipes and structures appear in 3D.

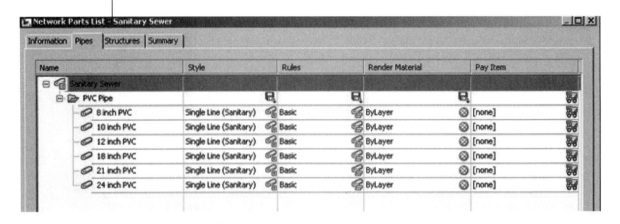

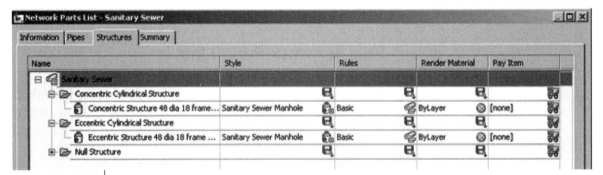

Figure 10–5

- To add a pipe size or structure size, click on the part type heading, right-click, and select **Add a part size**. Then select a new part size from the size list, as shown in Figure 10–6.

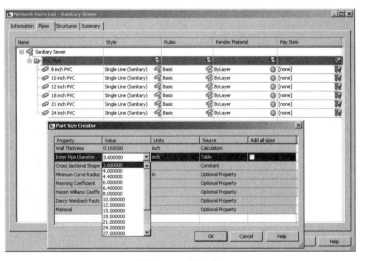

Figure 10–6

- To add a new part family (e.g., concrete pipes for a sanitary system), select the name of the part list, right-click, and select **Add a part family**. Then select a new part family from the list of available parts in the catalog, as shown in Figure 10–7.

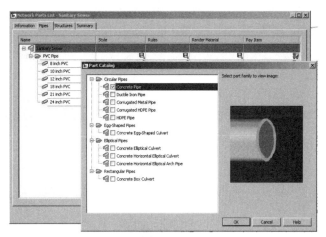

Figure 10–7

Pipe and Structure Styles

The pipe style defines how a pipe appears in plan, profile, and section views. The most critical tab of a Pipe Style is the *Display* tab. By turning on or off Component display, a style affects how a network appears on the screen (e.g., as a single or double line), its layer name, and color.

A structure style defines how a structure is displayed in plan and profile views. The plan settings include the plan view symbol and how a structure displays in profile and section views (the outline of the 3D shape).

Pipe styles include the **Clean up Pipe to Pipe Intersections** option for networks, where one pipe connects to another (rather than to a structure). This enables the pipes to appear to fillet together. For this option to work, the pipes must be connected with a *null* structure.

Pipe and Structure Rules

Since pipes and structures often need more than one rule applied to them, individual rules are organized into collections called **rule sets**. You can have different sets for different types of pipe sizes and/or systems.

- Pipe rules define minimum/maximum slopes, cover, and maximum pipe segment length.

- Pipe rule sets are located in the *Settings* tab, *Pipe Rule Set* collection, as shown in Figure 10–8. To view or edit a rule set, right-click on it and select **Edit**.

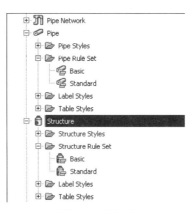

Figure 10–8

- Structure rules define the across structure drop's default value, maximum value, and maximum pipe size.
- Structure rule sets are located in the *Settings* tab, *Pipe Rule Set* collection.

Some pipe and structure rules directly control the layout of new pipes and structures, such as minimum and maximum slope. Some rules are simply checks that are made after creation, such as maximum pipe length. Rules like maximum pipe length do not prevent you from creating a pipe that is over the maximum length, for example. However, if a pipe is over the maximum length, you are notified with a warning in the *Prospector* tab and in the Pipe Network Vistas, as shown in Figure 10–9.

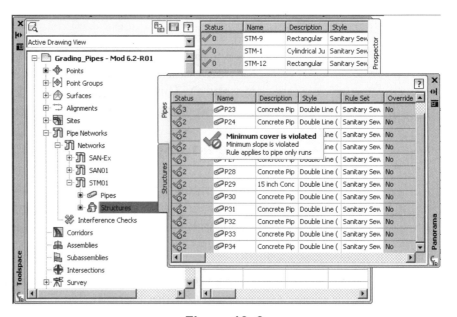

Figure 10–9

Re-Applying Pipe Rules

Structure Invert Out elevations are automatically calculated when the structure is first created. Therefore, if new connecting pipes are added to a structure below the lowest invert in, the outlet is not automatically lowered until you run the command **Modify > Pipe Network > Modify > Apply Rules…**. An example is shown in Figure 10–10.

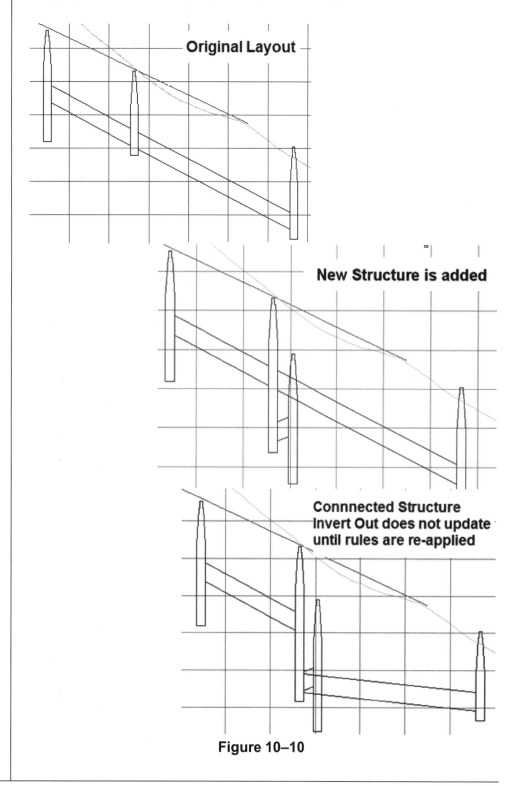

Figure 10–10

Pipe Layers

Unlike most AutoCAD Civil 3D objects, pipe network layers typically need to be manually reassigned when a pipe network is created. Layers need to be assigned for pipes and structures in plan, profile, and section views. For example, the default AutoCAD Civil 3D templates default to layers appropriate for storm drainage structures. The Pipe Network Layers dialog box is shown in Figure 10–11.

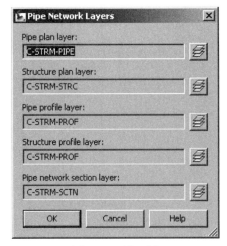

Figure 10–11

If creating a water line, each one needs to be remapped to layers specific to water utilities, such as the examples shown in Figure 10–12.

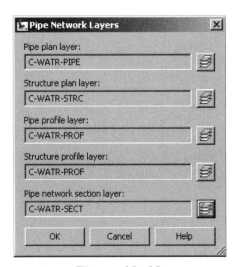

Figure 10–12

10.3 The Network Layout Toolbar

The Network Layout Tools toolbar contains commands for creating pipe networks by layout (interactively, similar to creating an alignment by layout) and for editing them after creation. This toolbar is opened by selecting **Home > Pipe Network > Pipe Network Creation Tools or Modify > Pipe Network > Edit Pipe Network**. The toolbar commands are shown in Figure 10–13 and are described below.

Figure 10–13

- ⬛ (Pipe Network Properties): Enables you to review and edit the properties of a pipe network. These include the default labeling, layers, and default parts list to be used.

- ⬛ (Select Surface): Enables you to select a surface model to calculate rim elevations and pipe invert elevations. This can be changed while laying out pipes and structures.

- ⬛ (Select Alignment): Enables you to specify an alignment to lay out components by station and offset. The chosen alignment can be changed while laying out pipes and structures.

- ⬛ (Parts List): Enables you to change the current parts list, even in the middle of a layout.

- ⬛ Concentric Structure 1. ▾ ⬛ 400 mm Concrete Pipe ▾ (*Structure* and *Pipe* pull-down menus): Enables you to select the next type of structure or pipe to add.

- ⬛ ▾ (Create pull-down menu): Enables you to select if you want to lay out pipes only, structures only, or both pipes and structures. When laying out pipes, you graphically select the location of the next structure (or pipe end point if laying out pipes only).

-  (Toggle Upslope/Downslope): Controls the direction of the next pipe to be laid out in gravity flow networks.

-  (Delete Pipe Network Object): Enables you to delete a pipe or structure from the network.

-  (Pipe Network Vistas): Opens a grid view where pipes and structures can be reviewed and have their properties edited. Here you can assign meaningful names to pipes and structures (such as **DMH-1**), which can be included in labels.

-  (Undo): Enables you to undo the last pipe network edit.

Connecting Pipes and Structures

When creating or editing networks with the Network Layout Tools toolbar, you can connect new pipes to previously created structures (in the same network) by hovering your cursor over that structure until the tool tip image appears, as shown in Figure 10–14. When displayed, left-click to connect the new pipe to the structure.

Figure 10–14

New pipes and structures can also be used to divide an existing pipe into two pipes. To do so, hover your cursor over the connection point until the tool tip image appears, as shown in Figure 10–15.

Figure 10–15

10.4 Creating Networks from Objects

In addition to creating networks by layout, a pipe network can be created from a 2D or 3D object, including a polyline or feature line. Select **Home > Pipe Network > Create Pipe Network from Object** to start the creation of a pipe network.

Since AutoCAD Civil 3D is geared for gravity flow networks, creating pressurized or conduit systems requires a few extra steps. For example, pipes connect to other pipes at a structure. Ideally, these null or nonexistent structures need to be managed to be hidden from the final display. Therefore, the following is recommended:

- To maintain a certain depth below grade, draw a layout as a polyline, convert it to a feature line, and assign elevations from a surface. Edit the feature line to include additional vertices and to lower the pipe to a specified depth, and then create a pipe network from the feature line.
- Use a pipe rule set that includes a pipe-to-pipe match drop value of 0.
- Use a structure rule set that includes a structure drop value of 0 and a sump value of 0.
- AutoCAD Civil 3D does not enable you to add pipe networks by object with null structures. Therefore create your own null structure type that appears with a symbol in plan view, but is not masked and is on a layer that does not print.
- To adjust the pipe network in plan view, manipulate the custom null structure to change the connection point of two pipes.
- To adjust the network manually in profile view, select both pipe ends and grip-edit them together.

The drawing **Grading_Pipes - Mod 6.4.dwg** includes a custom Water Line part list, rules, and styles that illustrates this approach.

Practice 10a | Creating Pipe Networks

Task 1: Review the Storm Drain Parts List and Rules.

Before creating a network, you should become familiar with the configuration you are about to use.

1. Open the file **Pip1-Sec1-PipeWorks.dwg** from the following folder:

   C:\Civil 3D Projects\Civil3D-training\Drawings

2. In the *Settings* tab, expand the *Pipe Network* collection, expand the *Parts Lists* collection, right-click on the Storm Sewer part and select **Edit...**, as shown in Figure 10–16.

Figure 10–16

3. In the *Pipes* tab, the parts list currently contains a large number of concrete pipes. They are all assigned to use the Storm Sewer rule set and a pipe style that shows double lines in plan view, as shown in Figure 10–17.

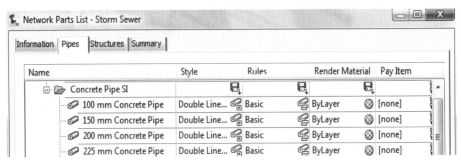

Figure 10–17

4. To add another Pipe type, under **Network Parts List - Storm Sewer**, select **Storm Sewer**, right-click, and select **Add part family...**, as shown in Figure 10–18.

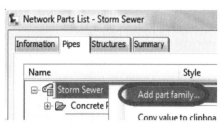

Figure 10–18

5. In the Parts catalog, select **PVC Pipe SI**, as shown in Figure 10–19. Click [OK] to close the dialog box.

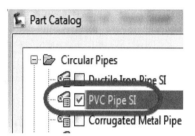

Figure 10–19

6. To add sizes to the part family, select **PVC Pipe SI**, right-click, and select **Add part size...**, as shown in Figure 10–20.

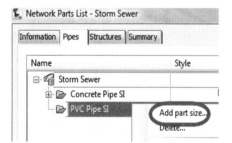

Figure 10–20

7. To add part sizes, you can either select individual sizes from the Value drop-down list or select the check box in the *Add all sizes* column to add all of the available sizes, as shown in Figure 10–21. Select and add the **200**, **250**, **300** and **400** mm Pipe sizes. Note you cannot select all four of these sizes; you will have to add each one separately. Click OK to add each one.

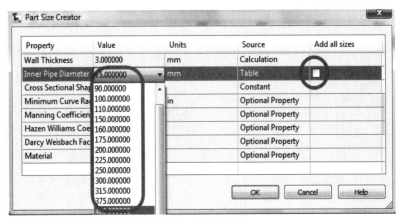

Figure 10–21

When finished, the Network Parts List - Storm Sewer dialog box appears as shown in Figure 10–22.

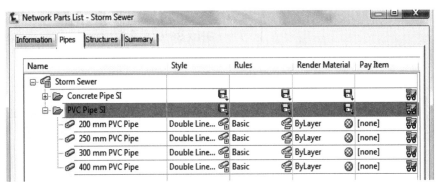

Figure 10–22

8. Select the *Structures* tab. The parts list includes a number of headwalls of different sizes, as well as catch basins and manholes. Each of these is assigned styles and rules specific to each type, as shown in Figure 10–23.

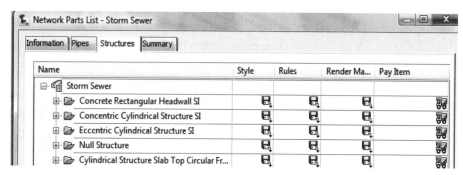

Figure 10–23

9. Click [OK] to exit.

10. In the *Settings* tab, expand the *Structure* collection, expand the *Structure Rule Set* collection, select the Storm rule set, right-click and select **Edit...**, as shown in Figure 10–24.

Figure 10–24

For this Manhole, you are allowed to use a maximum pipe length of 4m. You have elevations based on Inverts and a drop across the manhole of 0.1m with a 3.0m maximum interior drop, as shown in Figure 10–25.

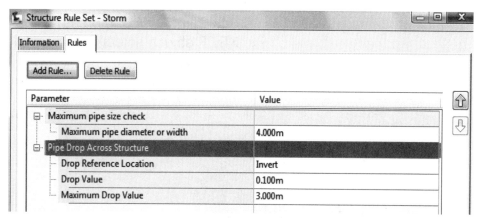

Figure 10–25

Note: Using the arrows at the right side of the Rules tab enables you to prioritize the rules. The rules are processed sequentially from bottom to top. Therefore, place the most important rule at the top of the list.

11. Review and click $\boxed{\text{OK}}$ to exit without changes.

Task 2: Create a Pipe Network by Object.

In a production environment, the line assignment for utilities is often based on the offsets from the Right -Of-Ways boundary. Based on the tools available in the Network Layout Tools toolbar, it is simpler to use AutoCAD's tools to lay out the utility line assignments and then convert it to a pipe network. In this task, you will review the process of converting a line assignment to a pipe network.

1. Continue working with the drawing from the previous task.

2. In the *View* tab > Views panel, select the preset view **C3D-PipeWork Object**. You may need to enter **Regen** at the Command Line.

3. In the *Home* tab > Create Design panel, select **Pipe Network > Create Pipe Network from Object**, as shown in Figure 10–26.

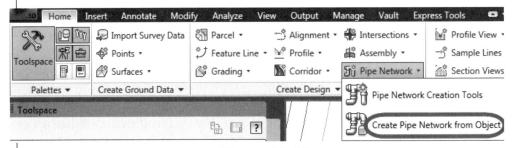

Figure 10–26

4. When prompted to select the object or Xref type, type **Xref** at the Command Line and press <Enter>. When prompted to select the XREF object, select the storm line (red line at the center of the road), as shown in Figure 10–27.

Figure 10–27

5. Accept the default flow direction. In the Create Pipe Network from Object dialog box, enter **STORM** for the *Network name*. For the *Pipe to create*, select **300mm PVC Pipe**. For the *Structure to create*, select **Slab Top Cylindrical Structure 900dia**. For the *Surface name*, select **Phase1-Site** and for the *Alignment name*, select **<none>**. Click [OK] to accept and close the dialog box, as shown in Figure 10–28.

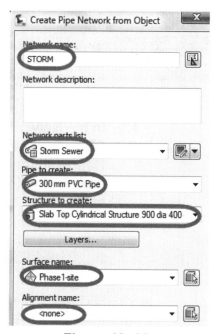

Figure 10–28

AutoCAD Civil 3D has created a Pipe network based on the rules and values entered in the Create Pipe Network from Objects dialog box. After you have completed building the network, you will go back and make adjustments to the design inverts, slopes, and part sizes.

6. Save the drawing.

Task 3: Create a Pipe Network by Layout.

In this task, you continue adding to the network using Civil 3D's Pipe Network creation tool.

If you want to modify or add to a pipe network that you have already defined, do not use the command **Pipes > Create Pipe Network by Layout**, as this creates a whole new network. Instead, use **Edit Network** when you want to modify a network you already have started.

1. Continue working with the drawing from the previous task.

2. In the *View* tab > Views panel, select the preset view
    C3D-PipeWork-Create.

3. In Model Space, select a part in the STORM network. In the
    contextual Ribbon tab > Modify panel, select **Edit Pipe Network**,
    as shown in Figure 10–29.

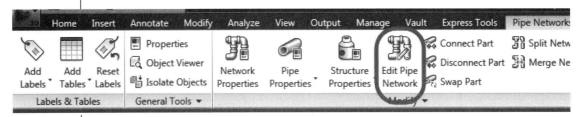

Figure 10–29

4. In the Network Layout Tools - STORM toolbar, select
    **1575x660x900 mm Concrete Rectangular Box Culvert
    Headwall** for the manhole structure and select **300mm PVC
    Pipe** for the Pipe part. Then click (Draw Pipe and Structure), as
    shown in Figure 10–30.

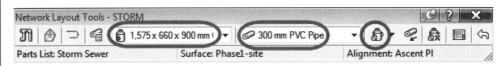

Figure 10–30

5. AutoCAD Civil 3D prompts you for the locations of the structures.
    Select end point pt1 and then select an approximate location
    near point pt2 for the next structure location, as shown in
    Figure 10–31.

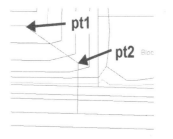

Figure 10–31

6. In the Network Layout Tools - STORM toolbar, select **Slab Top Cylindrical Structure 900 dia** for the manhole structure, as shown in Figure 10–32.

Figure 10–32

7. At the Command Line, you should still be prompted for a structure insertion point. Type **S** <Enter> for a start point.

   You will insert manholes based on Figure 10–33. The first structure, pt1, is located at the intersection of Jeffries Ranch Rd and Ascent Blvd. The next structure, pt2, is located at the beginning of the curve, pt3 is at the intersection of Jeffries Ranch Rd and Ascent Pl, and pt4 is at a station of 0+098.87 along the Jeffries Ranch Rd alignment. Refer to Figure 10–33 as a guide.

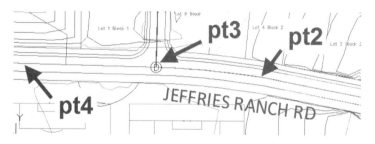

Figure 10–33

8. Civil 3D prompts you for the locations of the structures. Select end point pt1 and select the **end point pt2** for the next structure.

9. When prompted for the next structure, type **C** <Enter> to draw a curved pipe. When prompted for the end of curve, select the manhole structure at the intersection of Jeffries Ranch Rd and Ascent Pl. You should see a symbol indicating that you are tying into a manhole, as shown in Figure 10–34.

Figure 10–34

10. You now want to use a different pipe size. In the Network Layout Tools - STORM toolbar, select **400mm PVC Pipe** from the list, as shown in Figure 10–35.

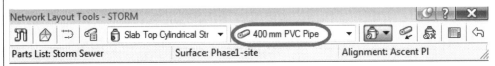

Figure 10–35

11. At the prompt for the end of curve, type **L** <Enter> to draw a line.

   When prompted to select the next structure location, click (Station offset), as shown in Figure 10–36.

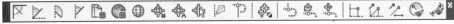

Figure 10–36

12. When prompted for an alignment, select the Jeffries Ranch Rd alignment. Enter **98.87** for the station, and enter **0** for the offset. Press <Esc> to exit the command and press <Enter> to exit the prompt for the insertion point of a structure.

13. You have made a design change and decided to insert a manhole east of the original intended location, as shown in Figure 10–37. This requires you to make further adjustments to the network. The following section and its practice will demonstrate how to do this.

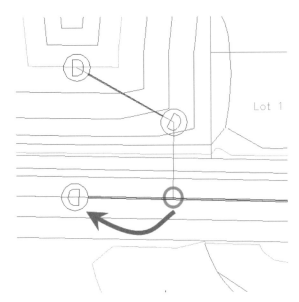

Figure 10–37

14. Close the Network Layout Tools toolbar by clicking on the **X**.

15. Save the drawing.

Review Questions

Question 1   What do Pipe Rules trigger and affect?

Question 2   Where do you find Parts Lists?

Question 3   How do you add a pipe size or structure size?

Question 4   What are the drafting modes of the Network Layout Tools toolbar?

Question 5   What is a Pipe Warning?

Section 2: Pipe Networks Editing and Annotation

10.5 Network Editing

You can edit pipe networks by graphically changing the components' locations in plan or profile views, through tabular fields in the *Prospector* and Grid View, and through the Object Properties dialog boxes. All of the commands listed below are available in the shortcut menu that appears after selecting and right-clicking on a part in plan. (Some, but not all, are available in profile.)

Pipe (and Structure) Properties

The Properties dialog box lists the object's name, dimensions, material, rotation angle, sump depth, etc., as shown in Figure 10–38. Those shown in black can be directly edited.

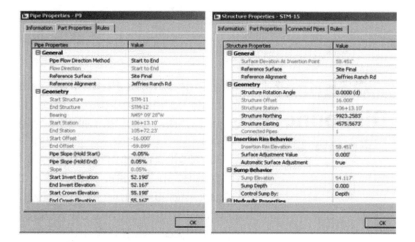

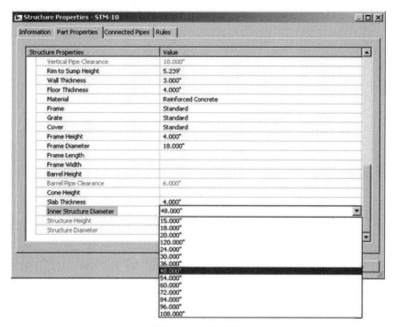

Figure 10–38

Swap Part

The **Swap Part** command exchanges one part for another from the same parts list but in a different size. When starting the command, AutoCAD Civil 3D displays the Swap Part Size dialog box containing all of the parts sizes from the parts list, as shown in Figure 10–39.

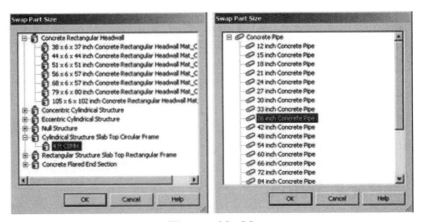

Figure 10–39

Connect / Disconnect From Part

The **Disconnect From Part** command detaches a selected object from its connected part. Once detached, you can move the selected object and any of its remaining attached items to a new location.

Whether the **Disconnect From Part** or **Connect To Part** command is displayed in the shortcut menu depends on the state of the selected object. For example, if the object is a structure attached to pipes, the shortcut menu shows only **Disconnect From Part**. If the object is a pipe not connected to any other object, the shortcut menu shows **Connect To Part**.

10.6 Annotating Pipe Networks

As with other AutoCAD Civil 3D labels, pipe network plan and profile labels are all style-based. A pipe label style can contain an extensive list of pipe network properties. The labels are scale- and rotation-sensitive, and use the same interface for creating or modifying styles.

- AutoCAD Civil 3D can label pipes and structures as you draft them or later on as needed.
- In the *Annotate* tab > Add Labels panel, select **Pipe Network > Add Pipe Network Labels...** to label individual objects or an entire network. The Add Labels dialog box is shown in Figure 10–40.

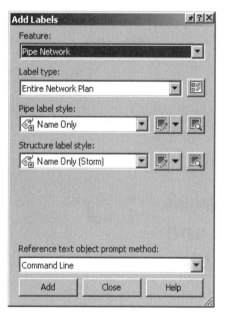

Figure 10–40

Most pipe labels annotate the length and slope of a particular pipe. If you have pipe bends and would rather not label each individual segment as a separate pipe, select the **Spanning** label type. This label type enables you to select multiple pipes that should be given a single label, which can include overall length, slope, and other properties.

Parts within a network can be renumbered quickly and easily by selecting **Modify > Pipe Network > Modify (panel) > Rename Parts**. Another method is to renumber each one manually through the Pipe Network Vistas view, which can be accessed in the Network Layout Tools toolbar, as shown in Figure 10–41. Labels automatically show the new part label.

Figure 10–41

Pipe Networks in Sections

To show pipe networks in sections, they need to be included as a data source for the sections' sample line group. If a sample line group has been created before a pipe network, they are not automatically included. To include them, open the sample line group Properties dialog box, select the *Sections* tab, and click **Sample more sources...**, as shown in Figure 10–42.

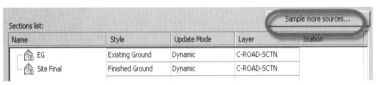

Figure 10–42

Pipe Network Reports and Tables

Pipe reports are available in the Toolbox (**Home > Palettes > Toolbox**), as shown in Figure 10–43.

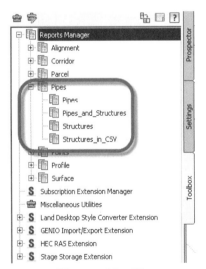

Figure 10–43

Pipe tables can be created inside of drawing files through **Annotate > Add Tables > Pipe Network > Add Structure and Annotate > Add Tables > Pipe Network > Add Pipe**.

Practice 10b | Pipe Networks Editing and Annotating

Task 1: Modify a pipe network.

1. Continue working with the drawing from the previous practice or open the file **Pip1-Sec2-PipeWorks.dwg** from the following folder: *C:\Civil 3D Projects\Civil3D-training\Drawings*.

2. Select the headwall structure. In the contextual Ribbon tab > Modify panel, select **Structure Properties**. Change the style of this structure to **Flared End Section**, and click ⬚ OK ⬚ to close the dialog box.

3. Select the headwall structure again. Notice the grips; the square grip enables you to relocate the structure and end of pipe, while the circular grip enables you to rotate the structure. Select the circular, rotation grip and rotate the structure as shown in Figure 10–44.

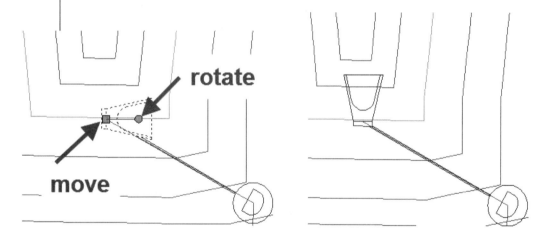

Figure 10–44

4. Press <Esc> to exit the command.

5. Using AutoCAD commands, select and erase the manhole structure that is located to the right of the headwall structure.

6. To connect the pipe to the STORM network, select the pipe structure, right-click, and select **Connect to part**, as shown in Figure 10–45.

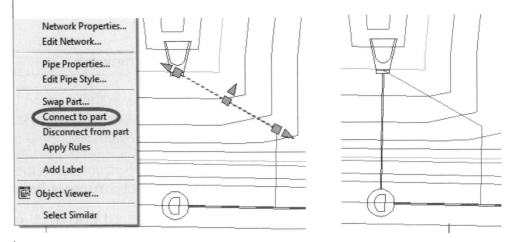

Figure 10–45

7. When prompted to select the network structure, select the manhole to the south of the headwall structure.

8. In Model Space, select the manhole structure that is south of the headwall structure, right-click, and select **Swap Part...**, as shown on the left in Figure 10–46. In the parts list, select **1500x750 Rect Structure 400 dia Frm...**, as shown on the right.

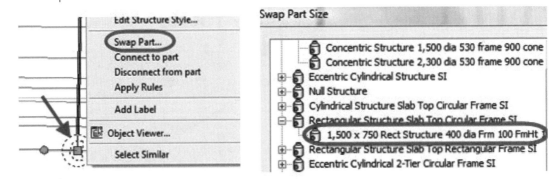

Figure 10–46

9. In Model Space, select the pipe that is connected to the headwall structure, right-click, and select **Swap Part....** In the parts list, select **600mm Concrete Pipe**.

Task 2: Edit network data.

When creating the Pipe network, Civil 3D assigned names to each part. In this task, you will rename these parts so that they conform to company standards.

1. Continue working with the drawing from the previous task.

2. In the *View* tab > Views panel, select the preset view **C3D-PipeWork-Create**.

3. In the *Modify* tab, select **Pipe Network**.

4. In the *Pipe Networks* tab > Modify panel, click the panel drop-down arrow and select **Rename Parts**, as shown in Figure 10–47.

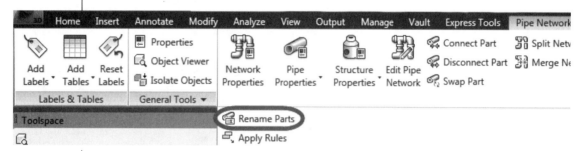

Figure 10–47

5. At the prompt to select the network parts to rename, select the manhole structure at the intersection of Jeffries Ranch Rd and Ascent Blvd and the headwall structure. Civil 3D will select all pipes and structures between these two selected structures. Then select the manhole structures at the end of the cul-de-sac. Notice that Civil 3D will select all parts in between. Press <Enter> to end the selection.

6. You have 11 structures and 9 pipes selected, as shown in the dialog box in Figure 10–48. Enter **STM - <[Next Counter(CP)]>** for the name of the *Structure name template* and enter **1** for the *Starting number*. Enter **Pipe - <[Next Counter(CP)]>** for the name of the *Pipe name template* and enter **1** for the *Starting number*. Select the **Rename existing parts** option in the *Name conflict options* section. Click [OK] to accept the changes and close the dialog box.

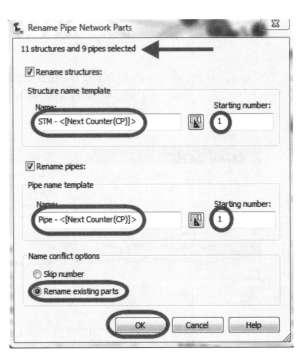

Figure 10–48

7. In the Status Bar, enable the **Quick Properties** icon, as shown in Figure 10–49.

Figure 10–49

8. In Model Space, select the headwall structure, and in the Properties view, change the name to **Headwall**, as shown in Figure 10–50.

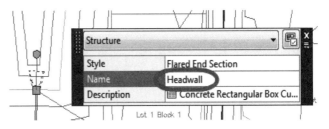

Figure 10–50

9. Save the drawing. Figure 10–51 shows the part names.

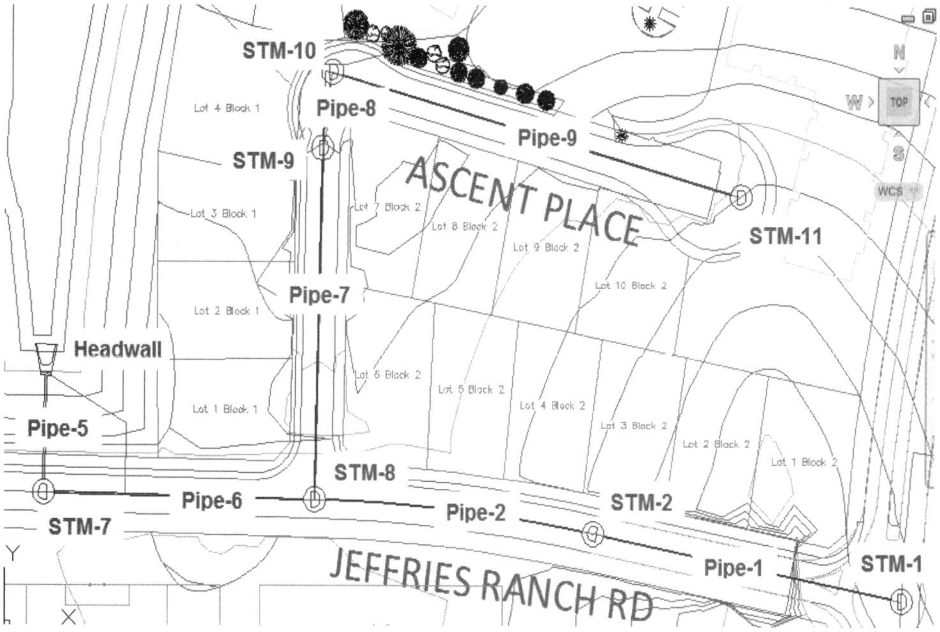

Figure 10–51

Task 3: Annotate Pipe networks.

---

1. Continue working with the drawing from the previous task.

2. In the *View* tab > Views panel, select the preset view **C3D-PipeWork-Create**.

3. In the *Annotate* tab > Labels & Tables panel, select **Add Labels**, as shown in Figure 10–52.

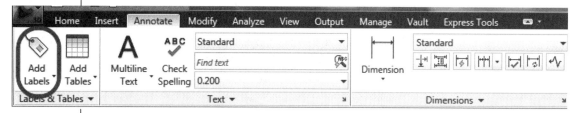

Figure 10–52

4. In the Add Labels dialog box, set the following parameters, as shown in Figure 10–53:

- Feature: **Pipe Network**
- Label type: **Entire Network Plan**
- Pipe label style: **Length Description and Slope**
- Structure label style: **Data with connected Pipes**

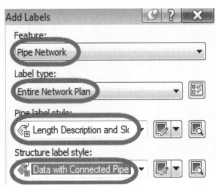

Figure 10–53

5. Click [Add]. When prompted, select any part in the network.

6. Click on the **X** or click [Close] to close the Add labels dialog box.

7. Save the drawing.

Task 4: Create a Structure table.

1. Continue working with the drawing from the previous task.

2. In Model Space, select any Pipe network part. In the contextual Ribbon tab > Labels & Tables panel, as shown in Figure 10–54, select **Add Tables > Add Structure**.

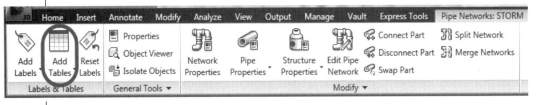

Figure 10–54

3. In the Structure Table Creation dialog box, select **Structure with Pipes** as the *Table style*. Select the **Dynamic** option and accept all the other defaults. Click  to close the dialog box, as shown in Figure 10–55.

Figure 10–55

4. Zoom to an open space and insert the table, as shown in Figure 10–56.

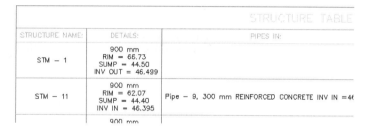

Figure 10–56

5. Save the drawing.

Task 5: Edit network data in plan view.

On reviewing the network labels, as well as the table, you notice that you need to make adjustments to the inverts.

1. Continue working with the drawing from the previous task.

2. In the *View* tab > Views panel, select the preset view **C3D-PipeWork-Create**.

3. The flow direction is incorrect. To fix this, select the pipe part in Model Space. In the contextual Ribbon tab > Modify panel, click the panel drop-down arrow and select **change flow direction**.

4. When prompted to select the Upstream starting point, select the Manhole STM-7. When prompted to select the Downhill starting point, select the Headwall. Press <Enter> to end the command. The drawing appears as shown in Figure 10–57.

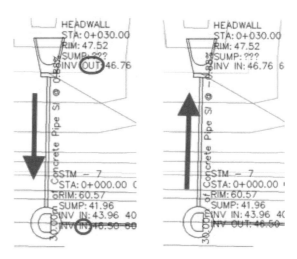

Figure 10–57

5. In Model Space, select a part in the STORM network. In the contextual Ribbon tab > Modify panel, select **Edit Pipe Network**, as shown in Figure 10–58.

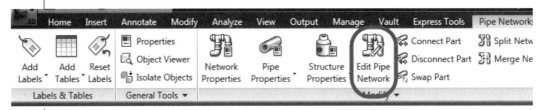

Figure 10–58

6. In the Network Layout Tools - STORM toolbar, click 🖻 , as shown in Figure 10–59, to open the Pipe network Vista.

Figure 10–59

7. In the Panorama, ensure that the *Rule Set* is set to **Storm**, as shown in Figure 10–60. Close the Panorama Vista and the Network Layout Tools toolbar.

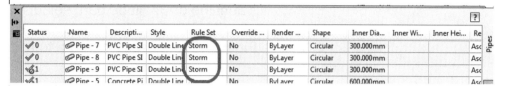

Figure 10–60

8. Apply the rule set to the network. In the *Modify* tab > Design panel, select **Pipe Network**.

9. In the *Pipe Networks* tab > Modify panel, as shown in Figure 10–61, click the panel drop-down arrow and select **Apply Rules**.

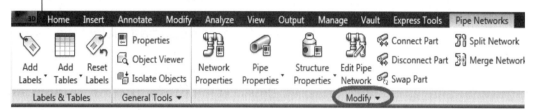

Figure 10–61

10. When prompted to select the up slope part, select the manhole at the end of the cul-de-sac (Pt1). When prompted to select the down slope part, select the manhole at the intersection (Pt2), as shown in Figure 10–62. Press <Enter> to apply the changes.

Figure 10–62

11. In the *Pipe Networks* tab > Modify panel, click the panel drop-down arrow and select **Apply Rules**. When prompted to select the up slope part, select the manhole at the intersection of Jeffries Ranch Rd and Ascent Blvd, (Pt1). When prompted to select the down slope part, select the manhole at the intersection of Jeffries Ranch Rd and Ascent Pl (Pt2), as shown in Figure 10–63. Press <Enter> to apply the changes.

Figure 10–63

12. In the *Pipe Networks* tab > Modify panel, click the panel drop-down arrow and select **Apply Rules**. When prompted to select the up slope part, select the manhole at the intersection of Jeffries Ranch Rd and Ascent Pl (Pt1). When prompted to select the down slope part, select the headwall (Pt2), as shown in Figure 10–64. Press <Enter> to apply the changes.

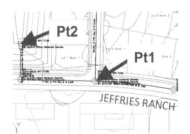

Figure 10–64

13. All labels have now been updated and the table you inserted earlier has also been updated. Review the design and save the drawing.

Task 6: View Pipe network in profile view.

---

1. Continue working with the drawing from the previous task.

2. In the *View* tab > Views panel, select the preset view **C3D-PipeWork Profile**.

3. In the *Modify* tab > Design panel, select **Pipe Network**. In the *Pipe Networks* tab > Network Tools panel, select **Draw Parts in Profile**.

4. At the Command Line, you can choose to select each part to be displayed in the profile or you can select the entire network. In Model Space, select any of the network parts and press <Enter> when done.

5. When prompted to select the Profile view, select the profile view to the right of the site plan.

6. To add all of the network parts, you will have to turn off the display parts that are not relevant to this profile view. Select the Profile view and in the contextual Ribbon tab > Modify Views panel, select **Profile View Properties**, as shown in Figure 10–65.

Figure 10–65

7. In the Profile View Properties - Jeffries Ranch Rd dialog box, in the *Pipe Networks* tab, ensure that only the following parts are enabled, as shown in Figure 10–66: **Pipe - 1, 2,** and **6,** and **STM - 1, 2, 8,** and **7.**

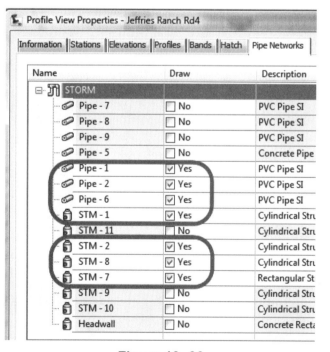

Figure 10–66

8. Label the network in the profile view. In the *Annotate* tab > Labels & Tables panel, select **Add Labels**.

9. In the Add Labels dialog box, set the following parameters, as shown in Figure 10–67:

    - Feature: **Pipe Network**
    - Label type: **Entire Network Profile**
    - Pipe label style: **Length Description and Slope**
    - Structure label style: **Data with Connected Pipe**

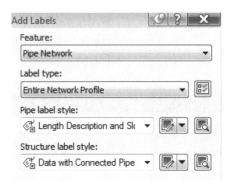

Figure 10–67

10. Click [Add].

11. When prompted, select any one of the network parts in the profile view, and click on the **X** to close the dialog box.

12. Save the drawing.

Task 7: Edit network data in profile view.

The design surface does not extend far enough into the intersection at Jeffries Ranch Rd and Ascent Blvd, as shown in Figure 10–68. The Pipe network rules set the rim elevations for STM - 1 to the existing ground elevation. You could go back and fix the corridors and surface to extend into the intersection, or to save time, you could fix it here.

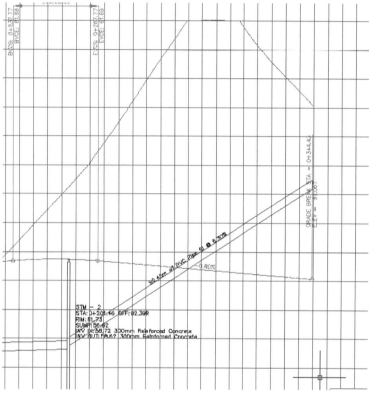

Figure 10–68

1. Continue working with the drawing from the previous task.

2. In the *View* tab > Views panel, select the preset view **C3D-PipeWorks Profile Edit**.

3. In the profile view, select the pipe that runs between STM - 1 and STM - 2. In the contextual Ribbon tab > Modify panel, select **Pipe Properties**, as shown in Figure 10–69.

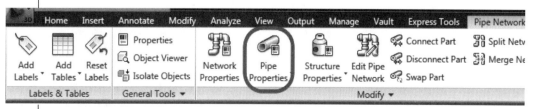

Figure 10–69

4. In the Pipe Properties - Pipe - 1 dialog box, change the *Start Invert Elevation* to **59.067**, which is 2m below the proposed ground elevation. As you want to hold this start invert, enter **-0.40** as the slope for the Pipe Slope (*Hold Start*), as shown in Figure 10–70.

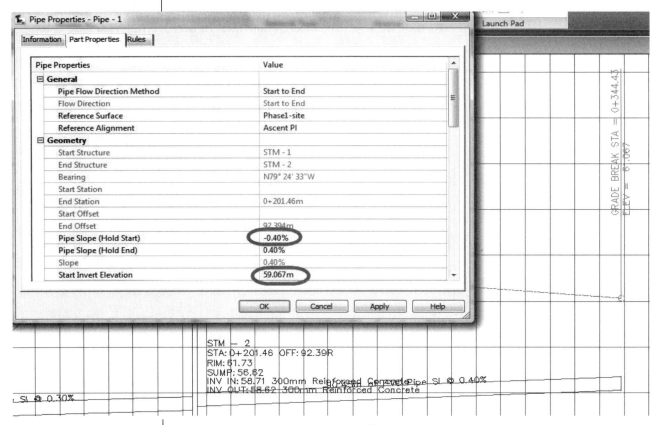

Figure 10–70

5. Click  to apply the changes.

6. Save the drawing.

Task 8: Generate a Pipe network report.

1. Continue working with the drawing from the previous task.

2. In the *Home* tab, toggle on the *Toolbox* tab, as shown in Figure 10–71.

Figure 10–71

3. In the *Toolbox* tab, expand the *Reports Manager* collection, expand the *Pipes* collection, and select **Pipes_and_Structures**, as shown in Figure 10–72. Right-click and select **Execute**.

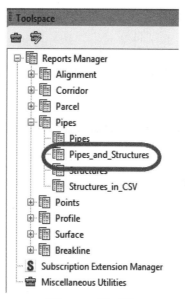

Figure 10–72

4. In the Export to XML Report dialog box, accept the defaults, since you only have one network. Click OK.

5. Accept the default name and ensure that the file type is **HTML**. Click Save. If prompted to overwrite the file, select **yes**. The report appears as shown in Figure 10–73.

Your Company Name

123 Main Street

Suite #321

City, State 01234

	Pipes and Structures Report	**Client:** Client Company
Project Name: C:\Civil 3D Projects\Civil3D-training\Drawings\PIP1-PipeWorks-Complete.dwg		**Project Description:**
	Report Date: 13/04/2010 7:27:54 PM	**Prepared by:** Preparer

Pipe Network: STORM
Pipes

Name	Shape	Size (mm)	Material	US Node	DS Node	US Invert (m)	DS Invert (m)	2D Length (m) center-to-center edge-to-edge	% Slope
Pipe - 7 (STORM)	Circular	D:300.00	Reinforced Concrete	STM - 8 (STORM)	STM - 9 (STORM)	53.40	53.66	88.34 87.44	-0.30
Pipe - 8 (STORM)	Circular	D:300.00	Reinforced Concrete	STM - 9 (STORM)	STM - 10 (STORM)	53.76	53.82	19.21 18.31	-0.30
Pipe - 9 (STORM)	Circular	D:300.00	Reinforced Concrete	STM - 10 (STORM)	STM - 11 (STORM)	53.92	55.51	122.35 121.45	-1.30

Figure 10–73

6. Save the drawing.

Review Questions

Question 1 What does the **Swap Part** command do?

Question 2 What does the **Disconnect From Part** command do?

Question 3 What do changes made in a profile view do to a plan view?

Question 4 How do you label individual objects or an entire network?

Module 11

Quantity Take Off/Sections Level 1

This module introduces:

Section 1: Sections
- ✓ **Sample Line Groups**
- ✓ **Section Views**

Section 2: Quantity Take Off
- ✓ **Section Volume Calculations**

Section 1: Sections

11.1 Sample Line Groups

Sample lines are objects that sample corridor elements for display in cross-sections and are used to form the basis for materials lists used in corridor volumetric calculations. Sections are organized into groups for ease of selection and for managing common properties. A drawing can have any number of sample line groups for the same alignment.

The **Sample Lines** command is located in the *Home* tab > Profile & Section Views panel, as shown in Figure 11–1.

Figure 11–1

Selecting this command opens the Create Sample Line Group dialog, as shown in Figure 11–2, and the Sample Line Tools toolbar.

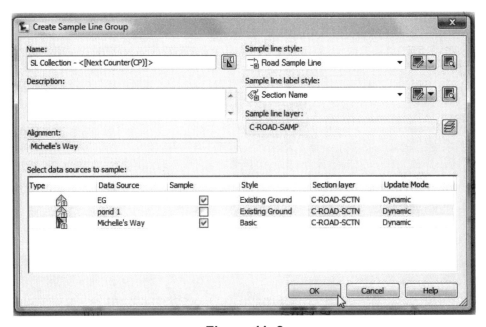

Figure 11–2

The Create Sample Line Group dialog box identifies all of the

elements that could be included in the section, such as (corridor

geometry), 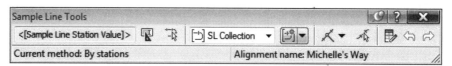 (terrain surfaces), (corridor surfaces) and
(pipe networks). The *Select data sources to sample* section shows the
type of object, where it comes from, whether or not to sample, the
style to use for the sections, the preferred layers, and the update
mode for the section.

After adjusting the values for the Create Sample Line dialog box and

clicking [OK], the Sample Line Tools toolbar becomes active, as
shown in Figure 11–3.

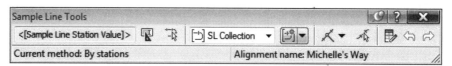

Figure 11–3

The Sample Line Tools toolbar is the control center for creating
sample lines. The default method is At a Station, as shown in
Figure 11–4, which means you are able to select a specific station at
which to add a sample line.

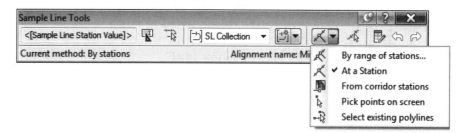

Figure 11–4

Other methods include:

- **By range of stations**: Enables you to specify a range of stations,
  sampling width, and other options where you want sample lines to
  be created.
- **From corridor stations**: Creates a sample line at all predefined
  corridor sections. This method also opens the Create Sample Line
  dialog box for you to define the station range and swath widths for
  the sections.
- **Pick points on screen**: Enables you to select points in the
  drawing to define the path of the section. This type of section can
  have multiple vertices.

- **Select existing polylines**: Includes section lines based on existing polylines in the drawing. The polyline does not have to be perpendicular to the center line and can have multiple segments.

The dialog box that opens for the **By range of stations** option is shown in Figure 11–5.

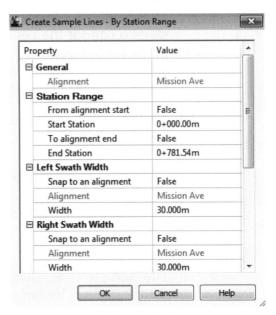

Figure 11–5

After creating the sample line group, the *Prospector* tab lists the individual sample lines under the sample line group's name. Each entry in the list includes all sampled elements for a section, as shown in Figure 11–6.

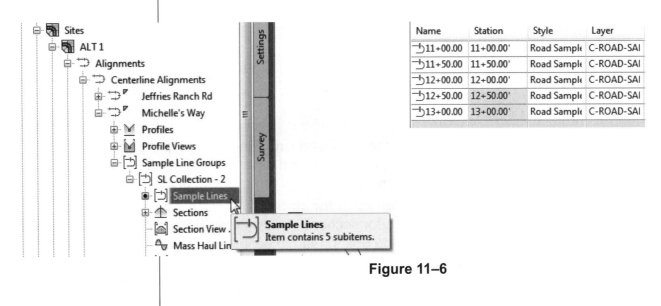

Figure 11–6

Modifying Sample Line Groups

New sample line groups can be added, existing groups can be deleted, swath widths (section sample width) can be adjusted, and new data sources can be added (such as newly created pipe networks) using the commands in the *Modify* drop-down list in the Sample Line Tools toolbar, as shown in Figure 11–7.

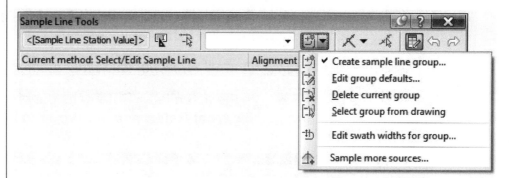

Figure 11–7

Sample line properties (such as display styles) can also be adjusted through the sample line group's properties, accessed through the *Prospector* tab.

Practice 11a	Creating Sections Part I

Task 1: Create a new drawing, XREF, and reference design data.

1. Open the file **QTO1-Sec1-Sections and Quantity Take Off.dwg** from the following folder:

   C:\Civil 3D Projects\Civil3D-training\Drawings

2. In the *Insert* tab > Reference panel, expand the panel, and select **External Reference**, as shown in Figure 11–8.

Figure 11–8

3. In the External References dialog box, click (Attach Drawing), as shown in Figure 11–9.

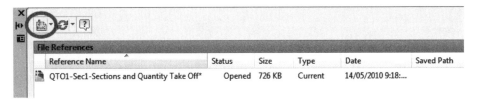

Figure 11–9

4. In the Select Reference File dialog box, browse to *C:\Civil 3D Projects\Civil3D-training\Drawings*. Select the file

   COR1-ProfileCorridor-Complete.dwg and click ⬛ **Open** .

5. In the Attach External Reference dialog box, select the **Attachment** and **Locate using Geographic Data** options, as shown in Figure 11–10. Click ⬛ **OK** to close the dialog box, and click the **X** to close the External References dialog box.

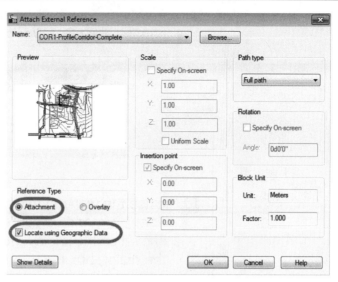

Figure 11–10

6. At the Command Line, type **ZE** <Enter>.

7. To import data, you must first ensure that Data Shortcut paths have been set. If this has not been done, set the working folder to point to the Data Shortcuts. If this has been done, skip to step 11.

8. In the *Prospector* tab in the Toolspace, expand the *Data Shortcuts* collection, right-click, and select **Set Working Folder**, as shown on the left in Figure 11–11. In the Browse For Folder dialog box, select the **Civil3D-training** folder from the following path: *C:\Civil 3D Projects*, as shown on the right. Click

   [OK] to exit and apply the selection.

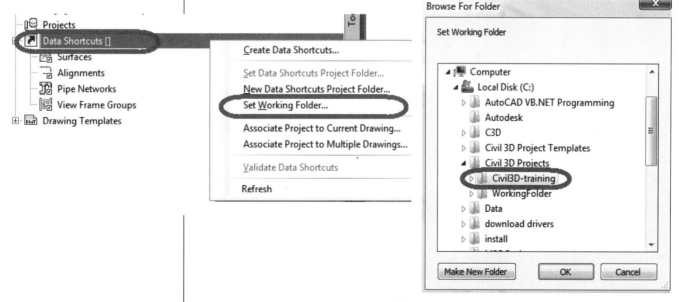

Figure 11–11

9. An alternative method is in the *Manage* tab > Data Shortcuts panel, select **Set Working Folder**, as shown in Figure 11–12.

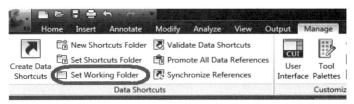

Figure 11–12

10. Once the working folder has been set, select **Data Shortcuts**, right-click, and select **Set Data Shortcuts Project Folder**, as shown on the left in Figure 11–13. Then select **DataShortCuts** in the dialog box that opens, as shown in Figure 11–13.

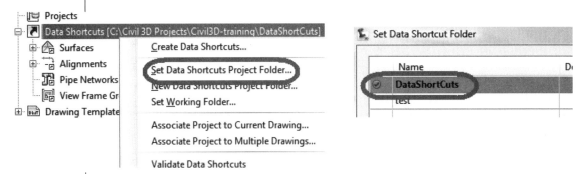

Figure 11–13

11. Once you have established the Data Shortcuts project, you can proceed to reference data. Expand the *Surfaces* collection and the *Alignments* collection, as shown in Figure 11–14.

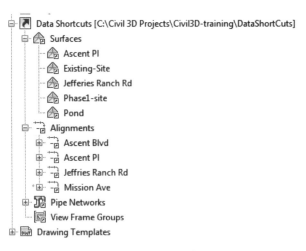

Figure 11–14

12. In the *Alignments* collection, select **Mission Ave**, right-click, and select **Create Reference...**, as shown in Figure 11–15.

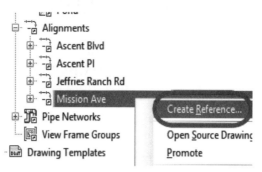

Figure 11–15

13. In the Create Alignment Reference dialog box, as shown in Figure 11–16, set the **Alignment label** set to **Major and Minor only**, accept all other defaults, and click [OK] to complete the reference to the surface. On the graphics screen, you will now see the surface based on the style selected.

Figure 11–16

14. Save the drawing.

Task 2: Create sample lines.

---

1. Continue working with the drawing from the previous task.

2. Change the *Annotation Scale* to **1:500** in the Status Bar, which is a scale more appropriate for viewing cross-sections.

3. In the *Home* tab > Profile and Section Views panel, select

    Sample Lines ⌐ᕽ . When prompted to select an alignment, press <Enter> and select Mission Ave or select the **Mission Ave**

    alignment in Model Space. Click [OK] to exit the dialog box. The Create Sample Line Group dialog box appears, listing multiple data sources.

4. Assign the styles shown in Figure. Make sure you clear the *Sample* column for all but the *Existing-Site, Mission Ave*, and *Mission Ave Mission Ave (Datum)*, as shown in Figure 11–17.

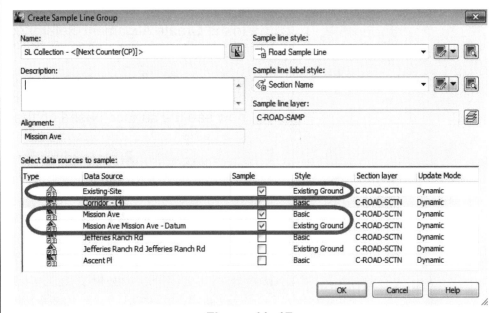

Figure 11–17

5. Leave the other settings at their defaults and click [OK].

6. In the Sample Line Tools toolbar, select to create sample lines **By range of stations...**, as shown in Figure 11–18.

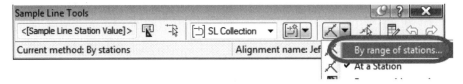

Figure 11–18

7. In the Create Sample Lines dialog box, review the settings, as shown in Figure 11–19.

- Under *Station Range*, set the *From alignment start* and *To alignment end* to **False**.

- Set the *Start Station* to **60** and the *End Station* to **585**. This is set because the alignment extends beyond where you have existing ground or design ground data.

- Set both the *Left and Right Swath Width[s]* to **30.00m**.

- Under *Sampling Increments*, set the *Increment Along Tangents* and *Increments Along Curves* to **25.00m**.

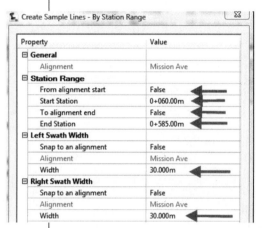
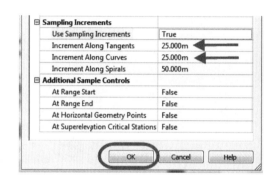

Figure 11–19

8. Click [OK] when done.

9. At the Command Line, press <Enter> to close the dialog box.

10. Save the drawing.

Task 3: Review Sample Line Data.

1. Continue working with the drawing from the previous task.

2. In the *Prospector* tab, expand the *Alignment* collection, expand the *Centerline Alignments* collection, expand the *Mission Ave* collection, expand the *Sample Line Groups* collection, and select **SL Collection**, as shown in Figure 11–20.

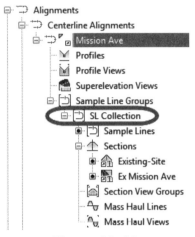

Figure 11–20

3. Right-click and select **Properties**. In the Sample Line Group Properties dialog box, in the *Sections* tab, you can re-assign styles and layers, and add new data sources.

4. The *Sample Lines* tab enables you to change the swath widths of individual sections numerically. Click **Cancel** to exit without making any changes.

5. Save the drawing.

11.2 Section Views

A section view can display sampled surface sections, corridor assemblies, and any pipes or structures. Similar to profiles, sections use a section view to annotate their elevations and center line offsets. Styles affect the look of a section view.

Section views can annotate an assembly's offsets, elevations, and grades. The All Codes style assigned to the assembly in the sample line group makes all points and links available for labeling. The Section Label styles do not interact with the assembly, only with the corridor surfaces.

*   Like Profile views, Section views can be moved and retain the correct information.
*   Section views can be created individually or in groups.

Section View Wizard

The Profile & Section Views panel in the *Home* tab enables you to create a single section view, multiple sections organized into columns and rows, and project objects to a section view. The single and multiple view commands open the Section View wizard, which walks you step by step through the process of creating Section views. There are six tasks in the Section View wizard, as shown in Figure 11–21.

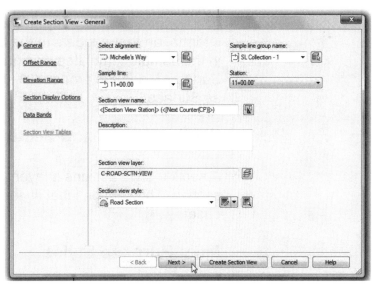

Figure 11–21

- **General**: Specifies basic information about the Section view, including which alignment to use, the sample group and line, as well as the view template. If creating multiple views, the *Group Plot Style* method specifies how to create multiple section views (**All** or **Page**). You can define page styles that define sheet sizes and plottable areas (sheet size minus margins and border).
- **Offset Range**: Enables you to set the width of the view.
- **Elevation Range**: Enables you to set the height of the view.
- **Section Display Options**: Enables you to select what gets drawn in the view and the section style.
- **Data Bands**: Enables you to specify one or more band set styles for the sections and their position in the view.
- **Section View Tables**: Enables you to add and modify volume tables calculated using the Section view (a material list must be created from the sample line group for this option to be available).

Section View Styles

A Section view style defines the vertical and horizontal grid and its annotation. The horizontal lines represent the elevations and the vertical lines represent the center line offset.

Section View Band Styles

A band style defines the offset and elevation annotation at the bottom of a Section view. The style affects the annotation's format and the information that appears in the band. Using the band styles provided in the sample templates, assign your existing ground surface as Surface 1, and the proposed surface (such as a Corridor Top surface) as Surface 2.

Section Styles and Section Label Styles

A section style assigns a layer and other layer properties to a surface section. The section label styles annotate grade breaks, slopes, and offsets.

Multi-Purpose Styles

In Multi-Purpose styles, the All Codes style assigns object and label styles for corridor assemblies. This is the most important style for section labeling.

The All Codes style defines object styles for points, links, or shapes. It specifies which labels appear in a Section view.

- All link styles annotate a grade or slope.
- All point styles annotate an offset and elevation.

Page Styles

A page style defines the plottable area of a sheet size. The plottable area is what remains after removing the non-printing margins and border from the sheet size. The page style also defines a sheet grid. The Plot Group styles use the grid to space sections on a sheet.

Practice 11b | Creating Sections Part II

Task 1: Create a single Section view.

1. Continue working with the drawing from the previous practice or open the file **QTO1-Sec2-Sections and Quantity Take Off.dwg** from the following folder:

   C:\Civil 3D Projects\Civil3D-training\Drawings

2. In the *View* tab > Views panel, select the preset view **C3D-QTO plot section**.

3. In the *Home* tab > Profile & Section Views panel, select **Section Views > Create Section View**, as shown in Figure 11–22. The Create Section View wizard opens.

Figure 11–22

4. On the *General* screen, enter **0+200** in the *Sample Line* field, as shown in Figure 11–23. Set the *Section view style* to **Road Section** and click Next >.

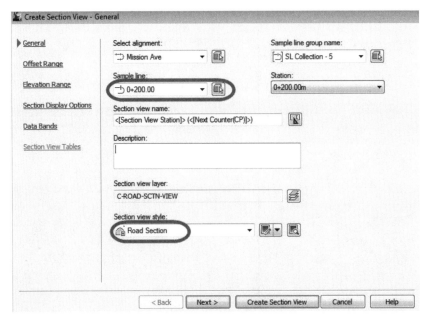

Figure 11–23

5. On the *Offset Range* and *Elevation Range* screens, accept the defaults and click [Next >].

6. On the *Section Display Options* screen, set the *Style* to **View-Edit with Shading** for the *Ex Mission Ave* section. Assign the label options and styles shown in Figure 11–24 and click [Next >].

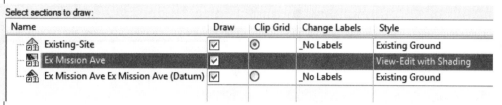

Select sections to draw:

Name	Draw	Clip Grid	Change Labels	Style
Existing-Site	☑	⦿	_No Labels	Existing Ground
Ex Mission Ave	☑			View-Edit with Shading
Ex Mission Ave Ex Mission Ave (Datum)	☑	○	_No Labels	Existing Ground

Figure 11–24

7. On the Data Bands screen, select **Existing-Site** for Surface 1 and select the **Mission Ave Mission Ave - Datum** surface for Surface 2, as shown in Figure 11–25.

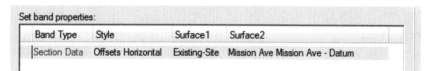

Set band properties:

Band Type	Style	Surface1	Surface2
Section Data	Offsets Horizontal	Existing-Site	Mission Ave Mission Ave - Datum

Figure 11–25

8. Click [**Create Section View**] and when prompted to Identify section view origin, click in an open space in model space to locate this section in the drawing.

9. Pan and Zoom to look at the section close-up. The labels shown are provided by the default AutoCAD Civil 3D template.

10. Adjust the section by dragging or deleting unwanted labels. (As a reminder, to remove or change the properties of all labels of one type, such as Grade Break labels, select one and they will all become selected. If you only want to remove one label, hold down <Ctrl> when selecting.) The drawing is shown in Figure 11–26.

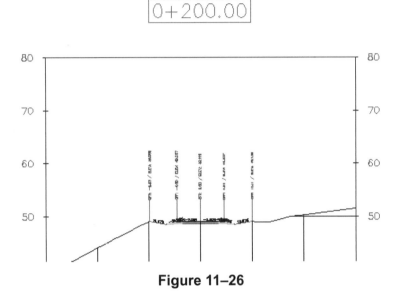

Figure 11–26

Task 2: Create a Multiple Section view.

1. Continue working with the drawing from the previous task.

2. In the *View* tab > Views panel, select the preset view **C3D-QTO plot section**.

3. In the *Home* tab > Profile & Section Views panel, select **Section Views > Create Multiple Section Views**.

4. In the Create Multiple Section Views dialog box, accept the defaults and click ⬚ Next > ⬚ .

5.   On the remaining screens, accept all the defaults values (*Offset Range, Elevation Range, Section Display Options,* and *Data Bands*). When done, click [Create Section View] and click in an open space in Model Space to insert all of the sections, as shown in Figure 11–27.

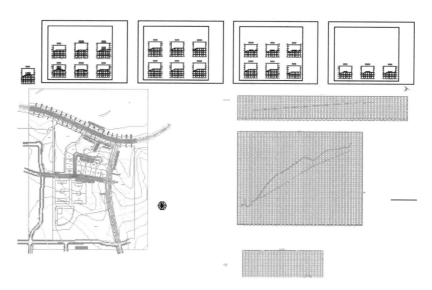

Figure 11–27

6.   Save the drawing.

Review Questions

Question 1 | What are sample line groups?

Question 2 | What is the default sample line method and what does it mean?

Question 3 | What does the Create Section View dialog box do?

Question 4 | What does the All Codes style define?

Section 2: Quantity Take Off

11.3 Section Volume Calculations

Two types of quantity takeoffs can be calculated based on sections: earthwork volumes and material volumes. Earthwork volumes represent the amount of cut (existing material above the vertical design) or fill (the vertical design above the existing material). Material volumes are the amount of materials needed to build the road. Materials include asphalt pavement, concrete curbing, sub base materials, and other materials.

Earthwork Volumes

Earthwork volumes represent an amount of displaced surface materials. The displacement represents the excavation of high areas or filling of low areas in the existing ground surface, relative to the vertical road design.

One goal road designers strive for is to balance the amount of excavated material (called cut) and the amount of material to be added (called fill). On any site, not all of the excavated material (cut) is reusable. For example, the spoil materials could be from a bog, a type of material that does not compact well, or rock debris. The reuse of cut material can be a percentage of the overall cut value and affects the overall earthwork calculation. An example is shown in Figure 11–28.

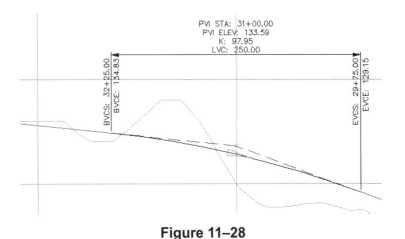

Figure 11–28

The earthworks calculations are applied between the existing ground surface and the datum surface of an assembly. The datum surface represents the roadbed on which the sub base gravel, asphalt, and concrete materials lie. Earthwork volumes affect which revisions occur to a roadway design. For example, excessive cut material (material needing excavation) could lead to raising the vertical design or, if possible, moving the horizontal alignment to create less cut.

Mass Haul

Starting in AutoCAD Civil 3D 2009, a mass haul diagram can be generated and used as a visual representation of the cumulative cut and fill material volumes along a corridor. Contractors use mass haul diagrams as a primary tool in determining and balancing haulage costs when bidding on an earthwork job. Mass haul is the volume of excavated material multiplied by the distance it is required to be moved. When the mass haul line is above the balance line, it indicates how much cut there will be at that station. When the mass haul line is below the balance line, it indicates the volume to be filled. To generate a mass haul diagram, you need an alignment, a sample line group, and a materials list. The mass haul diagram calculates and displays the following:

- The distance over which cut and fill volumes balance.
- Free haul and overhaul volumes.
- Volumes offset by borrow pits and dump sites.

Construction costs can be reduced by enabling the designer to compare alternative designs, add dump sites, and borrow pits at key locations within the free haul distance, thus eliminating a portion of the overhaul volume. An example of a mass haul diagram is shown in Figure 11–29.

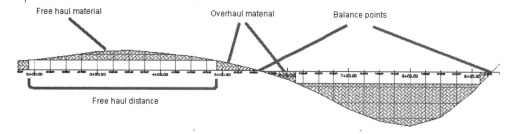

Figure 11–29

Material Volumes

Subassembly shapes represent materials available for quantity takeoffs. These quantities come from the subassembly shapes (e.g., curb, pave, shoulder, sidewalk, etc.).

Quantity Takeoff Criteria

The Quantity Takeoff Criteria defines the surfaces and materials to be analyzed. Takeoff criteria can identify two surfaces for earthwork calculations and/or a list of shapes for material volumes.

The criteria style entries are generic since they are intended to be used on multiple corridors, which may contain different subassembly components. When computing section calculations, you are prompted to identify which entries correspond to the corridor shapes. The Quantity Takeoff Criteria dialog box is shown in Figure 11–30.

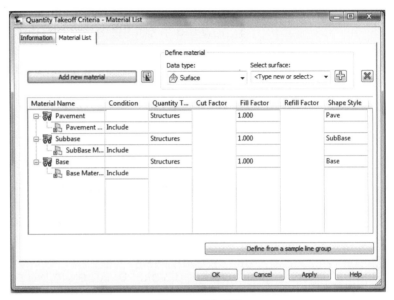

Figure 11–30

Define Materials

After defining the volume criteria, you create data from the criteria settings. In the *Analyze* tab > Volumes and Materials panel, select **Compute Materials** to set the alignment and a sample line group to use for data extraction. The command is shown in Figure 11–31.

Figure 11–31

When the Edit Material List dialog box appears, you associate surfaces and/or structures (subassembly shapes) to the appropriate entries. Click OK to exit and AutoCAD Civil 3D then calculates the needed report data.

Practice 11c | Quantity Take Off Part I

Task 1: Generate Earthworks Quantities.

In this task you will compute the site cut and fill required to create the datum surface below the corridor. You then calculate the construction materials that will be placed above the datum (asphalt, gravel, etc.).

1. Continue working with the drawing from the previous practice or open the file **QTO1-Sec3-Sections and Quantity Take Off.dwg** from the following folder:

    C:\Civil 3D Projects\Civil3D-training\Drawings

2. In the *View* tab > Views panel, select the preset view **C3D-QTO-plot section**.

3. In the *Analyze* tab > Volumes and Materials panel, select **Compute Materials**, as shown in Figure 11–32.

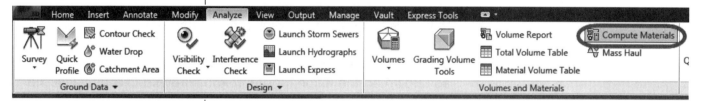

Figure 11–32

4. In the Select Sample Line Group dialog box, accept the default alignment **Mission Ave** and sample line group **SL Collection**, as shown in Figure 11–33. Click [OK].

Figure 11–33

5. In the Compute Materials dialog box, select **Existing-Site** for the *EG* and **Mission Ave Mission Ave - Datum** for the *DATUM*, as shown in Figure 11–34. Click OK when done.

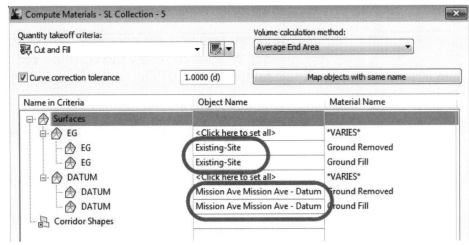

Figure 11–34

6. Generate a volume report. In the *Analyze* tab > Volumes and Materials panel, select **Volume Report**.

7. In the Report Quantities dialog box, ensure that you select the correct XSL file. Click next to the *Select a style sheet* field, as shown on the left in Figure 11–35. Browse to and select the file **earthwork.xsl**, as shown on the right, and open it. Click OK to close the Report Quantities dialog box.

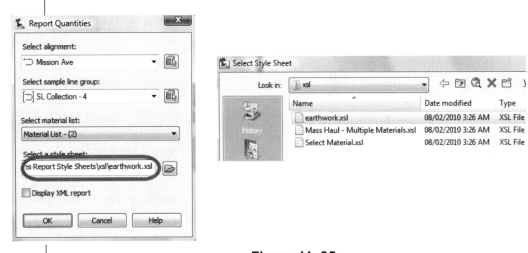

Figure 11–35

8. Windows Internet Explorer will open as Civil 3D creates an HTML format report. Depending on your IE security settings, you may be prompted to allow the script to run. Select **Yes** if this prompt appears. Your report will display, as shown in Figure 11–36.

Volume Report

Project: C:\Users\Mal\appdata\local\temp\QTO1-Sections and Quantity Take Off_1_1_1081.sv$

Alignment: Mission Ave
Sample Line Group: SL Collection - 4
Start Sta: 0+075.000
End Sta: 0+575.000

Station	Cut Area (Sq.m.)	Cut Volume (Cu.m.)	Reusable Volume (Cu.m.)	Fill Area (Sq.m.)	Fill Volume (Cu.m.)	Cum. Cut Vol. (Cu.m.)	Cum. Reusable Vol. (Cu.m.)	Cum. Fill Vol. (Cu.m.)	Cum. Net Vol. (Cu.m.)
0+075.000	0.00	0.00	0.00	0.00	0.00	0.00	0.00	0.00	0.00
0+100.000	5.10	63.75	63.75	0.00	0.00	63.75	63.75	0.00	63.75
0+125.000	6.01	139.00	139.00	0.00	0.00	202.75	202.75	0.00	202.75
0+150.000	7.16	165.17	165.17	0.00	0.00	367.92	367.92	0.00	367.92
0+175.000	6.19	167.47	167.47	0.00	0.00	535.39	535.39	0.00	535.39
0+200.000	5.02	140.31	140.31	0.18	2.24	675.70	675.70	2.24	673.46
0+225.000	5.02	125.51	125.51	0.00	2.27	801.21	801.21	4.51	796.71
0+250.000	5.15	127.13	127.13	0.00	0.00	928.34	928.34	4.51	923.83
0+275.000	5.02	127.13	127.13	0.32	3.94	1055.47	1055.47	8.45	1047.02
0+300.000	5.02	125.53	125.53	0.00	3.94	1180.99	1180.99	12.40	1168.59

Figure 11–36

9. Close the HTML report.

10. Create an AutoCAD table listing earthwork volumes. In the *Analyze* tab > Volumes and Materials panel, select **Total Volume Table**, as shown in Figure 11–37.

Figure 11–37

11. Accept the defaults in the Create Table dialog box, as shown in Figure 11–38, and click OK. When prompted, click in an unused portion of your drawing to create the table.

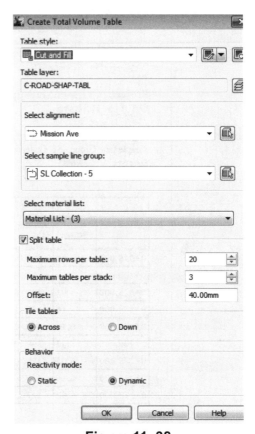

Figure 11–38

12. Select a point in Model Space to insert the table, as shown in Figure 11–39. Note that the top left of the table is the reference point.

Total Volume Table						
Station	Fill Area	Cut Area	Fill Volume	Cut Volume	Cumulative Fill Vol	Cumulative Cut Vol
0+075.00	0.00	0.00	0.00	0.00	0.00	0.00
0+100.00	0.00	5.10	0.00	63.75	0.00	63.75
0+125.00	0.00	6.01	0.00	139.00	0.00	202.75
0+150.00	0.00	7.16	0.00	165.17	0.00	367.92
0+175.00	0.00	6.19	0.00	167.47	0.00	535.39
0+200.00	0.18	5.02	2.24	140.31	2.24	675.70
0+225.00	0.00	5.02	2.27	125.51	4.51	801.21
0+250.00	0.00	5.16	0.00	127.17	4.51	928.34

Figure 11–39

13. Save the drawing.

Task 2: Calculate Material Quantities.

Your assemblies include five defined shapes: Pave1 and Pave2 (the top two courses), Base, Sub base, and Curb. The default Material List only includes one material for Pavement so you will need to adjust it. You will not calculate curb volume at this time.

1. Continue working with the drawing from the previous task.

2. In the *Analyze* tab > Volumes and Materials panel, select **Compute Materials**, as shown in Figure 11–40.

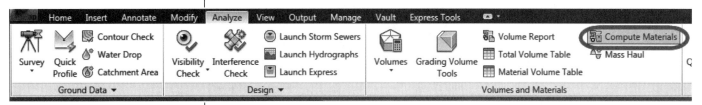

Figure 11–40

3. In the Select Sample Line Group dialog box, accept the default alignment **Mission Ave** and sample line group **SL Collection**, and click OK .

4. In the Edit Material List dialog box, click Add new material . In the *Material Name* column, select the new Material name and rename it as **Asphalt**, as shown in Figure 11–41. Change the *Quantity* value to **Structures**.

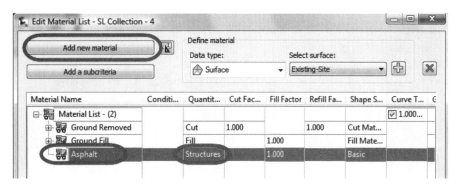

Figure 11–41

5.   Select **Corridor Shape** from the *Data type* drop-down list and select **Ex Mission Ave Pave 1** from the *Select corridor shape* drop-down list. Click 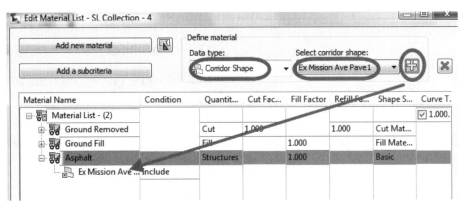 to add the branch to the list, as shown in Figure 11–42.

Figure 11–42

6.   Click [OK] to close the dialog box and calculate the material.

7.   Generate a volume report. In the *Analyze* tab > Volumes and Materials panel, select **Volume Report**.

8.   In the Report Quantities dialog box, ensure you select the correct XSL file from the Select a style sheet drop-down list. Click  next to the drop-down list. Browse to and select the file **Material.xsl** and open it. Click [OK] to close the Report Quantities dialog box.

9. Windows Internet Explorer will open as Civil 3D creates an HTML format report. Depending on your IE security settings, you may be prompted to allow the script to run. Select **Yes** if this prompt appears. The report will display with the volume of Pavement 1 from your corridor, as shown in Figure 11–43.

Material Report

Project: C:\Users\Mal\appdata\local\temp\QTO1-Sections and Quantity Take Off_1_1_1081.sv$

Alignment: Mission Ave
Sample Line Group: SL Collection - 4
Start Sta: 0+075.000
End Sta: 0+575.000

	Area Type	Area	Inc.Vol.	Cum.Vol.
		Sq.m.	Cu.m.	Cu.m.
Station: 0+075.000				
	Ground Removed	0.00	0.00	0.00
	Ground Fill	0.00	0.00	0.00
	Asphalt	0.23	0.00	0.00
Station: 0+100.000				
	Ground Removed	5.10	63.75	63.75
	Ground Fill	0.00	0.00	0.00
	Asphalt	0.23	5.82	5.82
Station: 0+125.000				
	Ground Removed	6.01	139.00	202.75
	Ground Fill	0.00	0.00	0.00
	Asphalt	0.23	5.82	11.64
Station: 0+150.000				

Figure 11–43

10. Close the HTML report.

11. The road design, specifically the corridor assembly, has a second shape called Pave 2. This is also Asphalt, but may be based on a different composition than Pave 1. You can quantify this value as a separate amount; however, for demonstration purposes, you will create a total volume for Asphalt.

12. In the *Analyze* tab > Volumes and Materials panel, select **Compute Materials**. In the Select Sample Line Group dialog box, accept the defaults and click OK.

13. In the Edit Material List dialog box, select **Asphalt** in the *Name* column. Select **Corridor Shape** from the *Data type* drop-down list and select **Ex Mission Ave Pave 2** from the *Select corridor shape* drop-down list, as shown in Figure 11–44. Click ⊞ to add **Ex Mission Ave Pave 2** to the *Asphalt* collection.

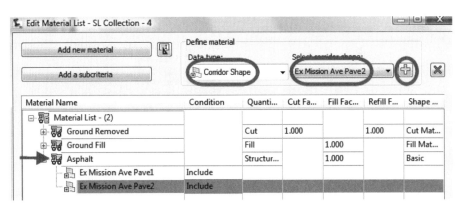

Figure 11–44

14. In the Edit Material List dialog box, click

    Add new material . In the *Material Name* column, select the new Material name and rename it as **Gravel**. Change the *Quantity* to **Structure**.

15. Select **Corridor Shape** from the *Data type* drop-down list and **Ex Mission Ave Base** from the *Select corridor shape* drop-down list. Click ⊞ to add the **Mission Ave Base** to the list, as shown in Figure 11–45.

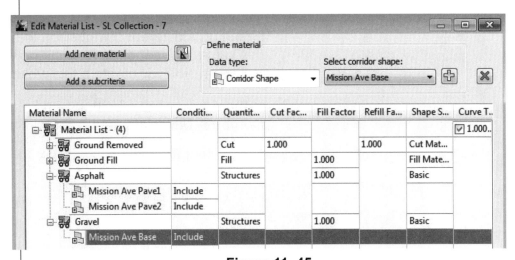

Figure 11–45

16. Click OK to apply the changes and close the dialog box.

17. As in steps 7-9, generate a volume report. In the *Analyze* tab > Volumes and Materials panel, select **Volume Report**.

- In the Report Quantities dialog box, ensure you select the correct XSL file from the Select a style sheet drop-down list. Click 📂 next to the drop-down list. Browse to and select the file Material.xsl and open it. Click [OK] to close the Report Quantities dialog box.

- Windows Internet Explorer will open as Civil 3D creates an HTML format report. Depending on your IE security settings, you may be prompted to allow the script to run. Select **Yes** if this prompt appears. Your report will display, as shown in Figure 11–46.

Material Report

Project: C:\Users\Mal\appdata\local\temp\QTO1-Sections and Quantity Take Off_1_1_7933.sv$

Alignment: Mission Ave
Sample Line Group: SL Collection - 4
Start Sta: 0+075.000
End Sta: 0+575.000

	Area Type	Area	Inc.Vol.	Cum.Vol.
		Sq.m.	Cu.m.	Cu.m.
Station: 0+075.000				
	Ground Removed	0.00	0.00	0.00
	Ground Fill	0.00	0.00	0.00
	Asphalt	0.47	0.00	0.00
	Gravel	1.01	0.00	0.00
Station: 0+100.000				
	Ground Removed	5.10	63.75	63.75
	Ground Fill	0.00	0.00	0.00
	Asphalt	0.47	11.77	11.77
	Gravel	1.01	25.17	25.17

Figure 11–46

18. Save the drawing.

You can also create drawing tables showing this information using the **Material Volume Table** command in the Volumes and Materials panel.

Practice 11d | Quantity Take Off Part II - Integrated Quantity Takeoff

Task 1: Assign pay item ID.

A tool available in AutoCAD Civil 3D enables you to automate the process of quantity takeoff. The traditional method involves a manual process of counting pay items individually (e.g., street lights) or performing linear measurements to obtain quantities of items such as curb and gutter.

1. Continue working with the drawing from the previous practice or open the file **QTO1-Sec3-Sections and Quantity Take Off.dwg** from the following folder:

    C:\Civil 3D Projects\Civil3D-training\Drawings

2. In the *View* tab > Views panel, select the preset view **C3D-QTO-takeoff**.

3. In the *Analyze* tab > QTO panel, select **QTO Manager**, as shown in Figure 11–47.

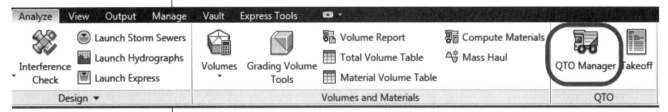

Figure 11–47

4. In the Panorama, expand ![icon] and from the drop-down list shown in Figure 11–48, select **Open pay item file**.

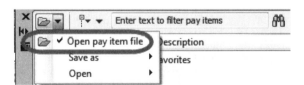

Figure 11–48

5. In the Open Pay Item File dialog box, select **CSV (Comma delimited)** as the file format and click 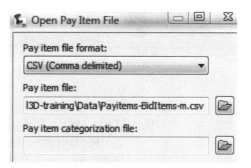 beside the Pay item file drop-down list, as shown in Figure 11–49. Select **Payitems-BidItems-m.csv** from the folder *C:\Civil 3D Projects\Civil3D-training\Data*. Click [OK] to accept the changes and close the dialog box.

Figure 11–49

6. The *Pay Item ID* list will be populated with pay item numbers from the CSV file. To display only the pay items you want, enter **shrubs** in the filter field at the top and press <Enter>. Only the shrubs pay items will be listed, as shown in Figure 11–50.

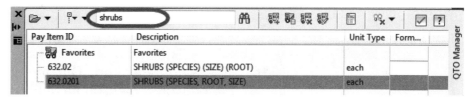

Figure 11–50

7. Assign a Pay Item ID to the object in the drawing. In Model Space, select a shrub, right-click, and select **Select Similar**, as shown in Figure 11–51.

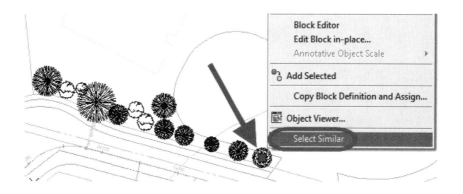

Figure 11–51

8. With all similar objects selected, select pay item **632.02** in the Panorama, right-click, and select **Assign pay item**, as shown in Figure 11–52. At the Command Line, you will see a message that pay items have been assigned to objects.

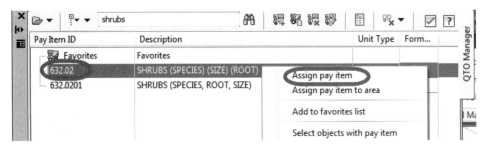

Figure 11–52

9. Use steps 6-8 above to apply Pay items to street light objects. Enter **lighting** in the filter field at the top and press <Enter>. Only pay items with the word *lighting* will be listed, as shown in Figure 11–53.

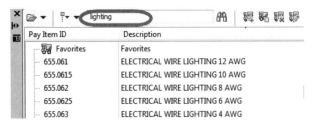

Figure 11–53

10. To assign a Pay Item ID to the object in the drawing, ensure that the previous selection set has been cleared by pressing <Esc>. In Model Space, select a street light, as shown in Figure 11–54, right-click, and select **Similar**.

Figure 11–54

11. With all similar objects selected, select pay item **659.07 Lighting units walkway** in the Panorama, as shown in Figure 11–55. Right-click and select **Assign pay item**. At the Command Line, you will see a message that pay items have been assigned to objects.

Figure 11–55

12. As these objects are now linked to QTO pay items, using the AutoCAD **Copy** command will also copy the reference to the pay item list. Press <Esc> to clear the selection set. Use the AutoCAD **Copy** command, select any of the street lights, and copy to the far west end of the parking lot, as shown in Figure 11–56.

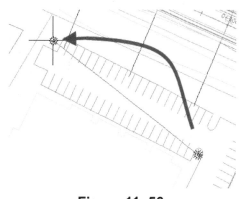

Figure 11–56

Task 2: Compute Quantity Takeoff.

Once pay items have been assigned to Civil 3D or AutoCAD objects in the model, you will be able to compute quantities and generate a report.

1. Continue working with the drawing from the previous task.

2. View the objects that have been tagged with Pay Item IDs. In the *Analyze* tab > QTO panel, select **QTO Manager**, as shown in Figure 11–57.

Figure 11–57

3. Enter **lighting** in the filter field at the top, and press <Enter>. Only the lighting pay items will be listed, as shown in Figure 11–58.

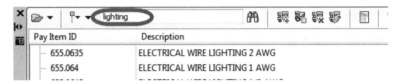

Figure 11–58

4. In the QTO Manager Panorama, select pay item **659.07**, right-click, and select **Select objects with pay item**, as shown in Figure 11–59. All tagged pay items in the drawing with the Pay Item ID 659.07 will be highlighted.

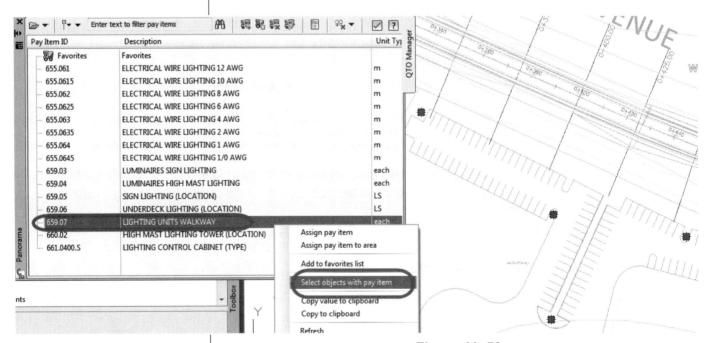

Figure 11–59

5. To generate a Quantity report, in the *Analyze* tab > QTO panel, select **Takeoff**, as shown in Figure 11–60.

Figure 11–60

6. In the Compute Quantity Takeoff dialog box, select the **Summary** option in the *Report type* section and select **Drawing** in the *Report extents* drop-down list, as shown in Figure 11–61.

Accept all other default values. Click [Compute] to accept the changes and calculate the quantities.

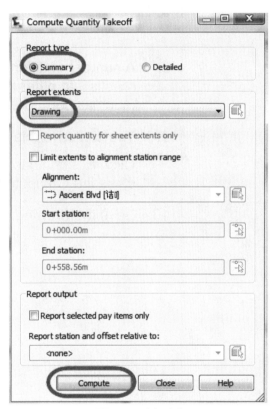

Figure 11–61

7. In the Quantity Takeoff report, select **Summary (HTML).xsl** as the output type, as shown in Figure 11–62.

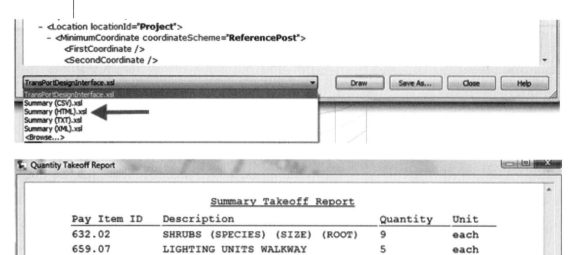

Figure 11–62

8. A number of different output formats will enable you to import the results into other software. You can also tag Civil 3D objects (such as corridor materials with Pay Item ID).

9. You can save this report or draw a table in your CAD drawing. Click Close to close the dialog box, and Close again to close the Compute Quantity Takeoff dialog box.

10. Save the drawing.

Review Questions

Question 1 What do takeoff criteria identify?

Question 2 What does a mass haul diagram represent?

Module 12

Plan Production Level 1

This module introduces:

Section 1: Productivity Tools
- ✓ **Plan Production Tools**
- ✓ **Plan Production Objects**
- ✓ **Plan Production Object Edits**
- ✓ **Creating Sheets**
- ✓ **Sheet Sets**

Section 1: Productivity Tools

12.1 Plan Production Tools

In the digital age, although a large amount of resources and time is dedicated to the creation of digital data, printed sets of plans are still necessary for a number of reasons. For example, hard copy plans are required when obtaining approval from a Client, review and approval from governing agencies, bidding, construction layout, and recording as-built conditions. AutoCAD Civil 3D includes a Plan Production system that enables the automated generation of plan, profile, or plan and profile sheet sets. The Plan Production tools are shown in Figure 12–1.

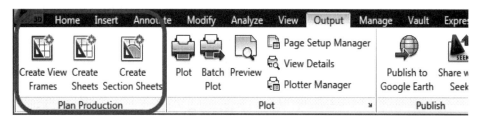

Figure 12–1

Overview

The process of creating plan and profile sheets follows this general workflow:

1. **Configure custom title blocks and styles**: Configure your own custom title blocks and styles or use those provided in the Autodesk templates.

2. **Create View Frames**: These are interactive, rectangular regions that represent the plan area to be included in individual sheets. The **Create View Frames** command organizes these frames into View Frame Groups and creates interactive Match Lines. A north arrow can automatically be included in the sheets.

3. **Adjust View Frames and Match Lines as desired**: This adjustment can be done through object properties or by manipulating the objects directly in Model Space.

4. **Create Sheets**: When you are satisfied with the layout of the frames and Match Lines, plotting layouts can be generated in the current drawing or in new ones.

5. **Plot and Manage**: Sheets generated from this system are automatically included in the Sheet Set Manager for ease of plotting and for organizing with other sheets. (See the AutoCAD Civil 3D Help system for more information on AutoCAD Sheet Sets.)

More Information

Describing how to customize a title block and styles can be an involved process. Due to time limitations, only the fundamentals of this system are covered in this Student Guide, not its configuration. For more information, it is recommended that you review the Plan Production Tools topic in the AutoCAD Civil 3D User's Guide.

12.2 Plan Production Objects

The first step in using the Plan Production tools is to assemble all of the relevant data. This process is the same, whether or not you choose to use the Civil 3D Plan Production tools. Some of the steps you may undertake in assembling this base plan will involve x-referencing pertinent data into your drawing to give the plan geographic reference (i.e., ROW lines, contours, survey data, aerial photographs, etc.). Civil 3D design objects will also be data-referenced into the base plan.

AutoCAD Civil 3D provides a tool to help automate plan and production sheet creation: the Create View Frames wizard. This tool is the next step in plan production after the base plan is created. Using this wizard, you create View Frames, View Frame Groups, and Match Lines, all of which are plan production objects. The wizard is shown in Figure 12–2.

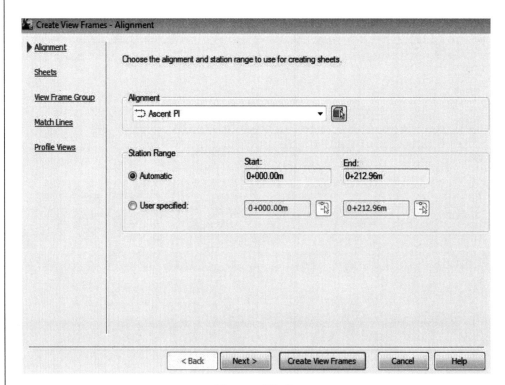

Figure 12–2

View Frames

View Frames are rectangular-shaped objects that are placed along a selected alignment. These rectangular shapes represent a view for each plan sheet that will be created in AutoCAD Civil 3D. View Frames divide the alignment into segments. These segments are based on the base drawing scale and the viewport settings on the layout tab from the drawing template that is used to define the views.

View Frame Groups

View Frame Groups are collections of the View Frames along a single alignment. View Frame Groups enable you to manage a group of views, including properties such as styles and labeling.

Match Lines

A Match Line is a line that designates a location along an alignment that is used as a common reference point for two adjacent plans. If you choose to create plan and profile or profile only sheets, the **Insert Match Lines** option is automatically selected and you cannot edit it.

Match Lines, like all other AutoCAD Civil 3D objects, are style-driven. Typically, they have labels that can identify both adjacent plans, one plan, or no plans. You also have the ability to have these labels displayed at the top, bottom, or middle of the Match Line.

12.3 Plan Production Object Edits

After using the AutoCAD Civil 3D wizard to create View Frame Groups, View Frames, and Match Lines, you may need to make some minor adjustments to best present your design. You can access three properties: *Name, Description* and *Object style*. In addition to adjusting the field properties of the object, you may also want to adjust the geometry properties of the object.

Name

The *Name* is a unique identifier that is appropriate to the object. For example, you may name the View Frame with the alignment name and station, or name the View Frame Group with the alignment name and the starting and ending station that the group encompasses.

Description

The *Description* field provides a detailed description of the View Frame or Match Line.

Object style

Adjusting the *Object style* impacts the presentation of the object. One application of this property is to ensure that the object conforms to company preferences or standards. The View Frame Properties dialog box is shown in Figure 12–3.

Figure 12–3

View Frame Geometry Properties Edits

You can change the View Frame's location and rotation along the alignment using the object grips, as shown in Figure 12–4.

- The *circle grip* (1) enables you to rotate the View Frame.
- The *square grip* (2) enables you to offset the View Frame relative to its original location.

- The *diamond grip* (3) enables you to move the View Frame along the alignment.

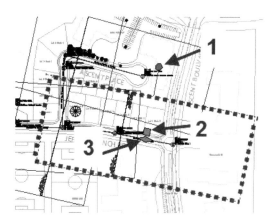

Figure 12–4

Match Line Geometry Properties Edits

Using the object grips, you can change the Match Line`s location, rotation, and length, as shown in Figure 12–5. However, you can only move the Match Line within the View Frame overlap area.

- The *circle grip* (1) enables you to rotate the Match Line.
- The *triangle grips* (2) enables you to extend the length of the Match Line.
- The *diamond grip* (3) enables you to move the Match Line within the overlap area of the two referenced View Frames.

Figure 12–5

Practice 12a | Plan Production Tools I

Task 1: Create View Frames.

---

1. Open the file **PPR1-Sec1-PlanProduction.dwg** from the following folder:

   C:\Civil 3D Projects\Civil3D-training\Drawings

2. You will create the plan - profile sheets at a scale of 1:500. The sheets will be created more consistently if the Model Space scale matches the final output scale. Set the *Annotation Scale* to **1:500** if it is not already set, as shown in Figure 12–6.

Figure 12–6

3. In the *Output* tab > Plan Production panel, select **Create View Frames**, as shown in Figure 12–7.

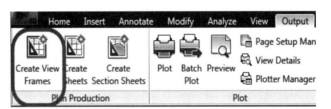

Figure 12–7

4. In the wizard, on the *Create View Frames - Alignment* screen, select **Jeffries Ranch Rd** as the *Alignment* and select the **Automatic** option in the *Station Range* section, as shown in Figure 12–8. Then click Next >.

Figure 12–8

5. On the *Create View Frames - Sheets* screen, in the sheet settings, select the **Plan and Profile** option. In the *Template for Plan and Profile sheet* section, click ▦.

6. In the *Drawing template file name* field, click 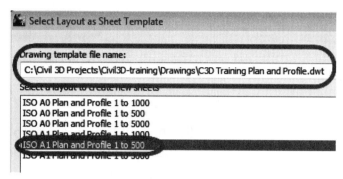 and browse to the file **C3D Training Plan and Profile.dwt**. This file is located in the folder *C:\Civil 3D Projects\Civil3D-training\Drawings*.

7. In the *Select a layout to create new sheets* section, select **ISO A1 Plan and Profile 1 to 500** from the list, as shown in Figure 12–9, and click ![OK] to close the dialog box.

Figure 12–9

8. For the *View Frame Placement*, select the **Along alignment** option, as shown in Figure 12–10. Click ![Next >] .

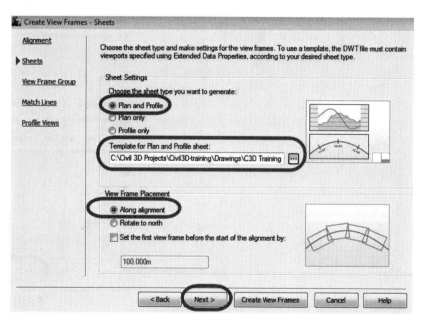

Figure 12–10

9. On the *Create View Frames - View Frame Group* screen, leave the default for the *Name*. This will append the alignment name and a counter to the VFG.

10. You want to name the View Frame with the starting station. Click ![icon] (Edit View Frame Name).

11. In the Name Template dialog box, enter **VF - sta** in the *Name* field. Select **View Frame Start Raw Station** in the *Property fields* drop-down list and click 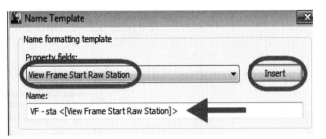, as shown in Figure 12–11. Click [OK] to close the dialog box.

Figure 12–11

12. Accept the default Label and Label style. Accept the Label location of **Top left**, as shown in Figure 12–12, and click [Next >].

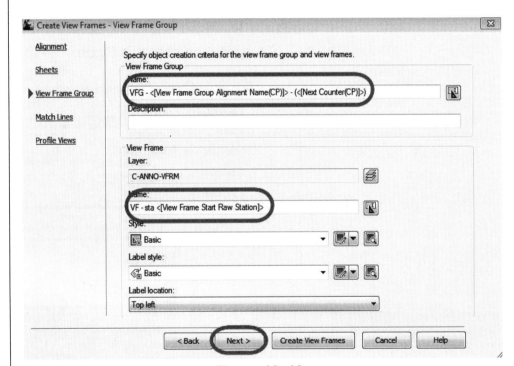

Figure 12–12

13. On the *Create View Frames - Match Lines* screen, change the Match Line name to **ML - <[Match Line Raw Station]>**, as shown in Figure 12–13. The procedure to do this is similar to the previous step. Accept all other defaults and click Next > .

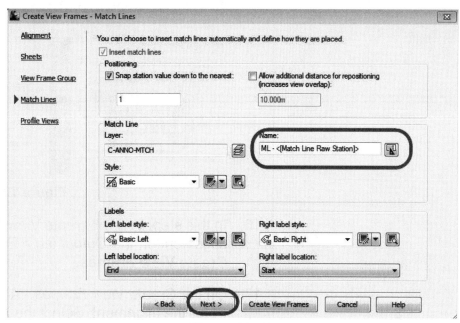

Figure 12–13

14. On the *Create View Frames - Profile Views* screen, accept the default values for the *Profile View Style* and the *Band Set*. Click **Create View Frames** , as shown in Figure 12–14.

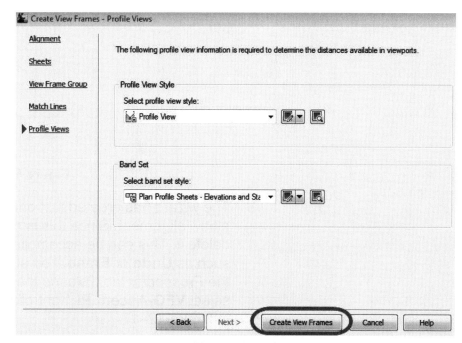

Figure 12–14

15. In the *Prospector* tab, expand the *View Frame Groups* collection, expand the *VFG - Jeffries Ranch Rd View* Frame Group, and then expand the *View Frames* collection and the *Match Lines* collection. Notice that the Create View Frame wizard has created three Plan Production objects, two View Frames, and one Match Line, as shown in Figure 12–15.

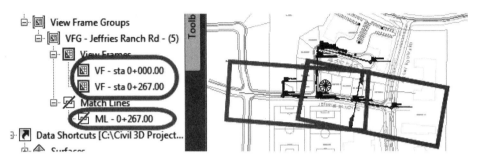

Figure 12–15

16. In this step, you will create View Frames for the Ascent Pl alignment. In the *Output* tab > Plan Production panel, select **Create View Frames**.

17. On the *Create View Frames - Alignment* screen, select **Ascent Pl** for the alignment. Select the **Automatic** option in the *Station Range* section. When you used the wizard to create View Frames for **Jeffries Ranch Rd.**, Civil 3D retained all the settings. Since you want to use the same settings for this alignment (Ascent Pl), simply select **Create View Frames** rather than step through each setting. The drawing appears as shown in Figure 12–16.

Figure 12–16

18. The wizard has created just one View Frame of the dog-leg or elbow alignment. Since this is not the desired View Frame, delete it. This can be accomplished using AutoCAD commands such as **Undo** or **Erase**. You also can erase the View Frame in the *Prospector* tab. Expand the *View Frame Groups* collection, select **VFG-Ascent Pl**, right-click, and select **Delete**, as shown in Figure 12–17.

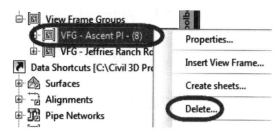

Figure 12–17

19. Because Civil 3D does not have the ability to add new View Frames into a pre-existing View Frame Group nor the ability to create Plan Production objects without the wizard, you will have to find another method to create two View Frames for this alignment. In the *Output* tab > Plan Production panel, select **Create View Frames**.

20. On the *Create View Frames - Alignment* screen, select **Ascent PI** for the alignment. Select the **Automatic** option in the *Station Range* section and click Next >.

21. On the *Create View Frames - Sheets* screen, select the **Set the first view frame before the start of the alignment by** option in the *View Frame Placement* section, and enter **100m** in the field below, as shown in Figure 12–18. This forces Civil 3D to add an additional view frame.

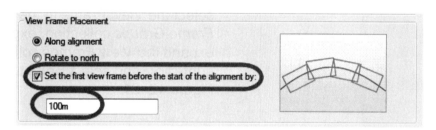

Figure 12–18

22. Since you do not need to make any other changes, click Create View Frames. The drawing appears as shown in Figure 12–19.

Figure 12–19

23. Although you still have to make some minor adjustments to the Plan Production objects, View Frames, and Match Lines, you now have the correct View Frames along the Ascent Pl alignment.

24. Save the drawing.

Task 2: Edit View Frames and Match Lines.

1. Continue working with the drawing from the previous task.

2. In the *View* tab > Views panel, select the preset view **C3D-PlanProduction-Edit View Frame**, as shown in Figure 12–20.

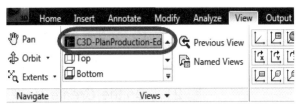

Figure 12–20

3. In Model Space, select the View Frame object **VF - Sta 0+000.00**, as shown on the left in Figure. This represents the View Frame for the Ascent Pl alignment. Alternatively, you can select the View Frame in the *Prospector* tab. Expand the *View Frame Groups* collection, expand the *VFG-Ascent Pl* collection, expand the *View Frames* collection, select **VF - Sta 0+000.00**, right-click, and select **Select**, as shown on the right in Figure 12–21.

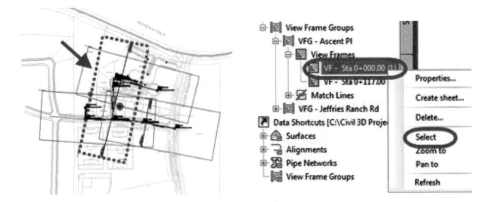

Figure 12–21

4. Select the rotation grip (the circular grip), and graphically rotate the View Frame so that it is parallel to the Ascent Pl alignment.

5. To adjust the Match Line in Model Space, select the Match Line **ML-0+117.00**, as shown on the left in Figure, that lies along the Ascent PI alignment. Alternatively, you can select the View Frame in the *Prospector* tab. Expand the *View Frame Groups* collection, expand the *VFG-Ascent PI* collection, expand the *Match Lines* collection, select **ML-0+117.00**, right-click, and select **Select**, as shown on the right in Figure 12–22.

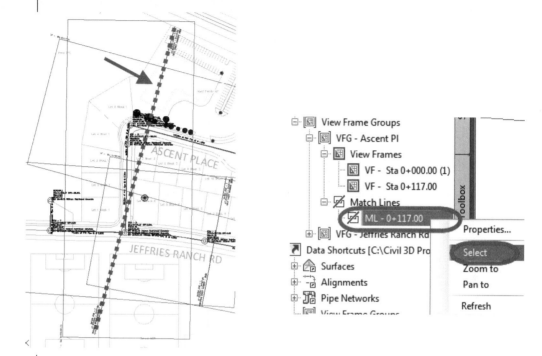

Figure 12–22

6. Select the Match Line station grip (diamond-shaped grip). You can drag the station grip as it follows the alignment. However, to establish a more precise location, enable the Dynamic Input icon (if not already active), as shown in Figure 12–23.

Figure 12–23

7. In the Dynamic input field, type **103** <Enter> as the station number for the Match Line. Select each of the Match Line stretch grips (the triangular-shaped grip at each end of the Match Line) and stretch them to an appropriate length so that they fall within the View Frames. Typing **67** <Enter> in the Dynamic input field will make this Match Line similar in length to the other existing Match Lines on Jeffries Ranch Rd.

8. Press <Esc> to exit the feature line selection.

9. Save the drawing.

12.4 Creating Sheets

Once the Match Lines, View Frames, and the associated View Frame Groups have been established, you can start the next phase of generating sheet sets.

AutoCAD Civil 3D provides a wizard that will step you through the process of creating sheets from the View Frames. The flexibility of this wizard, in addition to the selection of styles, enables you to create sheets automatically that will conform to many of your existing standards. The wizard is shown in Figure 12–24.

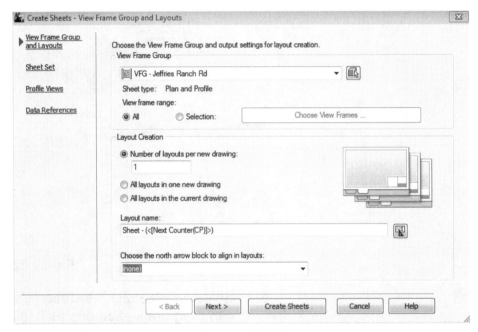

Figure 12–24

Since no dynamic link exists between the View Frames and the sheet, it is imperative that the desired View Frames are established before creating the sheets. Changing or editing View Frames after the sheets are created has no effect on the sheets.

In addition to using the wizard for creating sheets, this workflow also uses the AutoCAD Sheet Set Manager.

Practice 12b	Plan Production Tools II

Task 1: Create sheet files and a new Sheet Set Manager file.

1. Continue working with the drawing from the previous practice or open the file **PPR1-Sec2-PlanProduction.dwg** from the following folder:

   C:\Civil 3D Projects\Civil3D-training\Drawings

2. In the *Output* tab > Plan Production panel, select **Create Sheets**, as shown in Figure.

3. In the wizard, on the *Create Sheet - View Frame Group and Layouts* screen, ensure that the *View Frame Group* is **VFG - Jeffries Ranch Rd**, and the *View frame range* is set to **All**. In the *Layout Creation* section, set the *Number of layouts per new drawing* to **1**.

4. For the *Layout name*, click ⬚ (Edit Layout Name). In the *Name* field, delete the current name and type **Sheet -**. Select **View Frame Start Raw Station** in the *Property fields* drop-down list and then click ⬚ Insert ⬚. Civil 3D will append the data string *<[View Frame Start Raw Station]>* to the text **Sheet -**, as shown in Figure 12–25. Click ⬚ OK ⬚ to close this dialog box.

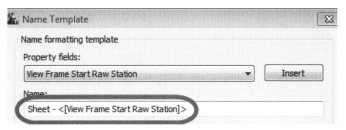

Figure 12–25

5. In the *Choose the north arrow block to align in layouts* drop-down list, select the **North** block, as shown in Figure 12–26. Once this is complete, click [Next >].

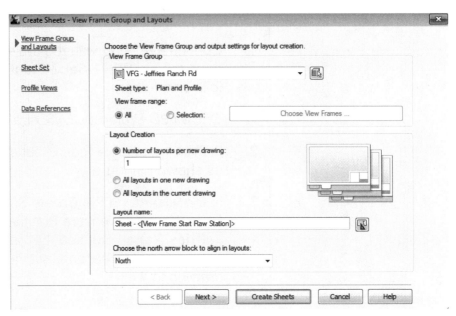

Figure 12–26

6. On the *Create Sheets - Sheet Set* screen, set the following:

- Select the **New sheet set** option, and enter **Ascent Phase1** in the *Sheet Set name* field. In the *Sheet set file (.DST) storage location* field, enter **C:\Civil 3D Projects\Civil3D-training\Drawings**.

- In the *Sheet files storage location* field, enter **C:\Civil 3D Projects\Civil3D-training\Drawings\PlanProduction**.

- In the *Sheet file name* field, delete the existing name and click [icon] (Edit sheet file name).

- In the *Property fields* drop-down list, select **View Frame Group Alignment Name** and click [Insert].

- Also in the *Sheet file name* field, append the text string **Sta**.

- In the *Property fields* drop-down list, select **View Frame Start Raw Station** and click [Insert].

- Also in the *Sheet file name* field, append a - (dash).

- In the *Property fields* drop-down list, select **View Frame End Raw Station** and click [Insert].

7. Once these steps are complete, the *Sheet file name* field will have the following format: *<[View Frame Group Alignment Name]> Sta <[View Frame Start Raw Station]> - <[View Frame End Raw Station]>*, as shown in Figure 12–27. Click Next > .

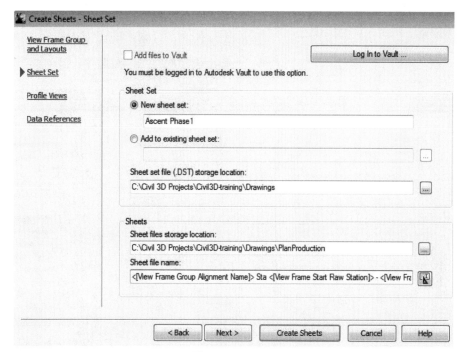

Figure 12–27

8. On the *Create Sheets - Profile Views* screen, accept the defaults, as shown in Figure 12–28, and click Next > .

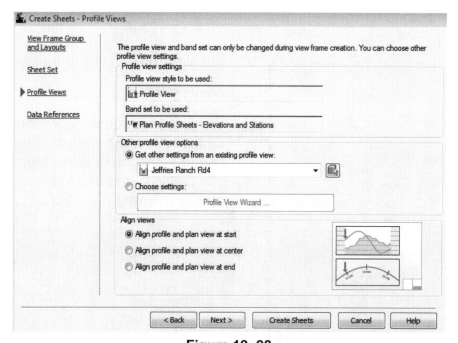

Figure 12–28

9. On the *Create Sheets - Data References* screen, you can add data-referenced objects to your Profile sheets. You will reference in the surface and Pipe network. Accept all the defaults, and select the **Phase1-site** surface, as shown in Figure 12–29. Also select the **Pipe Networks, Networks,** and **STORM** entries. Click **Create Sheets** to exit the wizard and create the sheets.

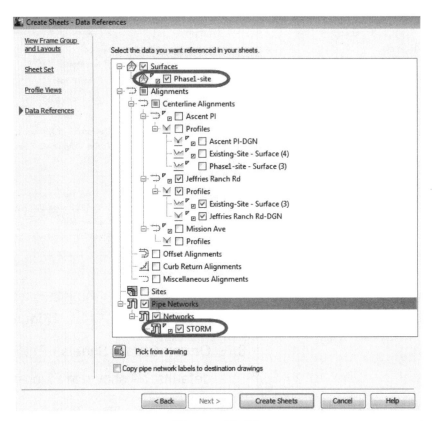

Figure 12–29

10. The wizard notifies you that the drawing will be saved before creating the new sheets. Click [OK] to accept this.

11. When prompted for the location of the profile, select a blank space in your drawing, as shown in Figure 12–30. Civil 3D will use this location to insert a profile of your alignment. Note that this profile is inserted in the newly created sheet and not in the current drawing.

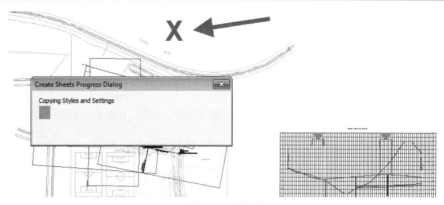

Figure 12-30

12. AutoCAD Civil 3D creates the two sheets and the Sheet Set Manager file. The Sheet Set Manager opens, as shown in Figure 12-31.

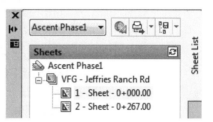

Figure 12-31

13. Hover the cursor over the file name in the Sheet Set Manager to see all of the properties of the sheet, including the name and location of the drawing file, as shown in Figure 12-32.

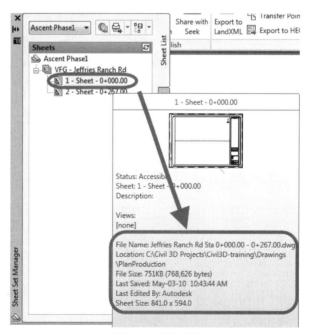

Figure 12-32

14. Save the drawing.

Task 2: Create sheet files and add to the new Sheet Set Manager file.

1. Continue working with the drawing from the previous task.

2. In the *Output* tab > Plan Production panel, select **Create Sheets**.

3. On the *Create Sheet - View Frame Group and Layout* screen, ensure that the *View Frame Group* is set to **VFG - Ascent Pl** and the *View frame range* is set to **All**. In the *Layout Creation* section, set the *Number of layouts per new drawing* to **1**.

4. Make sure the Layout name is set to **Sheet - <[View Frame Start Raw Station]>**.

5. In the *Choose the north arrow block to align in layouts* drop-down list, select the **North** block. Once this is complete, click ⌈ Next > ⌋. On the *Create Sheets - Sheet Set* screen, select the **Add to existing sheet set** option. Click ⌈···⌋ and select the file **Ascent Phase1.dst** located in *C:\Civil 3D Projects\Civil3D-training\Drawings*. This is the Sheet Set Manager file you created in Task 1.

6. In the *Sheet files storage location* field, enter **C:\Civil 3D Projects\Civil3D-training\Drawings\PlanProduction**, as shown in Figure 12–33. Click ⌈ Next > ⌋.

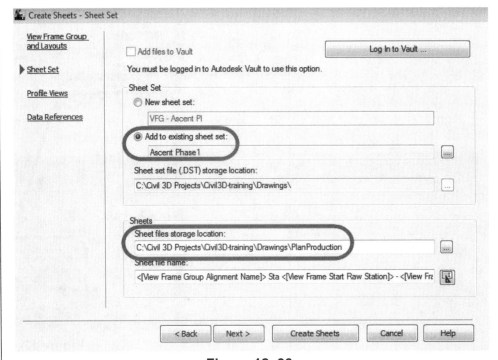

Figure 12–33

7. On the *Create Sheets - Profile Views* screen, accept the defaults, as shown in Figure 12–34, and click Next > .

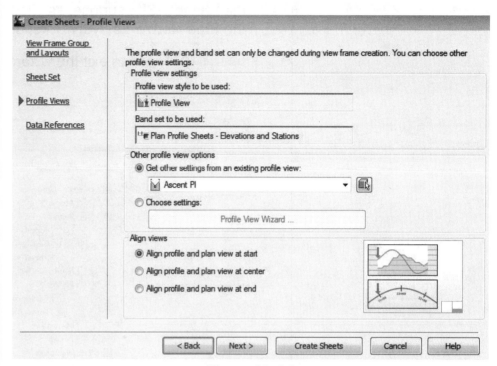

Figure 12–34

8. On the *Create Sheets - Data References* screen, you can add data-referenced objects to your Profile sheets. You will reference in the surface and Pipe network. Accept all defaults, and select the **Phase1 -Site** surface, as shown in Figure 12–35. Also select the **Pipe Networks**, **Networks**, and **STORM** entries. Click

Create Sheets to exit the wizard and create the sheets.

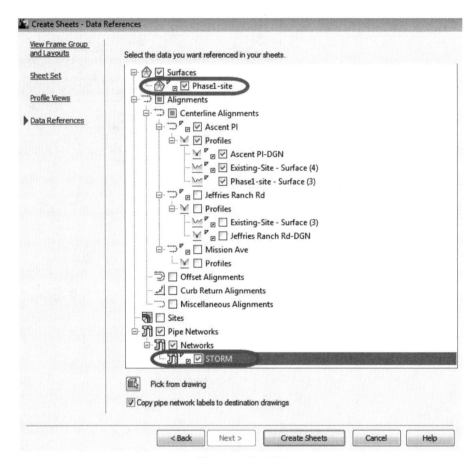

Figure 12–35

9. You are notified again that the drawing will be saved. Click

OK to accept this.

10. When prompted for the location of the profile, select a blank space in your drawing. Civil 3D will use this location to insert a profile of your alignment. Note that this profile is inserted in the newly created sheet and not in the current drawing.

Civil 3D creates the two sheets in the Sheet Set Manager file, as shown in Figure 12–36.

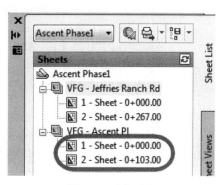

Figure 12–36

11. Save the drawing.

12.5 Sheet Sets

The preceding sections have covered only a fraction of this highly productive tool and workflow. The sheet set is not exclusive to AutoCAD Civil 3D, but is used in all AEC products. More detailed training on this topic is covered in the CAD manager's training.

A sheet set is a collection of sheets that are created from a combination of several different drawings. Sheets listed in the Sheet Set Manger file (DST) refer to layouts in a drawing file. The sheet set can reference any number of layouts from any number of drawings.

For example, you may be working on a commercial site plan or a highway project drawing. Using the Sheet Set Manager, you can create a construction set or tender documents by compiling a sheet set that lists all of the required sheets from the two master plans. Additionally, if the project is a multi-disciplined project that includes structural engineers and architects, you will be able to compile a list of sheets from those sources as well. Figure 12–37 outlines the structure of sheet sets in a project.

1. Drawings residing in various folders from various disciplines

2. Layouts within those drawings organized into sheet sets

3. Final documents

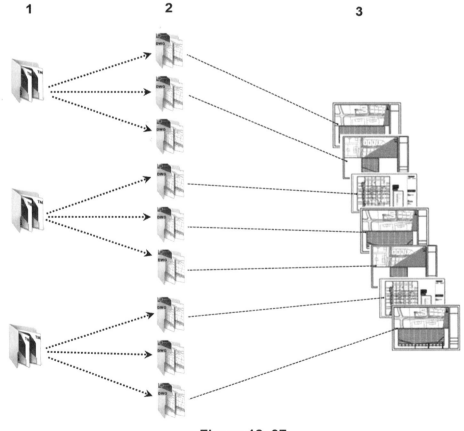

Figure 12–37

Structuring Sheet Sets

Figure 12–38 displays a typical hierarchical structure of the sheet set elements.

- The *Sheet Set Name* (1) identifies the sheet set (i.e., the DST file). This file can reside anywhere on your server.
- The *Sheet* subset (2) is used to organize sheets in a logical manner (i.e., Plan Profiles, Structural, Electrical, etc.).
- The *Individual Sheets* (3) are layouts from drawings imported into the sheet set.

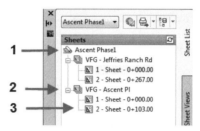

Figure 12–38

Each of the elements shown above represents a core component in a typical sheet set. Corresponding to the other Civil 3D object functionality, right-clicking on any of these elements will list all of the available options for that element.

Editing Sheet Sets

You have the ability to modify and re-organize sheet sets in a number of ways. For example, you can reorder the sheets in the set, rename or renumber sheets, create new sheets or subsets, and import new layouts as sheets. To reorder elements in the sheet set, drag the element to a new location. Reordering sheets using this method does not automatically renumber the sheets. The options to edit sheet sets are shown in Figure 12–39.

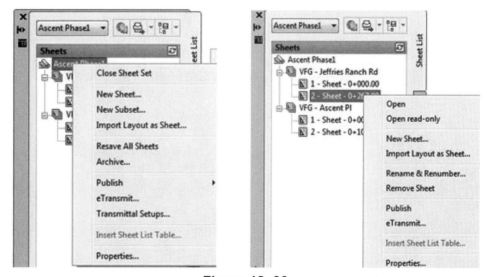

Figure 12–39

To rename and renumber sheets automatically, enter a *Number* and *Sheet title*. To change the associated file name, enter a new *File name*. You also have the ability to have the associated file name change anytime you rename the sheet. To enable this feature, simply select the **Sheet title** option to rename the drawing file to match the sheet title, as shown in Figure 12–40.

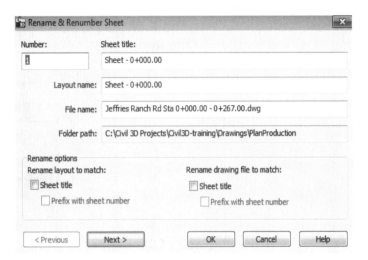

Figure 12–40

Sheet Set Manager Properties

In the Sheet Set Properties dialog box, you can change the name, the path of the drawing files or template associated with the sheet set, as well as any custom properties associated with the sheet set.

To access the properties, right-click on the Sheet Set Manager name and select **Properties**. Information specific to the sheet set will display.

The sheet set properties dialog box contains the following, as shown in Figure 12–41:

- Sheet Set properties (1)
- Project Control properties (2)
- Sheet Creation properties (3)

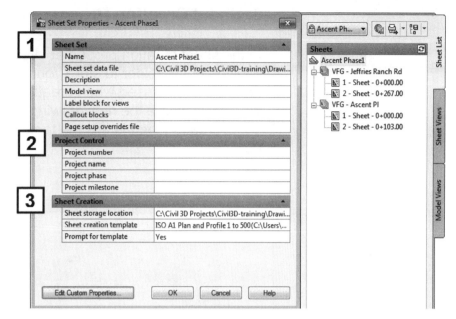

Figure 12–41

1. Sheet Set Properties

The sheet set properties give you access to the following:

*   Name of the sheet set.
*   Sheet set data file location (read only).
*   Description.
*   Model view drawing location (the location of the resource drawings).
*   Label block for views (the location of the drawing and blocks that will contain the block, which can be used for the views).
*   Callout blocks (a list of blocks that can be used for callouts).
*   Page setup override file (a drawing template that contains the page setup overrides for the sheet set). The page setup override enables you to override existing page setups for individual drawings in the sheet set.

2. Project Control Properties

You can use four preset project properties: *Project Number, Name, Phase,* and *Milestone*. These four properties can also be displayed on the individual sheets. In addition to these four properties, you can create custom properties. There are two types of properties:

*   *Sheet Set properties* are applied to all the sheets in the set.
*   *Sheet properties* are only applied to a single sheet.

3. Sheet Creation Properties

In the sheet creation properties dialog box, you have access to the location of the folder to store your sheets, as well as the default template that is used when creating a new sheet. The sheet storage location is where the new drawing sheet that is created is stored. The sheet creation template is the template that is used when creating the new sheet.

Practice 12c | Plan Production Tools III

Task 1: Define the Sheet Set Manager properties.

1. Continue working with the drawing from the previous practice or open the file **PPR1-Sec2-PlanProduction.dwg** from the following folder:

    C:\Civil 3D Projects\Civil3D-training\Drawings

2. If the Sheet Set Manager is not visible, open it in the *View* tab > Palettes panel. Expand the panel and select the Sheet Set Manager from the drop-down list, as shown in Figure 12–42.

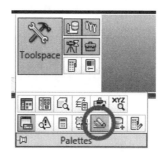

Figure 12–42

3. Select the **Ascent Phase1** sheet set from the list in the sheet set drop-down list at the top of the manager palette. If it is not in the list you will have to open and browse to the file Ascent Phase1.dst in the following folder: *C:\Civil 3D Projects\Civil3D-training\Drawings*, as shown in Figure 12–43.

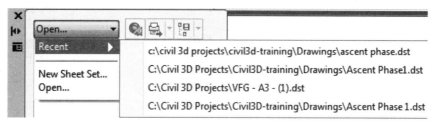

Figure 12–43

4. Select **VFG - Jeffries Ranch Rd**, right-click, and select **Rename Subset...**, as shown on the left in Figure 12–44. For the *Subset Name*, enter **PlanProfile - Jeffries Ranch Rd**, as shown on the right. Click ⟨ OK ⟩ to close the dialog box.

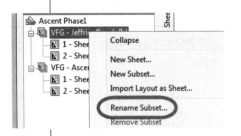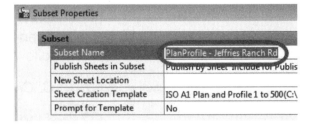

Figure 12–44

5. Do the same for **VFG - Ascent Pl** and rename it to **PlanProfile - Ascent Pl**.

6. In the *PlanProfile - Ascent Pl* collection, select **1 - Sheet - 0+000.00**, right-click, and select **Rename & Renumber**, as shown in Figure 12–45.

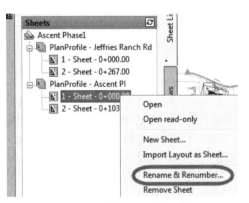

Figure 12–45

7. In the *Rename & Renumber Sheet* dialog box, change the *Number* to **3**, and select **Sheet title** in the *Rename layout to match* section, as shown in Figure 12–46. Click ⟨ Next > ⟩.

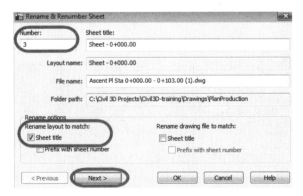

Figure 12–46

8. Change the next sheet number to **4**, as shown in Figure 12–47. Click [OK] to accept the changes and close the dialog box.

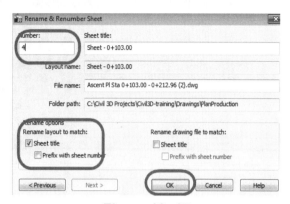

Figure 12–47

9. Notice the changes to the subsets and sheet names, as shown in Figure 12–48.

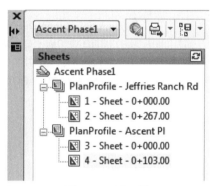

Figure 12–48

10. Save the drawing.

Task 2: Define the Sheet Set properties.

---

1. Continue working with the drawing from the previous task.

2. If the Sheet Set Manager is not visible, open it in the *View* tab > Palettes panel. Open the drop-down list by expanding the panel, and select the Sheet Set Manager from there.

3. Select the **Ascent Phase1** sheet set from the list in the sheet set drop-down list at the top of the manager palette. If it is not in the list you will have to open and browse to the file Ascent Phase1.dst in the following folder: *C:\Civil 3D Projects\Civil3D-training\Drawings,*

4. To navigate to one of the drawings, double-click on the **3-Sheet - 0+100.00** entry or right-click on the *3-Sheet - 0+103.00* entry and select **Open**, as shown in Figure 12–49.

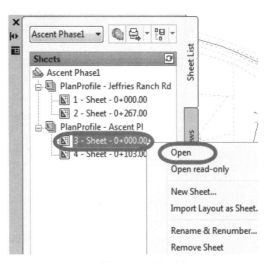

Figure 12–49

5. Once the drawing is open, zoom in to the lower right corner of the drawing, as shown in Figure 12–50. Note the title block. The values for the **Project Name**, **Project Number**, and **Drawn By fields** do not display any values.

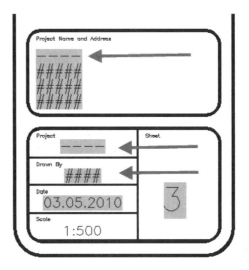

Figure 12–50

6. In the Sheet Set Manager for *Ascent Phase1*, select the sheet set name **Ascent Phase1**, right-click, and select **Properties**, as shown in Figure 12–51.

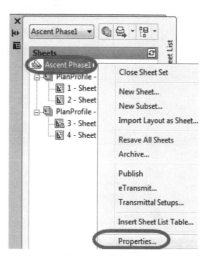

Figure 12–51

7. In the Sheet Set Properties - Ascent Phase1 dialog box, enter **30052010** in the *Project Number* field and enter **C3D Training** in the *Project Name* field. Click [OK] to complete the procedure. You may have to type **regen** <Enter> at the Command Line to show the updated fields. You should now see the values in your drawing title sheet, as shown in Figure 12–52.

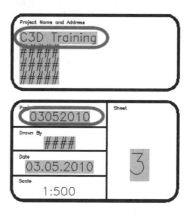

Figure 12–52

8. You do not have a field called *Drawn By* in the Sheet Set Manager properties, which means you have to create a custom property. In the Sheet Set Manager for *Ascent Phase1*, select the sheet set name **Ascent Phase1**, right-click, and select **Properties**.

9. In the Sheet Set Properties - Ascent Phase1 dialog box, click **Edit Custom Properties...** . In the Custom Properties dialog box, click **Add...** . In the Add Custom Property dialog box, enter **Drawn By** for the Name. Enter **??** for the Default Value, as this property is based on a per sheet value rather than the entire sheet set. At the bottom of the dialog box, select the **Sheet** option. Click **OK** to close the Add Custom Property dialog box. Click **OK** again to close the Custom Properties dialog box. The process is shown in Figure 12–53.

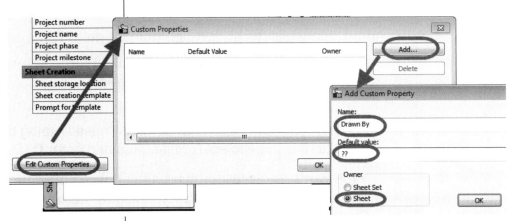

Figure 12–53

10. You now need to set the field properties for this sheet. In the Sheet Set Manager for *Ascent Phase1*, select **3 - Sheet - 0+000.00**, right-click, and select **Properties**, as shown in Figure 12–54.

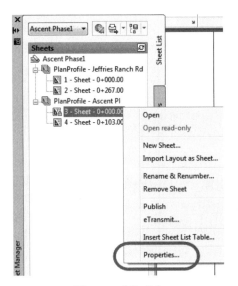

Figure 12–54

11. In the Sheet Properties dialog box, under *Sheet Custom Properties*, enter **ME** for the *Drawn By* value, as shown in Figure 12–55. Click [OK] to close the dialog box.

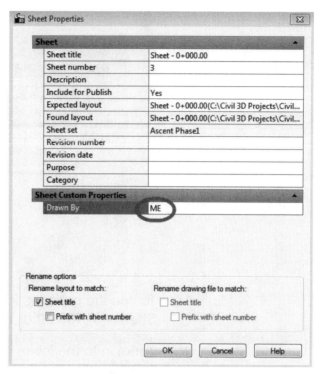

Figure 12–55

12. You may have to type **regen** at the Command Line to see the changes, as shown in Figure 12–56.

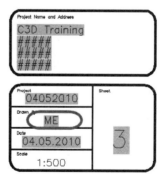

Figure 12–56

13. Set a different value for another sheet. In the Sheet Set Manager for *Ascent Phase1*, select **4 - Sheet - 0+103.00**, right-click, and select **Properties**. Set the *Drawn By* value to **You**, as shown in Figure 12–57, and click ⬛ OK ⬛ to close the dialog box.

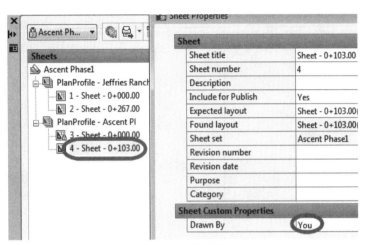

Figure 12–57

14. To see the changes in the sheet, double-click on the sheet **4 - Sheet - 0+103.00** or right-click on it and select **Open**.

15. Zoom in to the lower right corner of the title block and confirm that both the sheet set and the sheet properties have been updated, as shown in Figure 12–58.

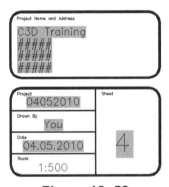

Figure 12–58

16. Save and exit all drawings.

Task 3: Define Sheet Set properties.

---

1. Open a new drawing session by selecting **File > New**. Then select **C3D Training.dwt** in the folder *C:\Civil 3D Projects\Civil3D-training\Drawings*.

2. If the Sheet Set Manager for *Ascent PL* is not active, you can open the Sheet Set .dst file using one of the following methods:

- Select the Civil 3D file and click **Open**. Select **Sheet Set** and browse to the **Ascent Phase1.dst** file, or select **Open the Sheet Set Manager** and select the **Ascent Phase1** from the drop-down list, as shown in Figure 12–59.

Figure 12–59

- In the *View* tab > Palettes panel, select the Sheet Set Manager from the drop-down list.

3. In the Sheet Set Manager dialog box, select the sheet set **Ascent Phase1**, right-click, and select **New Subset**, as shown on the left in Figure 12–60. Enter **Base Plans** for the *Subset Name*, as shown on the right. Set the *Prompt for Template* to **No**, so that all new sheets use the preset template. Click [OK] to exit the dialog box.

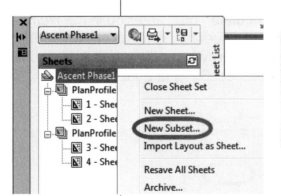

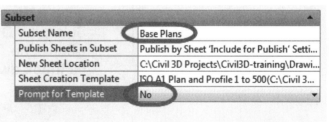

Figure 12–60

4. In the Sheet Set Manager, select the subset **Base Plans** and drag it to the top, as shown in Figure 12–61.

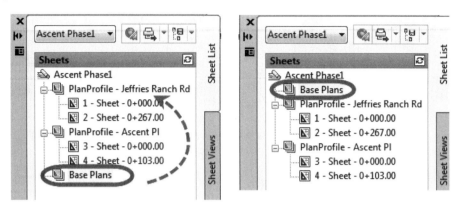

Figure 12–61

5. To create a new sheet, select the subset **Base Plans**, right-click, and select **New Sheet**, as shown in Figure 12–62.

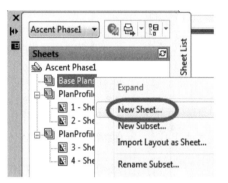

Figure 12–62

6. In the New Sheet dialog box, enter **00** in the *Number* field, and enter **Index** in the *Sheet title* field, as shown in Figure 12–63. Select the **Open in drawing editor** option to open the drawing when done. The Sheet Set Manager will create a drawing named **00 Index.dwg**.

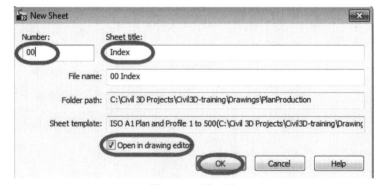

Figure 12–63

7. The Sheet Set Manager has created a new drawing based on the template and the sheet set properties. You can select and delete the two viewports, since they are not necessary. Zoom in so you can see the entire title block.

8. In the Sheet Set Manager, select the sheet set **Ascent Phase1**, right-click, and select **Insert Sheet List Table**, as shown in Figure 12–64.

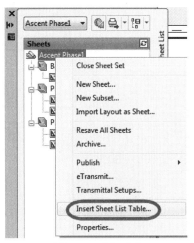

Figure 12–64

9. In the Sheet List Table dialog box, select **Legend** in the *Table Style name* drop-down list. Select the **Show Subheader** option and click [OK] to close the dialog box, as shown in Figure 12–65.

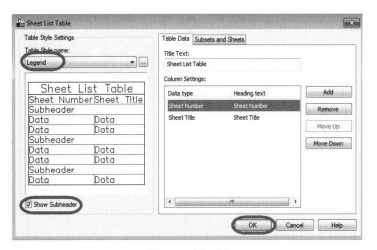

Figure 12–65

10. When prompted for the location of the table, select a point in the middle of the title block, as shown in Figure 12–66. Since the table scale is too small, use the AutoCAD **Scale** command to scale the table by a factor of **30**.

Sheet List Table	
Sheet Number	Sheet Title
Base Plans	
00	Index
PlanProfile —	Jeffries Ranch Rd
1	Sheet — 0+000.00
2	Sheet — 0+267.00
PlanProfile —	Ascent Pl
3	Sheet — 0+000.00
4	Sheet — 0+103.00

Figure 12–66

11. Save the drawing.

Review Questions

Question 1   What are two of the steps needed to create plan and profile sheets using the Plan Production tools?

Question 2   How can you integrate AutoCAD Civil 3D's Plan Production system layouts into an existing sheet set?

Appendix A

Design Data

A.1 Set Up Data Shortcuts Working Folder

1. Set the working folder as the location in which to store data shortcut projects. The default working folder for data shortcut projects is *C:\Civil 3D Projects*.

2. Open a new drawing, as shown in Figure A–1, using the **C3D Training.dwt** template from the following folder:

   C:\Civil 3D Projects\Civil3D-training\Drawings

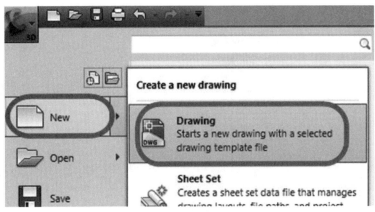

Figure A–1

3. In the *Manage* tab > Data Shortcuts panel, select **Set Working Folder**, as shown in Figure A–2. In the Browse For Folder dialog box, select the **Civil 3D-training** folder (*C:\Civil3D Projects\Civil 3D Training*). Finally, click OK to close the dialog box.

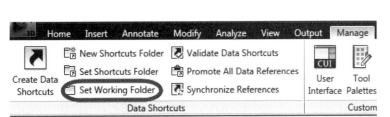

Figure A–2

4. In the *Manage* tab > Data Shortcuts panel, select **Set Shortcuts Folder**, as shown in Figure A–3. In the Set Data Shortcut Folder dialog box, select **DataShortCuts** and click OK .

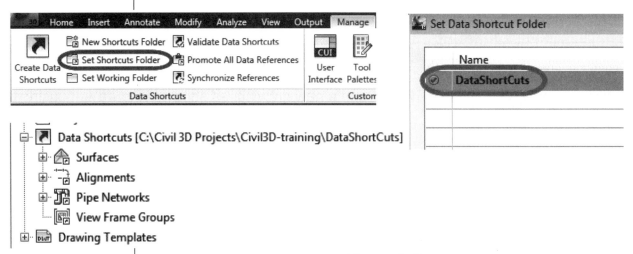

Figure A–3

A.2 Design Data

Parcel Size

The following data, shown in Figure A–4, describes the parcel size used in the training dataset:

- **Minimum Area:** 950sq m
- **Minimum Frontage:** 20m
- **Frontage Offset:** 6m
- **Minimum Width:** 20m

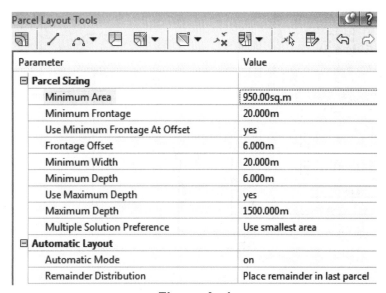

Parameter	Value
⊟ **Parcel Sizing**	
Minimum Area	950.00sq.m
Minimum Frontage	20.000m
Use Minimum Frontage At Offset	yes
Frontage Offset	6.000m
Minimum Width	20.000m
Minimum Depth	6.000m
Use Maximum Depth	yes
Maximum Depth	1500.000m
Multiple Solution Preference	Use smallest area
⊟ **Automatic Layout**	
Automatic Mode	on
Remainder Distribution	Place remainder in last parcel

Figure A–4

Pipe Size Conversion

The following table contains a listing of pipe size conversions between metric and imperial.

Metric Size in mm	Imperial Size in mm	Metric Size in mm	Imperial Size in mm
-	-	1050	42
150	6	1200	48
200	8	1350	54
250	10	1500	60
300	12	1650	66
375	15	1800	72
450	18	1950	78
525	21	2100	84
600	24	2250	90
675	27	2400	96
750	30	2700	108
825	33	3000	120
900	36		

Road Design Criteria

Figure A–5, Figure A–6, Figure A–7, and Figure A–8 plus the corresponding tables specify the design criteria for the expressway design on Mission Avenue, the grand boulevard on Ascent Blvd., the collector streets at Jeffries Ranch Rd., and the residential street design for Ascent Place.

Expressway: Mission Avenue

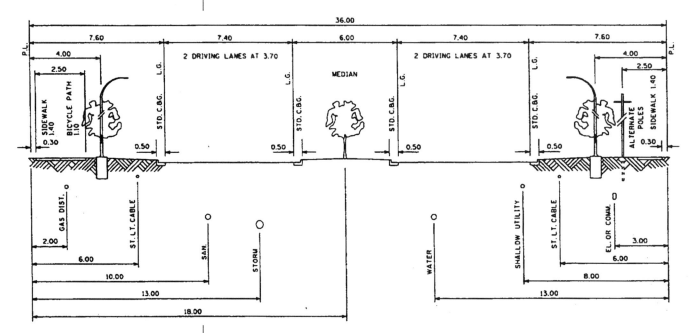

Figure A–5

Daily Traffic Volume (vehicles/day)	Number of Lanes	Right-of-way Requirement	Minimum Intersection Spacing
30,000 - 90,000	4, 6, or 8	60.0 m (min.)	800 m

Function

- To permit relatively unimpeded flow for through traffic between major elements.
- To function as part of the Truck Route System.

Access Conditions

- Intersections are grade separated where warranted.
- Divided roadways with full control of access.
- Direct access to abutting property is prohibited.
- Only roadways of Major category or higher can intersection with Expressways.
- Intersections should be 800m apart but in special circumstances can be a minimum of 450 m apart.
- At-grade intersections should be signalized.

Traffic Features

Posted Speed (kph)	60-80	On-street Bikeway	No
Parking	None	Bus Route	No
Sidewalk	None	Truck Route	Yes
Traffic Signals	For interim condition only	Sound Attenuation	Yes

Pedestrian Crossing	Grade-separated, at-grade for interim condition		

Note

- Interchange spacing is generally similar to that of Freeways. However, closer spacing might be considered under special circumstances.
- Expressways are designed in accordance with TAG standards and for capacity conditions based on Level of Service D'.
- Pedestrian crosswalks are permitted at intersections. However, grade separated walkways are used where warranted.
- The right-of-way varies from a minimum of 60 m depending on the number of lanes, sloping requirements, road grades, and noise attenuation requirements.
- A noise attenuation study is required at the Outline Plan application stage for residential lots adjacent to interchange areas, including the Transportation Utility Corridors (TUG) areas, to determine noise attenuation and right-of-way requirements.

Typical Cross Section	See TAC Standards

Classification	Design Speed	Intersection Design
Urban Arterial Divided (UAD) 50 Urban Arterial Divided (UAD) 60 Urban Arterial Divided (UAD) 70	50-70 kph	See Appendix II-A Sheets/ -9

Horizontal Alignment

Minimum Stopping Sight Distance	Minimum Radius of Curvature
Major UAD 50 = 65 m Major UAD 60 = '5 m Major UAD 70 = 110 m	Major UAD 50 = 90 m, 130 m - 6000 m (desirable) Major UAD 60 = 120 m, 260 m - 6000 m (desirable) Major UAD 50 = 170 m, 400 m - 6000 m (desirable)

Median and Left Turn Bay

- The minimum median width on a Major street is 6.0 m for a parallel left turn lane and 9.5 m for parallel dual left turn lanes.
- The introduced median is used to transit an undivided road to a divided road with a left turn median.
- Slot left turn bays are required as an interim design on wide medians, such as those reserved for future LRT or future widening in the median.
- No left turn bays are permitted on curves with a center line radius of less than 400 m nor within 60 m of the end of a center line transition curve (spiral) if the radius is less than 440 m.
- Standard left turn bays shall be provided on Major streets at all intersections. For left turn bay designs.
- The minimum storage length for a left turn bay is 60 m with a 3.5 m wide left turn lane.
- Dual left turn bays and slot turn bays are to be designed to TAG standards.

Note

- Major streets are classified as Urban Arterial Divided (UAD) roadways and are designed for speeds of 50, 60, and 70 kilometers per hour. Most Major streets fall within the 60 kph category. However, developers must be informed by the approving authority of Land Use and Mobility of the applicable design speed.
- A standard curb with a 0.5 m gutter is to be used on the median and on the outside edges.
- A reverse gutter is used where necessary.
- Street light poles, power poles, and traffic signal poles are to be located a minimum of 3.5 m from the lip of gutter.

Vertical Alignment

Minimum and Maximum Grades

- Maximum grade: Major UAD 50 = 7.0%
  Major UAD 60 – 6.0%
  Major UAD 70 = 5.0%

- Minimum grade: 0.6%

- The maximum and minimum grades also apply to the development of superelevation.

Grade at Intersections

- The grade line of the approaching street (maximum approach grade of 4%) shall tie to the lane line of the Major street with a vertical curve of a minimum length of 30m. I.e., the crossfall of the Major street shall be extended and intersects the grade of the approaching street. The resulting vertical curve ends at the lane line of the Major street.

- The maximum profile grade on a Major street at an intersection shall be 4% for a minimum distance of 100 m measured from the Vertical Point of Intersection (VPI) to the center line of the intersecting street on both sides of the intersection.

Vertical Curves and Superelevation

- The length of a vertical curve is calculated based on the stopping sight distance.

- The length of a vertical curve is calculated based on the stopping sight distance.
- For Major streets, crest vertical curves are to be designed using the "K" values for 20 kph higher than the design speed.
- Superelevation shall be developed through the transition spiral by using the following superelevation tables:
  - Major UAD 50 emax = 0.06
  - Major UAD 60 emax = 0.08
  - Major UAD 70 emax = 0.08
- The superelevation through all Major street intersections shall not exceed 4%.
- A right turn ramp on a Major street shall have a minimum of 4% crossfall within the length of the island.

Grand Boulevard: Ascent Boulevard

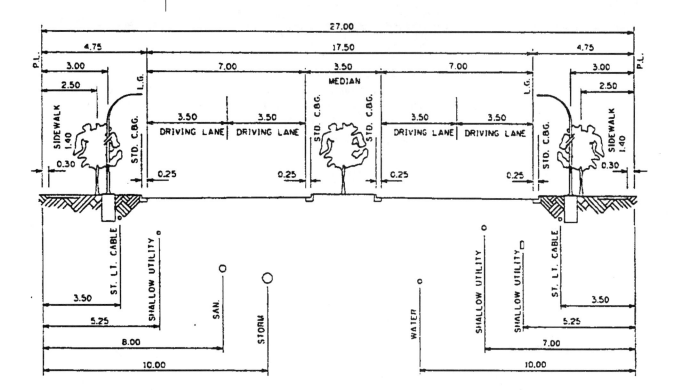

Figure A–6

Daily Traffic Volume (vehicles/day)	Number of Lanes	Right-of-way Requirement	Minimum Intersection Spacing
5,000 - 10,000	2	26.0 m (min.)	120 m/60 m

Function

- Functions are similar to Primary Collector and Collector streets.
- To serve as secondary traffic generators.
- To serve as a main route within the community to accommodate substantial traffic volumes.
- Might be used as bus routes and are designed to accommodate Frequent Transit Service.

Access Conditions

- A minimum intersection spacing of 120 m shall be provided between a Major Street and the first intersection on the Grand Boulevard from the Major Street.
- Intersection spacing for those subsequent to the above condition shall be a minimum 60 m spacing.
- No access to abutting commercial properties.
- Access to abutting multi-family residential properties is permitted and is generally restricted to right turns in and out.
- Residential frontage of single and multi-family development is permitted.
- Single family, semi-detached, and duplex style homes must access from a rear alley.

Traffic Features

Posted Speed (kph)	50	On-street Bikeway	Signed Bicycle Route
Parking	Yes	Bus Route	Yes

Sidewalk	1.4 m separate walk on both sides	Truck Route	Yes
Traffic Signals	As warranted	Sound Attenuation	Yes
Pedestrian Crossing	At Grade		

Note

• Undivided roadway with intersections controlled by signage.
• Parking is permitted on both sides but might be restricted under special circumstances.
• Sidewalk is normally only required on one side, but is preferable on both sides. Refer to Section E - Sidewalks and Walkways for more details.

Typical Cross Section	

Collector Streets: Jeffries Ranch Road

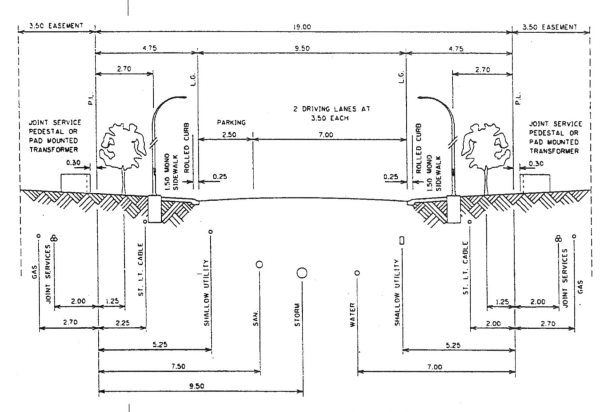

Figure A–7

Daily Traffic Volume (vehicles/day)	Number of Lanes	Right-of-way Requirement	Minimum Intersection Spacing
1,000 - 5,000	2	18.0 m 1nd 21.0 m	60 m

Function

• To be used where the Daily Traffic Volumes exceed the volumes for a Residential Road but are less than 5,000 vehicles/day.
• To collect and distribute traffic from Major streets to lesser standard streets.
• To serve as secondary traffic generators, such as neighbourhood commercial centers, parks, and golf courses, and from neighbourhood to neighbourhood.
• All Collector streets designated as bus routes must use the 21.0 m right-of-way cross-section.
• Might be used as bus routes.

Access Conditions

- Direct access is permitted to abutting properties.
- Minimum intersection spacing is 60 m. Wherever possible, a desirable intersection spacing of 80 m should be used.
- Collector streets might intersect with Residential streets, Residential Entrance streets, other Collector streets, Primary Collector streets, Local Major streets, and Major streets.

Traffic Features

Posted Speed (kph)	50	On-street Bikeway	Signed Bicycle Route
Parking	Except at bus zones	Bus Route	Yes
Sidewalk	1.4 m separate walk or 1.5 m mono walk on both sides	Truck Route	No
Traffic Signals	As warranted	Sound Attenuation	No
Pedestrian Crossing	At grade		

Note

- Collector Streets are undivided roadways.
- There are two types of Collector Streets:
    - 21.0 m R.O.W.: 2 driving lane of 3.5 m wide and 2 parking lane of 2.25 m wide.
    - 19.0 m R.O.W.*: 2 driving lanes of 3.5 m wide and 1 parking lane of 2.5 m wide.
- This standard can only be used where residential and/or commercial frontage occurs on one side of the road and where no bus route is planned.

Typical Cross Section

Classification	Design Speed	Intersection Design
Urban Collector Undivided (UCU) 50	50 kph	

Horizontal Alignment

Minimum Stopping Sight Distance	Minimum Radius of Curvature
Collect UCU 50 = 65 m	Collector UCU 50 = 90 m

Median and Left Turn Bay

- Medians, left turn bays, and intersection channelization are not normally required.
- A tear-drop median is required on a Collector street when the Collector street is designated as a bus route and intersecting with a Major street.

Note

- The cumulative length of Collector streets before feeding onto Major streets shall not be excessive. The maximum number of dwelling units serviced shall not exceed 500.
- Low profile rolled curb with 0.25 m gutter is to be used except in areas identified as bus zones and adjacent to parcels which that do not contain residential development (e.g., commercial sites, parks, school reserves, etc.) where a standard curb is to be used.
- Standard curb is to be used on Collector streets if the grade is greater than 6%.
- Reverse gutter is used where necessary.

Vertical Alignment

Minimum and Maximum Grades

• Maximum grade:	8.0%	
• Minimum grade:	0.6%	

Grade at Intersections

- The grade line of the approaching street (maximum approach grade of 4%) shall tie to the Collector street in the following manner:
  - Tie to the property line grade if the approaching street is undivided.
  - Tie to the lane line of the Collector street with a vertical curve of a minimum length of 30 m if the approaching street is divided. I.e., the crossfall (or 2% if the road is crowned) of the Collector street shall be extended and intersects the grade of the approaching street and the resulting vertical curve ends at the lane line of the Collector street.
- It is desirable to ensure that the grade on the Collector streets is less than the permitted maximum of 8% at intersections to improve operational aspects, such as stopping and starting in winter conditions.

Vertical Curves and Superelevation

- The length of vertical curve is calculated based on the stopping sight distance.
- The maximum superelevation rate for a Collector street shall not exceed emax=4%.

Residential Street: Ascent Place

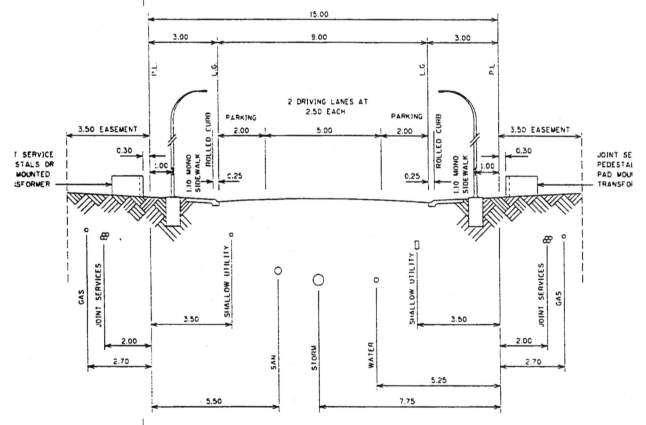

Figure A–8

Daily Traffic Volume (vehicles/day)	Number of Lanes	Right-of-way Requirement	Minimum Intersection Spacing
<1,000	2	15 m (min.)	60 m

Function

- To provide direct access to properties.
- To collect and distribute traffic from residential properties to Collector and Residential streets.

Access Conditions

- Direct access is permitted to abutting residential properties.
- Access is not permitted to commercial properties.
- Residential streets might intersect with other Residential streets, Residential Entrance streets, Collector streets, and Primary Collector streets.

Traffic Features

Posted Speed (kph)	50	On-street Bikeway	Signed Bicycle Route
Parking	Yes	Bus Route	No
Sidewalk	1.1 mono walk on at least one side, preferable on both sides	Truck Route	Yes
Traffic Signals	No	Sound Attenuation	Yes
Pedestrian Crossing	At Grade		

Note

- Undivided roadway with intersections controlled by signage.
- Parking is permitted on both sides but might be restricted under special circumstances.
- Sidewalk is normally only required on one side but is preferable on both sides. Refer to Section E - Sidewalks and Walkways for more details.

Typical Cross Section	See

Classification	Design Speed	Intersection Design
Urban Local Divided (ULD) 50	50 kph	

Horizontal Alignment

Minimum Stopping Sight Distance	Minimum Radius of Curvature
Residential ULD 50 = 65 m	Residential ULD 50 = 80 m

Median and Left Turn Bay

- Minimum median width is 3.5 m.
- Left turn bays and intersection channelization are not required.

Note

- Same requirements as Residential streets.
- Standard curb with 0.25 m gutter is to be used on the median and low profile curb with 0.25 m gutter on the outside edges, except in areas adjacent to parcels which do not contain residential developments where standard curb is to be used.

Vertical Alignment

Minimum and Maximum Grades

- Maximum grade: 8.0%
- Minimum grade: 0.6%

Grade at Intersections

- The grade line of the intersecting street (maximum approach grade of 4%) shall tie to the property line grade of a Residential Entrance street.

Vertical Curves and Superelevation

- The length of vertical curve is calculated based on the stopping sight distance.
- Superelevation is not required.

Traffic Circle Design Criteria

The following specifies the design criteria for the traffic circle at Jeffries Ranch Road and Accent Boulevard, as shown in Figure A–9.

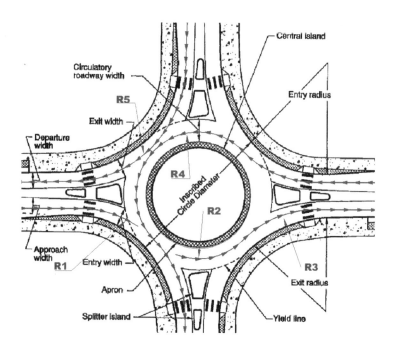

Inscribed Circle Diameter (m)	Approximate R_4 Value		Maximum R_1 Value	
	Radius (m)	Speed (km/h)	Radius (m)	Speed (km/h)
Single-Lane Roundabout				
30	11	21	54	41
35	13	23	61	43
40	16	25	69	45
45	19	26	73	46

Figure A–9

Five critical path radii must be checked for each approach:

- **R1 (entry path radius):** The minimum radius on the fastest through path before the yield line.
- **R2 (circulating path radius):** The minimum radius on the fastest through path around the central island.
- **R3 (exit path radius):** The minimum radius on the fastest through path into the exit.
- **R4 (left-turn path radius):** The minimum radius on the path of the conflicting left-turn movement.
- **R5 (right-turn path radius):** The minimum radius on the fastest path of a right-turning vehicle.

It is important to note that these vehicular path radii are not the same as the curb radii. First the basic curb geometry is laid out, and then the vehicle paths are drawn.

Intersection Design

The following specifies the design criteria for the intersection design at Mission Avenue and Accent Boulevard, as shown in Figure A–10.

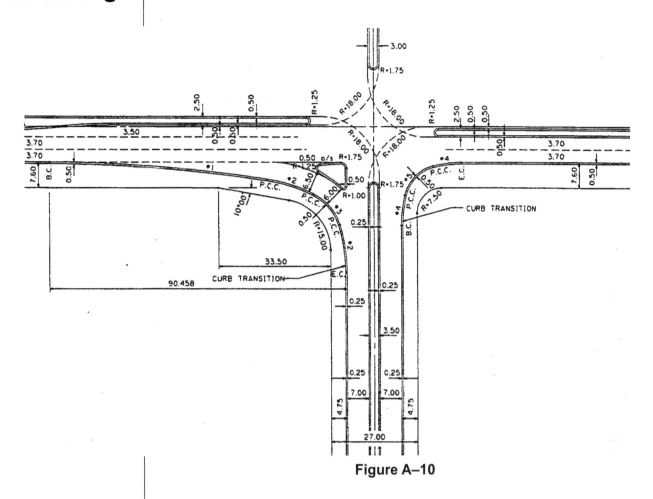

Figure A–10

A.3 Drawing Settings

Use Map3D to assign the coordinate system, as shown in Figure A–11, because the one in AutoCAD Civil 3D 2011 does not work correctly when using CA83-VI.

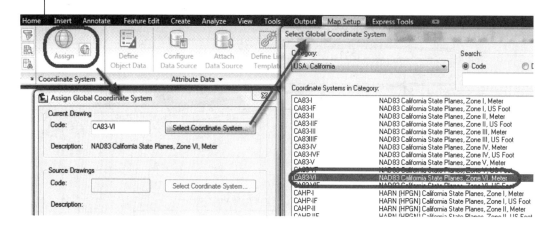

Figure A–11